BANARAS: CITY OF LIGHT

DIANA L. ECK

BANARAS
CITY OF LIGHT

Princeton University Press

PRINCETON, NEW JERSEY

Published by Princeton University Press, 41 William Street,
Princeton, New Jersey 08540

Copyright © 1982 by Diana L. Eck
All Rights Reserved

First Knopf edition, 1982
First Princeton Paperback printing, 1983
Second printing, 1990

LCC 82-48566   ISBN 0-691-02023-x pbk.

Reprinted by arrangement with Alfred A. Knopf, Inc.

Princeton University Press books are printed on acid-free paper
and meet the guidelines for permanence and durability of the
Committee on Production Guidelines for Book Longevity of the
Council on Library Resources

Printed in the United States of America

4   6   8   10   9   7   5   3

TO
Kuber Nāth Sukul,
Ambika Datta Upādhyāya,
J. L. Mehta, and Vimalā Mehta—
all Banārsīs

Are there not many holy places on this earth?
Yet which of them would equal in the balance one speck
    of Kāshī's dust?
Are there not many rivers running to the sea?
Yet which of them is like the River of Heaven in Kāshī?
Are there not many fields of liberation on earth?
Yet not one equals the smallest part of the city never forsaken by
    Shiva.
The Ganges, Shiva, and Kāshī: Where this Trinity is watchful,
    no wonder here is found the grace that leads one on
    to perfect bliss.

(KKh 35. 7–10)

CONTENTS

PREFACE
xiii

1
BANARAS: AN INTRODUCTION
3

2
BANARAS IN HISTORICAL PERSPECTIVE
43

3
THE CITY OF SHIVA
94

4
THE SACRED CIRCLE OF ALL THE GODS
146

5
THE RIVER GANGES AND THE GREAT *GHATS*
211

ix

6

SEASONS AND TIMES

252

7

CITY OF ALL INDIA

283

8

CITY OF THE GOOD LIFE

304

9

CITY OF DEATH AND LIBERATION

324

APPENDIX I

Sanskrit Sources for the Study of Banāras

347

APPENDIX II

The Zones of the Sacred City

350

APPENDIX III

The Shiva Lingas of Kāshī

358

APPENDIX IV

The Cycles of Kāshī Goddesses

360

APPENDIX V

Other Deities of Kāshī

362

APPENDIX VI

The Year in Banāras: A Partial Calendar

364

Note on Transliteration and Pronunciation

367

GLOSSARY

369

NOTES

379

BIBLIOGRAPHY

399

ACKNOWLEDGMENTS

407

ILLUSTRATIONS

409

INDEX

413

PREFACE

I FIRST knew Banāras fifteen years ago when I studied for a year at Banāras Hindu University. It was an awesome city—captivating, challenging, and endlessly fascinating. Banāras raised some of the questions about the Hindu tradition which have interested me ever since—its complex mythological imagination, its prodigious display of divine images, its elaborate ritual traditions, and its understanding of the relation of life and death. It was Banāras that turned me to the study of India and the Hindu religious tradition. I have returned to Banāras many times since then, for extended periods of research and for short visits. Over these years it has become a familiar city to me. I know its streets and lanes as well as I know those of Cambridge, and perhaps better, for the time I have spent mapping the city and searching for its hidden temples. And yet, while Banāras has become familiar, I remember vividly how foreign it once seemed.

This book is a study and interpretation of Banāras from the standpoint of one who is close enough to the Hindu tradition to see its religious significance and close enough to Western religious and academic traditions to know the problems of understanding that Banāras and the Hindu tradition it represents might pose. My work is based on two primary sources: a voluminous literature of Sanskrit texts which describe and praise Banāras, and the city itself, with its patterns of temples, its seasons of pilgrimage, and its priestly and lay interpreters. It is a study of "text and context," or perhaps more accurately, of classical Sanskrit texts and the "text" of the city, brought together so that we may see this city and understand its sacred structure and meaning as it has been seen and understood by Hindus.

The Sanskrit texts alone present a complex interpretive task, and those that deal primarily with Banāras—the *Kāshī Khanda* and the *Kāshī Rahasya*—have not previously been translated or studied by Western scholars. In reading these texts, I found that they contain diverse types of literature requiring different interpretive approaches. Much of this literature is praise-literature called *māhātmya,* the purpose of which is to extoll, expand, and even exaggerate the glories of its subject. Such *māhātmya* is a product of that particularly Hindu structure of consciousness which is pluralistic and polycentric, but which at any one time, against a vivid and variegated backdrop, brings but one center, one deity, one sacred city, or one temple into sharp focus for adoration and praise. Here that center is Kāshī. In addition to and often as part of the *māhātmya* there is the mythological literature. Here, many of the major Hindu myths, which are always set in the particular context of one or another human or divine drama, are told in the context of Banāras and its holy history. Some of these myths must be understood as primarily theological in intent in that they reveal and describe the nature of the divine. Others lend themselves to a quasi-historical interpretation in that they reveal the gradual emergence and pre-eminence of the worship of Shiva in Banāras. A third type of literature contained here is ritual literature, which must be understood and interpreted in the wider context of brahminical ritual and injunction. There are ritual instructions for pilgrims, for brahmins, for kings, and there are lists of the great fruits to be won from such rituals. Finally, this literature contains detailed geographical descriptions, locating temples in relation to one another with such precision that it enables one to construct a picture of the city and its pattern of temples as it existed nearly a thousand years ago.

The city "text" presents an equally diverse task of study and interpretation. First, there is its geography—its ancient streams and pools, its temples and ruins, its lanes and pilgrimage routes. The sacred geography of the city provides information the Sanskrit texts cannot provide. Some of the temples I sought out, which had clearly been important in the era of the Sanskrit literature, no longer exist. Some such sites are now occupied by mosques. Others are marked only by tiny shrines or have been moved to new locations. Conversely, some temples barely mentioned in the Sanskrit texts have achieved great fame and popularity. Reading the text of the city's geography has often been difficult, for most of the city has changed in the past 700 years, with hardly a stone left upon stone. Parts of it, including many major temples, were destroyed by Muslims several times between the twelfth and the seventeenth centuries, and in the eighteenth century whole new sectors of what is now the dense urban heart of the city were constructed. And yet with all this change, most of the temples of the great Sanskrit tradition are still here, somewhere.

The geographical text of the city is supplemented by a revealing art-historical text. The record of artistic and archeological remains is virtually unbroken since Mauryan times in the fourth century B.C., and each era contributes something to understanding the growth of the city and the emergence of its population of divinities. Still, we must remember that, except for one brief decade of archeological work at Rājghāt, nothing in Banāras proper has been systematically excavated. Occasionally in digging graves or foundations, some new image will be unearthed and added to the city's record of artistic remains, but that record, while useful, is far from complete.

Another important source of information are the brahmins of Banāras, especially those who are the knowledgeable keepers of the tradition and who act as interpreters of myth and *māhātmya*. Here my informants included pandits (teachers), *pūjārīs* (temple priests), *pandās* (pilgrimage priests), *mahants* (heads of a large temple complex), and *vyāsas* (storytellers). These people were invaluable guides, safeguarding against either over-interpreting parts of the Sanskrit literature or neglecting important aspects of it. While the movements and actions of the pilgrims themselves tell us something about the sacred city today, the pilgrims' knowledge of the city and its traditions is very quickly exhausted. They would inevitably refer me to "those who know," and indeed the many hours I spent with "those who know" through the years of my research helped to refine my understanding of the city.

A final aspect of the "city-text" is simply what happens. The days, weeks, and months with their rhythms of worship and cycles of pilgrimage contributed greatly to my sense of the sacred order of Banāras as a whole. The brahmins may know little of temples and tanks they have never visited. But when, for example, ten thousand people arrive at Lolārka Kund on a day in September, we hear the voice of ordinary people and villagers who "vote with their feet." Part of the task of researching a place such as Banāras is to see where the people cast their vote, month after month.

Finally, I have for the most part avoided the temptation to compare Banāras with other places of pilgrimage and sacred centers, both in India and elsewhere. The comparison of the sacred structure and *māhātmya* of Banāras with that of Jerusalem, Mecca, or Peking is in many respects obvious to historians of religion; more significant, perhaps, is the historical layering of traditions, age after age, in these centers. As for its relation to other centers in India, let it suffice to say that because of the polycentric nature of the Hindu imagination, the sacred structure and *māhātmya* of a place as important as Banāras are widely duplicated and serve, therefore, to reveal something fundamental about the nature of such sacred places in India generally. Here, however, the story of Banāras alone is told, and that in itself is a lengthy undertaking. Even in restricting myself to Banāras I have had to omit a great deal. Both in my fieldwork and in my writing, I have often felt like the pilgrim described in the *Padma Purāna:* "Making a pilgrimage there in Banāras every day for a whole year, still she did not reach all the sacred places. For in Banāras there is a sacred place at every step."

BANĀRAS
February 1981

BANARAS: CITY OF LIGHT

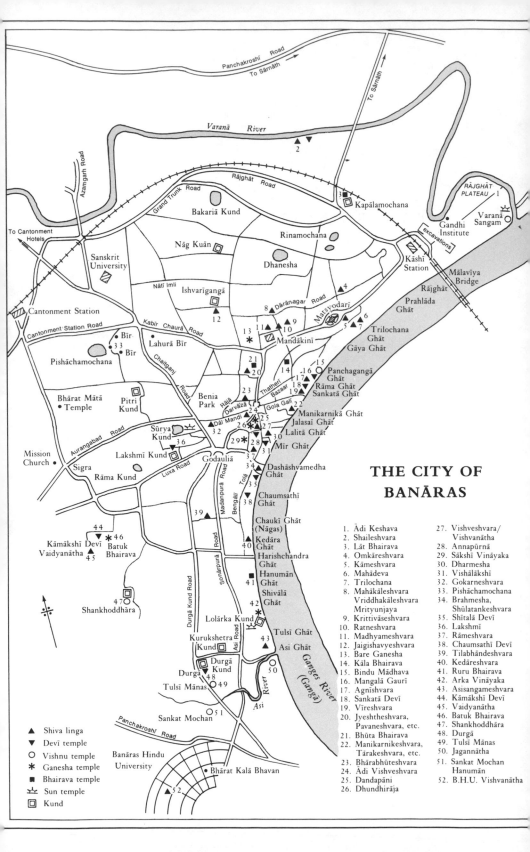

THE CITY OF
BANĀRAS

1. Ādi Keshava
2. Shaileshvara
3. Lāt Bhairava
4. Omkāreshvara
5. Kāmeshvara
6. Mahādeva
7. Trilochana
8. Mahākāleshvara
   Vriddhakāleshvara
   Mrityunjaya
9. Krittivāseshvara
10. Ratneshvara
11. Madhyameshvara
12. Jaigishavyeshvara
13. Bare Ganesha
14. Kāla Bhairava
15. Bindu Mādhava
16. Mangalā Gaurī
17. Agnīshvara
18. Sankatā Devī
19. Vīreshvara
20. Jyeshtheshvara,
    Pavaneshvara, etc.
21. Bhūta Bhairava
22. Manikarnikeshvara,
    Tārakeshvara, etc.
23. Bhārabhūteshvara
24. Ādi Vishvanātha
25. Dandapāni
26. Dhundhirāja

27. Vishveshvara/
    Vishvanātha
28. Annapūrnā
29. Sākshī Vināyaka
30. Dharmesha
31. Vishālākshī
32. Gokarneshvara
33. Pishāchamochana
34. Brahmesha,
    Shūlatankeshvara
35. Shītalā Devī
36. Lakshmī
37. Rāmeshvara
38. Chaumsathī Devī
39. Tilabhāndeshvara
40. Kedāreshvara
41. Ruru Bhairava
42. Arka Vināyaka
43. Asisangameshvara
44. Kāmākshī Devī
45. Vaidyanātha
46. Batuk Bhairava
47. Shankhoddhāra
48. Durgā
49. Tulsī Mānas
50. Jagannātha
51. Sankat Mochan
    Hanumān
52. B.H.U. Vishvanātha

▲ Shiva linga
▼ Devī temple
○ Vishnu temple
✳ Ganesha temple
■ Bhairava temple
☀ Sun temple
▣ Kund

I

BANARAS: AN INTRODUCTION

B A N Ā R A S is a magnificent city, rising from the western bank of the River Ganges, where the river takes a broad crescent sweep toward the north. There is little in the world to compare with the splendor of Banāras, seen from the river at dawn. The rays of the early-morning sun spread across the river and strike the high-banked face of this city, which Hindus call Kāshī—the Luminous, the City of Light. The temples and shrines, ashrams and pavilions that stretch along the river for over three miles are golden in the early morning. They rise majestic on the high riverbank and cast deep reflections into the waters of the Ganges. Long flights of stone steps called *ghāts*, reaching like roots into the river, bring thousands of worshippers down to the river to bathe at dawn. In the narrow lanes at the top of these steps moves the unceasing earthly drama of life and death, which Hindus call *samsāra*. But here, from the perspective of the river, there is a vision of transcendence and liberation, which Hindus call *moksha*.

The riverfront reveals the sources of Kāshī's ancient reputation as the sacred city of the Hindus. Along the river there are over seventy bathing *ghāts*, literally "landings" or "banks," reaching from Asi Ghāt in the south to Ādi Keshava in the north, beyond the bridge. Some are quiet neighborhood *ghāts*, while others are crowded with pilgrims from all over India. Bathing in the Ganges, a river said to have fallen from heaven to earth, is the first act of Banāras pilgrims and a daily rite for Banāras residents. Also along the river are dozens of temples with high spires, most of them dedicated to Lord Shiva, who according to tradition makes this city his permanent earthly home. Great temples, like Kedāreshvara, sit atop their own *ghāts,* while innumerable small shrines along the river are barely large enough for a single *linga,* the simple stone shaft that is the symbol of Shiva. Along with the temples are the ashrams, such as the Ānandamayī ashram, built at the top of the *ghāt* steps. They continue a tradition of spiritual education for which Kāshī has long been famous. At dawn, students of all ages practice yogic exercises, breath control, or meditational disciplines on the steps by the river. Finally, there are the riverside cremation grounds at Harishchandra Ghāt and Manikarnikā Ghāt, recognizable by the smoke that rises from the pyres of the dead. Elsewhere in traditional India, the cremation ground is outside of town, for it is polluted ground. Here, however, the cremation grounds are in the midst of a busy city, adjacent to the bathing *ghāts,* and are holy ground, for death in Kāshī is acclaimed by the tradition as a great blessing. Dying here, one gains liberation from the earthly round of *samsāra.*

For over 2,500 years this city, also called Vārānasī, has attracted pilgrims and seekers from all over India. Sages, such as the Buddha, Mahāvīra, and Shankara, have come here to teach. Young men have come to study the Vedas with the city's great pandits. Householders have come on pilgrimages, some to bring the ashes of a deceased parent to commit to the River Ganges. *Sannyāsins,* "renouncers" who have left the householder stage of life behind, have come to gather in the monasteries *(mathas)* and ashrams of Kāshī, especially during the rainy season when they are unable to continue their lives as homeless way-farers. Widows too have come to Banāras, out of piety or out of misery, to take refuge in its temples and to live on the alms of the faithful. And the very old or very ill have come to Kāshī to live out their final days until they die.

Banāras is one of the oldest living cities in the world, as old as Jerusalem, Athens, and Peking. It occupied its high bank overlooking the Ganges in the cradle days of Western civilization. Its antiquity has caught the imagination of many, such as the Reverend M. A. Sherring, a mid-nineteenth-century missionary in Banāras, who wrote effu-sively:

Twenty-five centuries ago, at the least, it was famous. When Babylon was struggling with Nineveh for supremacy, when Tyre was planting her colonies, when Athens was growing in strength, before Rome had become known, or Greece had contended with Persia, or Cyrus had added lustre to the Persian monarchy, or Nebuchadnezzar had captured Jerusalem, and the inhabitants of Judaea had been carried into captivity, she had already risen to greatness, if not to glory.[1]

On the antiquity of Banāras, which he visited in his journey around the world, Mark Twain quipped, "Benares is older than history, older than tradition, older even than legend, and looks twice as old as all of them put together!"[2]

Unlike these other ancient cities, however, Banāras is a city whose political history is little known. It has rarely been an important political center, and the rise and fall of kings through its long history have no role in the tale of the city's sanctity told by its own people. Kāshī is said to be the city of Shiva, founded at the dawn of creation. It is not the events of its long history that make it significant to Hindus; rather, it has such a long history, and it has survived and flourished through the changing fortunes of the centuries *because* it is significant to Hindus.

There is another important difference between Banāras and its contemporaries: its present life reaches back to the sixth century B.C. in a continuous tradition. If we could imagine the silent Acropolis and the Agora of Athens still alive with the intellectual, cultural, and ritual traditions of classical Greece, we might glimpse the remarkable tenacity of the life of Kāshī. Today Peking, Athens, and Jerusalem are moved by a very different ethos from that which moved them in ancient times, but Kāshī is not.

Lewis Mumford, in *The City in History,* wrote that a city is "energy converted into culture."[3] There are a few great cities in the world which have converted the energy of an entire civilization into culture, and have come to symbolize and embody that whole civilization in microcosm. Again, we think of Peking, Mecca, Athens, Jerusalem, and Rome. It is no wonder that such cities have become places of pilgrimage for the cultures they have produced, and that pilgrims speak of the whole world as radiating from and being present in the great "world-city," the cosmopolis.

In launching the Crusades, Pope Urban II cried, "Jerusalem is the center of the earth!"[4] Indeed, medieval maps sometimes depict Jerusalem at the center of the world, with whole continents spreading out

from it like petals. Similarly, Mecca was said to be the first place of
creation, situated on the axis of the universe directly below the throne
of God.[5] For Chinese culture, Peking was the city at the center of the
world, the "Pivot of the Four Quarters."[6] And so Hindus say of
Banāras that it stands at the center of the earth as the place of creation,
and gathers together the whole of the sacred universe in a single
symbolic circle, a *mandala*. Yet it is not an earthly city. Kāshī is said to
sit above the earth as a "crossing place" *(tīrtha)* between this world
and the "far shore" of the transcendent Brahman.

There are few cities in India as traditionally Hindu and as symbolic
of the whole of Hindu culture as the city of Banāras. And there are few
cities in India, or in the world for that matter, as challenging and
bewildering to Western visitors as Banāras. It is a city as rich as all
India. But it is not an easy city to comprehend for those of us who
stand outside the Hindu tradition. As we survey the riverfront at
dawn, we are challenged to comprehend the whole of India in one
sweeping glance.

The India we see here reflects the elaborate and ancient ritual tradition of Hinduism. It is a tradition of pilgrimage to sacred places,
bathing in sacred waters, and honoring divine images. It is a tradition
in which all of the senses are employed in the apprehension of the
divine. Its shrines are heaped with fresh flowers and filled with the
smell of incense, the chanting of prayers, and the ringing of bells. It is
a tradition that has imagined and imaged God in a thousand ways, that
has been adept in discovering the presence of the divine everywhere
and in bringing every aspect of human life into the religious arena. It is
a religious tradition that understands life and death as an integrated
whole. Here the smoke of the cremation pyres rises heavenward with
the spires of a hundred temples and the ashes of the dead swirl through
the waters of the Ganges, the river of life.

At the outset, we cannot even *see* the scope and dimensions of this
religious tradition. We do not know the myths, the symbols, and the
images that are the language of access to Hinduism. In an important
sense, we do not see the same city Hindus see. We see the waters of
the River Ganges, we see stone images adorned with flowers, and we
see cows browsing with leisurely sovereignty through the streets. So
do the Hindus. We see a city of narrow lanes surging with life, streets
noisy with the jangling of rickshaw bells, buildings crumbling about
the edges and sagging in the balconies. So do the Hindus. But it is as if

The narrow lanes and lofty houses of Banāras.

we see these things in one dimension, while Hindus see them in many dimensions. What Hindus "see" in Kāshī only begins with the city that meets the eye. To know what else they see we must know what Kāshī means and has meant in the Hindu tradition. What is its symbolic significance? What stories do Hindus tell of it? What mighty events do they ascribe to this place? What hopes and expectations do they bring when they come here? What vision do they see of the City of Light?

It is our purpose here to try to see the city Hindus see. We will explore the Sanskrit texts that praise this city. We will hear the popular Hindi tales and listen to the voices of priests and pilgrims. We will walk the ancient streets of Banāras, visit its temples, ponder its ruins,

and learn of its gods. And all the while we will attempt to see, in and
through the facts we have gathered, a vision of the city Hindus have
seen.

Seeing Banāras Through Western Eyes

To visitors from the West, the great commercial cities of
India—Madras, Bombay, Calcutta, and Delhi—seem far more familiar
than Banāras. These are the modern cities of India, and they were all
built by foreigners: Delhi by the early Muslim dynasties in the twelfth
and thirteenth centuries, Bombay by the Portuguese in the sixteenth
century, and Madras and Calcutta by the British in the seventeenth
century. Banāras is older than all of them, by over two thousand years.
Although parts of Banāras were destroyed repeatedly between the
twelfth and the seventeenth centuries by the armies of the various
Muslim kings who ruled North India, they were rebuilt, right on top
of the ruins and rubble. Despite the fact that few of its buildings are
ancient, the city looks very old.

The heart of urban Banāras has few streets wide enough for a two-
seat bicycle rickshaw, and even fewer wide enough for automobile
traffic. It is a maze of lanes, barely wider than a footpath. The last two
centuries of "modernization" have left this part of the city little
changed, at least on the surface. Of course, there is electricity and
running water where once there were oil lamps and wells. There are
high-fashion *sārīs* and stainless-steel utensils for sale in the same celebrated shops that for centuries have carried only silk and brass. There
are bicycles, taxis, and, more recently, motorcycle rickshaws, which
vie with the horse-drawn tongas, the camels, and the pedestrians in the
traffic of the main streets. And through the arched doorways of two-
and three-story houses in the narrow lanes, there are kitchens
equipped with refrigerators and blenders. But the dense structure of
the old city has not changed. And in these years, while Calcutta has
grown from a small trading fort to one of the largest and most complex
cities in the world, the splendid riverfront face of Banāras has retained
its old and ageless character.

To linger in Banāras is to linger in another era, an era which one
cannot quite date by century. It is very old, and yet it has continued to

gather the cumulative Hindu tradition, right to the present. While the loudspeaker on the *ghāts* blares the chanting of devotional hymns—the latest notion of a public charity!—people bathe in the river and splash an ancient tree trunk with Ganges water on their way home, as they may have done for three thousand years. The city displays the layering of the Hindu tradition like a palimpsest, an old parchment that has been written upon and imperfectly erased again and again, leaving the old layers partially visible.

It is precisely because Banāras has become a symbol of traditional Hindu India that Western visitors have often found this city the most strikingly "foreign" of India's cities. The city is a living text of Hinduism. Men and women descend the *ghāts* to bathe in the Ganges and they crowd into temples along the river with their hands full of flowers and sweets destined for the lap of a multi-armed image. They sip the waters of the Ganges and they carry these waters home in polished brass pots. In the market, bronze-cast or clay images of different gods are bought and sold. In the wayside shrines, worn old stones are daubed and smeared with vermilion paste. In a thousand temples, stone *lingas* of Shiva are touched, sprinkled, and strewn with flowers. Along the river, the burning of the dead is a common sight. As we read this visible, living text, we ask some of the same questions that Western visitors have posed in their minds for centuries: Who is Shiva and who are these multi-armed gods? Why do Hindus bathe in the Ganges? Why do they come here to die?

For over four hundred years Banāras has both astonished and bewildered visitors from the West. Merchants and missionaries, civil servants and travelers have written extensively of this city in letters, journals, and books. Although they rarely understood what it all meant, they described what they saw with energy and with vivid visual detail. Their writings are interesting and important, in part because they provide the only descriptive accounts of Banāras in the past centuries. Because of their very different sense of the "individual," Hindus have no tradition of keeping journals or personal reflections of their travels. However, these foreign diaries give us more than a description of Banāras. They allow us to see how our Western predecessors, with little knowledge of India, saw and understood a culture that was so markedly different from their own.

In 1584, Ralph Fitch was the first English visitor to record his impressions of "Bannaras." Fitch was traveling with a small party of merchants carrying letters of introduction from Queen Elizabeth to the great monarchs of India and China. They arrived in Banāras by boat, having come down the Ganges from Allahabad. Fitch wrote,

In this place they be all Gentiles, and be the greatest idolaters that ever I sawe. To this towne come the Gentiles on pilgrimage out of farre coun-treyes. Here alongst the waters side bee many faire houses, and in all of them . . . they have their images standing, which be evill favoured, made of stone

and wood, some like lions, leopards, and monkeis; some like men and women, and pecocks; and some like the devil with foure armes and 4 hands.[7]

Fitch went on to describe the rites he saw people performing along the riverbank:

And by breake of day and before, there are men and women which come out of the towne and wash themselves in Ganges. And there are divers old men which upon places of earth made for the purpose, sit praying, and they give the people three or foure straws, which they take and hold them betweene their fingers when they wash themselves; and some sit to marke them in the forheads, and they have in a cloth a litle rice, barlie, or money, which, when they have washed themselves, they give to the old men which sit there praying. Afterwards they go to divers of their images, and give them of their sacrifices. And when they give, the old men say certaine prayers, and then all is holy.[8]

The "divers old men," of course, were the brahmin *ghātiās* or *pan*

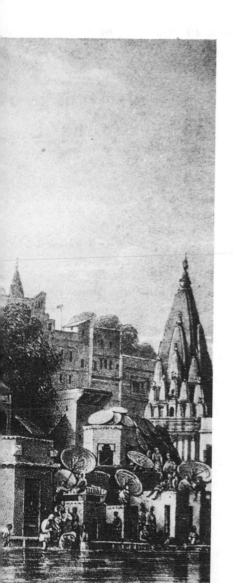

"Munikurnika Ghat" as drawn by James Prinsep, Benares Illustrated, *1831, showing bathers at the water's edge and brahmin* ghātias *on their stone platforms. The temple at the center is Tārakeshvara, the "Lord of the Crossing." The temple at the right has since fallen into the river. Prinsep writes, "In the rains the temples are submerged to the cornice; many Hindoos, notwithstanding, are bold enough to swim through an impetuous current, and to dive under the porch and door-way, for the honor of continuing their customary worship in despite of perils and personal inconvenience."*

dās who tend to the needs of pilgrims and bathers even today. They
receive the token offerings of grain in exchange for their services. The
straws are of the sacred *kusha* grass, held in the hand during the
performance of many Hindu rites.

About a century after the time of Fitch came the French traveler
Jean Baptiste Tavernier, a dealer in jewels who made six voyages to
India between 1636 and 1668. Tavernier visited Banāras on his last trip
and saw the great riverside temple, which he called a "pagoda," of
Bindu Mādhava. His account is especially interesting because the
temple was demolished shortly afterwards by the armies of the Mughal
Aurangzeb and it has never been rebuilt on its old foundations. Tavernier arrived during the morning *āratī*, a service of worship which
takes its name from the offering of camphor lamps to the deity. People
had gathered for the *darshana*, the "sacred sight" of the image. Tavernier did not know it was an image of Vishnu, nor did he know
anything about Hindu ritual, but he described the rite with care:

As soon as the door of the pagoda was opened, and after a large curtain had
been drawn, and the people present had seen the idol, all threw themselves
upon the ground, placing their hands upon their heads and prostrating themselves three times; then having risen they threw a quantity of bouquets and
chains in the form of chaplets, which the Brahmins placed in contact with the
idol, and then returned to the people. An old Brahmin who was in the front
of the altar, held in his hand a lamp with nine lighted wicks, upon which,
from time to time, he threw a kind of incense when approaching the lamp
toward the idol.[9]

Tavernier saw one of the most common rites of Hindu worship, called
pūjā or *āratī*, which includes the offering of flowers, the presentation
of oil lights, the burning of fragrant camphor, and the libations of
Ganges water. The flowers, water, and even food offerings placed in
contact with the image are considered to have been consecrated and
are received by the worshippers as what is called *prasāda*, the "grace"
of the Lord.

In 1823 and 1824, Bishop Reginald Heber, Anglican Bishop of Calcutta, made a circuit trip across North India and stopped in Banāras.
He stayed in the British cantonment to the west of Banāras, but ven-
tured into the city and, like Tavernier, into its temples. As is still the
case today, the priests would present such a guest with a consecrated
garland of flowers as a courtesy. Heber wrote,

During my progress through the holy places I had received garlands of flowers in considerable numbers, which I was told it was uncivil to throw away, particularly those which were hung around my neck. I now, in consequence, looked more like a sacrifice than a Priest, and on getting again into the gig was glad to rid myself of my ornaments![10]

Heber found Banāras "a remarkable city, more entirely and characteristically Eastern than any which I have yet seen."[11] Like other travelers, he was impressed with the tight web of city lanes. He wrote, after his first trip into the center of the city,

No Europeans live in the town, nor are the streets wide enough for a wheel-carriage. Mr. Frazer's gig was stopped short almost at its entrance, and the rest of the way was passed in tonjons,* through alleys so crowded, so narrow, and so winding, that even a tonjon sometimes passed with difficulty. The houses are mostly lofty, none I think less than two stories, most of three, and several of five or six, a sight which I now for the first time saw in India. The streets, like those of Chester, are considerably lower than the ground-floors of the houses, which have mostly arched rows in front, with little shops behind them. Above these, the houses are richly embellished with verandahs, galleries, projecting oriel windows, and very broad overhanging eaves, supported by carved brackets. The number of temples is very great, mostly small and stuck like shrines in the angles of the streets, and under the shadow of lofty houses.[12]

Shortly after the visit of Bishop Heber, Miss Emma Roberts, who wrote a series of sketches on India for the *Asiatic Journal* and collected them in *Scenes and Characteristics of Hindostan,* gave her account of the temples of the city. Unlike Tavernier and Heber, she was not inclined to linger for the rites of worship:

As soon as it is broad day, the priests repair to the temples, and devotees are seen conveying the sacred water from the Ganges to the several shrines. At the doors of the pagodas, persons are stationed with baskets of flowers for sale. Long rosaries of scarlet, white, or yellow blossoms, seem to be in the greatest request, and are purchased by the pious as offerings to their gods: the pavements of the temples are strewed with these floral treasures, the only

---

* A *tonjon* is described by one author as "a sort of open sedan chair which is carried by poles resting on the shoulders of the bearers." (Norman Macleod, *Days in North India,* p. 116.)

pleasing ceremonial connected with Hindoo worship. The too-abundant supply of water, the dirty throng of religious beggars, and the incessant vociferations of "Ram! Ram!" compel all save determined antiquaries to make a speedy exit from the noise and crowd of these places.[13]

Above all, these early visitors were struck by the "spectacle," the "panorama" of the Banāras riverfront. Especially as the nineteenth century drew to a close and the "exotic" India had caught the imagination of the West, a great many writers and adventurers set their hand to the description of this scene. In his around-the-world adventures, *Following the Equator,* Mark Twain wrote:

The Ganges front is the supreme showplace of Benares. Its tall bluffs are solidly caked from water to summit, along a stretch of three miles, with a splendid jumble of massive and picturesque masonry, a bewildering and beautiful confusion of stone platforms, temples, stairflights, rich and stately palaces—nowhere a break, nowhere a glimpse of the bluff itself; all the long face of it is compactly walled from sight by this crammed perspective of platforms, soaring stairways, sculptured temples, majestic palaces, softening away into the distances; and there is movement, motion, human life everywhere, and brilliantly costumed—streaming in rainbows up and down the lofty stairways, and massed in metaphorical gardens on the miles of great platforms at the river's edge.[14]

About the same time, W. S. Caine described the people "streaming in rainbows" in more detail:

Up and down the *ghats,* all day long, but especially in the early morning, stream the endless course of pilgrims, ragged tramps, aged crones, horrible

James Prinsep's view of "Dusaswumedh Ghat" from Benares Illustrated, *1831.*

beggars, hawkers, Brahmin priests, sacred bulls and cows, Hindu preachers, wealthy *rajas* or bankers in gay palanquins, Fakirs, pariah dogs, and scoffing globetrotters from Europe and America.[15]

Edwin Arnold, already well known for the *Light of Asia,* wrote in *India Revisited* of the rite of bathing in the Ganges, and he described with emotion the people he observed at their prayers:

Some are old and feeble, weary with long journeys of life, emaciated by maladies, saddened from losses and troubles; and the morning air blows sharp, the river wave runs chilly. Yet there they stand, breast-deep in the cold

Bathing in the Ganges.

river, with dripping cotton garments clinging to their thin or aged limbs, visibly shuddering under the shock of the water, and their lips blue and quivering, while they eagerly mutter their invocations. None of them hesitates; into the Gunga they plunge on arrival, ill or well, robust or sickly; and ladle the holy liquid up with small, dark, trembling hands, repeating the sacred names, and softly mentioning the sins they would expiate and the beloved souls they would plead for.[16]

These descriptive accounts, vivid and impassioned as they are, raise continually the question of meaning. This may be awesome, poignant, spectacular, but what is going on? How are we to understand this place, these religious acts, these people? Since most of these early visitors, Arnold being an exception, knew little of Hinduism but what presented itself to the eye, they were unable to broach these questions. Banāras was somehow too much for the mind to comprehend, and their writings are replete with expressions of speechless amazement. They had few interpretive resources with which to make sense of what they saw.

Some tried to understand Banāras by comparison with something "comparable" in the West. François Bernier called it the "Athens of India," and Edwin Arnold called it "the Oxford and Canterbury of

India in one," referring to its pre-eminence as a seat of learning and religious authority.[17] Lieutenant-Colonel Davidson, in his 1843 *Diary of Travels and Adventures in Upper India,* wrote, "It is the Hindoo Jerusalem, to which their dying thoughts are directed by pious Hindoos, expire where they may."[18] Another traveler, Norman Macleod, wrote, "Benares is to the Hindoos what Mecca is to the Mohammedans, and what Jerusalem was to the Jews of old. It is the 'holy' city of Hindostan."[19]

There was considerable disagreement on just how "holy" this city was. Here the question of interpretation is raised with special clarity. Some of these writers were utterly appalled, like James Kennedy, who lived in Banāras as an employee of the London Missionary Society. Of the Hindu tradition, so visibly embodied here, he wrote, "Everything you see is wild, grotesque, unnatural, forbidding, utterly wanting in versimilitude and refinement, with nothing to purify and raise the people, with everything fitted to pervert their taste and lower their character...,"[20] There were others who, at least from a distance, could sense and appreciate the holiness of Banāras, which Norman Macleod described as the "visible embodiment of religion."[21] A few, however, were completely captivated by Banāras. Count Hermann Keyserling, who left Europe shortly before World War I to journey around the world, wrote an account of the city that could hardly present a sharper contrast to Kennedy's:

Benares is holy. Europe, grown superficial, hardly understands such truths anymore.... I feel nearer here than I have ever done to the heart of the world; here I feel every day as if soon, perhaps even to-day, I would receive the grace of supreme revelation.... The atmosphere of devotion which hangs above the river is improbable in its strength: stronger than in any church that I have ever visited. Every would-be Christian priest would do well to sacrifice a year of his theological studies in order to spend this time on the Ganges: here he would discover what piety means.[22]

Most of the accounts and journals, however, reveal neither revulsion nor intoxication alone, but rather a curious mixture of the two. Although there is some genuine attempt to understand and to appreciate the significance of the city, there is clearly a point at which appreciation or fascination yields to condemnation. The city might be awesome, but in the world view of nineteenth-century civil servants and missionaries, it could not be "holy." The most striking examples of this complex attraction-repulsion response are in the writings of the Christian missionaries. M. A. Sherring, for example, spent many years in Banāras in the mid-nineteenth century and was clearly fascinated by the city. He took great interest and care in his research into its history and its sacred sites, and he described what he learned and saw with thoroughness and zeal. At the same time, as a Christian he could not include the city in his religious imagination. The poignant ambivalence of a man who had come to love Banāras and yet felt he must finally condemn it is expressed in Sherring's *The Sacred City of the Hindus.* Note both voices in his portrayal of the aging pilgrim making his way to Banāras:

. . . [He comes] as of old, from the remotest corners of India, as the sands of time are slowly ebbing away, and, fearful lest the last golden grains should escape before his long journey is ended, makes desperate efforts to hold on his course, till, at length, arriving at the sacred city and touching its hallowed soil, his anxious spirit becomes suddenly calm, a strange sense of relief comes over him, and he is at once cheered and comforted with the treacherous lie, that his sins are forgiven and his soul is saved.[23]

While the general sense of a "sacred city" and the triumph of reaching sacred ground were things Sherring and others could understand by comparison with the sacred cities of the West, there were many aspects of Kāshī that remained inaccessible to them. Their writings are filled with the language of the "treacherous lie" and "idolatrous worship." They saw a city about which Hindus had "superstition," not faith. They saw sacred waters which were "stagnant," "unsufferably foul," and "loathsome," not cleansing. And they saw Hindus who were "deeply perverted," not religious.

More than anything else, it was the multitude of divine images or "idols," as they called them, that elicited the strongest response of Westerners in their encounter with Banāras and with Hinduism generally. Virtually everyone who visited the city, from Ralph Fitch in the 1500s through those who went there in subsequent centuries, expressed astonishment and even repugnance at the panoply of images. Fitch wrote, "Their chiefe idols bee blacke and evill favoured, their mouths monstrous, their eares gilded and full of jewels, their teeth and eyes of gold, silver, and glassé, some having one thing in their handes and some another."[24] Three hundred years later, the English assessment of these images had changed little. In the 1800s, Norman Mac-leod, in the midst of his exuberance for the vistas of Banāras, referred to "that ugly looking monster called God," [25] and Sherring wrote of "the worship of uncouth idols, of monsters, of the *linga* and other indecent figures, and of a multitude of grotesque, ill-shapen, and hideous objects."[26] Mark Twain had a certain imaginative humor about it all, but he too added his voice to the chorus: "And what a swarm of them there is! The town is a vast museum of idols—and all of them crude, misshapen, and ugly. They flock through ones dreams at night, a wild mob of nightmares."[27]

These divine images bring into sharp focus the issue of what Western visitors thought they saw in the temples and along the riverfront of Kāshī, and they raise the question of what it is that Hindus see—both in the images of the temples and in the larger divine image of the city itself.

Seeing Kāshī Through Hindu Eyes

A MULTITUDE of Hindu deities is visible everywhere in Banāras. Over the doorways of temples and houses sits the plump, orange, elephant-headed Ganesha. On the walls of tea stalls and tailor shops hang gaudy polychrome icons of Lakshmī or Krishna. And on the whitewashed walls of houses and public buildings the episodes of Shiva's marriage to Pārvatī, or Rāma's battle with the ten-headed Rāvana, are painted afresh after the season of rains by local folk artists.

In temples one sees the *linga* of Shiva, or the four-armed image of Vishnu, or the silver mask of the goddess Durgā. Such images are crafted according to carefully prescribed rules of iconography and iconometry. When they are finished, the "breath" or "life" of the deity is invited to be present in the image. In some Hindu sectarian movements, the sense of God's presence here is so powerful that they see it as an image-incarnation of the Supreme Lord.[28] The last act of the elaborate consecration rites is opening the eyes of the image, which is done symbolically with a golden needle or by placing large enameled eyes upon the image. Contact between God and the worshipper is exchanged most powerfully, they say, through the eyes.

The Hindu tradition has entrusted the senses, especially the eyes,

with the apprehension of the holy. When Hindus go to the temple,
they do not say, "I am going to worship," but rather, "I am going for
darshana." The word *darshana* means "seeing." In the religious sense,
it means beholding the divine image and standing in the presence of
God. Hindus go for *darshana* especially at those times of day when the
image is beautifully adorned with flowers, and when offerings of incense, water, food, and camphor lamps are presented to the deity. The
central acts of Hindu worship are having the *darshana* of the Lord and
receiving the *prasāda,* the consecrated food offerings, which are the
Lord's special "grace" or "blessing." For Hindus, therefore, the image
is not an object at which one's vision halts, but rather a lens through
which one's vision is directed. Even the nineteenth-century missionary James Kennedy, who found the images of the gods "wild" and
"grotesque," acknowledged that he had "never met a Hindu who
would allow he worshipped the material objects before which he
bowed down."[29]

Of course, it is not only the divine image, but the fact that there are
so many different images that invites our understanding. It is fundamental to the Hindu tradition and to the Hindu way of thinking that
the Divine, the Supreme Lord, can be seen in a great variety of ways
and from many different perspectives. From one perspective it is perceived that there are more gods, or faces of God, than we can count—
330 million, they say. And yet, from another perspective, it is obvious
that there is One. The fact that there may be many gods does not
diminish their power or significance. Each one of the great gods may
serve as a lens through which the whole may be clearly seen.

When Hindus travel on a pilgrimage to a holy place such as Banāras,
it is also for *darshana*—not sight-seeing but "sacred sight-seeing."
They want to have the *darshana* of the place itself as well as that of its
presiding deity, who in Kāshī is Shiva Vishvanātha, the "Lord of All."
Their vision is sharpened and refined by the rigors of the pilgrim
journey. Some travel long distances by train or bus. Some come on
foot, as the many generations before them have done, walking the
dusty roads of rural India, balancing a bundle of provisions on their
heads.

Those who travel as pilgrims follow the path of the "holy men"
(sādhus) or "renouncers" *(sannyāsins),* those perpetual seekers and
pilgrims who have given up the settled life of home to live out the
spiritual truth that all people, finally, are travelers and pilgrims on

earth. Very few people become *sannyāsins* or *sādhus,* but in going on a pilgrimage, ordinary householders become, for a short time, renouncers of sorts. Leaving home, they take only those few things they can carry, and their life is the simple life of the road. Their destinations are spiritual ones, and they are often difficult to reach. Going on foot to a distant place becomes for these pilgrims a kind of asceticism in which the journey itself is as purifying as the sacred destination. In the *Aitareya Brāhmana,* the god Indra, protector of travelers, urges the life of the road upon a young man named Rohita:

There is no happiness for him who does not travel, Rohita! Thus we have heard. Living in the society of men, the best man becomes a sinner. . . . Therefore, wander!

The feet of the wanderer are like the flower, his soul is growing and reaping the fruit; and all his sins are destroyed by his fatigues in wandering. Therefore, wander!

The fortune of him who is sitting, sits; it rises when he rises, it sleeps when he sleeps, it moves when he moves. Therefore, wander! [30]

Hindus have taken up with great zeal the injunction to wander, and pilgrimage has long been the major reason for Hindus to travel. Modern bus and train service has brought a new dimension to Indian pilgrimage, enabling Hindus to take to the road by the millions each year for the *darshana* of the far-flung sacred places of India. The organization of this new style of pilgrimage is a thriving business.

In a city like Banāras, pilgrimage is a thriving priestly business as well. There are priests and sacred specialists to assist in every aspect of pilgrimage. There are the *pandās,* who meet the pilgrims at the train station, arrange their rest houses, and oversee the entire pilgrimage. For many pilgrims, the *pandā* will be the same man or of the same family who has cared for their ancestors. There are the *karmakāndīs,* priests who assist in particular rites; the *ghātiās,* priests of a somewhat lower class who have proprietary rites along the *ghāts* and who tend to the needs of the bathers; the *pūjārīs,* who officiate in the temples; and the *mahāpātras,* who specialize in death rites. [31]

As pilgrims arrive in Kāshī and travel by bicycle rickshaw from the train station to their rest house, the city that meets the eye is not so different from the city described by its Western visitors—the narrow streets, the cows, the temples, the *ghāts,* the river. For Hindus, however, the city they see is not only the city that meets the eye; it is also the city that engages the religious imagination. For hundreds of generations, Kāshī has received pilgrims like themselves, who have seen this city through the eyes of the collective imagination and the power of religious vision.

From childhood, these pilgrims have known of Kāshī, not through the diaries of travelers, but through a type of traditional literature called *māhātmya*. A *māhātmya* is a laud, a hymn of praise, a glorification. These praises, of particular places or of particular gods, form a part of the many Purānas, the "ancient stories" of the gods, kings, and saints. Kāshī *māhātmyas* are found in many of the Purānas, the most famous and extensive being the *Kāshī Khanda* of the *Skanda Purāna* and

The riverfront near Manikarnikā.

the *Kāshī Rahasya* of the *Brahmavaivarta Purāna*.[32] These *māhātmyas* are not descriptive statements of fact about an ordinary city, but statements of faith about a sacred city.

Kāshī is the whole world, they say. Everything on earth that is powerful and auspicious is here, in this microcosm. All of the sacred places of India and all of her sacred waters are here. All of the gods reside here, attracted by the brilliance of the City of Light. All of the eight directions of the compass originated here, receiving jurisdiction over the sectors of the universe. And all of time is here, they say, for the lords of the heavenly bodies which govern time are grounded in Kāshī and have received their jurisdiction over the days and months

right here. Thus, all the organizing forces of space and time begin
here, and are present here, within the sacred boundaries of Kāshī.

And yet Kāshī is not of this earth, they say. While it is in the world
and at the very center of the world, it is not attached to the earth. It
sits high above the earth on the top of the trident of its lord and
protector, Shiva. Kāshī is not subject to the relentless movement of the
great cycles of time, the eras of universal creation and dissolution. It is
the still center which anchors the perpetual movement of time and
space, without participating in the ever-turning world of *samsāra*.

Kāshī is the permanent home of Shiva, they say. Here he dwells in
order to bestow the enlightening wisdom of liberation. Although Shiva
is omnipresent, there are a few places that are especially transparent to
his luminous presence. And of these few, the City of Light is the most
brilliant of all.

Kāshī is Light, they say. The city illumines truth and reveals reality.
It does not bring new wonders into the scope of vision, but enables one
to see what is already there. People have called this Light the Eternal
Shiva (Sadā Shiva) or Brahman. Where this Light intersects the earth,
it is known as Kāshī.

Kāshī is famous for Death, they say. People come to this place from
all over India to die here, for "Death in Kāshī is Liberation."[33] Kāshī is
the final destination of a long pilgrimage through many lives. From
Kāshī one makes the great "crossing" to the "far shore." Death in
Kāshī is not a death feared, for here the ordinary God of Death,
frightful Yama, has no jurisdiction. Death in Kāshī is death known and
faced, transformed and transcended.

As pilgrims stand at the top of the *ghāts* and see the famed riverfront of
Kāshī and the great sweep of the Ganges for the first time, what do
they know of the *māhātmyas* that glorify this city? There are thousands
of hymns and stories of Kāshī's pilgrims and temples in the *māhātmya*
literature and in the oral traditions of different regions and even different families. Pilgrims may know very little, and perhaps no two
pilgrims know quite the same stories. During the two or three days
they spend here, they will learn a little more, from the *pandās,* storytellers, and charlatans, or from the penny-paperback *māhātmyas* for
sale in the bazaars. But even as they arrive, they bring with them the
wealth of tradition which has drawn their ancestors here for as long as

the mind can imagine, since "the days before the Ganges came from heaven to earth," they might say. And the city they see, they see in the light of a long tradition of faith.

The Names of the Sacred City

L I K E a loved one, the sacred city is called by many names. The names express the various powers and attributes of the city and reveal the dimensions of its sacred authority. All the names occur frequently in the Sanskrit *mahātmyas* which praise the city. Sometimes they are used to refer to progressively smaller units of the sacred city.* More often, however, they are used interchangeably, as we will use them here.

KĀSHĪ. THE CITY OF LIGHT

This name is the most ancient. It was used nearly three thousand years ago to refer to the kingdom of which this city became the capital. In time, the name came to refer to the capital city as well. It was to the outskirts of Kāshī that the Buddha came to preach his first sermon in the sixth century B.C. The somewhat later Jātaka tales of the Buddhist tradition speak of the "town of Kāshī."[14]

As for its etymology, it has been suggested that the name Kāshī comes from Kāsha, the name of an ancient king, whose dynasty later produced the famous legendary King Divodāsa of Kāshī, or that it comes from *kāsha*, the name of the tall silver-flowering grass which

---

* Kāshī is the largest unit—a symbolic circle with a radius of five *kroshas* or about ten miles. This sacred zone extends far beyond the city itself into the countryside to the west and is circumambulated on the famous Panchakroshī Road. Vārānasi is, roughly, the urban city today, from the Varanā to the Asi Rivers. Avimukta is a still smaller unit, and the Antargriha or "Inner Sanctum" is smaller still, including only the dense center of the city surrounding the Vishvanātha Temple. Thus, the structure of the sacred city, in this view, is a series of concentric sacred zones like the symbolic structure of a *mandala*. (*See* Appendix II for a more detailed description of these boundaries and Map 5 for an approximation of these zones.)

grows wild along the riverbank. Most commonly, however, it is said to
derive from the Sanskrit root *kāsh,* "to shine, to look brilliant or beautiful."

Kāshī, sometimes called Kāshikā, is the shining one, the luminous
one, the illumining one. Its most famous *māhātmya,* the *Kāshī Khanda*
explains: "Because that light, which is the unspeakable Shiva, shines
[*kāshate*] here, let its other name be called Kāshī."[35] The wordplay of
Sanskrit continually underlines the relation of the City of Light to the
light of enlightenment. For example, the city is called "City of Light,
which illumines liberation"—*moksha-prakāshikā Kāshī.*

VĀRĀNASĪ: BETWEEN THE VARANĀ

AND THE ASI

Vārānasī is also an ancient name, found in both the Buddhist Jātaka
tales and in the Hindu epic, the *Mahābhārata.* From the Pali version of
this name—Bārānasi—comes the corrupted name Banāras, by which the
city is most widely known today. In both Muslim and British India, the
city was "Benares," but in independent India, Vārānasī has been revived as the official name of the city.

Any resident of the city will readily explain that Vārānasī sits between the Varanā River, which flows into the Ganges on the north,
and the Asi River, which joins the Ganges on the south. Vārānasī
stretches along the river between the two. According to the *Padma
Purāna,* "The Varanā and the Asi are two rivers, set there by gods.
Between them is a holy land [*kshetra*] and there is none more excellent
on earth." And in the *Kūrma Purāna,* we find it simply put: "Vārānasī
is the city between the Varanā and the Asi."[36]

It is likely, however, that the city did not receive its name from
these two rivers, but rather from the single river that bordered it on
the north, known to early literature as the Vārānasī River, not the
Varanā.[37] As we shall see in the next chapter, it is clear from archeological excavations and from old descriptions of the city that ancient
Vārānasī was situated primarily in the north, on the high Rājghāt
Plateau where the Vārānasī River met the Ganges. The city may have
been built on both sides of the Vārānasī River; it certainly did

not stretch along the Ganges to the south as it does today. It might be added that the Asi, the alleged southern boundary, hardly merits the status of a river except during the rainy season. It is little more than a rivulet, and one Purāna rightly calls it the "Dried-Up River."[38]

While the popular derivation of Vārānasī is probably a false etymology, it is nonetheless extremely important for our discussion. What interests us in the name is not only that from which it really derives, but rather that toward which it points in helping us understand what Hindus have commonly understood by the name Vārānasī. The rivers are the boundaries of this sacred zone; they define and protect the city. According to the myth, the two rivers were created by the gods and placed in position to guard against the entrance of evil. One river was named "The Sword" *(asi)* and the other was named "The Averter" *(varanā)*.[39]

In the *Vāmana Purāna*, the two rivers are said to originate from the body of the primordial person, Purusha, at the beginning of time. The Varanā issued from the right foot of the cosmic giant and the Asi issued from its left foot. "The tract of land lying between them is the best place of pilgrimage in the three worlds and is potent enough to destroy all sins. Its peer does not exist in heaven, earth, and the netherworld."[40]

In the *Jābāla Upanishad*, the two rivers are described not as geographical rivers, but interior rivers, the mystical veins of the body's subtle physiology. "It is called Varanā because it obstructs [*vārayati*] all sins of the senses. It is called Nāsī because it destroys [*nāshayati*] all sins of the senses."[41] When the seeker asks where this place between the Varanā and the Nāsī is located, the sage replies: "It is the place where the nose and the eyebrows meet. That is the meeting place of heaven and the world beyond." Here Vārānasī is given an esoteric interpretation. It is the highest of the six *chakras,* the "circles" of power in the yogic anatomy. It is the place of the eye of wisdom.

AVIMUKTA: THE NEVER-FORSAKEN

In one Purānic *māhātmya*, Shiva says, "Because I never forsake it, nor do I let it go, this great place is therefore known as Avimukta."[42] Avimukta means "not let loose,"* and in this context it means the city "Never Forsaken" by Lord Shiva. According to the city's mythology, this was the place where the *linga* of Shiva was first established and worshipped on earth as the symbol of the Lord's perpetual presence. It is said that even in the *pralaya*, the periodic universal destruction, Shiva never lets go of Kāshī, but holds the city up above the flood-waters on his trident. "Oh silent sages, even in the time of the *pralaya* that land is never let loose by Shiva and Pārvatī. Therefore it is called 'Avimukta.' "[43]

The name Avimukta is often used to emphasize the fact that people should never leave this place. Visitors say of many a place of pilgrimage or retreat that it is so lovely or peaceful one should settle and stay forever. In Avimukta this is taken quite seriously, making this city unique among places of pilgrimage. The "Never Forsaken" is not a place the true pilgrim should merely visit, although many pilgrims do just that. Rather, it is a place one should come to live. Those pilgrims who come to live are called Kāshīvāsīs, the "dwellers in Kāshī," who have come to live out their lives here until they die.

Every Banāras householder knows a tale or two of some unfortunate friend or relation who lived for years in Vārānasī, only to die on a chance trip to Calcutta or on family business in Allahabad. The most conservative say it is best not to leave at all, even to go to the Banāras Hindu University hospital, less than one hundred feet beyond the limit of sacred Kāshī to the south. Some take a vow never to leave, a vow called *kshetra sannyāsa*. Dozens of injunctions in the Purānic *māhātmyas* urge the pilgrim to think twice before leaving Avimukta. With Death holding out the ultimate spiritual promise of liberation, who of sane mind would leave? Who but a fool would cast away a

---

* *Mukti* is another word for *moksha*, "liberation," literally to be "loosed" from the bonds of this world, to be set free. There is much wordplay on the notion that this city which makes people *mukta*, "set free," is never set free by the Lord who makes his home here.

priceless ruby to snatch up a piece of glass?[44] Indeed, it is said, having gained this holy ground one should smash one's feet with a stone to make certain that the priceless treasure of Kāshī is not negligently lost![45]

ĀNANDAVANA: THE FOREST OF BLISS

In one *mahātmya*, Shiva explains, "My *lingas* are everywhere there, like little sprouts arisen out of sheer bliss. Thus it is called the Forest of Bliss."[46] A forest with Shiva *lingas* as thick as the fresh sprouts of spring: this is the vision of the sacred city as the Forest of Bliss, the Ānandavana or Ānandakānana. The name refers to this place in the idyllic times of its mythical beginnings. It was not the urban Vārānasī that sat on the Rājghāt Plateau, but the forest paradise that spread out to the south. Its groves, streams, and pools provided a beautiful setting for temples and ashrams. Here teachers could gather their students, yogis could practice their yoga, and ascetics and hermits could find a place for their disciplines.

The city today is so dense that it is difficult to imagine it as a garden paradise. But the extensive settling of Vārānasī is relatively recent. In the twelfth century, the city still had its center in the north, around the confluence of the Ganges and the Varanā. Even in the late eighteenth century, when William Hodges and William Daniell sketched the riverfront of Banāras, it was a long spectacular bluff crowned with trees and a few prominent temples. By that time, however, the urban center of the city had already shifted southward and the dense area around Chaukhambā and Thatherī Bazaar called the *pakka muhalla,* the "well-built quarter," was completed. Even so, the people in that neighborhood still refer to their quarter as the Ban Kati, the "Cut-Down Forest," for the memory of the time when this was indeed a forest is not many generations past. Farther south and west, the Forest of Bliss remained a forest until still more recently. Even at the beginning of the twentieth century, there are maps which show much of the southern part of the city in gardens and fields, and people in their old age today remember when areas around Lahurā Bīr and Durgā Kund were jungles.

The Forest of Bliss is a vivid part of Vārānasī's sense of its own history. Today when priests or partisans of some particular temple

"View of the City of Benares" by William Hodges, Select Views in India, *1798.*
Hodges's sketch is made looking north along the Ganges from about Kedāra Ghāt.
The minarets of Aurangzeb's Mosque at Panchagangā are in the distance, and the
Ganges bank is still, for the most part, a high, tree-covered bluff.

insist, as they commonly do, that it existed when Kāshī was the Ānandavana, they are making a claim to venerable antiquity. One priest at
the temple of Madhyameshvara, the "Lord of the Center," right at the
center of Kāshī, attempted to persuade me that his temple was among
the oldest in Kāshī. It had been standing on its present site, he said,
since the very beginning, when Kāshī was the Ānandavana, even before the Ganges fell from heaven to earth. This temple was so very
old, he said, that pilgrims used to make their way through the Forest of
Bliss on a footpath when they came to Madhyameshvara from Kāshī
Station! Somewhat surprised, I asked if Kāshī Station had indeed been
there, in that time when Kāshī was the Ānandavana, even before the
Ganges had fallen to earth. He did not get my point, but seemed to
conclude that I was assailing the authenticity of the Kāshī Station. He
replied, in typical *māhātmya* style, "Of course. It's the oldest train

station in Kāshī!" In India the mythic imagination is still flourishing, and for this man, as for many Hindus, the ancient time when Kāshī was a forest paradise or when the Ganges fell to earth is part of a far more vivid, meaningful, and important history than the kind of record-keeping that concerns itself with the advent of train service. While he was certain there was a time when the wise King Bhagīratha petitioned the Ganges to come down from heaven and led the river from the mountains, through the plains of North India, past Banāras, and on to the sea, it had never occurred to him that there was a time when the railroad first arrived in Banāras.

The Purānic *māhātmyas* describe the Forest of Bliss as a garden paradise, sprinkled with the waters of the heavenly Ganges, abundant with flowers and blossoms, filled with the songs of birds, the buzzing of bees, and the tinkling of the anklets of lovely women. In its blessed groves even animals who are natural enemies dwell in peace with one another. The mouse nibbles the ear of the cat, the cat sleeps peacefully in the tail feathers of the peacock, the crane leaves the fish alone, the hawk pays no attention to the quail, and the jackal befriends the antelope.[47] Its peace and beauty are attractive even to the gods, who begin to feel dissatisfied with heaven once they have seen the Forest of Bliss.

In the Hindu philosophical traditions there are very few words used to describe the supreme and attributeless *(nirguna)* Brahman. *Ānanda* is one of these words. Brahman is *sat* (being), *chit* (consciousness), and *ānanda* (bliss). The bliss of the knowledge of Brahman is likened to the unitive bliss of lovers in close embrace. The word *ānanda* certainly carries the weight of its association with Brahman when it is used to describe the essential nature of Kāshī, which the *Kāshī Rahasya* calls the "Forest of the Bliss of Brahman."[48]

RUDRAVĀSA: THE CITY OF SHIVA

This is the dwelling place of Shiva, who is known also by his ancient name, Rudra. Here the Supreme God has taken up permanent residence. In Banāras there is a popular saying, *"Kāshī ke kankar Shiva Shankar haim,"*—"The very stones of Kāshī are Shiva." Shiva dwells not only in the city's great temples, but in the very ground and substance of the place itself.

Not only are the stones saturated with Shiva, but, according to the *māhātmyas,* so is everything else in Kāshī: the trees, animals, and people of the city. "Whatever touches Kāshī, that thing becomes her, just as a stream of wine poured into the River Ganges becomes like the Ganges. Just as iron touching the philosopher's stone becomes gold, so does one obtain the very form of Brahman, which is the form of Shiva, in Kāshī."[49] Kāshī transforms what is ordinary into what is called *Rudramaya*—"made of the substance of Rudra himself."[50] Kāshī is called Rudravāsa not only because Rudra lives here, but because everyone who lives here *is* Rudra. In the *Kāshī Khanda* Shiva explains that those who dwell in Kāshī take on the form, the attributes, and the ornaments of Rudra, and they should be honored as one would honor Rudra, and at death they are absorbed into Rudra-Shiva himself.[51]

Although Shiva dwells everywhere and in everyone, he is said to dwell with special intensity here, where the membrane between this world and the transcendent reality is so thin as to be virtually transparent. Because dying in Kāshī brings liberation, living here is an anticipatory participation in that liberation. Those who dwell in Kāshī, intending to die here, are called *jīvan muktas,* "liberated while yet alive." In this sense they are thought of as Shiva incarnate. They are to be honored, even worshipped, for it is said that they are the recipients of the sidelong glances of the alluring goddess Mukti, who is only as far away as the moment of death.[52]

MAHĀSHMASHĀNA: THE GREAT
CREMATION GROUND

"Kāshī is the Mahāshmashāna. You can burn the dead anywhere here," volunteered a very old brahmin. The discussion took place in the home of one of Kāshī's most eminent priests and had turned to the subject of cremation in Kāshī. "The whole of Kāshī is a cremation ground," he said. Lest the brahmin's point be missed, let us remember that in India the cremation ground, called the *shmashāna,* is specifically marked off outside of town, often to the south, the direction of Yama, the Lord of Death. The cremation ground is the most inauspicious of places because of the ritual pollution imparted to it by the bodies of the dead. When members of the funeral party return to their homes from the cremation ground they must undergo rites of purification. Yet in

Kāshī, the cremation ground, particularly at Manikarnikā Ghāt, is considered the most auspicious of places.

In an episode in the *Shiva Purāna,* the pretentious demigod Daksha sponsors a great Vedic sacrificial rite to which he invites everyone in the universe, except the renegade god Shiva. As the rite opens, the sage Dadhīchi stands up and rails against Daksha for not inviting Shiva, calling his sacrificial arena, without the presence of Shiva, a cremation ground. It was intended and taken as the greatest of insults.[53] On a scale of sanctity, the sacrificial ground is supposed to be the most sacred and the cremation ground the most polluted of places. It is of some importance, then, that the holy city of Kāshī has as one of its most famous epithets the "Great Cremation Ground."

As we learn more about Shiva, it will become clearer why his earthly capital city should take the name and, indeed, the nature of the most inauspicious of places. Shiva is the holy One who challenges ordinary distinctions of pure and impure, auspicious and inauspicious. He is the deity who may be beautiful or terrifying, who may anoint his body with the fragrant oil of sandalwood or with the gray ashes of the dead. It is fitting that his city be called the Great Cremation Ground as well as the Forest of Bliss.

The cremation grounds of prominence in the city today are at Manikarnikā Ghāt and Harishchandra Ghāt, although there is evidence to substantiate the old brahmin's claim that cremations once took place everywhere. There are *satī* stones, carved with the relief images of a man and a woman, which mark the places where a "good woman" *(satī)* was burned upon the funeral pyre of her husband. Such stones may be found in the area called Brahma Nāla, which was formerly a stream bed, extending up and into the city from Manikarnikā Ghāt. They are also found at a number of prominent *ghāts* along the river.[54]

The city is more than a place of mortal cremations, however. As the Great Cremation Ground, it is said to be the final resting place of the corpse of the entire universe at the end of its vast cycle of life. The *Kāshī Khanda* explains the "etymology" of the word *shmashāna:*

Shma means *shava,* a corpse. *Shāna* means *shayana,* a "bed." Thus do those who are skilled in the meaning of words say about the meaning of *shmashāna.*

When the general dissolution comes, even great beings sleep here, having become corpses. Thus the *shmashāna* is called "great."[55]

Banāras and the Sacred "Crossings" of India

B A N Ā R A S does not stand alone as India's sacred city. It is part of an extensive and intricate pattern of sacred places in India. For Hindus, the landscape of India is holy, from the Himālayas, the home of the gods, in the North, to Cape Comorin or Kanyā Kumārī, where the Goddess dwells at the southernmost tip of the subcontinent. The land that stretches out between is a land of sacred hills, rivers, and cities, webbed with pilgrimage routes. Going on a pilgrimage for the *darshana* of such places has long been an important and vibrant aspect of the Hindu religious tradition.

Hindus call the sacred places to which they travel *tīrthas,* "fords" or "crossing places." Some of India's great *tīrthas* were indeed fords, where the rivers could be safely crossed. Banāras itself is located at that ford where the old trade route through North India crossed the River Ganges. As a place of pilgrimage, however, the *tīrtha* is a spiritual ford, where earth and heaven meet, or where one "crosses over" the river of *samsāra*—this round of repeated birth and death—to reach the "far shore" of liberation. The *tīrtha,* like the river ford, is a place where that "crossing" might be easily and safely made.

A *tīrtha* is an earthly place, charged with power and purity. We call it a "sacred" place, but it is important for us to realize that there is not a Hindu term which means quite what we mean by "sacred." The term "pure" *(shuchi, pavitra)* is used, as is "good" *(punya)* and "auspicious" *(shubha, mangala).* As for sacred, in the sense of bearing the essence of the Divine, we might say that in the Hindu view the whole earth is sacred, for it is all the embodiment of the Divine. In Hindu creation myths, the earth and all the plenitude of life spring from the very body of God.[56] Like the body, the creation is differentiated in power and in function. Some earthly places reveal the Divine more readily than others. As the *Mahābhārata* puts it, "Just as certain parts of the body are called pure, so are certain parts of the earth and certain waters called holy."[57] The right ear, for example, which receives the *mantra* of the guru at the time of initiation, is especially pure, while the feet, which touch the dust, are not. So it is with the land itself. Those places most luminous, most powerful, and most transparent to the heavens are called *tīrthas*.

As a place of power, the *tīrtha* is a doorway between heaven and earth, or between "this shore" and the "far shore." There, according to Hindus, one's prayers are more quickly heard, one's petitions more readily fulfilled, and one's rituals more likely to bring manifold blessings. In the praises of a place such as Kāshī, this amplification of power is described at length:

There whatever is sacrificed, chanted, given in charity, or suffered in penance, even in the smallest amount, yields endless fruit because of the power of that place. Whatever fruit is said to accrue from many thousands of lifetimes of asceticism, even more than that is obtainable from but three nights of fasting in this place.[58]

The *tīrthas* are primarily associated with the great acts and appearances of the gods and the heroes of Indian myth and legend. As a threshold between heaven and earth, the *tīrtha* is not only a place for the "upward" crossings of people's prayers and rites, it is also a place for the "downward" crossings of the gods. These divine "descents" are the well-known *avatāras* of the Hindu tradition. Indeed, the words *tīrtha* and *avatāra* come from related verbal roots: *tṝ*, "to cross over," and *avatṝ*, "to cross down." One might say that the *avatāras* descend, opening the doors of the *tīrthas* so that men and women may ascend in their rites and prayers. The appearance of the Divine in this world is what Mircea Eliade has called hierophany, the "showing forth" of the gods.[59] In India it is clear that the gods have shown forth in thousands of places, some known and famous throughout India and some visited only by people from the immediately surrounding districts.

The stories of India's *tīrthas* are told in the popular praise literature, the *māhātmyas*, sometimes called *sthala purāṇas*, the "ancient stories of the place." This literature contains a thousand variations on the themes of divine hierophany. Considering this vast corpus of Indian mythology, which recounts the deeds of the gods and heroes, it is not difficult to imagine that the whole of India's geography is engraved with traces of mythic events. It is a living sacred geography. In Mathurā, Lord Krishna was born. In the groves of nearby Brindāvan, he danced at night with the milkmaids. In a high Himālayan cave at Amarnāth in Kashmīr, Lord Shiva appeared as a *linga* of ice. In a dozen places from

the Himālayas to the tip of Southern India, Shiva split the earth as a
linga of fire. A number of places claim the glorious victory of the
goddess Durgā over the demon Mahisha. And thousands of places
claim to have been visited by Rāma, Sītā, and Lakshmana in their
journey described in the *Rāmāyana,* or by the Pāndava brothers in
their forest exile recounted in the *Mahābhārata.*

A great *tīrtha* such as Kāshī collects a vast array of such mythic
events. In the eyes of those who love this city, everything of significance happened here—the *linga* of fiery light pierced the earth, the
goddess Durgā defeated her foes, the heroes and heroines came here on
a pilgrimage, and the saints came here to teach.

It is not only the legends and myths that communicate the power of
a place, however. The world's great *tīrthas,* in India and elsewhere,
match Mark Twain's description of Banāras as "older than history,
older than tradition, older even than legend." Whether it is Kāshī,
Jerusalem, or Guadalupe, the place itself has traditions of pilgrimage
and a reputation for sanctity and power that are far more ancient than
the particular traditions now associated with it.

In India, the wide-ranging popular cults of vegetative divinities
(yakshas), aquatic divinities *(nāgas),* and goddesses *(devīs)* set their
seal upon groves, pools, and hillocks long before the Purānic tales
were compiled. *Tīrthas* such as Kāshī and the River Ganges are symbols shaped by geography, and because geography is slow to change,
these symbols have had a tenacious hold upon the religious imagination. The particular myths and stories may come and go; the narrative may change or be forgotten; but the hilltop, the pool, and the
grove remain. Today Ganesha may sit under the great tree where the
yaksha was worshipped three thousand years ago. Shiva may stand
in a small shrine next to the ancient pool of the *nāgas.* The great
Durgā may lend her name to some local hilltop *devī.* But while the
story and the names have changed, the place attracts its worshippers
much as before.

Of India's thousands of *tīrthas,* a few places and cycles of pilgrimage
have risen to pre-eminence through the centuries. First, there are the
seven sacred cities *(sapta purī)* which are said to bestow the highest
spiritual goal, liberation. The seven are famous, and known to practi-
cally every literate brahmin in the verse:

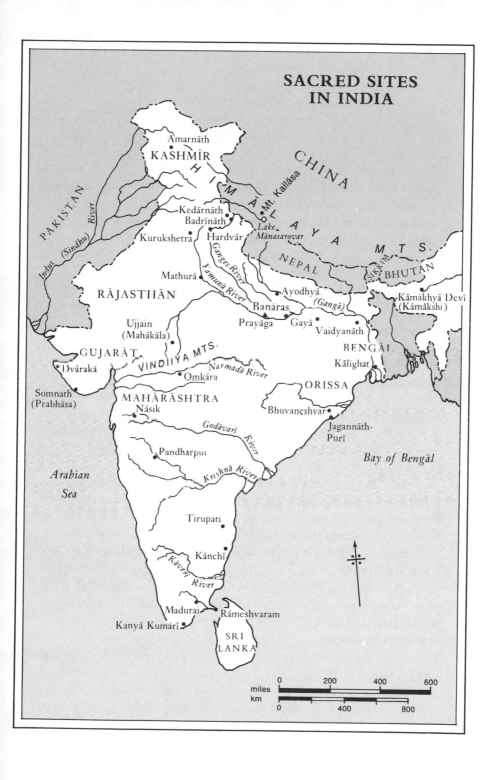

SACRED SITES IN INDIA

PAKISTAN

Indus (Sindhu) River

KASHMIR

Amarnāth

HIMĀLAYA

CHINA

Mt. Kailāsa

Kedārnāth
Badrīnāth

Lake
Mānasarovar

Kurukshetra   Hardvār

Ganges River

NEPAL

M T S.

SIKKIM   BHUTAN

Mathurā

Yamunā River

Ayodhyā

(Gangā)

Kāmākhyā Devī
(Kāmākshi)

RĀJASTHĀN

Banāras

Prayāga   Gayā

Vaidyanāth

Ujjain
(Mahākāla)

GUJARĀT

VINDHYA MTS.

Narmadā River

BENGĀL

Kālīghat

Dvārakā

Omkāra

ORISSA

Somnath
(Prabhāsa)

MAHĀRĀSHTRA

Nāsik

Bhuvaneshvar

Jagannāth-
Purī

Godāvarī River

Pandharpur

Krishnā River

Bay of Bengāl

Arabian
Sea

Tirupati

Kānchī

Kāverī
River

Madurai   Rāmeshvaram

Kanyā Kumārī

SRI
LANKA

miles
km

0   200   400   600

0   400   800

> *Ayodhyā, Mathurā, Māyā*,*
> *Kāshī, Kānchī, Avantikā,*
> *And the city of Dvārakā,*
> *These seven are* mokshada.

Mokshada means "bestower of liberation," and these seven are said to
grant liberation to all who die within their boundaries. In Kāshī it is
commonly said, however, that those who die in the other six cities are
liberated indirectly, by being reborn for a final lifetime in the City of
Light, from which they make their final journey to the "far shore."
We shall have more to say of these seven in discussing Kāshī's own
sacred geography in Chapter 7.

In addition to the seven cities, there are the four "divine abodes"
(dhāmas) at the four compass points of India, marking with sanctity
the furthest limits of the land: Badrīnāth in the Himālayan North, Purī
in the East, Rāmeshvaram in the South, and Dvārakā in the West.
There are 108 "benches" or "seats" *(pīthas)* of the Goddess, associated with the various parts of the body of the Goddess, each a manifestation of the divine female "power" called Shakti. Other cycles of
tīrthas include the twelve places where the *linga,* Shiva's emblem,
shone forth in a fiery column of light; the sixty-eight places where
Shiva's *lingas* are said to have emerged "self-born" *(svayambhū)* from
the earth; and the seven sacred rivers. Some *tīrthas* are primarily important for the people of a particular region or sectarian group.[60]

For Hindus, pilgrimage to the *tīrthas* has been an important unifying
force, not only for sects and regions, but for the wider Hindu perception of what constitutes the land of India. Everyone knows how diverse India is, in race, language, religion, and sect. In its long history
there have been few centuries of political unity until modern
times. But one thing Hindu India has held in common is a shared sense
of its sacred geography. What is India, or Bhārat, as Hindus call it? It
is that land stretching from Badrīnāth in the North to Rāmeshvaram and Kanyā Kumārī in the South. It is that land rimmed by the
Himālayas, the abode of the gods, and watered by the Ganges and the
other rivers of heaven.

In Banāras there is a modern temple called Bhārat Mātā, "Mother
India," containing no ordinary image in its sanctum, but rather a large

---

* Māyā is better known today as Hardvār, and Avantikā as Ujjain.

relief map of India, with its mountains, rivers, and sacred *tīrthas* carefully marked. It is a popular temple with today's pilgrims, who circumambulate the whole map and then climb to the second-floor
balcony for the *darshana* of the whole. Looking down at this map, they
can see at a glance the great distances many of their ancestors traveled
on foot. Most of these pilgrims will know of someone, even today, who
has made the trip to the four divine "abodes" at India's compass points,
a pilgrimage called the "Great Circumambulation" *(Mahāparikramā)*
of India. It is said that such pilgrims would carry a pot of Ganges water
from the Himālayas in the North all the way to Rāmeshvaram at
India's southern tip in order to pour that water on the Shiva *linga*
there. And from Rāmeshvaram, they would carry the sands of the
seashore back to deposit in the Ganges on their return north.

Among India's *tīrthas,* Kāshī is the most widely acclaimed. Pilgrims
come from all over India to bathe in the Ganges at Kāshī and to visit
her temples, and they come from all sectarian groups—Shaiva, Vaishnava, and Shākta alike. From one perspective, Kāshī is a single *tīrtha*
among others—one of the seven cities, one of the *lingas* of light, one of
the benches of the Goddess. At the same time, Kāshī is said to embody
all the *tīrthas.* One may visit the far-off temple of Shiva, high in the
Himālayas at Kedāra—right here in Kāshī. And one may travel to the
far South to Rāmeshvaram on the island that stretches toward Shrī
Lankā—right here in Kāshī. And even if one does not visit the sites of
these transposed *tīrthas* in Kashī, the power of all these places has been
assimilated into the power of this one place, and the pilgrims who visit
Kashī stand in a place empowered by the whole of India's sacred
geography.

One will hear that Kāshī is supreme among India's *tīrthas,* but in the
Hindu world view this does not mean what the Westerner might
imagine. It does not mean that Kāshī is unique, *the* most holy of *tīrthas.*
Singularity is not especially prized as a cultural value in India. Fitting
in is more important in this interdependent world than standing out. It
is sometimes said, for example, that in India the "individual" as we
think of it in the West does not exist. A person thinks of himself or
herself not as a singular entity, but rather as part of a larger interdependent whole, in which the parts mirror one another in an infinite,
intricate pattern. This is useful for our understanding of Hindu notions of the gods and the *tīrthas.* A place such as Kāshī is important,
even supreme, without being unique. Such is the nature of truly

pluralistic, polytheistic, consciousness. The German Indol-
ogist Max Müller coined a
term to describe the religious
consciousness of the Vedas:
kathenotheism—the worship of
many gods, one at a time. The
supremacy of the god one worships now and in this place is
taken for granted, but not that
god's uniqueness. It is assumed
that the Supreme Reality can be
approached and apprehended
in many ways. To celebrate
one god or one *tīrtha* need not
mean to celebrate only one.

Far from standing alone,
Kāshī, like a crystal, gathers
and refracts the light of other
pilgrimage places. Not only are other *tīrthas* said to be present in
Kāshī, but Kāshī is present elsewhere. In the Himālayas, for example,
on the way to the headwaters of the Ganges, the pilgrim will come
to a place called the "Northern Kāshī" (Uttara Kāshī). Just like its
prototype on the plains below, this Kāshī has its own Vishvanātha
Temple and its circumambulatory pilgrim circuit called the Panchakroshī Road. This kind of "transposition of place" is a common phenomenon in Indian sacred topography. One can readily apprehend that
the Divine dwells with equal potency in many places. Here, however, the affirmation is that the place itself, with its sacred power, is
present in more than one place. In addition to the northern Kāshī,
there is a southern Kāshī and a Shiva Kāshī in the Tamil South. There
are hundreds of temples, large and small, called Kāshī Vishvanātha,
and many of them have local *māhātmyas* claiming for that temple the
very benefits that one might receive from going to distant Kāshī. In a
similar way, the River Ganges is a prototype for other sacred waters,
and her presence is seen in countless rivers and invoked into ritual

waters all over India. To some extent all of India's great *tīrthas* are duplicated and multiplied elsewhere in India, but none as widely as Kāshī. What is "unique" about Kāshī is that this city has most powerfully collected and refracted the light of India's *tīrthas* to become the City of All India.

The symbol that condenses the whole into the part is common in the Hindu world. The whole of the sacred Vedas, they say, may be packed in a single powerful *mantra*. Or the whole of the complexity of the Divine may be visualized in a single multi-armed deity. Or the whole of the universe may be depicted in the "sacred circle" of a cosmic map called a *mandala*. Kāshī is this kind of symbol, which condenses the whole of India into a great "sacred circle," a geographical *mandala*.

The great Panchakroshī Road circles the whole of Kāshī. The sacred

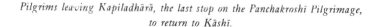

Pilgrims leaving Kapiladhārā, the last stop on the Panchakroshī Pilgrimage, to return to Kāshī.

circle of the city has its center at Madhyameshvara, the "Lord of the Center." To follow the Panchakroshī Road around Kāshī is, they say, to circle the world. The pilgrims who circumambulate Kāshī on this sacred way take five days for the trip and visit 108 shrines along the way. And, of course, it is fitting that if one cannot make the long trip around the Panchakroshī Road, there is a single temple in the heart of the city—the Panchakroshī Temple—which one can visit. By circumambulating the sanctum of this temple, with 108 wall reliefs of the stations of the sacred way, one honors the whole of Kāshī and, in turn, the whole world.

BANARAS
IN HISTORICAL
PERSPECTIVE

FROM its commanding position on the River Ganges, Banāras has witnessed the entire history of Indian civilization as it evolved in North India. From the ancient Aryan kingdoms and their rivalries, through the golden Mauryan and Gupta empires, to the thousand years of Muslim and then British domination, the historical currents of the times have passed through Banāras. Here the great sages have propounded their philosophies and here reformers have come with new ways of seeing. Yogis and ascetics have made their retreats and hermitages here, orthodox brahmins have articulated and elaborated their rituals, poets and saints have sung their songs. And here all the Hindu gods have emerged from the shadows into bold relief, as people have come to understand them, have seen their faces, and have created their multi-form images. As we attempt to see what Banāras has seen through the ages, we will see some of the great movements in the history of Indian civilization.

The Rājghāt Plateau and
the Ancient City

AT THE northern end of present-day Banāras the great Mālavīya bridge spans the Ganges at the same place where, for three thousand

years, ferries plied the river transporting the traffic and commerce of
the famous Northern Road which stretched from Bengāl in the East to
the far Northwest. In the sixth century B.C., the Buddha must have
traveled along the Northern Road from Gayā in Bihār, where he
attained enlightenment, to Banāras. Here he forded the River Ganges
to make his way to the suburb of Sārnāth, where he preached his first
sermon. Today the Grand Trunk Road follows virtually the same
route.

Just beyond the bridge to the north is a high plateau called the
Rājghāt Plateau. Today it is a rural area, containing the grounds of the
Annie Besant College, the Krishnamurti Foundation, and the Gan-
dhian Institute. There is one important temple on the plateau today, the
temple of Ādi Keshava, which has a lofty perch right at the confluence
of the Varanā River with the Ganges. On this plateau stood the oldest
part of the city of Banāras. It was an excellent, well-protected location
for a city: high, stable ground, bordered by the Ganges on its east and
by the River Varanā, skirting both its western and northern sides.

What do we know of the city that sat on this high plateau? When
the Aryan peoples moved from their stronghold in Northwest India
into the Gangetic plains at the end of the second millennium B.C., was
this an outpost of the Aryan tribe called the Kāshīs? When the Kāshī
kings took sides in the great war described in the *Mahābhārata,* was
this the city from which they came and to which they returned? Although we hear of the Kāshī kingdom in the first part of the first
millennium B.C. in the traditions and royal genealogies preserved in
the Vedic literature, the *Mahābhārata,* and the Purānas, we can only
speculate that this place was its capital.

The history of North India becomes somewhat clearer in the eighth
to sixth centuries B.C. with the emergence of the sixteen great kingdoms. These kingdoms were called *janapadas,* which literally means
the "foothold of a tribe," and they were indeed the places where
Aryan culture gained a foothold in its expansion through North India.
Kāshī was one such kingdom, as were its powerful neighbors Koshala
to the north and Magadha to the east.

The history of North India in this period is sketched out not only by
the genealogies and battles described in the *Mahābhārata* and the
Purānic texts, but also by the Buddhist literature, particularly the
Jātaka tales which tell the fables of the former lives of the Buddha.
While all of this literature dates from a later time, it contains historical

traditions, legends, and cultural information that shed some light upon the time of the great kingdoms.[1] In the Jātaka tales, for example, it is clear that the city of Vārānasī was the capital of the Kāshī kingdom, and that it was a magnificent city indeed. "Bārānasi," as they called it, had walls that were twelve leagues around,[2] and it is said to have been "the chief city in all India."[3] Elsewhere the Jātakas tell us that "all the kings round coveted the kingdom of Bārānasi."[4]

At the outset, Kāshī was one of the strongest of the kingdoms. Through this period of the great kingdoms, however, the balance of power constantly changed and by the seventh century B.C. Koshala began to grow in strength, contending first with Kāshī and then with Magadha for commanding position. It was in this time of Koshala's ascendancy that the Shākya kingdom in which the Buddha would be born a generation later was subsumed. This shift in power is also noted in the Jātakas, a number of which describe the victories of the Koshala kings over Kāshī. Finally we see the king of Koshala dubbed "Bārāna siggaho"—"Conqueror of Vārānasi."[5]

Vārānasī must have been quite a plum for Koshala in that kingdom's rise to the top. Not only was it a city of some size, but it was also a significant trading and commercial center, set as it was at the crossroads of North India's two great trading routes: the River Ganges and the Northern Road. Kāshī's wealth is famous in the Jātakas. In several such tales, for example, the Buddha-to-be, called a *bodhisattva,* is said to have been born as a rich merchant in Banāras, going about his commercial ventures with some 500 carts full of goods.[6]

In the sixth century B.C. Magadha challenged the power of Koshala. The kingdom of Kāshī and the city of Vārānasī on its high plateau became a pawn between them. The threatened king of Koshala, eager for his neighbor's goodwill, wed his daughter to King Bimbisāra of Magadha and gave Kāshī away to him as a wedding gift on the condition that the revenues of the city go to the queen for her bathing and perfume expenses.[7]

Bimbisāra was succeeded on the Magadhan throne, however, by his son Ajātashatru, who killed his father to claim the throne. Bimbisāra's Koshalan wife is said to have died of grief.[8] Presumably, the king of Koshala did win the city back and subdued Ajātashatru, but then, of all things, he gave Kāshī away again to Ajātashatru as a dowry with yet another marriage alliance! In the sixth century B.C., Magadha was clearly the ascendant power. Koshala finally had to capitulate. With the increase in Magadhan suzerainty both Kāshī and Koshala became absorbed into that kingdom.

We can only speculate about these early centuries of the "chief city in all India." Nothing of it remains. The excavations carried out on the Rājghāt Plateau revealed parts of the old city wall, datable to the ninth century B.C., as well as pottery and artifacts from this period on.[9] The excavation began quite by chance in 1940, when railroad contractors, digging for landfill for the Kāshī train station reconstruction, unearthed part of an ancient settlement. Archeologists worked in the early 1940s and again in the mid-1960s to discover the layers and the extent of the settlement at Rājghāt. Even so, the excavations have been very limited considering the magnitude of the site.

While Rājghāt is a grassy plateau today, it was the very heart of urban Vārānasī for nearly two thousand years. Its last century of glory was the twelfth century, when it became the capital of the Gāhadavāla kingdom. According to Gāhadavāla inscriptions, the kings of this great dynasty bathed in the Ganges below the temple of Ādi Keshava on the northern edge of the Rājghāt Plateau and there made pious donations to the brahmins they patronized. At the end of the twelfth century, however, this part of Vārānasī was completely destroyed by the Muslim armies of Qutb-ud-din Aibak, the chief general of Muhammad Ghūrī. The city on the high plateau never recovered.

The Geography of the Forest of Bliss

T O T H E south of the Rājghāt Plateau a high ridge continues along the Ganges, broken only by the entry of small streams. Gradually the city expanded along this ridge and spread out to the west behind it. Today, from the river, one can see that the *ghāt* steps which lead up into the city from the water's edge are treacherously steep in some places. The lofty location of Vārānasī, fifty to seventy-five feet above the river, has made it magnificent to behold and has given it a stable foundation immune from the tempests of the Ganges.[10]

The river rises and falls dramatically, rainy season and dry, up and down this high escarpment. The sacred topography of the *ghāts*, therefore, is seasonal. During the rains, from July to September, the river swells, rising as much as fifty feet up the *ghāts*. The great stairs,

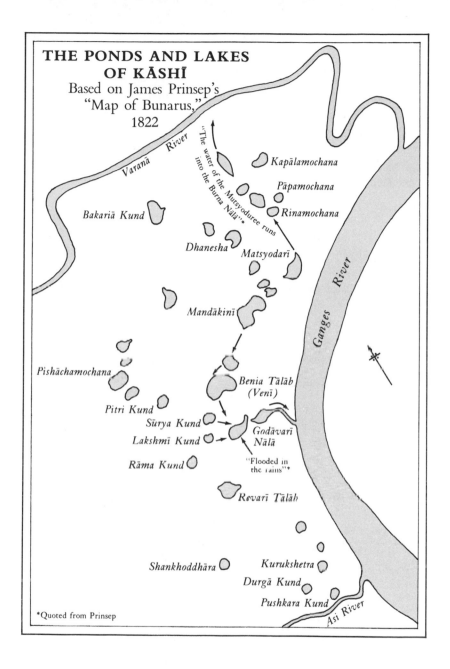

THE PONDS AND LAKES
OF KĀSHĪ
Based on James Prinsep's
"Map of Bunarus,"
1822

Varanā River

"The water of the Mutsyoduree runs into the Burna Nālā"*

Kapālamochana

Pāpamochana

Rinamochana

Bakariā Kund

Dhanesha

Matsyodarī

Mandākinī

Ganges River

Pishāchamochana

Benia Tālāb
(Venī)

Pitri Kund

Sūrya Kund

Godāvarī
Nālā

Lakshmī Kund

Rāma Kund

"Flooded in
the rains"*

Revarī Tālāb

Shankhoddhāra

Kurukshetra

Durgā Kund

Pushkara Kund

Asi River

*Quoted from Prinsep

the myriad shrines, and even a few major temples are under water
during these months. When the river subsides, the entire riverfront
must be reclaimed from beneath the tons of silt and sand deposited
there by the Ganges. The city on the high ridge, however, is rarely

touched by this seasonal cycle, although every few decades the river rises to flood level and inundates the city streets, as it did during the most recent floods of 1948 and 1978.

To the west of this high river ridge are lowland basins. In ancient times, these low areas were dotted with small pools and inland lakes and laced with small streams. The four major bodies of water were the Mandākinī (now Maidāgin) lake and the Matsyodarī (now Macchodarī) lake in the North, which drained northward into the Varanā River, and the Venī (now Beniā) lake farther south, which drained through the stream called Godāvarī (now Godauliā) into the Ganges at Dashāshvamedha. Many of the pools and streams of inland Vārānasī were named after the sacred waters of all India. For example, the Mandākinī is the name of the Ganges as it runs through the heavens and is the name of one of the first major tributaries of the earthly Ganges in the high Himālayas. The Venī is the confluence of the Ganges and the Yamunā at Prayāga or, according to some, the Krishnavenī River of South India. The Godāvarī is a great river of Central India, running eastward toward the Bay of Bengāl. In these and in other tanks and pools

"Benares from the Mundakinee Tulao" as drawn by James Prinsep, Benares Illustrated, 1831. Looking east, the minarets of the mosque at Panchagangā in the distance. Bare Ganesha Temple in the grove on the right. One of the famous tame turtles being fed at center.

of Kāshī, all the sacred waters of India were named and were said to be symbolically present.

The 1822 map of Banāras made by the British scholar James Prinsep* shows how numerous these pools and lakes were. His drawing of the

---

* James Prinsep (1799–1840), an archeologist, numismatist, and epigraphist, was stationed in Banāras in the late 1820s, where he conducted a city census. His map of the city is unsurpassed, even today, and his drawings of the city were published in the early 1830s, when Prinsep was the Assay Master of the Calcutta Mint as well as the editor of the *Journal of the Asiatic Society of Bengal.* During these years he did the work for which he is most well known: the deciphering of the Kharoshthī and Brāhmī scripts, which enabled him to read the famous inscriptions of the Mauryan Emperor Ashoka.

Mandākinī shows it to be a lake of substantial size. As the city spread, the proper drainage of these waters was obstructed and they became polluted. During the 1820s the Mandākinī and the Matsyodarī were drained and the two, much reduced in size, became small lakes, surrounded by municipal parks. Prinsep estimated that while the Maidāgin was being drained, conscientious Hindus transported some 1,500 stranded turtles to the Ganges!

By the time Mr. Bax mapped the city in 1863, the Godauliā stream had become the broad commercial street which still brings pilgrims and tourists to the great bathing *ghāt* at Dashāshvamedha. In his day, the Venī lake still remained, but by the beginning of this century it too was drained and named "Victoria Park," today called Beniā Park.

There are still many smaller lakes and pools in Banāras today. They are called *kunds,* and in addition to their mundane uses they serve as waters for ritual bathing. Most of them still remain as natural, clay-banked pools, such as Rāma Kund, Sūrya Kund, and Shankhoddhāra. Some of them, however, have been converted into artificial tanks, with stone steps leading to the water along all four sides. Durgā Kund, where the famous Durgā Temple of southern Banāras sits, is a good example of such a tank, as is nearby Kurukshetra Kund and Lakshmī Kund, near Godauliā.

A thousand years ago, when these pools and lakes were pure and the water moved without obstruction, when Kāshī was luxuriantly forested, and when temples and ashrams sat in relative isolation on the banks of each lake and stream, the sacred precincts of Banāras must have been very inviting indeed. The fact that there was so much water here—with the Ganges on one side of the long river ridge and all these inland pools on the other—certainly contributed to its popularity as a religious center. Hindu concern with sacral waters and ritual purity is as ancient as the tradition itself, and Kāshī was a place of abundant waters. As the Chinese traveler Hiuen Tsiang noted in his seventh-century journal, streams of pure and clear water flowed throughout the city.[11] From the Sanskrit Purānas of about the same time, it seems that in years of exceptional flooding, the city on the high ridge was completely surrounded by water, becoming virtually an island. These times, when the holy Ganges encircled the holy city, were praised as the most auspicious of times, as we shall see in exploring the Omkāra Temple in Chapter 3.

The visitor to the city today would hardly notice this unusual geography. Its many tanks and pools are hidden in crowded sections of the city, accessible only by very narrow lanes. The basins that were once lakes have become city parks, and the running streams have become streets. But knowing something of its ancient geography, it is possible to glimpse what the Forest of Bliss must have been like a thousand years ago.

The Ancient Religion of the Yakshas

E A R L Y I N T H E first millennium B.C., long before the emergence of Vishnu and Shiva as the great gods of Hinduism, this Forest of Bliss was inhabited by a host of ancient deities associated primarily with trees and pools. They were not worshipped in temples, but may have had a small shrine or bench at the base of a tree. They had no images, save perhaps a stone. They were not worshipped for salvation from this world; rather their realm of jurisdiction was life and death, health and disease, fertility and mortality. One scholar has called the propitiation of these deities the *yakshadharma*, the "religion of the *yakshas*"; another has called it the "life-cult."[12] Whatever it is called, this was the prevalent religious tradition of the non-Aryan people of ancient India.

By the term *yakshas*, "honored ones," we wish to include a whole range of deities, some of which were actually called *yakshas*, while others were called *rakshasas* ("demons"), *ganas* ("troops" or "attendants"), *ganeshas* ("troop-leaders"), or *bhairavas* (the "frightful" ones). On the female side, they were called *yakshīs*, *yoginīs* ("enchantresses"), *mātrikās* ("mothers"), or simply *devīs* ("goddesses"). In addition, there were *nāgas*, the "serpents" inhabiting the waters and the netherworlds. The names of these deities were not interchangeable, but it is very difficult to draw firm lines between these types of tutelary deities. All were local deities, associated with particular villages or regions. They may be called autochthonous, literally "sprung up from the land itself." They have in common their jurisdiction over the mundane concerns of life, and their ambiguous capacity to heal and to harm, to work for protection or for mischief, within their areas of jurisdiction. Some of these deities are theriomorphic, having an "animal form."

The worship of these deities with flowers and incense, banners and bells, milk and food offerings, contained the elements that were later to become standard in Hindu *pūjā*. One difference, however, is that some of these ancient deities were offered meat, blood, and spiritous liquors, a practice which still exists in some parts of rural India, especially in the worship of the goddesses. This type of worship is called *bali*. For the most part, this blood offering has been replaced by the practice of smearing the stone or icon with vermilion. In modern North India, one can use the smearing of vermilion in worship as a virtual color code for identifying the heirs of these ancient autochthonous deities.

The *yakshas* were the first Indian deities to be depicted in iconic, anthropomorphic form, beginning in the Mauryan period in about the third century B.C. They were shown as stout, sturdy, and often pot-bellied. The *yaksha* leader, Kubera, was said to dwell in the Himālayas, where he guarded the jewels and minerals of the earth. He was rich as well as fat. Like Kubera, other *yakshas* were also associated with beneficent abundance. Most often they dwelt in trees, which are the most common natural symbol of continuous generativity: the birth, growth, death, and rebirth which are the jurisdiction of the deities of the life-cult. *Yakshas* were sometimes depicted spewing vegetation from their mouths. Similarly, their female counterparts, the *yakshīs,* were first depicted as tree-spirits: shapely, full-breasted, and full-hipped women, embracing the trunks of flowering trees.[13]

The Hindu Purānas bear witness to this ancient popular religion of the *yakshas*. Amidst their abundant mythologies, the Purānas contain the rudiments of Hindu "history."[14] There one will find the genealogies of kings and the fragmentary tales of kingdoms and tribal rivalries, victories and calamities. In addition, the Purānic corpus of many volumes composed over many centuries preserves several layers of a single myth, thus revealing something of an historical development. In the Kāshī literature, one instance of the "history of a myth" takes us from the age of the *yakshas* to the apotheosis of Shiva.

To begin with, the *Brahmā Purāna* tells of the rivalry between two clans, the Kāshīs and the Haihaiyas. In the context of this mytho-history, it tells us that the Kāshī king named Divodāsa was expelled from the city by a *rākshasa* named Nikumbha. For a long time thereafter the city was occupied by another *rākshasa* named Kshemaka.[15] It is not much of a story.

In the *Harivamsha* and in the *Brahmānda* and *Vāyu Purānas,* we are given the reason for Divodāsa's expulsion: The King was cursed because he had propitiated this deity Nikumbha for a son and, having failed to receive the desired son, he flew into a rage and ordered Nikumbha's shrine destroyed. Here Nikumbha and Kshemaka are not *rākshasas,* but are called *ganas* or *ganeshas.* Nikumbha is portrayed as a very popular deity, posted at the city gate, granting boons by the thousands to those who propitiate him there.[16] His position at the city gate certainly presages what we know of Ganesha in later times as the Guardian of the Threshold. In addition, Nikumbha has the same double nature we see in Ganesha as Vighnesha, the "Lord of Obstacles," who removes obstacles by granting boons, and who also poses obstacles, in this instance by withholding the desired boon and later pronouncing a curse upon the city. Ganesha as a particular deity had not yet emerged at this time in history, but *ganas* and *ganeshas* were probably worshipped widely in North India as indigenous classes of deities.

Hindu stories all have a context, a larger story of which they are a part, like intricate sets of nesting boxes. This story of Divodāsa's rivalry with the Kāshī cult-deity Nikumbha is set in the context of a very important story: the story of Shiva's search for a home to which to bring his new bride Pārvatī. The time is after the wedding of Shiva and Pārvatī, and Shiva, who hitherto has lived in the snowy highlands of the Himālayas, has been pressured by his bride and his mother-in-law to find a proper home, as a bridegroom should. Scanning the whole earth, he saw lovely Vārānasī and decided that this city alone was fit to be their home. Unfortunately, Vārānasī was already the capital of King Divodāsa. Shiva plotted to get Divodāsa out of Vārānasī, and in this context summoned Kshemaka and Nikumbha to help him. The entire episode, therefore, is seen as part of Shiva's plot to get hold of the city for himself.

The involvement of Shiva here is clearly a later version of the story, but it is of great interest because it points to the time when Shiva did not dwell in Kāshī, when the city was in the hands of other kings and in the worship of other gods. When Shiva chose this place to be his capital, he had to wrest its possession from someone else.

A still later and very elaborate transformation of this myth occupies many chapters of the *Kāshī Khanda.* In this story, Divodāsa adheres to a *dharma* which rejects all the gods, i.e., the Buddhist *dharma.** In

* Here *dharma* means "religious tradition" or "religious ethic."

becoming king, he expels them all from Kāshī. In order to gain possession of the city once again, Shiva sends not only *ganas* like Kshemaka and Nikumbha, but all the deities of the pantheon. They go as spies and emissaries to attempt to get rid of Divodāsa. The story of how they inhabited the sacred city once again and prepared the way for Shiva to return will be told and examined in Chapter 4. In this one myth, then, we can glimpse the ancient *yakshadharma* in Kāshī, as well as a time when Buddhism held sway, and we can see the triumph of Shaivism in claiming the city for the "Great Lord," Shiva Maheshvara.

The Buddhist Jātaka tales, like the Purānas, tell of the worship of *yakshas*, *nāgas*, and other deities in ancient Kāshī. Many of the Jātaka tales have the formulaic beginning "Once upon a time when Brahmadatta was reigning in Bārānasi. . . ."[17] Brahmadatta is not the name of a single king, but rather the name of an entire line of kings who reigned in Kāshī in the centuries before the time of the Buddha. Such an introduction is so standard that one cannot presume the ensuing story to be a revelation of ancient Banāras life; but neither can one entirely dismiss the evidence of these stories. Taken as a whole, they open windows upon the cultural milieu of old Banāras. In these tales, the Buddha was born repeatedly in Banāras in his previous lives—as a dice-player, an ascetic, an acrobat, a gardener, a snake-bite doctor, a rich brahmin. What is especially interesting to us is that in many of these tales various *yakshas*, *yakshīs*, and *nāgas* are converted to the worship of the *bodhisattva*. These *yakshas* are said to be tree-dwelling deities who are to be propitiated with offerings of meat as well as the traditional incense and flowers. It is clear that the cultus of ancient Banāras included the form of worship called *bali*.

The remnants of this ancient cultus are plainly visible today. When we see the trunks of great trees daubed with orange *sindūr*, swathed about with string, and sprinkled with water by circumambulating worshippers; when we see a plain stone in a "shrine" consisting of nothing but two bricks surmounted by a slab of rock; when we see worshippers bathing in a pool or tank; when we see them smearing Ganesha or Hanumān with vermilion and sprinkling flowers in his lap—we are seeing something of this city's religious life that is pre-Shaiva, pre-Buddhist, and probably more than three thousand years old.

The Forest Hermitages and the Wisdom Traditions of Kāshī

I N S O M E Hindu weddings, even today, the groom will appear at the doorway of the bride's home, shortly before the extensive marriage rites are about to begin, and announce to his future father-in-law that he is going to renounce the world and go to Banāras to study the Vedas. This is a ritual threat, and it initiates a round of pleading, bantering, and bargaining in which the bride's family, with gifts and with promises, inevitably dissuades the young man from his noble goal.

Similarly, in some parts of India the initiation sacrament for young men includes a mock journey to Banāras. The rite is called the *upanayana samskāra*, the sacrament of "leading forth" the young student to the guru, from whom he receives the sacred thread worn by all twice-born males and the initiatory *mantra* which he will repeat every morning of his life. Immediately afterwards, the initiate takes seven steps in the direction of Banāras, a ritual enactment of the ancient journey to the fountainhead of all wisdom.

Perhaps as early as 1,000 B.C. the Forest of Bliss, which attracted the worshippers of *yakshas* and *nāgas*, also attracted religious seekers, ascetics, and yogis, who found this to be an ideal place for their hermitages. The centuries that saw the rise of the great kingdoms of North India were also a time of religious unrest and new philosophical thinking. The sages and seekers of this period were not primarily the brahmins, who guarded the traditional Vedic rites of the Aryans, but were called *shramanas*, "ascetics" who were teachers of a new, introspective, non-brahminical wisdom. This period produced a whole range of new philosophical perspectives, from the idealism of the Upanishadic sages, who claimed that Reality lay beyond the apprehension of the senses, to the materialism of the Lokāyatas, who contended, rather, that Reality is precisely what can be apprehended by the senses. This time also saw the rise of new spiritual disciplines, like those of the Jainas, the Buddhists, and the yogis. In this period Vārānasī became known as a center of learning. By the sixth century B.C. it was not as important a political center as were Shrāvastī to the north, the capital of Koshala,

or Rājagriha to the east, the capital of Magadha. But Vārānasī was
more than a city; it was also the sacred *kshetra,* the "field" or the
"precincts" that stretched out to the adjacent land of pools and groves,
where seekers and sages had their retreats.

The most famous seeker of this age was Siddhārtha Gautama, born a
prince in a small kingdom that had been subsumed by Koshala. The
story of his quest is well known: how he left a life of luxury to wrestle
with the questions of sickness, old age, and death; how he spent years
in the forest, practicing spiritual disciplines and asceticism with one
teacher and then another; how he left his companions and teachers
behind to seek a "middle way" in an age of extremism; how he sat in
deep meditation at the place called Gayā and saw deeply into the
nature of things. He came to be called the Buddha, the "Awakened
One," and after his enlightenment or awakening, he struck out for
Vārānasī to teach what he had seen to his companions, for he knew
they would be there. He walked the two hundred miles from Gayā and
crossed the Ganges by ferry to reach Vārānasī. There in a park in the
suburbs of the city he found his former companions and preached to
them the teachings that have come to be called the Four Noble Truths
and the Eightfold Noble Path. In this first sermon of the Buddha he
"turned the wheel of the *dharma,*" which has been in motion ever
since. As the historian Motī Chandra writes, "Vārānasī at this time
was so celebrated that it was only suitable for the Buddha to teach a
new way and turn the wheel of the law there."[18]

The park was called Rishipatana, for its *rishis* or "sages," and also
Mrigadāya, "Gift to the Deer."[19] The place has long been known as
the "Deer Park" and is associated with a Jātaka tale in which the king
of Vārānasī gave the park to the deer as an asylum. The modern name,
Sārnāth, is said to come from the "Lord of the Deer," Sāranganātha.

There at Rishipatana the Buddha is also said to have attracted his first
lay followers. He taught a young man named Yasha, the son of a
Vārānasī merchant. The story of how Yasha turned from a life of
worldly pleasure and riches to a life of renunciation and seeking is
similar to the Buddha's own story. Yasha was enlightened by the Buddha's teachings and became a monk. His parents also came to hear the
Buddha and became his first lay followers.

The Buddha is said to have spent his first rainy season retreat there
at Rishipatana before beginning his life as an itinerant teacher. Each
year he and his monks would spend the four months of the rains in a

park or retreat center on the outskirts of one of the major cities of North India, such as Shrāvastī, Rājagriha, or Vaishālī. Several times during his long career, he returned to Vārānasī's Deer Park for the rainy season.[20] A monastic retreat, called a *vihāra*, was soon established there, and after the Buddha's death this was one of the four places mentioned where a shrine or *dāgaba* was to be built and to be visited by pilgrims with "reverence and awe."[21]

For 1,500 years Sārnāth continued to be an active monastic center of Buddhism. In the third century B.C. the Buddhist Emperor Ashoka had a great *stūpa* constructed there. In the Gupta period of the fourth to sixth centuries A.D. Sārnāth became one of the great centers of Buddhist art, producing exquisite sandstone images of the Buddha. When Hiuen Tsiang visited Vārānasī, which he called "Polonisse," in the seventh century, he reported that there were some thirty monasteries and 3,000 monks. While Vārānasī grew increasingly famous as a Hindu place of pilgrimage, it continued to have a significant Buddhist monastic presence until the twelfth century, when Qutb-ud-din Aibak's armies demolished Sārnāth as well as Vārānasī's great Hindu temples. While the Hindus recovered from the blow, the Buddhist tradition, dependent entirely upon its monks, monasteries, and centers of learning, was virtually eliminated.

In addition to the Buddha and his followers, Vārānasī also attracted seekers of the other great heterodox tradition, the Jainas The Jaina spiritual leaders were called *jinas*, "victorious ones" or *tīrthankaras*, the "ford-makers," and the line of these legendary leaders extends far back into the dim past. According to Jaina tradition, the seventh *jina*, Suparshva, was born in Vārānasī and his mother was the earth herself. The twenty-third *jina*, Pārshvanātha, is the first to be dated historically. He lived in the eighth century B.C. and is also said to have been born in Vārānasī.[22] Pārshvanātha was followed in the sixth century B.C. by the *jina* Mahāvīra, a younger contemporary of the Buddha, who also visited Vārānasī during his forty-two years of itinerant teaching.

From the time of Pārshvanātha to the present the Jainas have continued to have a presence in Vārānasī and to count it among their own sacred *tīrthas*. In the fourteenth century, the Jaina scholar Jina Prabha Sūri traveled throughout India and wrote about the major *tīrthas* of the Jainas in a book called the *Vividha Tīrtha Kalpa*. There in his chapter on Vārānasī he mentions a temple of Pārshvanātha, perhaps the same temple that today still stands in the Jaina compound in the Bhelupura district of the city. He describes the life of the city with its yogis and rogues, its temples, tanks, and monkeys—a familiar description even today. Jina Prabha Sūri closes his account of the city saying, "Who does not love the city of Kāshī, shining with the waters of the Ganges and with the birthplace of two *jinas*?"[23]

The period that produced the speculations and the disciplines of Mahāvīra and the Buddha also produced the philosophers and seers whose teachings and dialogues are found in the Upanishads. While they may be called orthodox in the sense that they took the Vedas as authoritative, their concern was not with the ritual dimensions of the Vedas, but rather with the interior knowledge of their meaning. The questions of these seekers, like those of their heterodox counterparts, were life's most profound questions: "What is the cause? What is Brahman? Whence are we born? Whereby do we live? And on what are we established?"[24] These were the questions seekers brought to the ashrams and hermitages of Banāras. The answers were not the possession of the privileged brahmins alone. Indeed, many of the great teachers of this age were *kshatriyas*, members of the ruling class. One Upanishad describes a striking reversal: the king of Kāshī, Ajātashatru, becomes the teacher of a brahmin sage, who has taught all he knows of Reality to the King. Ajātashatru asks, "Is that all?" The brahmin replies, "That is all." The brahmin then becomes Ajātashatru's pupil. The King then goes on to teach him of the nature of the One Brahman, concluding: "As a spider might come out with his thread, as small sparks come forth from the fire, even so from this Soul come forth all vital energies, all worlds, all gods, all beings."[25]

The pursuit of wisdom, *jnāna*, has always been an important strand of the Hindu tradition. *Jnāna* is not conventional knowledge, but liberating insight, the deep-seeing that changes one's entire consciousness of oneself and the world. It was the pursuit of such insight into the nature of things that gave rise to the philosophies of the Upanishads and the disciplines of yoga and later produced the various schools of philosophical thought. It is significant that the views of the Upanishads and the philosophies that emerged from them were called *darshanas*, "points of view" or "perspectives." *Darshana* comes from a verb meaning "to see," and it conveys the understanding that any philosophy is one way of seeing a truth that can be viewed from different angles. The Sānkhya and Yoga, the Mīmāmsā and Vedānta, the Nyāya and Vaisheshika—all emerged as "orthodox" *darshanas,* in that they assume the authoritative nature of the Vedas. Although they articulate different theories of causation and enumerate different means of arriving at valid knowledge, they share a common goal: liberation, *moksha.* In this they might all be considered "religious philosophies." Through the centuries, the *darshanas* emerged and refined their views in debate and dialogue with one another.

Vārānasī has long been associated with the pursuit of this transforming wisdom. The ashrams of ancient India were its universities, so to speak. Around the great urban centers of Mithilā, Taxila, and Vārānasī were whole colonies of ashrams, where students would apprentice themselves to teachers in order to learn the Vedas. Vārānasī outlived all the others as such a center and became synonymous with classical learning. The ritual journeys to Kāshī "to study the Vedas" became, as we have seen, a part of initiatory and wedding rites in distant parts of India. This place of learning came to be called Brahmavārdhana, the "Increase of Brahman," meaning the place where the wisdom of Brahman increases.[26] And, of course, the name Kāshī also referred to the city as a center of "enlightenment," the place where the nature of Brahman is illumined.

Through the centuries, students would have encountered many of India's greatest philosophers and scholars in Vārānasī's ashrams: the grammarian Patanjali in the second century B.C., the philosopher Shankara in the eighth and ninth centuries, the theologian Rāmānuja in the eleventh. With the increasing organization of the *sannyāsins,* instigated by Shankara in his grand tour of India, monastic centers began to develop. Each of the great orders of *sannyāsins* and each of the major sectarian movements had a monastery or a forest retreat in Kāshī. The representation of all the major religious movements in Kāshī remains an important part of the city's sacred geography today. The followers of Shankara and Rāmānuja, Madhva and Vallabha all have their monastic centers, as do the Tantric Gorakhnāthī yogis and the frightful Aghorīs, the South Indian Vīra Shaivas and the North Indian Kabīr Panthīs.[27]

The ancient traditions of renunciation and the seeking of wisdom are still visible in the streets of Banāras, as the *sannyāsins,* distinctive in their faded orange clothing, carrying a staff and a water pot, make

their way to the river to bathe or collect their daily alms from householders in the neighborhood of their monasteries. Particularly during
the four months of the rainy season the *sannyāsins* gather here in large
numbers, interrupting their otherwise itinerant lives with a period of
rest and retreat, much as the holy men of India have done for over 2,500
years.

Kāshī and the Rise of
the Great Gods

W H E N the first Western travelers and traders visited Banāras, they
were overwhelmed by its multitude of temples and gods. But the holy
city the Buddha sought out in the sixth century B.C. was not a city of
temples, renowned for its association with Shiva. What happened in
the intervening centuries is of great interest, for it was nothing less
complex and fascinating than the emergence of the Hindu tradition as
it is known today: the rise to prominence of Shiva, Vishnu, Krishna,
and the Goddess; the emergence of the temple cults; the crafting of
mūrtis, the "images" or "forms" of the gods which came to be worshipped in the temples; and the development of the popular rites of
pūjā and pilgrimage.

The notion which came to the fore in these centuries is "theism"—a
religious life which focuses on God. The Vedic tradition had been
primarily oriented toward the *yajna*, the ritual "sacrifice." It had no
images or temples, but focused upon the fire-altar, a symbol of the
entire universe, and the elaborate rites whereby the universe was periodically re-created in the fire-sacrifice. The wisdom traditions of the
Buddhists and Upanishadic sages were primarily oriented toward the
interior universe and the transforming knowledge of its source and
destiny. Their rites were the rites of spiritual discipline, harsh asceticism, and yoga. While the "gods" were part of the Vedic and Upanishadic world, and were even recognized in the Buddhist world, they
were never the center and anchor of that world. Not until the rise of
theism did the gods take a place at the center. Vishnu, Krishna-
Vāsudeva, Rudra-Shiva, the Devī, even the Buddha gradually emerged in
these centuries as the focal point of a new type of religiousness. Many

of the ritual forms of this religiousness came from the *yaksha* tradition: the offering of flowers, water, incense, cloth, etc. But the deities worshipped were no longer strictly local spirits. They developed a wider and more universal appeal. And the attitude in which they were worshipped was expressed by a new term: *bhakti*. *Bhakti* means devotion, honor, love. The spirit with which these great gods were approached was not strictly the propitiatory spirit of approach to the *genii loci* and the tutelary deities of health and life; propitiation yielded to devotion.

We have noted how each of these great deities, in rising to prominence, incorporated various *yakshas, nāgas, ganas,* and *devīs,* as well as some of the earlier Vedic deities. Many lesser or local deities were subsumed under the canopy of a deity with a more universal outreach. The *nāga* stretched his hood out over the infant Krishna or the meditating Buddha, offering protection. The *ganas* and *ganeshas* joined in the entourage of Shiva as his henchmen. The village *devīs* came to be seen as facets of a Great Goddess. Many autochthonous and theriomorphic deities became associated with Vishnu as *avatāras* or "descents" of the wide-striding, rescuing god. It is important to remember, however, that many such "minor deities" resisted incorporation too, for one sees their evidences widely in India even today.

The rise of the great gods can be followed in the textual developments from the Brāhmanas, to the Epics, to the Purānas. And it is also evident in the sculptural artifacts and remains of early Banaras. We will follow the rise of these deities as witnessed in Banāras by beginning with some of these visual texts—the Kāshī artifacts that can be found in the Bharat Kalā Bhavan museum on the campus of Banāras Hindu University and in the Sārnāth museum.

The period of time under consideration here is many centuries, beginning after the first great Buddhist empire, that of the Mauryas in the fourth century B.C., and extending through the Gupta empire from the fourth to the sixth centuries A.D. These thousand years saw the emergence of theistic Hinduism and Mahāyāna Buddhism. In Banāras, the first half of this millennium saw the dominance of rulers with a disposition toward Buddhism, beginning with the Mauryas, whose great Emperor Ashoka is said to have visited Sārnāth. There a fragment of one of his celebrated inscribed pillars still stands, and its famous lion capital may be seen in the Sārnāth museum. While the Shunga kings in the first and second centuries B.C. apparently supported brahminism and Pushyamitra Shunga twice performed the Vedic *ashvamedha*** sacrifice at Vārānasī, they were followed in the first century A.D. by the Kushāna kings of Central Asia, who extended their rule over Vārānasī. Kanishka was a patron of the Buddhist tradition, and it was through the heartland of his kingdom in present-day Afghanistan that the first Buddhist monks made their way to China. Following the fall of the Kushāna empire, however, the Banāras area came under the jurisdiction of kings who patronized the Hindu tradition, with its various theistic movements. The Bhāra Shivas, a local dynasty, followed by the great Gupta dynasty, ushered in an age of Hindu revivalism, after centuries of Buddhist domination.

The whole sweep of this thousand-year period from the imperial Mauryas to the imperial Guptas is rich and complex in its literature, its art, and its emerging philosophies. Here, however, we focus on the emergence of theism, for this development was of overwhelming significance for the sacred city of Kāshī. And Kāshī, of course, was not simply a witness to these events, but an active participant in them.

The Divine Buddha

O N   E N T E R I N G the museum at Sārnāth one sees an enormous image of the Buddha. He is larger than life. He stands flat-footed, broad-shouldered, and open-faced, gathering up the folds of his thin robe with a very strong arm. The figure was produced by the artisans of Mathurā, two hundred miles to the west, in the first century A.D.[28] While it is a Buddha, its sturdy strength is that of the *yakshas,* who were among the first deities to be imaged in stone three centuries earlier. The inscription notes that during the third regnal year of King Kanishka, this image was donated by a monk named Bāla and established in Vārānasī, where the Buddha had turned the wheel of the *dharma.* According to the inscription, the donation was made in order

---

* The ancient Vedic *ashvamedha* rite, revived by Pushyamitra, was extremely complex. Simply, a horse was consecrated and let to roam for a whole year. The land over which it roamed, unchallenged, submitted to the power of the sponsoring king. As a royal rite, this became extremely rare in later India. So auspicious was this rite, however, that other rites, including pilgrimages, were later compared to it in sanctity.

to benefit Bāla's mother, father, and teacher, as well as all monks and, indeed, all living creatures.

While the image has a certain friendly humanness about it, one must ask what it meant to make an image of the Buddha in Bāla's day. From whom were the benefits of donating the image expected to derive? If the Buddha in his *nirvāna* had passed away into that complete passing away of which not a trace remains, then what was the religious intent and meaning of Bāla's gift?

These were the very questions with which Buddhists, monks and laity alike, had long been concerned at the time this image was made. Who was and is the Buddha? A human teacher and pathfinder? Or a divine being, who even now can receive gifts and bestow blessings in return? One may be certain that even during the lifetime of the Buddha there were many villagers and seekers who heard him and saw him and immediately considered him to be a divine being; but now in these centuries that view was elaborated and articulated by the Buddhists whose way was called the Mahāyana, the "Great Path," and who spoke of the Buddha, in the *Lotus Sūtra,* for example, as the "God of Gods," Devatideva. They developed a notion of the divine "descents" of the Buddha into the world of *samsāra.* Siddhārtha Gautama was only the most recent of these descents. Even now there are *bodhisattvas,* working with mercy and with wisdom in the world.

The increasingly sublime understanding of the Buddha is reflected in the Buddha images crafted by the artists of Sārnāth during the Gupta period. The figures have an exquisite delicacy, made possible by the fine-grained sandstone of Chunār and the canons which prescribe that such figures conform to a divine prototype of physical perfection. In the most famous of these images in the Sārnāth museum, the Buddha sits cross-legged, his limbs in the perfect proportions prescribed by the iconometry of the day, his hands in a teaching pose, his eyes downcast, half-shut in meditation, his head backed by a beautifully ornamented circular nimbus. Below the seat on which he sits is the wheel, the symbol of the *dharma* he taught at Sārnāth, and six kneeling figures, who perhaps represent those ascetic companions whom he first taught.

There are many other Gupta images of the Buddha and the *bodhisattvas* in the Sārnāth museum and in the Bhārat Kalā Bhavan of Banāras. They all portray a sublime Buddha, who certainly came in these centuries to be revered as a deity.

The Buddha from Sārnāth. Gupta period. His mudrā *or "hand gesture" here is one of teaching, for at Sārnāth the Buddha began his long career as a teacher.*

Not only the Buddha, but the Jaina *tīrthankara* was imaged in this sublime fashion during the Gupta period. In the Bhārat Kalā Bhavan, one can see three sixth-century images of Mahāvīra whose depiction in this age closely paralleled that of the Buddha.*

---

* Bhārat Kalā Bhavan, Nos. 161, 212, 294.

Vishnu and Krishna-Vāsudeva

V I S H N U appears briefly in the ancient Vedic hymns, sometimes as
the helper of the great god Indra and sometimes in his own right as the
"Wide-Striding" one. He is famous for his three great strides, with
which he stretches through the universe, pervading the earth, the atmosphere, and the heavens. The etymology of his name conveys his
ability to "spread" or to "extend." It is this extensiveness that made
Vishnu a god of universal dimensions, identified with India's most
universal of symbols: the Sun and the Vedic world-creating Sacrifice.
And as an all-pervading god, Vishnu came to be seen as having many
avatāras, his divine incarnations or, more precisely, "descents" into
the world. Some of India's most powerful folk deities, such as the
man-lion Narasimha, were ultimately recognized as *avatāras* of
Vishnu.* Many divinities came to be seen as the expressions of One.
Banāras watched Vishnu come to prominence during this millennium. So powerful was Vaishnava theism that the city's own legends
preserve the memory of a time when this was the City of Vishnu, and
several of Kāshī's most important ancient temples were dedicated to
Vishnu.

One of the most famous of the *avatāras* of Vishnu is Krishna. In the
first half of this thousand-year period, Krishna emerged from being an
ancient hero god remembered by the Yadava clan to being a great god,
with universal appeal to rival that of Vishnu. In the Bhagavad Gītā, the
"Song of the Lord," which began to take shape in the second century
B.C., the hero Krishna serves as charioteer to the warrior Arjuna, and
in the course of their dialogue, he reveals himself to Arjuna as the
Supreme Lord, the creator of the universe who supports this world
with but a fraction of his being. In the centuries that followed, and
certainly by the Gupta period, the legend of this great Krishna included not only that of the hero-god of the Yādavas, but of another
important North Indian god: the pastoral cowherd god, whose playful
childhood and romantic youth are celebrated in the area around
Mathurā, known as Braj, the homeland of Krishna. Krishna—the clan

* Narasimha, No. 215; Varāha, No. 22018.

hero, the lovable cowherd, and the great god—became the center of one of the most important of India's theistic movements.

Was there a cult of Krishna in Banāras during these centuries? This question is especially interesting since the Purānas record an old rivalry between Krishna and Kāshī, said to go back several generations before the Mahābhārata War.[29] In these tales, Krishna is said to have beheaded the king of Kāshī and burned the city down. There is no textual evidence of any more positive relation between Krishna and Kāshī. In fact, Krishna is remarkably and notably absent from the Kāshī *māhātmyas.* Yet while the brahmins may have conspired to keep Krishna out of the *māhātmyas,* the artisans were busy crafting his image for the temples. The visual texts tell us that Krishna was indeed honored in Banāras.

In the main hall of the Bhārat Kalā Bhavan museum is a prize piece, unearthed in a Muslim graveyard in the northern part of the city. It is an enormous, larger-than-life figure of a strong man standing with his weight shifted onto one leg, one hand on his hip, the other effortlessly lifting a mass of stone above his head. His long hair is pulled back by a headband, and his Sun-disc necklace is set between two curving lion claws. It is the cowherd god, perhaps once a local hero or a *yaksha,* lifting the holy hill of Braj, called Govardhana.[30] The mythic episode is famous: Krishna won the cowherds' loyalty away from the god Indra, and then lifted up the mountain to protect them from the rain of Indra's wrath. The image dates from the Gupta period.

The temple that housed such an image must have been magnificent indeed. It occupied a lofty bank on the west side of Bakariā Kund in northern Kāshī and was destroyed during the early Muslim raids on the city. It was not only important enough for the Muslims to destroy, but important enough to replace with a mosque, which now sits atop its ruins. The massive old foundation stones of this Gupta temple still lie in disarray on the banks of Bakariā Kund.

In the halls of the Bhārat Kalā Bhavan are other pieces that testify to the existence of the Krishna cult in Kāshī. There is a first century B.C. image of Balarāma, the *naga* deity, whose head is backed by the multi-headed hood of a cobra.* Balarāma, long worshipped in his own right, became associated with Krishna as his brother. In addition there is a

* No. 279.

Krishna lifting Mt. Govardhana. Bhārat Kalā Bhavan No. 147.

small sixth-century image of the baby Krishna engaged in one of his
most beloved pranks: stealing butter from the churn.*

There have clearly been times when Krishna *bhakti* has been strong
in Kāshī—in the Gupta period and again in the new wave of devotionalism in the fifteenth and sixteenth centuries. Yet today, while Krishna
is honored in family shrines in Kāshī, there is but one major Krishna
temple in the city: the Gopāla Temple in the heart of the Chaukhambā
district.

---

* No. 180.

Shiva Maheshvara, the "Great Lord"

O N E intriguing fragment of sculpture in the Bhārat Kalā Bhavan shows a man balancing a *linga* on his head with his hand.* Only the head, the *linga*, and the hand remain of what must have been quite a large image. It is attributed to the third century A.D. We can only imagine that the man is going somewhere with this extraordinary load, perhaps to Vārānasī to establish this emblem of Shiva in a shrine or temple.

Some clues to the meaning of this piece may be found in the records of a local dynasty, the Bhāra Shivas, who ruled in the vicinity of Vārānasī and were the first of the Hindu revivalist empires, which included the Vākātakas and then the Guptas. As their name indicates, these were Shaiva kings. According to an inscription, they are said to have performed ten *ashvamedhas* ("horse sacrifices") on the banks of the River Ganges to signify their suzerainty. The inscription reads:

> . . . Of [the Dynasty of] the Bhāra Shivas whose royal line owed its origin to the great satisfaction of Shiva on account of their carrying the load of the symbol of Shiva on their shoulders—the Bhāra Shivas who were anointed to sovereignty with the holy water of the Bhāgīrathī [Ganges] which had been obtained by their valour—the Bhāra Shivas who performed their sacred bath on the completion of their Ten Ashvamedhas.[31]

According to one historian who has studied this period carefully, the place of this "Ten Horse Sacrifice" may well have been Banāras, where this is the name of one of the great river *ghāts*: Dashāshva-medha.[32]

Today Kāshī is the City of Shiva *par excellence*. Perhaps this has long been so, but today this surely means something much larger than it could have meant 2,500 years ago, when the name Kāshīshvara Shiva, "Kāshī's Lord," first appeared.[33] Then Shiva was closely linked with

---

* No. 223.

ascetics and yogis, and his cult was the cult of *tapas*. During the period we are considering, however, the lord of the yogis became the "Great Lord"—Maheshvara—and his cult became a cult of devotion.

For early evidence of Shiva's rise to supremacy, we must look back to the Vedic god Rudra-Shiva and to the celebrated "Shatarudriya" hymn of the *Shatapatha Brāhmana,* a hymn still chanted in Shiva temples today.[34] It describes the awesome weapons and powers of Rudra, it appeals for his mercies, and it tells of the many places where he may be found—by the wayside, in the high mountain passes, in the brook, in the forest, in fact, everywhere. A few centuries later, in the third or fourth centuries B.C., the *Shvetāshvatara Upanishad* confirms the beginning of a theistic view in which Shiva is the omnipresent One God, the Supreme Lord.

Shiva brought many of the *yaksha* deities into his entourage. Local autochthonous deities, the kindly and fearsome spirits of nature, became his *ganas,* his "group." The most prominent among them became *ganeshas,* the "lords of *ganas.*" In the Kāshī literature, for example, we will find the story of a certain Harikesha *yaksha* who became a great devotee of Shiva and was rewarded for his devotion by being made the chief *ganesha* of all Kāshī.[35]

In Shiva's rise to prominence, he incorporated into his entourage a much wider range of *yaksha* deities than did Vishnu. Perhaps it was the paradoxical ambiguity of Shiva—both auspicious and frightening—that enabled him to assimilate the similarly ambiguous *yakshas* and *ganeshas,* who were both the cause and the cure of problems, the posers and removers of obstacles.

It is impossible to say how long Shiva has been honored in the aniconic *linga,* in which Shiva takes no bodily form but is present in a simple stone shaft. Beginning in the first or second century B.C., however, there are icons and images of Shiva in anthropomorphic form. Especially famous is the Gudimallam *linga* from South India, an erect phallic shaft from which an armed figure emerges in relief. While he has the sturdy strength of a *yaksha,* it is Shiva who stands forth from the stone shaft of the *linga.* This motif, combining the aniconic *linga* with the anthropomorphic icon of Shiva, becomes a common one. While Shiva is indescribable and represented only by his emblem or mark *(linga),* he is also personal and shows his face to those who honor him. Sometimes a single face emerges from the shaft of the *linga,* and

sometimes four faces emerge, one in each direction.*

In the Bhārat Kalā Bhavan there is one tenth-century bas-relief that tells a story of Shiva's ascendancy that is very important in Kāshī lore: the famous myth in which Shiva's *linga* splits open the earth as a fiery column of light. The shaft is flanked by the four-faced god Brahmā on the one side, and Lord Vishnu on the other, both kneeling in reverence upon their divine lotus blossoms. The shaft, with flames shooting from its sides, has been broken, but one can see most of the story. Beneath Vishnu there is another image of Vishnu, as a boar, who is said to have searched deep in the earth for the source and base of this marvel, to no avail. Brahmā must have been duplicated at the top left as well, soaring high into the heavens on his divine goose to look for the top of this wondrous light. Finding neither the

* No. 22755 in the Bhārat Kalā Bhavan, for example. There is a one-faced *linga* at Dehalī Vināyaka on the Panchakroshī Road, and there are four-faced *lingas* in the Trilochana Temple and in the Brahmeshvara shrine of the Ādi Keshava Temple.

Gudimallam linga. *Āndhra Pradesh. Second century* B.C. *Shiva, standing on the world-bearing giant, emerges from the shaft of the* linga.

source nor the top, the two gods submit to the *linga* as the manifestation of Shiva's supremacy.

By the Gupta period, a Shaiva sectarian movement called the Pāshupatas was well under way. It combined the old Shaiva asceticism with a new note of devotion. In the post-Gupta era, Hiuen Tsiang visited Vārānasī, where he reported that most of the worshippers in the more than one hundred temples of the city honored "Maheshvara Deva," and some were radical ascetics, going without clothing and smearing their bodies with ashes.[36] The Shaiva character of the city visited by Hiuen Tsiang predominates in Banāras even today.

The fiery appearance of the linga. *Bhārat Kalā Bhavan No. 154. Ninth to tenth century. From Etah, Uttar Pradesh.*

The Great Goddess

I N O N E I M A G E , found in the dense Chaukhambā district of central
Vārānasī, a ten-armed goddess, wielding all the weapons of the great
male deities, surrounded by a host of female *shaktis,* crushes the demon
underfoot. The wily demon changes form, from lion to bull to man, in
an effort to escape. She is about to deliver the blow of death. This
image—a visual theology in itself—stands at the culmination of the long
history of goddesses, *devīs,* in India. The female deity has many
names, but in this all-powerful form she is often simply called Devī, *the*
Goddess, or Mahādevī, the Great Goddess. Although this particular
image is from the eleventh century, it tells a story which by Gupta
times had become known in the famous *Devī Māhātmya,* the hymn in
praise of Devī. In the post-Gupta period, and especially with the rise of
Tantra, this story of the Goddess who transcends the gods, takes their
weapons, fights their battles, and is, indeed, their very life-energy, is
one of the most powerful stories to shape the Hindu religious imagination.

Goddesses have always been part of the religious life of the indigenous culture of India. In India's earliest civilization in the Indus Valley, goddesses with full breasts, rounded hips, and the hipline belt or
girdle called the *mekhalā* were roughly shaped in terra-cotta. We do
not know how such figurines were used ritually, but we may assume
that they did have a religious purpose. The early *yakshīs,* as depicted at
the Buddhist *stūpa* sites of Bhārhut and Sānchī in the second and first
centuries B.C., were stone figures, far more elegantly crafted than their
terra-cotta ancestors, but with the same well-endowed figure and the
same hipline *mekhalā.* The *yakshīs* were closely associated with fecun-
dity, especially the ever-renewing cycle of vegetative life and growth.
They were often depicted with an arm wrapped about a tree, and with
the twist of their body and the grace of their limbs conveying the same
vegetative vitality as the tree itself.

Goddesses of local and regional significance have attracted supplicants for their blessings and protection for nearly three thousand
years. The word *shakti* came to be used to describe these female divinities. *Shakti* means "energy" or "power" and these, indeed, are the

Durgā, Slayer of the Bull Demon. Bhārat Kalā Bhavan No. 177. Eleventh century. From Chaukhambā, Vārānasī.

life-energies of the world, firmly associated with both the nourishment and the vagaries of nature. All the various aspects of nature became the *pīthas*, the "seats" or "benches" of the goddesses. The rivers of India were praised, even in the *Rig Veda*, as "mother rivers," and their

nurturing waters were compared to the milk of mother-cows. Trees
and groves were, as we have seen, commonly associated with female
yakshīs as well as male *yakshas*. Also from the organic world, one of the
most persistent visual emblems of abundance and auspicious generosity
was the lotus, and the goddesses associated with the lotus were known
locally by hundreds of names. The earth was also seen as a female
divinity, and in some parts of India its cycles of fertility and production were explicitly likened to the monthly cycles of women. The
mountains too were linked to the goddesses: Pārvatī, the name of
Shiva's wife, means "Woman of the Mountain," and her sister,
Gangā, is also a child of the mountains. Finally, the *genii loci* of towns
and villages were predominantly female. These deities, called *grāma
devatās* or *nagara devatās,* had their benches at the boundaries of town.
Even the great cities of India, such as Ayodhyā, Madurai, and Ujjain,
had female tutelary deities, and such was the case for Vārānasī as well,
where Vārānasī Devī and Kāshī Devī have an ancient reputation.[37] All
these *devīs*—embodied in trees, rivers, mountains, and towns—were
place-specific and often known simply as *mātā* in the North or *amman*
in the South, both of which mean "mother."

   In the first half of this thousand-year period, stretching from the
Mauryan to the Gupta empire, it would not have been meaningful to
speak of "*the* Goddess," for there were thousands of goddesses. The
second half of this period, however, saw the rise of a larger conception
of Devī, of whom these many *devīs* were particular manifestations.
Early evidence of this process is seen in the long lists of goddesses,
grouped together as if they all belonged together, in such texts as the
Mahābhārata and the *Matsya Purāna*.[38] Elsewhere, the various *shaktis* of
nature are described as the manifestations of the Great Goddess: "In
the frightful mountains, in the rivers, and in the caves, in the forests
and in the winds, dwells Mahādevī!"[39] The most powerful goddess
shrines came to be seen as the *pithas,* the "benches," of the Goddess.

   The great hymn to Devī, the *Devī Māhātmya,* which appears in this
period, praises a goddess named Chandika as the eternally existent
One, from whom the universe was stretched forth in the beginning.[40]
It tells of her gathering up the weapons or the *shaktis* of the male gods
in order to slay mighty demons. And it calls her by the names of many
goddesses: Ambikā, Durgā, Shrī, Gaurī, and others. In the wrath of
battle, the terrible Kālī, also called Chāmundā, emerges from Chandikā's forehead wearing a garland of skulls, her tongue lolling out for

blood; she fills the entire universe with her roar. In the *Devī Māhātmya* and in this eleventh-century stone image, it is clear that the Great Goddess has fully emerged, gathering together the powers and the domains of countless *devīs* into a grand theistic vision of a single Mahādevī.

In Kāshī, this whole history of the rise of the Great Goddess is witnessed and recorded. From the oldest layer of archeological evidence found in the Rājghāt excavations come ringstones, the circular discs that seem to have been associated with goddesses since the Indus Valley civilization.[41] The use of these circular aniconic symbols for female deities may be fruitfully compared to the later symbolism of the female *yoni*, the counterpart of the male *linga*, and to the use of the geometric *yantra* as a representation of the Goddess. On one of the Rājghāt ringstones from the Mauryan period in the fourth or third century B.C., there are relief carvings of full-hipped *devīs* with honeysuckle between them.

Although there are no major goddesses from the Gupta period in the museum collections, one might conjecture a Gupta date for dozens of fragments of stone sculpture found beneath trees and in temple courtyards throughout the city and around the Panchakroshī Road. However, if we move beyond this period into the centuries of Tantric efflorescence that followed, there is a great burst of *devī* sculptural depiction. She stands on an equal footing with Shiva in a seventh-century Umā-Maheshvara. In the eighth century, she appears as the fierce Chāmundā, dancing wildly on a demon, wearing a necklace of skulls. In the tenth century, she appears as Vaishnavī, carrying the weapons of Vishnu. In the eleventh century, she is Durgā Mahishamardanī, bearing the weapons of all the gods and breaking the back of the demon.*

The goddesses of Kāshī today still display the full historical range of goddess types. There are innumerable *devīs* local to each district in the city; there are independent *devīs* such as Shitalā, who wields influence over fever diseases, both causing and curing them; there are *devīs* who have become associated with gods as their consorts, such as Umā or Pārvatī; and there are *devīs* who have achieved a universal appeal and stand on their own as embodiments of the Great Goddess.

---

* Umā-Maheshvara, Rāmnagar Fort; Chāmundā, Nos. 20926, 205; Vaishnavī, No. 174; Hara-Gaurī, No. 173; Durgā Mahishamardanī, Nos. 153, 177.

Other Deities of the Gupta Age

T H E imperial Guptas also patronized other deities, who in that age may well have been as important as the emergent "great" gods of Hinduism—Vishnu, Shiva, and Devī. The god Skanda is an example of such a deity who, in Gupta times, was clearly very popular in Banāras, but did not retain a hold in North India in later times.[42] Skanda is also called Kārttikeya, after the Krittikās, the six stars who nursed him as foster mothers, and Kumāra, the "Youth," for he is eternally young and virile. Two fifth-century Gupta kings, Kumāragupta and Skandagupta, took their names to honor this deity. The worship of Skanda is attested to by one of the finest pieces of sculpture from Gupta Banāras. Here Skanda is shown with the peacock, his animal mount (vāhana). He holds his war staff and wears the large ring ear-ornaments and the double-clawed necklace that we see on other youthful strong men, like the one who lifts Govardhana. Skanda Kārttikeya is clearly one of India's ancient indigenous deities, the "strong ones," called bīrs or vīras. He is still very popular in South India under the name Murugan. In the North, however, despite his identification with Shiva as one of Shiva's sons, the worship of Skanda died out, although the group with which he is associated—the vīras/bīrs—is still prominent in local traditions. There is even some evidence of an attempt to suppress his worship in Kāshī; the Skanda Purāna, in which the Kāshī Khanda occurs, reports that Skanda was living on holy Shrī Shaila mountain in South India, having been exiled from Kāshī for not properly honoring its guardian deity Dandapāni.[43]

Another deity of some significance in Gupta times was Sūrya, the Sun. Despite the antiquity of Sūrya and the Sun-symbol, even in Vedic India, a new impetus was given to Indian Sun-worship by Hindu interaction with people of the Zarathustrian and Mithraic traditions of Iran during the first several centuries of our era.[44] In this time, the rulers of North and West India were the Shakas and the Kushānas, both tribal groups from Central Asia, which adjoined the empires of the Parthians and the Sassanians. It was in their time that the Sun, which has so often inspired a monotheistic vision in human religious history, was again the center of theistic devotion in India.

Skanda Kārttikeya. Bhārat
Kalā Bhavan No. 206.
Gupta period, Sixth century.
Gāya Ghāt, Vārānasī.

When these Central Asian kings were replaced by the imperial Guptas in North India, the new zeal for the Sun was taken up by the Guptas themselves. The worship of Sūrya continued through the time of King Harsha in the seventh century, and was taken up by the Pālas of Bengāl in the ninth and tenth centuries and the Senas in the twelfth century. The temple of Konārak in Orissa, built in the form of the Sun's chariot, is India's greatest standing monument to the Sun. It is also clear, however, that the temple of Somnāth, on the Gujarāt coast in far West India, was powerfully connected to the worship of the Sun as well as Shiva. That temple was destroyed by the first Muslim incursions into India. The appearance of many late Purānas dealing with the Sun cult indicates the full development of a sectarian movement of Sun devotion called the Saura cult. About the thirteenth century, the sectarian worship of the Sun began to decline. Yet, for nearly one thousand years, the Sun had been the center of a developed cult and had been a major figure in the Hindu pantheon. In Vārānasī, as we shall see, there were numerous Sun temples, and in the collection of

the Bhārat Kalā Bhavan there are prominent images of the Sun, beginning in the seventh century.*

Ganesha did not become one of the "great" gods, at least in this part of India, but he did outlive Skanda and Sūrya in his significance and he continues to be honored as a tutelary deity by virtually all Hindus. As guardian of the "thresholds" of space and time, he is honored at the doorways of temples and homes and propitiated at the outset of rites and ceremonies.

There is no doubt that Ganesha emerged from the "group" of *ganas* by the beginning of Gupta times to become an individual, particular deity. There are no Ganesha images from the Gupta period that one can identify in Banāras, although most of the city's Ganeshas have been coated with so many layers of vermilion that it is impossible to know what shape lies beneath. Among the images of Ganesha at Bhārat Kalā Bhavan, there is one striking eighth-century image from the western "border station" of Kāshī, called Dehalī Vināyaka.† In this image, the fat, elephant-headed deity is dancing, standing with his

---

* Nos. 160, 179, 181.

† No. 158.

great weight shifted to his right leg, his left leg slung out, and his foot pointing delicately forward. His dancing is but one of the many delightful twists of consciousness that Ganesha demands of his worshippers. The corpulent elephant dances. Enormous as he is, he rides a mouse. Seemingly friendly and benevolent as he is, he carries fierce weapons. Part animal that he is, he is the scholar among the gods, to whom the entire *Mahābhārata* was dictated in one sitting. We shall consider Ganesha more extensively in discussing Kāshī's pantheon.

From the Guptas to the Great Kingdom of the Gāhadavālas

B Y T H E end of the Gupta period in the sixth century, the religious life of Kāshī included flourishing sectarian devotional movements of all kinds—Buddhist, Vaishnava, Shaiva, Shākta, and Saura. The basic Hindu cultus was established. These deities were imaged in anthropomorphic and aniconic forms, and there were temples and shrines of stone to house the images. Presumably the sponsorship and installation of such images accrued spiritual benefits to the patron, and the worship of such images moved into the forefront of the religious life of India.

During the period from the end of the Gupta dynasty in the sixth century to the establishment of the Delhi Sultanate and Muslim power at the beginning of the thirteenth century, Banāras was under the control of different Hindu kingdoms in North India. These centuries saw Banāras established as the stronghold of brahminical Hinduism. The theistic developments we have surveyed continued and flourished. While there are no temples that survived intact from this time, it is clear from the ruins and sculptural remains found in Banāras that this was a time of prolific architectural and sculptural achievement. It was also a time in which many of the Purānic traditions about the sacred city were elaborated. Many of the Puranas as we now know them took their shape during these centuries.

As this period began, in the seventh century, during the reign of King Harsha at Kanauj, Hiuen Tsiang visited Vārānasī and described the city as being about three miles long and one mile wide, containing clusters of villages. Leafy trees shaded the temples and shrines, and streams of clear water flowed in all directions. He described the city as a luxuriant place covered with vegetation, where wealthy families lived in houses stocked with rare and precious things, and where people were cultured, polished, and given to study.[45] As we have seen, the city he described, with its hundred temples, its groves and streams, was very much the Forest of Bliss described in the imaginative vision of the Purānas.

We have another glimpse of Banāras in the eighth century in an extensive inscription by a certain individual named Pantha, who apparently visited the city as a pilgrim and established a goddess image here. He described Vārānasī as a city which has collected the three worlds—the netherworld, the earth, and the heavens—together in one place. He wrote that people come here from afar to live, die, and obtain *moksha;* that the city is never abandoned by Shiva and his attendants; and that the city is so pure as to remove the sin of killing a brahmin. He described the city itself, with its high temple spires, its beautiful women, and its wide and narrow streets. And, finally, he described the image of the goddess Bhavānī, called Chandī, which he established in Vārānasī: horrific, wearing a necklace of skulls, creeping snakes hanging from her throat, diced meat stuck to the blade of her axe, dancing playfully, her eyes rolling! For this fine image he established a temple, famous for its fluttering banners and the sound of its bells.[46]

Pantha's inscription is representative of what was surely the most vibrant movement of the age: Tantra. In the Tantric movement, the Goddess in her various forms rose to wider prominence than she had known before, both as Great Goddess and as the *shakti* of the male deities. As we noted earlier, the Bhārat Kalā Bhavan collection includes quite a number of goddess images from this period and confirms the significance of Tantrism in all the religious traditions of Kāshī— Buddhist, Jaina, Vaishnava, and Shaiva.

The apogee of Kāshī's prestige during this period came during the Gāhadavāla kingdom, which rose to power in the Gangetic plain in the late eleventh century and held sway for about one hundred years. The Gāhadavālas provided strong Hindu leadership and saw themselves as the protectors of the *tīrthas,* especially four of the great *tīrthas* of their realm, the most important of which were Kāshī and, farther north along the Ganges, ancient Kanauj.[47] Kanauj was the city which, for three centuries, had been the political heart of North India, following the Gupta age. Now, Kanauj and Kāshī became not only the recipients of the religious patronage of the Gāhadavālas, but the administrative centers of their empire as well.

With the Gāhadavāla kingdom, the city of Kāshī came into political prominence for the first time in nearly two thousand years. Not since the days when Kāshī vied with other North Indian kingdoms for prestige in the sixth and seventh centuries B.C. had this been an imperial capital. Now Kāshī entered a golden age.

The Gāhadavālas were liberal and eclectic in their religious patronage. In their inscriptions the kings described themselves as "great worshippers of Shiva," the Lord of Kāshī.[48] Nonetheless, the most famous of the kings, Govindachandra, had two queens who espoused and patronized Buddhism. For the most part, however, the Gāhadavālas were worshippers of Vishnu, and in one inscription, Govindachandra is praised as an incarnation of Vishnu, commissioned to protect Vishnu's favorite abode, the city of Vārānasī.*[49]

The center of the royal capital was then on the Rājghāt Plateau, and there Govindachandra made numerous ritual donations *(mahādānas)* at the temple of Ādi Keshava, the "Original Vishnu." A typical donation would have been the gift of the tax revenues of a small village to the support of some particular brahmin or temple. Govindachandra left over fifty inscriptions recording such charitable donations to temples of Shiva, Vishnu, and Sūrya.

Govindachandra gave himself the lofty epithet "Spokesman for Reflection upon All Knowledge" *(sarvavidyā-vichāra-vāchaspati).*[50] He was indeed a great patron of learning, and perhaps the most important thing he did in his entire reign was to hire the learned brahmin named Lakshmīdhara as chief minister. Almost single-handedly, Lakshmīdhara inaugurated a new era in Hindu religious literature by compiling one of the earliest, most reputable, and most extensive digests *(nibandhas)* of literature on *dharma*. Here he brought together quotations from the vast literature of the Epics, Purānas, and Dharmashāstras, topic by topic, covering such subjects as the duties of householders and kings, the establishing of divine images, the rites of worship, the rites for the dead, the giving of charitable donations, and, of course, the visiting of *tīrthas*. The entire work of fourteen volumes is called the *Krityakalpataru*, the "Magical Wishing Tree of Duties," and later

---

* About the same time, in the spirit of the late Purānas, Vārānasī is sometimes called Nārāyanavāsa ("Abode of Vishnu") and Harikshestra ("Field of Hari/Vishnu").

compilers of digests borrowed extensively from this pioneering work.

In his volume, "The Discussion of *Tīrthas*" *(Tīrthavivechana Kānda)*, Lakshmīdhara leads off with a discussion of Vārānasī, a precedent that later digests followed, and he devotes nearly half the work to this one *tīrtha*. Not only does he compile scriptural references to over 350 shrines in Kāshī, he contributes, by his selection of verses and his brief commentaries, to a theory of Hindu pilgrimage, emphasizing the interior pilgrimage of the heart that must accompany the earthly pilgrim journey. He is attentive to both the letter and spirit of the tradition.

Since Lakshmīdhara's work was produced in the mid-twelfth century, it also serves as a clear guidepost in the wilderness of Purānic proliferation. Lakshmīdhara cites what was accredited, sacred literature in his day, and many works—including the famous and extensive *Kāshī Khanda*—are notably absent from his discussion. The *Kāshī Khanda* expresses a vision of the city which must have been clear as never before in the golden age of the Gāhadavālas, although the final compilation of this work may have been as much as a century and a half later.

The greatest flaw of this era was nearsightedness. While the Gāhadavālas nourished religious culture at home, they also skirmished with their rivals in North India, the Chāhamānas to the west. The Chāhamānas, under King Prithvīrāja, wanted to establish hegemony over all of North India; the Gāhadavālas, under King Jayachandra, apparently wanted the same. They wasted their efforts in the rivalry and both were the losers. Prithvīrāja, having spent his strength against the Gāhadavālas, was defeated by the advancing Muslim armies of Muhammad Ghūrī in 1192, and Jayachandra, whose kingdom was now exposed on the west, was defeated in 1193/94. Jayachandra was beheaded, his army was humiliated, and the forces of Muhammad Ghūrī, under the leadership of General Qutb-ud-din Aibak, advanced to Vārānasī. They sacked and looted the city. According to a Muslim historian of the age, they destroyed nearly one thousand temples in Vārānasī alone and "raised mosques on their foundations."[51] It took 1,400 camels to haul away their plunder. The glorious century of the Gāhadavālas ended in catastrophe.

The Muslim Centuries

IN 1206, with the establishment of the Delhi Sultanate, the entire Ganges valley came under Muslim domination. It remained in Muslim hands for over five hundred years. The history of this period is complicated, and the various Muslim dynasties which came to power through the centuries were far from monolithic in their policies toward the sacred sites of the Hindus. There were certainly high moments in these centuries, when Kāshī recaptured something of its lost glory. There were times of ambitious temple construction and stimulating scholarly activity. But for the most part these were hard centuries. The religious life of the city was under almost constant threat. At least six times during these years the temples of Kāshī were destroyed.

Following the sack of the city by the forces of Muhammad Ghūrī, temples were destroyed again in the 1300s under Firūz Shāh Tughluq. In the 1400s, the city came under the rule of the Sharqī kings of Jaunpur, and temples were again destroyed, their blocks hauled away for the construction of a mosque in Jaunpur. When the Lodīs seized power from the Sharqīs in the last years of the 1400s, Vārānasī came into Lodī hands and parts of the city were destroyed by Sikandar Lodī. In the 1500s, the situation improved for a short time during the liberal reign of the Mughal Emperor Akbar, who not only permitted, but in some cases sponsored the rebuilding of temples. Some of the Hindu Rājputs of Rājasthān, who were allies of Akbar, participated actively in the construction of Banāras *ghāts* and temples during this part of the Mughal period. During the reign of Akbar's grandson Shāh Jahān, however, imperial policy changed again. By his order, the temples that were being constructed—no fewer than seventy-six in Banāras alone— were destroyed. His successor, Aurangzeb, was even more zealous in his disdain for the sacred sites of the Hindus. Some of the city's greatest temples, including Vishveshvara, Krittivāsa, and Bindu Mādhava, were razed during the reign of Aurangzeb, and their sites were forever sealed from Hindu access by the construction of mosques. In his zeal for crushing Hindu idolatry, Aurangzeb even tried to rename the city "Muhammadabad," but the name did not stick. In short, although the

history of Banāras during these centuries was not an unmitigated tale
of woe, the scenes of destruction were repeated and frequent enough
in the drama of those years that the city must have seemed constantly
to be regaining its footing only to stagger again.[52]

There is no major religious sanctuary in all Banāras that pre-dates
the time of Aurangzeb in the seventeenth century. The sacred geography of the city changed considerably in these centuries. The city of
the Purānic *mahātmyas* was no more. Its greatest temples—Krittivāsa,
Omkāra, Mahādeva, Madhyameshvara, Vishveshvara, Bindu Mādhava,
and Kāla Bhairava—were in ruins. Some never recovered, like the
Shiva temple of Krittivāsa, the site of which is today occupied by a
run-down mosque. Others went into hiding, like the guardian deity
Kāla Bhairava, who was housed in humble quarters for hundreds of
years and did not appear in a fitting temple until the eighteenth century. Likewise, the Vishnu image of Bindu Mādhava, whose site was
usurped by a huge mosque, was moved to a nearby house. And some
temples were continually resurgent, like Vishveshvara, Kāshī's supreme sanctum of Shiva, which was destroyed and rebuilt at least three
times during these centuries. The sacred city could not be destroyed,
but it could certainly be defaced. The memory of Kāshī as the brilliant
capital of Lord Shiva, set amidst the Forest of Bliss, faded into a time
almost as distant as the time before the Ganges fell from heaven to
earth.

Despite the discouraging, repeated ruin of this period, Banāras continued to be an important center of intellectual life and religious
thought. The traditions of learning for which the city was famous
could not easily be broken, for they were independent of the rise and
fall of temples. During the latter part of this period, the French scholar
and medical doctor, François Bernier, visited Banāras, which he called
the Athens of India, and recorded his observations in a letter to one
Monsieur Chapelain:

The town contains no colleges or regular classes, as in our universities, but
resembles rather the schools of the ancients; the masters being dispersed over
different parts of the town in private houses, and principally in the gardens of
the suburbs, which the rich merchants permit them to occupy. Some of these
masters have four disciples, others six or seven, and the most eminent may
have twelve or fifteen; but this is the largest number. It is usual for the pupils
to remain ten or twelve years under their respective preceptors. . . .[53]

The Forest of Bliss was still famous for its teachers.

What kind of scholarly activity took place in Kāshī during this era? As always there were great masters of philosophy here, especially of the schools of Nyāya (Logic) and Advaita (Non-Dualism). And there were masters of Sanskrit grammatical science. Most important for our study were the further developments in the Purānic traditions about Kāshī during these centuries. The *Kāshī Khanda*, which according to one scholar did not reach its final form until around 1350, gained popularity and importance in this period, in part because it evoked the vivid memory of Kāshī in its time of glory.[54] Other great *māhātmyas* were also written: the *Kāshī Rahasya*, with its eclectic and mystical view of the city, and the *Kāshī Kedāra Māhātmya*, with its glorification of the southern sector of the city. During the Mughal period, the poet Jagannātha composed what is still the most popular praise poem of the River Ganges, the "Gangā Laharī."

In religious and ethical thought, this was a time of great productivity. Digests on various matters of *dharma* were compiled, following the earlier tradition of Lakshmīdhara. Manuals on everything from temple rites to cremation rites appeared. This activity was stimulated in no small part by six families of pandits from what, in Banāras, is called the "South"—the Deccan Plateau of Central India.[55] They were Mahārāshtrian brahmins who, after their migration to Banāras, became the most prominent leaders of the city's intellectual life. One of their number, Nārāyana Bhatta, was the moving force behind the grand reconstruction of the Vishvanātha Temple in the late 1500s. Nārayana Bhatta also compiled the *Tristhalīsetu* ("Bridge to the Three Sacred Places"), a famous digest of scriptural verses on the three great pilgrim cities of North India—Kāshī, Prayāga, and Gayā.

This period in Indian history also saw the rise and spread of a new wave of popular *bhakti* devotionalism in North India. It was largely a people's movement, in which the classical Sanskrit literature yielded to a vibrant new poetic literature composed in the languages of the people. Some devotees and poets of *bhakti* expressed an intensely personal form of love for a personal God, "with attributes" *(saguna)*, such as Rāma or Krishna. Others praised a God who transcends every name and description, without the limit of any of the characteristics ascribed to God by the human imagination *(nirguna)*. These latter devotees called God by many names, but spoke of a reality beyond all names and, indeed, beyond all the distortions of "religion," whether Muslim or Hindu.

Despite its reputation as a stronghold of Hindu orthodoxy and conservatism, Banāras participated in the vibrant devotional resurgence of this era. In the fifteenth century, a teacher named Rāmānanda, said to be from the South Indian Vaishnava devotional tradition of the great Rāmānuja, settled in Banāras at Panchagangā Ghāt. He was a most unusual Banāras teacher, for his pupils were not shaven-headed brahmin boys, but among them was an untouchable, a barber, and, it is said, even a woman. Although little more is known of him, Rāmānanda stood at the dawning of a new age of religiousness all over North India, an age in which full participation in a life of devotion was not the prerogative of the elite few, but the claim and faith of all—the illiterate, the downtrodden, and the outcastes. It is not surprising that this new counter-culture in India shared certain things in common with the old ascetic and Tantric counter-culture, which also experienced a revival in this age in various movements such as the ragged and outrageous Gorakhnāthī yogis. They shared a distaste for the brahminical establishment, for the caste system, and for an orientation to ritual which they considered to be mechanical and mindless.

One of the great poets of the age and, indeed, one of the greatest in all of Indian literature, was Kabīr, whose terse colloquial songs are still sung today. Kabīr, was from a group of very low-caste Banāras weavers, called *julāhās*, who were recent converts to Islam. He was born a Muslim and was a pupil of a Muslim *pīr*, said some. He was a Hindu, a Vaishnava, a pupil of the *bhakta* Rāmānanda, according to others. When he died, it is said that followers of both religious traditions bickered over his remains. But when the cloth covering his body was lifted, there was nothing there but a spray of flowers. This apocryphal legend captures the essence of Kabīr's own message: he would not be classified by any religion. He ridiculed with equal vehemence the sacred books of the Muslims and Hindus, the Muslim *mullās* and the Hindu brahmins, the Muslim Mecca and the Hindu Kāshī.

Although Kabīr lived in Kāshī, he delighted in heaping disrespect upon its traditions of pilgrimage. God—by the name of Rām, or Hari, or Allah—is to be found deep within.

> *Going on endless pilgrimages, the world died,*
> *exhausted by so much bathing!*[56]

Kabīr went nowhere on pilgrimage, and when death approached, he refused to die in Kāshī and claim the lifelong dream of Hindus who believe that death in Kāshī brings liberation. Kabīr, disdainful as always, went to die in the dusty rural town of Magahar, so impure and disreputable, according to Kāshī brahmins, that those who die there will be reborn as asses. Kabīr said:

> *My whole life, I have wasted in Kāshī*
> *But, at the time of death, I have risen and come to Magahar!*[57]

Perhaps more telling of his devotion is Kabīr's famous line, "If Kabīr dies at Kāshī, what homage will he render Rām?"[58] The point, of course, is that God alone, Rām alone, can save, no matter where one dies.

Despite Kabīr's disdain for Kāshī and for organized religion, his followers soon generated a sectarian movement called the Kabīr Panth and established a major center right in Kāshī. The center has lent its name to an entire sector of the city, now called Kabīr Chaurā.

Kabīr was at his height in Kāshī during the fifteenth century. In the sixteenth century, he was followed in Banāras by another great poet of the Hindu *bhakti* tradition, Tulsī Dās. Like Kabīr, Tulsī Dās wrote in Hindi, the vernacular language of the people, rather than in Sanskrit. Unlike Kabīr, who was little concerned with scriptures, Tulsī Dās rendered sacred literature—the very province of the Sanskrit pandits—into Hindi. His famous version of the *Rāmāyana,* called the *Rāmcharitmānas,* was attacked at first by orthodox pandits, but it was loved by the people. It remains today the single most popular classic, the Bible of the Hindi-speaking people.

Tulsī Dās was a *bhakta* of Rāma, the Lord whose tale is told in the *Rāmāyana.* Hanumān, the monkey-servant of Lord Rāma, was also important to Tulsī's devotion, and ever since the time of Tulsī Dās, Hanumān has had an increasingly prominent place in North Indian religious life. Compared with his revolutionary predecessor Kabīr, Tulsī Dās was in the Hindu Vaishnava mainstream. For him there was no doubting the particularity of the Lord's name and the powerful story of his deeds. Rāma was, indeed, the incarnation of Vishnu. The story of Rāma was popularized by Tulsī Dās, not only in his Hindi saga, but in the annual performances of the tales of Rāma in the Rām Līlā, which Tulsī is said to have launched in Kāshī. The Kāshī Rām

Līlās, enacted at various places throughout the city, are today among
the most famous in India, and across the river in Rāmnagar the
Mahārāja sponsors an elaborate Rām Līlā with an episode enacted
every day for some three weeks.

Tulsī Dās lived through the best days of the Mughal period in
Banāras. During his lifetime, the great Vishvanātha Temple was rebuilt, with the sponsorship of the Emperor Akbar. The huge Vishnu
temple called Bindu Mādhava, praised in a number of Tulsī's poems,
sat at the top of Panchagangā Ghāt. Within a century, both would
again lie in ruins. Tulsī Dās is said to have lived at several places in
Banāras: at Panchagangā Ghāt, Hanumān Phātak, and the Gopāla
Temple—all in the heart of the city—and, finally, near Asi Ghāt, in a
house right next to the river. That *ghāt* is now called Tulsī Ghāt, and
his house at the head of the *ghāt* still contains a shrine, where the great
poet's sandals are kept.

Unlike Kabīr, Tulsī Dās was not disdainful of the great city where
he lived. The sanction of Kāshī for his new Hindi scripture was no
small matter. According to one legend, the pandits of Kāshī, attempt-
ing to ascertain the value of this new "scripture," placed it in the
Vishvanātha Temple overnight, at the bottom of a stack of scriptures
which included the Vedas, a Shāstra, and a Purāna. In the morning,
they found that the *Rāmcharitmānas* had moved to the top of the pile.[59]

At the outset of one of the sections of this work, Tulsī Dās praises
Kāshī and its Lord, Shiva. Although in his worship of Rāma one might
call Tulsī Dās a Vaishnava, the poet consistently displays a non-sec-
tarian spirit in his apprehension of the Divine. He begins one hymn to
Kāshī:

Serve with love all life through Kāshī, the wishing-cow of this Dark Age,
It banishes woe, affliction, sin, disease, and it amasses all things auspicious.[60]

The magical wishing cow of which Tulsī Dās writes is the bestower of
all desires. At the close of his last collection, the *Kavitāvalī*, Tulsī
blesses Kāshī as that place where all men are as Shiva and all women as
Pārvatī. And he takes his leave, with a note of mourning for the plague
which was then causing great suffering to the citizens.[61] Tulsī Dās died
in 1623 at the age of eighty, and his ashes were consigned to the
Ganges.

In the mid-twentieth century a great marble temple was erected in the southern part of Kāshī to honor Tulsī Dās. It is called the Tulsī Mānas Temple, and it is of stone so white that it is known locally as the Vimala Temple, the "flawless" one. Next to the new temple at Banāras Hindu University, this is the largest temple in the city. On its interior walls are marble slabs on which the entire *Rāmcharitmānas* is inscribed. At the back of the temple is a display which delights the villagers who flock to this temple from the rural areas around Banāras: Three-dimensional, brightly attired, animated figures from the Rāmāyana are shown in the various scenes Hindus know by heart. Rāma bends the great bow and wins Sītā for his bride. Exiled from his rightful kingdom by a petty family rivalry, Rāma leaves the great city of Ayodhyā with Sītā to live in the forest. Sītā is kidnapped by the wicked Rāvana. The great bird Jatāyu, the only witness to the kidnapping, flops his wings in agony and tells what he knows before he dies. And the tale continues, acted out in perpetual motion by those mechanical heroes. As the people watch these scenes, wonderstruck, they repeat to one another the episodes from Tulsi's epic they all know so well.

The memory of Tulsī Dās is vividly preserved in this temple today. He too is cast in plastic and sits in mechanical animation at the temple door, turning the pages of his epic and repeating the name, "Rām, Rām." The four hundredth anniversary of his *Rāmcharitmānas* was celebrated in this temple at the beginning of 1974, when 108 brahmins of Banaras sat in its spacious hall for days, while they read together the entire sacred book.

The Modern Period

AFTER the disintegration of the Mughal empire in the late seventeenth century, Banāras passed into the hands of a ruling family which has retained the throne of Banāras and the title of Kāshīrāj ever since. For the first time in over five hundred years, the city was under the jurisdiction of Hindu kings. There was Mansārām and his successor Balwant Singh in the early eighteenth century. Then there was the famous Chet Singh, who resisted the tax demands of the British, even when the Governor-General of India, Warren Hastings, came personally to Banāras to confront the local ruler. Chet Singh, imprisoned

in his own palace at Shivālā Ghāt, escaped on a makeshift rope of
turbans and rallied a local rebellion strong enough to make Hastings
flee for his life. That was in 1781. By 1794, however, Banāras came
under British administration. The Mahārājas continued to play a significant leadership role, especially in culture and religion, from the
great Mahārāja Īshvarī Prasād Nārāin Singh in the nineteenth century
to Mahārāja Vibhūti Nārāin Singh today. They have patronized fine
arts and music; they have sponsored festivals and fairs; and they have
continued to see themselves and to be seen by the people of Kāshī as
the earthly representatives of Lord Vishvanātha.

During the eighteenth century, Banāras had to be substantially rebuilt. The city which had sheltered the rebel Marāthā hero, Shivājī, in
his challenge to Mughal power, now became the recipient of the gratitude, the wealth, and the energy of the Marāthās. As one historian has
put it, "Modern Banāras is largely a creation of the Marāthās."[62]
Marāthā rulers and patrons sponsored the rebuilding of some of the
city's most important temples: the Shiva temples of Vishvanātha and
Trilochana, the Devī temple of Annapūrnā, the Ganesha temple of
Sākshī Vināyaka, and the temple of Kāla Bhairava. A number of *ghāts*
were also constructed under Marāthā patronage.

The face of the sacred city also changed considerably under the
administration of the British. Broad roads were cut through the city
where formerly there had been narrow lanes. The Dashāshvamedha-
Luxa Road was built running west from the river toward the Cantonment train station. The north-south artery called Chauk was cleared
through the business district. Many of the inland lakes, ponds, and
streams were drained and filled. The inland *tīrtha* waters dried up and
shrank away from the steps of the temples which had been located on
their banks.

In education, the British years brought a change from the ancient
pandit-student pattern of learning which had predominated in Kāshī
for 2,500 years. In 1791, the Governor-General, Warren Hastings, who
had presumably recovered from the indignities of his flight from
Banāras, approved the proposal of Jonathan Duncan for a Sanskrit
College in Banāras, where Sanskrit texts would be collected and pandits employed. In 1853, the present buildings for this college were
erected in a Gothic style strikingly out of place in Banāras. The
Sanskrit College, preserving the most traditional Hindu learning, was

oddly called Queen's College.[63] Today the pendulum has swung the other way, and it is called by a proper Sanskrit name: Vārānaseya Sanskrit Vishvavidyālaya, "The Vārānasī Sanskrit Ocean of All Learning."

When Bishop Heber visited this new British venture in Indian education in 1825, he was shocked to find that the pandit of one class apparently identified Mt. Meru with the north pole, and taught that at the south pole the earth was held up by a tortoise. In other words, he was shocked that Hindu cosmology was indeed being taught at a Sanskrit College.[64]

In 1904, the great Banāras pandit and reformer, Madan Mohan Mālavīya, began campaigning for a very different kind of university in Banāras: a modern Hindu university which would preserve the best Hindu philosophical and cultural traditions and also train students in the modern sciences. He made this proposal at the 1905 meeting of the Indian National Congress, which met in Banāras that year, and he found support from the influential British reformer and founder of the Theosophical Society, Annie Besant. Pandit Mālavīya toured India to raise money for the university. It is said that people from all levels of society responded to his vision. A woman would offer her bangles for the cause, a sweeper his day's wages. The Mahārāja of Banāras donated the land for the university. In 1916, the Viceroy of India, Lord Hardinge, laid the foundation stone of what would become one of the largest and most beautiful universities in Asia: Banaras Hindu University. The grounds were laid out with the symmetry of a half-wheel: at its core were the administrative buildings, in the inner circles were the various colleges, and at the outer rim were the residences of faculty and the hostels of students. It developed faculties not only in Sanskrit and Indology but in Commerce, Engineering, Agriculture, and Medicine. Pandit Madan Mohan Mālavīya became its Vice-Chancellor, and he remained active in the University until he died in his university lodge in 1946. The University is located just beyond the southern borders of the sacred zone of Kāshī. Those who knew Pandit Mālavīya tell the story of how he refused to move into Kāshī to die. He did not want liberation yet, he said, for there was so much left to do in his next lifetime in this world.

Another aspect of the modern period that deserves notice is the effort, beginning in the nineteenth century, to spread the Gospel of

Christianity among the inhabitants of Banāras. There were a number of mission projects in the city, beginning with the Baptist Missionary Society in 1819. The Church Missionary Society of the Church of England, with a church at Sigra and another right in the center of the city at Godauliā crossing, began its work about the same time. The London Missionary Society was located in the British Cantonment beginning in 1820. It was with this mission that the most noted authors among Banāras missionaries were affiliated: William Buyers, James Kennedy, and M. A. Sherring. Their writings give us a view of missions and the thoughts of missionaries in Banāras through the middle decades of the nineteenth century. Later in the century, the Wesleyan Missionary Society launched its Banāras mission, and the Zenana Bible and Medical Mission started a hospital for women. Today the church in Godauliā crossing is closed. The churches in Sigra and in the Cantonment have very small congregations. The hospital for women, however, continues to thrive.

The Christian missions never had a chance of gaining momentum in Banāras, but the early missionaries, steeped as they were in the cultural chauvinism of that era, did not know this. They could not comprehend how a reasonable person might speak of Mt. Meru as the center of the world and the River Ganges as a liquid form of divine grace. If there were a center of the world it was Jesus, and if there were a liquid form of grace surely it was the wine of his blood. Hindus were not impressed or attracted by such symbols, and could not comprehend the exclusivism of the Christian view.

To their credit, however, the missionaries recognized the great power and significance of Banāras for Hindus. For this reason they poured their energies into the conversion of Banāras, convinced that if only Banāras could be won for Christianity the tide would surely turn throughout India. As Kennedy wrote, "The news would soon spread that Hinduism was drying up at its fountain, and that its power could not much longer be maintained." He concluded, with some passion:

Are we allowing imagination to take the reins at the expense of judgment, when we indulge the hope, that as in former days Buddhist preachers went forth from Benares to the millions of Eastern Asia with the lessons of Gautama, the Brahmans of Benares, accepting Jesus as their Saviour, will go forth with His Gospel to diffuse it far and wide among the nations of India, and then, with their converts, make their way to the remotest East?[65]

Little did Kennedy dream that when the brahmins of Banāras went forth, it would be to the West, and they would teach Indian music, Vedānta philosophy, Ayurvedic medicine, Hindu meditation, and yogic exercises to the many millions in Europe and America who would appreciate their message.

3

THE CITY OF
SHIVA

The Lord of Kāshī

W H E N Lord Shiva, the mountain ascetic, left his perpetual meditation and married the lovely Pārvatī, daughter of the Himālayas, he
needed to find a suitable home for the two of them. Scanning the entire
earth from the high Himālayan peaks, he chose the city of Vārānasī, a
beautiful place five *kroshas* large, luminous with its countless palaces,
gardens, and temples.[1] Thus Shiva, the mountain god, who had long
lived on the fringes of culture and was associated with the ascetic
traditions of the Himālayas, became not only a family man but a city
man dwelling in the very center of culture. The move from Mt.
Kailāsa to the city of Kāshī played no small role in the ascendancy of
Shaivism in North India.

Kāshī is the city of Shiva. Its Shiva temples number in the thousands.
Shaiva ascetics and renouncers come to the city to the monasteries of
their respective orders.[2] Of course, as we have seen, the city's religious history began long before the rise of Shaivism as such. What is
significant, however, is that over the centuries Kāshī's connection with
Shiva became so firm that by the time of the *Kāshī Khanda* this city
was said to have been the "original ground" created by Shiva and
Pārvatī, upon which they stood at the beginning of time when no other
"place" existed; the place from which the whole creation came forth in
the beginning and to which it will all return in the fire of time's end;
the place where Shiva's *linga,* as the unfathomable symbol of the Supreme Lord, first pierced the earth.

We can see the history of Shiva's association with this city in those myths that tell how Shiva, from his vantage point in the high Himālayas, chose this city from all the earth to be his abode. It was already the most beautiful place on earth, and it captivated the imagination of the Lord himself. In the earliest versions of this story, such as that of the *Vāyu Purāna*, Shiva could not immediately bring his bride to Vārānasī because the city was already occupied by King Divodāsa. He had to win the city first, and the story of Shiva's eviction of the King is told:

Shiva summoned one of his attendants named Nikumbha and told him to go to Vārānasī and to empty out the city. Nikumbha went and appeared in a dream to a barber, telling him to establish and worship the image of Nikumbha *gana* at the edge of the city. The barber did this, and Nikumbha was worshipped as the "Lord of Ganas" [Ganesha] at the city gate. He was honored with incense, flowers, and food offerings, and he became popular with the citizens by granting boons to those who propitiated him there. He granted all earthly desires. The King's wife Suyasha, who was childless, came repeatedly and worshipped Nikumbha in order to get a son, but Nikumbha did not answer her prayers. At length King Divodāsa became angry and ordered the shrine of Nikumbha Ganesha destroyed. Then Nikumbha pronounced a curse upon the King and his city: "Because my sacred place has been destroyed, this city shall be empty of all its inhabitants."[3]

When the city was vacant, Shiva arrived and established his residence there. In place of Divodāsa, Shiva and his entourage of *ganas* and *ganeshas* took over the rule of Kāshī. Apparently Pārvatī was not fond of the city at first, but Shiva said to her, "I will not leave my home, for my home is 'Never-Forsaken'—Avimukta."[4]

While Kāshī is the City of Shiva, it clearly does not derive its sanctity from Shiva's presence alone, for in the beginning it was this place, they say, which attracted Shiva's presence and was chosen by the Lord as his home.

SHIVA THE OUTSIDER

To know Kāshī it is important to know something of the theology and mythology of its lord. Shiva is called Maheshvara or Mahādeva, the "Great God," and he confounds and transcends human presupposi-

Decorating the Ādi Vishveshvara linga for the evening ārati̇̄. The linga is washed with water and with milk, and then honored with fragrant sandalwood paste, flowers, and bilva leaves.

tions of the Divine. He displays many faces. He wields weapons and bestows blessings with his many arms and hands. In his supremacy, Shiva stands outside, even contradicts, human categories and conventions. Shiva's traditional home is in the distant Himālayas on Mt. Kailāsa. He is a yogi who sits focused inward in meditation. He is an outsider who lives on the fringes of culture.

In a historical sense, Shiva is an outsider to the Indo-Aryan pantheon. While Rudra-Shiva claims several hymns of the *Rig Veda* and receives attention in the *Atharva Veda* and *Shatapatha Brāhmana,* it is nonetheless clear that this god emerged from the shadows of non-Aryan India to a position of increasing prominence in the Hindu pantheon. A well-known seal from the ancient Indus Valley civilization, which flourished in the early second millennium B.C., shows a three-headed figure with an erect phallus, seated in a yogic posture, surrounded with animals in the style of Shiva as Pashupati, the "Lord of Beasts." One cannot say that this figure *is* Shiva, but it has many of the characteristics that came to be Shiva's.

Even in his later mythological development as a full-fledged member of the pantheon, Shiva contradicts the conventions of Hindu custom and ethics called *dharma*. He has none of the concern for purity, the love of the auspicious, the disdain of the polluted, the reverence for family, lineage, and status which are characteristically Hindu. He wanders naked, or clothed in the bloody skin of a slain elephant or tiger. When he leaves the Himālayas to dwell in the heart of the culture, he makes his home in the cremation ground. He anoints his body with the ashes of the dead from the cremation pyre. He wears snakes about his neck for ornaments. He rides upon a bull and carries a trident as a weapon. He has no wealth, no family, no lineage, nothing of worldly value to recommend him. At times he presents himself as the very epitome of the horrible and inauspicious. And yet he is called "Shiva"—the "Auspicious," the "Gentle."

Shiva first appears in Indian mythology as a god of ambiguous nature. In the Vedic hymns to Rudra he appears to be one whose presence is terrible as well as blessed.[5] He is repulsive as well as attractive; he destroys and yet he creates; he wounds and yet he heals. His many weapons, like the rod and staff of the biblical Yahweh, make Shiva dangerous and destructive as well as comforting and protective. He is associated with disease in the same ambiguous way, as its cause as well as its cure. Using the categories of Rudolf Otto, Shiva is the "Holy," the *mysterium tremendum et fascinans:* the frightening and captivating One.[6] In addressing him, the early Vedic hymnists would one moment invite him to be present and the next entreat him to keep his distance. He has multiple names and multiple natures: he is Rudra ("The Weeper" or "The Roarer"), Bhava ("Being"), Hara ("The Robber"), and Pashupati ("Lord of Creatures").

When Pārvatī, the "Mountain's Daughter," child of Himālaya and his wife Mena, fell in love with the yogi Shiva, she subjected herself to severe and difficult austerities in order to win him as her husband. In the myth, as it is recounted in the *Shiva Purāna*, the ascetic Pārvatī is tested to see if she knows who Shiva really is.[7] In one instance, the seven sages come to her to attempt to change her mind. They explain to Pārvatī that Shiva is too inauspicious and ugly to be her husband. He had no clothing, no home, no lineage, and he associates with ghouls and goblins. She should marry Vishnu, a more fitting bridegroom— auspicious, wealthy, and with many excellent and lordly attributes. Pārvatī responds with true understanding. Yes, she says, the Supreme

शंकर

Shiva (here called "Shankara")
seated in meditation. He has
three eyes and is therefore
omniscient. The nāga is his
necklace. The Ganges flows
from his head. His drum of
creation and trident of
destruction are at his side.
Banāras folk art. Wall
painting.

Shiva is without the valued attributes of this world. Why? Because
Shiva is Brahman and transcends the display of worldly lordship and
wealth. The embellishments and ornaments the world adores are not
to be found in him, for he is beyond what is merely beautiful and
merely auspicious.

In the Hindu tradition, there are two kinds of sacredness: the "auspicious," which sums up everything that is good and valuable, and the
"holy," which challenges and transcends the conventional distinctions
of good and bad, valuable and valueless. Particularly this latter type of
sanctity is Shiva's. He may wear the crescent moon as an ornament in
his hair, and yet he carries the skull in his hand. He may appear one
moment wearing the flayed skin of an elephant and the next wearing
the silken garments of a bridegroom. Appropriately, Shiva's city is the
Mahāshmashāna as well as the Ānandavana. An encounter with such a

god wrenches away the worldly conventions which tend to create "god" in the image of human society. Although Shiva's name means "auspicious" and "gracious," it is used euphemistically, for Shiva often displays himself in precisely those things that are neither auspicious nor gracious in the eyes of the world.

Shiva thus challenges any facile distinctions between sacred and profane, rich and poor, high and low. Shiva's critics among the gods and the sages often cast him as an outsider and a misfit for this reason. In one famous story, Shiva is the one god of the entire host of heaven who is not invited to the great sacrifice held by the pretentious demigod, Daksha. All the sacred rivers and mountains, all the gods and sages, all the denizens of heaven have come. And Daksha addresses the crowd to explain why Shiva is not there:

What is his lineage and what is his clan? What place does he belong to and what is his nature? What does he do for a living and how does he behave, this fellow who drinks poison and rides a bull?

He is not an ascetic, for how can one who carries a weapon be an ascetic?

Shiva and Pārvatī, in the Himālayas. Wall painting on the Ratneshvara Temple, Vārānasī. Note the Ganges flowing from Shiva's head, which is also decked with the crescent moon and a triple bilva leaf. Shiva's drum of creation and trident of destruction stand in the background.

He is not a householder, for he lives in the cremation ground. He is not a celibate student, for he has a wife. And he cannot be a forest-dweller, for he is drunk with the conceit of his lordship.

He is not a brahmin, for the Vedas do not know him as one. Since he carries a spear and a trident, he might be a *kshatriya*, but he is not. Since he delights in the destruction of the world, he cannot be a *kshatriya*, who protects the world from harm. And how can he be a *vaishya*, for he never has any wealth? He is not even a *shūdra*, for he wears the snake as a sacred thread. So he is beyond the castes [*varna*] and the stages of life [*āshrama*].*

Everything is known by its original source [*prakriti*], but Shiva the Immovable has no original source. He is not a man, because half his body is female. And yet he is not a woman, because he has a beard. He is not even a eunuch, because his phallus [*linga*] is worshipped. He is not a boy, for he is great in years, that fearsome one, and he is proclaimed in the worlds as beginningless and ageless. How can he be young when he is so ancient? And yet he is not old, for he is without old age and death.[8]

Shiva cannot be categorized in any way—not by *varna*, or *āshrama*. He cannot be known by his clan or lineage. "He" cannot even be known by sex, since Shiva is half Shakti, his female energy. He is a bafflement to conventions, including religious conventions. It is not surprising, therefore, that his followers were sometimes called *veda-bāhyas*, those who are "outside the Vedas."[9]

THE MANY-FACED AND FACELESS SHIVA

One way of seeing Shiva's enigmatic many-sidedness is in his many faces. Usually there are five faces, depicted by multiple heads or multiple gestures.[10] The faces are not entirely separate, but cohere in a single image of the Lord and are "moments" of his activity. There is

---

* The four traditional stages of life *(āshramas)* for a Hindu male are the celibate student, the householder, the retired forest-dweller, and the wandering renouncer. The four traditional "castes" *(varnas)* are: brahmins (priests and teachers); kshatriyas (warriors and kings); vaishyas (merchants and cultivators); and shūdras (servants). Of course, the real caste unit, the *jāti* (literally, "birth-group"), sometimes called the sub-caste, is the unit one claims as one's community and within which one marries. Nonetheless, the term *varnāshrama dharma* has come to mean one's duty according to caste and stage of life.

the face of creation *(srishti)* and that of preservation *(sthiti)*. There is the more horrific face of destruction *(samhāra)* and the playful face of concealment *(tirobhāva)*. Finally, there is the fifth, the indescribable face of revelation and salvation *(anugraha)*.

Shiva's creative moment is expressed in many ways. It is well known, for instance, in his dance, when he calls creation into being with the beat of his drum.[11] His creative power is most vividly displayed, however, in the symbol of the *linga* which, in one sense, is the erect phallus of a god who is creative, procreative, and, indeed, erotic.[12] Shiva's creative aspect is sensuous. He is the beautiful bridegroom of Pārvatī, anointed with perfumed sandal paste, decked with the crescent moon in his crown. This attractive aspect of Shiva as procreative god and husband is often shown in Hindu popular art in which Shiva is flawlessly beautiful. He is seated next to Pārvatī, perhaps with their small offspring, Ganesha and Skanda, at their feet. This is the aspect of Shiva that runs with the grain of life and upholds the social norms of marriage and family, peculiar as his family is. Shiva and Pārvatī have no normally conceived offspring. Shiva's seed is too hot for Pārvatī to carry, so Agni conveys it to the River Ganges where it is mothered by the six female deities called the Krittikās. Thus the child Skanda has six heads and is called Kārttikeya. Ganesha is produced by Pārvatī alone, out of the rubbings from her skin, according to one account. Nonetheless, Shiva and Pārvatī are praised in the tradition as the ideal married couple and Shiva is often depicted in the inconographical pose called Kalyānasundara, which shows Shiva at his wedding to Pārvatī.

Shiva shows his second face to maintain and preserve the ordered cosmos, a task he is frequently called upon to perform. The Hindu cosmos is a systemic whole, consisting of heaven, earth, and the netherworlds. When one part of it is out of balance the whole suffers. When there are too many sinners on earth the Earth complains. When there are too many people who have made it to heaven the gods complain, for they depend on the people of the earth for their sustenance through sacrifice. And when the anti-gods or demons called *asuras**** gain too much power, everyone complains. In one myth, the great

---

* *Asuras* are frequently called "demons," but we should note that they are characterized primarily by being the "other side" in the cosmic struggle with the *devas*, or "gods." Sometimes the *asuras* are not demonic at all, but devotees of Shiva or virtuous

citadel of the *asuras* called the Triple-City waxes strong, and the gods
plead with Shiva to destroy it. Shiva burns it up with a single blazing
arrow. In another myth, the *asura* Tāraka, who can be killed only by
the son of the yogi Shiva, becomes the strongman of the universe. The
gods plead with the celibate Shiva to marry and beget a son, so Shiva
marries Pārvatī and deposits his blazing seed into the Ganges, where it
becomes the hero Skanda, who slays Tāraka. Shiva as preserver is
constantly called upon to maintain order, to restore the balance that
keeps the universe in operation. The triple world is supported by
dharma, the "right order," the "law" of society and of nature, and
Shiva repeatedly acts to restore order when it has gone awry. Even for
this yogi-god, the world is here to be supported, not merely to be
transcended.

Shiva's third and fourth faces counterpose the first two. They run
against the grain and counter to the conventions of this world and
society. His third face is destruction, symbolized by his weapons, the
arrow and trident. His destruction of such anti-gods as Jalandhara and
Andhaka is well known, as is his destruction of the Triple City of the
asuras and his final destruction of the world at the end of time's cycle.
More important, Shiva as the yogi may also be seen as destructive, for
yoga is essentially the reversal of the process of creation, the disci-
plined return to oneness of the evolved elements of the human organ-
ism. "Yoga," it is said, "is stopping the whirlpools of the mind."[13] It is
"drawing in" *(nivritti)* rather than "evolving out" *(pravritti).* The
yogi and the ascetic stand apart from social *dharma.* In this moment,
Shiva is no longer the beautiful bridegroom, but the ugly and horrific
haunter of cremation grounds. His fragrant sandal paste becomes
ashes, his ornaments become snakes, and his silken garments become
animal hides. Here he stands outside *varnāshrama dharma* and is no
family man, but a seeming madman.

Fourth is Shiva's moment of concealment or obscuration. Shiva is
not easily discoverable, for he often hides himself in creation and is the
master of disguise and impersonation. Assuming many forms in his
cosmic play, Shiva is apt to be in one's very presence, unknown or
unrecognized. In this aspect, Shiva is the wielder of the power of

---

observers of *dharma.* Even so, they are the "other side" as far as the gods are concerned.
Remember that in the Zarathustrian branch of the Aryan family, the *daivas* became the
demons and the *ahuras,* the lords.

delusion *(māyā)* which veils human perception of the truth. As readily as Shiva shows himself he hides himself. Thus, one of the great themes of Shiva's mythology is the back-and-forth movement between the recognition and the veiling of truth, between beholding Shiva for an instant and then having the veil of *māyā* drawn over that vision so that the plot of ordinary life can go on.

The fifth of Shiva's faces is supreme: he bestows grace, revealing his mercy to his devotees. It is a face he shows in all his other aspects as well, for he may save in the act of destruction or disguise as easily as in the act of creation or preservation. For example, in destroying the Triple-City with his flaming arrow, Shiva purifies and saves the anti-gods with that same flame. This face of Shiva is ever present, behind his other masks. It is the face Shiva shows when he is fully known. And it is the face called "grace," for it can be known only by the Lord's favor, and the knowing of it brings liberation.

THE LINGA OF SHIVA

In Banāras, one will see anthropomorphic images of Shiva as they are painted by the folk artists of the city upon the walls of temples, public buildings, and private homes. Shiva may be seated alone in meditation, or he may be encamped in the high Himālayas with Parvatī, or he may be riding in procession on his bull surrounded by a host of attendants. Yet such images, while they remind the passerby of the heritage of myths and stories associated with Shiva, are relatively rare as the focus of worship in the many temples and wayside shrines of the city. There Shiva is honored in the form of the *linga,* the rounded vertical shaft of stone implanted in a circular base.

The word *linga* means both "phallus" and "emblem," and the worship of this erect shaft alarmed and horrified many early Western visitors to India. The Abbé Dubois, for instance, writing in the early nineteenth century, called it an "obscene symbol" and an "insult to decency."[14] While the sexual symbolism of the *linga* cannot be disregarded, neither should it be exaggerated. Insofar as its sexual connotations are significant, the *linga* is certainly a bisexual symbol and not a phallic symbol alone. The shaft of the *linga* of Shiva is invariably set in a circular base, called a "seat." It is the seat of that divine energy

Five-faced linga *from Panna, Madhya Pradesh. Fifth century.*

Linga *at Kedāra Ghāt, honored with a* bilva *leaf.*

(shakti) personified as Shivas's female half and often called by the proper name Shakti. From the womb-seat of the base a wedge-shaped channel opening extends the female symbolism and serves, in practical terms, as a drain for the water offerings which are poured so liberally upon the *linga* by worshippers. Shiva's ancient link with the autoch thonous deities of India is sometimes manifested in the snake which swims up the channel of the *pītha* or coils around the shaft of the *linga*. The *linga* is a vivid reminder that Shiva himself is really both Shiva and Shakti, unable to be cast even in the mold of sexual convention. Shiva is called Ardhanārīshvara, the "Half-Woman Lord," and is sometimes depicted as a one-breasted deity, clad half in *sārī* and half in *dhotī*. The *linga* as the "emblem" of Shiva is to be understood as both *linga* and *pītha*.

The symbolism of the *linga* extends far beyond its sexual dimensions and has been elaborately articulated in the philosophy, theology, and mythology of the tradition. The *linga* is, in a wider sense, *the* symbol of the wholeness of the Hindu universe. *Pravritti,* the evolution of the One into the multiplicity of the created universe, the centrifugal movement of expansion into the infinite variety of "names and forms," is represented by Shakti, the energy of life. *Nivritti,* the balancing involution of the multiplicity back into the One, the centripetal movement of condensation, is represented by Shiva, the still center which anchors and transcends the whirl of *saṃsāra.* The movement of *pravritti* and *nivritti,* Shakti and Shiva, is at the heart of the universe.

The term Sadā Shiva, the "Eternal Shiva," has been used to indicate that One reality which embraces both Shiva and Shakti, both Shiva and the many faces of Shiva. Nonetheless, most people speak simply of "Shiva," and when they bring their water and flower offerings to the temple, utter the *mantra* "Om Namah Shivāya," and linger for the evening *āratī** and the singing of the "Shiva Mahimna Stotra," the deity they worship is the Supreme One. Any of them would readily say that this One includes the whole array of multiple faces and gods, and that this One includes both Shiva and Shakti. And as the city of Shiva, Kāshī is called the "Embodiment of Shiva and Shakti" *(Shiva-shakti svarūpiṇī).*

In the *linga* Shiva is both the manifest and unmanifest Lord. In his manifest forms, Shiva has many phases or parts *(kalā),* like the moon. Shiva "with-parts" *(sakala)* has the four faces described earlier. He is active, energetic, and involved in the world of creation and destruction. Sometimes these faces emerge from the shaft of the *linga,* facing in the four directions. But Shiva is also "without-parts" *(nishkala),* like the unmanifest moon, present but not seen. Like the uncarved shaft of the *linga,* this Shiva is the unfractured whole, the source, the unutterable Brahman.

In an interview, the *mahant* of Kāshī's Vishvanātha Temple summarized the transcendent significance of the *linga* by explaining that the word itself comes from the Sanskrit root *lī*—"to dissolve," "to rest on," "to dwell in"—for in the *linga* everything that is comes to rest. He said, "Everything in the world is *in* the *linga* at all times, and not outside it. We too are in the *linga* and not separated from it." It is often said, in mythological terms, that the sky is the shaft of the *linga,* and the earth is its base. Since everything that is, including all gods, originates and dwells and rests in this whole, it is called the *linga.*

---

* *Āratī* means "lamp offering" and refers to the five-wick oil lamp or camphor lamp the priest circles before the image of the deity. This is one of usually sixteen offerings *(upachāras)* made in worship, including incense, flowers, water, cloth, fresh leaves, etc. *Āratī* has become the name of the entire rite, however.

THE LINGA OF LIGHT

There are many myths that tell of the origin of the *linga* as it is worshipped here on earth. Among them are vivid myths of the castration of Shiva. For example, it is said in one myth cycle that sages of the Pine Forest castrated Shiva because they believed him to have seduced their wives.[15] Most prominent, however, in Shaiva theology and most significant in the context of Kāshī is the great myth of the fiery appearance of the "*linga* of light," the *jyotirlinga*. This myth is one of the most popular of the entire Purānic corpus and is told many times in various settings.[16] It recounts the first appearance or hierophany of Shiva's *linga* which pierced the three worlds as a brilliant shaft of light and was witnessed by Brahmā and Vishnu long ago. In some versions, it is Shiva's castrated *linga* which is the *linga* of fire. In the versions treated here, however, the fiery *linga* is not a part of Shiva, but rather Shiva is a part of it. The *jyotirlinga* is the supreme "partless" reality, out of which Shiva may sometimes appear in bodily form as a "partial" reality. The myth of the *jyotirlinga* is of major importance to the mythology and symbolism of Kāshī, for here in this city that fiery column of light is said to have appeared.

The story begins with Brahmā, the Creator, and Vishnu, the Sustainer of the Universe, arguing about which of them is supreme. In some accounts of this myth, such as that of the *Kāshī Khanda* and the *Kūrma Purana*, Brahmā and Vishnu call in the four Vedas to settle their dispute. The Vedas, however, testify one by one that neither Brahmā nor Vishnu, but Shiva is supreme. As the two stand in disbelief, a huge column of fire splits the earth between them and blazes up through the sky to pierce the highest heavens. Astounded, Brahmā and Vishnu decide to determine the source and extent of this brilliant pillar of light. Vishnu becomes a boar and burrows deep into the netherworlds. Brahmā mounts his goose and flies as far up as the heavens reach. But even after thousands of years they cannot find the bottom or the top of the shaft of light. When they have returned to their starting place, Shiva emerges from the light in his "partial" bodily form. Vishnu honors the Lord, but Brahmā is still conceited and deluded.

In the *Shiva Purāna* version of the myth Brahmā lies about having

seen the top of the pillar and recruits the *ketakī* flower as a false witness
to support him. In the *Kāshī Khanda* version, Brahmā speaks conde-
scendingly to Shiva, as an elder would speak in recognizing the antics
of a youth. Whatever the cause, Brahmā's slander against Shiva is
punished. Shiva, taking the fearsome form of Bhairava, cuts off one of
Brahmā's five heads, leaving him with the four by which he is traditionally recognized. However, the skull of Brahmā, tangible evidence
of the worst of sins—killing a brahmin—sticks to Bhairava's hand and
will not come loose.* Even the Lord must pay for the sin of killing a
brahmin, so Bhairava wanders all over India, the skull clinging to his
hand, until he comes, finally, to Vārānasī, where the skull drops and
Bhairava becomes free of that sin. In some versions of the myth, the sin
is embodied not by a skull, but by an ugly hag with jagged teeth, who
follows Bhairava relentlessly until he reaches Vārānasī.

The first theme of interest in these myths is that of Shiva's supremacy over Brahmā and Vishnu. In this myth cycle Shiva suppresses the
slanderous Brahmā by stripping him of his power and his cultus and
relieving him of one of his heads. This is one of many mythic expla-
nations of how it is that Brahmā is no longer worshipped in India.
Shiva is pleased with Vishnu's devotion, however, and allows him a
high status and an active cultus. In some variations it is Vishnu who
points out the way to Vārānasī to the wandering Shiva.

The second theme here will be important later on in our discussion
of Kāla Bhairava: Shiva's expiation of the sin of killing a brahmin,
requiring a long pilgrimage which ends at the Kapālamochana
("Where the Skull Fell") Tīrtha in Vārānasī. Although he is supreme,
Shiva must atone for the decapitation of Brahmā. As Bhairava, Shiva
makes a pilgrimage to all the various *tīrthas* and finally to Vārānasī.
One of the claims made for this city is that merely entering its boundaries destroys all sins, for even this worst possible sin, killing a brahmin, fell here. Lord Shiva himself carried that sin as a skull and acted
out the drama of its expiation.

Most important is the *linga* of light itself—the image of the supremacy of Shiva. It is what Mircea Eliade has called the *axis mundi*, the
pillar at the center of the world, originating deep in the netherworlds,

---

* Lord Brahmā here is seen as the archetypal brahmin. Killing a brahmin is one of the
five "great sins" *(mahāpātakas)*. The others are stealing, drinking liquor, sleeping with
one's guru's wife, and associating with people who do such things.

cracking the surface of the earth, and splitting the roof of the sky.[17] In this *linga* Shiva is not one god among others, but the unfathomable One. In this "partless" form, Shiva transcends even Shiva himself, in embodied "partial" form. This is not Shiva, beautiful or ugly, dressed in silks or tiger skins, wearing the crescent moon or the necklace of skulls. This light is the *mysterium tremendum* which finally cannot be described or comprehended by any or all faces and attributes.

The *linga* of light was the first *linga*. After that, Shiva vowed that this unfathomable *linga* would become small so that people might have it as an emblem for their worship. Wherever the *linga* is, there is a *tīrtha*, because the *linga* by nature is a "crossing place" where the worlds are knit together by the shaft of Shiva. Other deities have *mūrtis*, images, but only Shiva has the world-spanning form of a *linga*.[18]

The myth of the fiery *linga* begins and ends in Kāshī. In Kāshī mythology this is the place where the light split the earth, and this is the place called Kapālamochana Tīrtha, "Where the Skull Fell." There are other Kapālamochana *tīrthas*, of course, just as there are other places in India that claim the *jyotirlinga* as their own, including an acknowledged cycle of twelve *jyotirlingas*. This entire myth cycle has a pan-Indian popularity, so it is one to which a great many places subscribe in telling the story of their own sanctity. The Hindu tradition, in contrast with the prophetic traditions of the West, is one in which every great hierophany is shared and multiplied, without exclusivist claim. In Kāshī alone there are three particular *lingas* that have claimed to be the *linga* of light: Omkāreshvara, Avimukteshvara, and Vishveshvara, each of which will be discussed later.

In Kāshī's spiritual tradition, however, it is affirmed that the *linga* of light did not merely burst forth from the earth *in* Kāshī. Rather it *was* Kāshī, the "Luminous." The entire sacred field included within the Panchakroshī Road *is* the *linga* of light, the blazing emblem of the Lord.

THE LINGAS OF BANĀRAS

In Kāshī it is said that there is a *linga* at every step, and that there is not a place as big as a sesame seed that does not sprout a *linga*.[19] Walking through the back streets and lanes of Banāras, one sees that this is not far from the truth. In the hundreds of small shrines found along every section of the riverbank, around every corner, and under every tree, there is a *linga,* very likely freshly adorned with a flower and sprinkled with water, no matter how obscure or broken with age it may be. In the *Kāshī Khanda,* there are several long enumerations of the city's Shiva *lingas.*[20] On page after page, these *lingas* are named and their locations described. Even so, only several hundred are mentioned. At the end of one of the long lists of *lingas,* it is said that there are 100,000 *lingas* in Kāshī and that the city is "made of *lingas.*"[21] The common saying in Banāras is "The very stones of Kāshī are Shiva."

Lingas are of two kinds: those that can be moved from place to place *(chala lingas),* and those that cannot *(achala lingas).* One can buy a small portable *linga* in the market to use for daily worship at home. Or one might wear such a *linga* around one's neck, as do the members of the Vīra Shaiva or Lingāyat sect. A momentary *(kshanika) linga* is also "movable": a small *linga* hand-fashioned of clay in which Shiva is invited to dwell for the moment of worship and which is thrown away into the Ganges or some other stream at the conclusion of worship. The *kshanika linga* dramatizes the Hindu understanding of divine images: they are a focal point for worship, a lens for *darshana,* and for a time they are imbued with the full presence and power of the Divine.

Of the non-moving *lingas* there are also two kinds. First, there are *svayambhū lingas,* which are said to have emerged miraculously from the earth as hierophanies of Shiva. One enumeration claims there are sixty-eight such self-manifest *lingas* throughout India, but in fact there are thousands of *lingas* which people call *svayambhū,* affirming that the Lord has appeared here by divine initiative. Second, there are *sthāpita lingas,* which have been "established" by people, sages, or gods. When they are consecrated, Shiva is invited to take up residence in the *linga.* Such *lingas* usually go by the name of their establisher as well as by the name of Shiva: Īshvara or Īsha, literally, the "Lord." Thus, the *linga* established by Brahmā is Brahmeshvara, and that established by the moon, Chandra, is Chandreshvara. The established *linga* partakes of the nature of the establisher as well as that of Shiva. Chandreshvara is especially associated with Mondays, the day of the moon, and with the bestowing of wisdom, also associated with the moon. The *linga* of the yogi Jaigishavya, called Jaigishavyeshvara, is particularly honored to obtain the high yogic attainments realized by its founder. Despite their

Rāma and Lakshmana, heroes of the Rāmāyana, honoring Shiva with flowers and bilva leaves. Banāras folk art. Wall painting.

multiplicity, Shiva is said to be fully present in all these *lingas*. As one Banāras pandit put it, "Shiva in his *lingas* is like the sun, reflected fully and individually in a thousand jars of water."

In the *Kāshī Khanda*, Shiva speaks to Pārvatī of the multiplicity of *lingas*, both in numbers and in kind, in Kāshī:

There are uncounted *lingas* in the Forest of Bliss, O Pārvatī. Some are material and others of a subtle and spiritual nature. They are made of various gems, made of many elements, made of stone. Many are self-born and many are established by gods and sages. . . . Those that have been established here are the cause of liberation. Some are not visible, some are visible, and some are in rather a miserable state. Even those that are broken down by the ravages of time are still to be worshipped, fair Pārvatī. One time I counted a hundred billion of them. Six million of them stand in the waters of the Ganges; those *lingas* bestow yogic achievement and have become invisible now in the Kali Age, O Goddess. And of course those *lingas* that were established here by my devotees after the day I counted have not been counted at all.[22]

Of these "hundred billion" *lingas* we will look at three in some detail here: Omkāra (Omkāreshvara), Vishvanātha (Vishveshvara), and

Kedāra (Kedāreshvara). The three are the anchor and namesake temples for the three traditional geographical sectors *(khandas)* of the sacred city: Omkāra in the north, Kedāra in the south, and Vishveshvara in the center. (*See* Appendix II and Map 7 for a description of the limits of these *khandas.*) These three will give some broader insight into the history and the structure of the city of Shiva, for they have different types of temple mythology and they have had very different histories in the past thousand years.

Omkāra

THE TEMPLE TODAY

A THOUSAND years ago, Omkāra was one of the most important Shiva *lingas* in Kāshī. Its grand temple complex stood on the banks of a large inland lake called the Matsyodarī Tīrtha. Today, however, only by persistent inquiry can one find Omkāra. It is not that the temple is hidden in the maze of Kāshī's narrow lanes, for unlike any other temple in the city it sits in the open on a prominent little hillock. Rather, Omkāra is simply not known today. It is located in a predominantly Muslim neighborhood which few Hindus would visit. Were one to stop at a roadside tea stall near the pond and park called "Macchodarī" after the ancient *tīrtha,* and inquire about, for instance, the Trilochana Temple toward the river to the south, anyone would be able to point out the precise lane to follow in order to reach it. But were one to ask about Omkāra, just about the same distance to the north, one would elicit at best a vague hand-waving reply that it's "off there" somewhere.

Omkāra, has today all but disappeared. Its lapse is due primarily to the Muslim conquest and occupation of what became known as the Adampura quarter of the city. In addition, the draining in the nineteenth century of the great Matsyodarī Tīrtha on which Omkāra stood has also contributed to its decline. "The whole quarter wears an aspect of decay," wrote Nevill in his 1909 *Gazetteer.*[23] Its fortunes have not changed for the better since then.

For centuries this has been a Muslim neighborhood, and the few Hindus who live in the vicinity are very poor and unable to support the temple. As the wife of the *pūjārī* said in an interview, "This is a neighborhood of poor people. They have to worry about bread. Of course, around Trilochana folks are well off. That is a neighborhood of big people. But here there are only little people, poor people. There is no one who gives a penny."

The ancient Omkāra Temple must have been an impressive structure, occupying the entire hilltop. The temple that sits there today is quite small, however. It is said to have been built upon that site by the patronage of the Marāthī Queen Bhavānī in the eighteenth century[24] and then given in patronage to a Banāras priestly family.* That same family has now delegated the daily worship and service of the deity to the *pūjārī* who resides at the temple. Thus, it is by patronage that the *linga* is cared for and that the temple is swept and whitewashed, for the temple does not have a constituency of its own.

While some pilgrims come to this temple in making their rounds of the city's *lingas* on the festival day of Shivarātri, ordinarily they do not come at any other time of year. On a daily basis, only a few worshippers come. One such worshipper is a local poet who goes by the name of Pāgal, the "Lunatic," and has recently published a small pamphlet of hymns in honor of Omkāreshvara Shiva. His "Garland of Hymns to Omkāreshvara" is a sign of some local enthusiasm for reviving the ancient reputation of this temple.

THE "OM" OF OMKĀRA

The mystical sound *"Om,"* sometimes written *"Aum,"* is said to consist of five separate sounds: "A," "U," and "M" plus the nasalization *(bindu)* and the resonance of the sound *(nāda)*. Similarly, the temple

---

* The term for this kind of patron-client relationship is *jajmānī,* which refers to the system of hereditary service exchanges in India. The *jajmān* is the employer, in this case the Queen, deriving from the Sanskrit term *yajamāna* ("sacrificer")—the one who hires the brahmin priest to perform the sacrifice and who, therefore, derives the spiritual benefit from the sacrifice. Here the priest is retained as an employee to see to the care of the temple on behalf of the *jajmān.*

Omkāreshvara Temple, with Muslim graves in the foreground.

of Omkāra, the "Syllable Om," is said to consist of five separate shrines, one for each part of this mystical sound. The A-Kāra* Temple is today a relatively small and neglected shrine located under a nearby *pīpal* tree. The U-Kāra, somewhat larger and more carefully attended, is set within a compound, where an ancient image of Shiva's bull, Nandin, guards the sanctum of the *linga,* which is now about three feet below the surface of the earth. Adjacent to this temple lives the *pūjārī*'s family. The most visible of the temples is simply called Omkāreshvara and is the hilltop temple. A stairway leads up the hill to the small temple, just large enough to contain the *linga* and one worshipper. This site is probably that of the old Ma-Kāra Temple, and Omkāreshvara itself probably stood on the adjacent larger hillock now occupied by the shrine of a Muslim saint and covered with Muslim graves. The other two temples formerly located here, the Nāda Temple and the Bindu Temple, are said to have disappeared.

---

* *Kāra* means "letter."

THE MYTH

According to the *Kāshī Khanda,* this is the place where Lord Brahmā, in ancient times, performed rigorous austerities. After a thousand years, a great shaft of light, illumining the four directions, shot up in front of him, splitting through the seven levels of the netherworlds and cracking the earth wide open. With that brilliant light was heard the five-fold sound of the mystical *mantra, Om.* Brahmā praised the *linga* and the *Om,* and Shiva appeared in personal form from the *linga* and granted Brahmā a boon: he made him the Grandfather and Creator of the world.[25]

The story is still told by the temple's attendant *pūjārī* and his wife, each recounting it eagerly, speaking of Shiva with the familiar and colloquial name, Bābā, "Father." The woman told me, "Bābā appeared out of the earth of his own accord. He appeared from below as a great light. This was the first *linga* in Kāshī. It had five parts then, but two have disappeared." The *pūjārī* added, "This *linga* was not established, mind you. But it appeared of its own accord. In that light, Brahmā first saw the syllable 'A,' then 'U,' and then 'M.' Finally he saw the *nāda* and *bindu,* and the five together were Omkāreshvara."

Sometimes Omkāra is called the "Five-Fold Abode" *(panchāyatana)* of Shiva who, as we have seen, is said to have five parts. Here the theological interpretation is that within the *Om,* Vishnu is the "A," Brahma the "U," and Rudra-Shiva the "M." The *bindu* is the completing fourth, and the *nāda* is the center of the quadrant, signifying transcendence. The manifold *Om,* although it is often given an abstract philosophical explanation, as in the commentaries on the *Māndūkya Upanishad,* in this instance appears to have a theistic significance. The myth of the appearance of the luminous *linga* is, then, not only a sectarian myth about the supremacy of Shiva; more important, it is a myth about the supremacy of the attributeless One, called Sadā Shiva or Brahman, over all forms and manifestations of god.

The word *panchāyatana* also has a specific meaning in the Hindu ritual tradition. Literally, it is the "Five-Altar" form of worship, in which five gods—usually Shiva, Vishnu, Ganesha, Sūrya, and Devī— are honored at once, in a quadrant with one occupying a central position as the "chosen" focus of worship *(ishtadevatā).*[26] The god occupying the center of the quadrant may vary. The *panchāyatana* form of worship is said to have been popularized by Shankara in his

tour of India, and it is propounded even today by one of his heirs, the
Shankarāchārya of Kāmakotipītha. Omkāra is said to have been famous
for this syncretistic ritual form.

Five is Shiva's number, a number symbolic of wholeness. There is
the circular wholeness of the four directions and their center. There is
the material wholeness of the five elements, and the bodily wholeness
of the five senses. On another level, a person is said to consist of five
koshas, or sheaths, the outermost sheath being the material body and
the inner sheaths being progressively more refined and spiritual. Kāshī
too has five *koshas* or *kroshas,* they say, referring not only to the
geographical area encircled by the Panchakroshī Road, but also to the
sheaths of the sacred city, its innermost core being the subtle and pure
linga of light.

The *Om,* like Shiva and the *linga,* is a five-fold symbol of wholeness.
It has four parts with a transcending fifth, just as Shiva has four faces
with a faceless fifth, and just as the *linga* has four faces or directions
with a centering fifth. Here at Omkāra, the *Om,* the *linga,* and Shiva
seem to merge into one:

This Omkāra is the supreme wisdom, worshipped five-fold, the bestower of
liberation, honored daily by the wise in Vārānasī. Here the great Lord, Shiva
himself, having a five-fold form, delights in granting liberation to creatures.
Since the five gods, Brahmā and the others, always dwell here, this *linga* is
called five-fold.[27]

THE CITY ENCIRCLED BY
THE GANGES

A thousand years ago, Omkāra was situated on the banks of the lake
called the Matsyodarī Tīrtha. During the rainy season, the Matsyodarī
River flowed by the very door of the temple. Today, Matsyodarī is
only a small elliptically shaped park and pond called "Macchodarī,"
which is a short distance to the south of Omkāra. The great Matsyodarī Tīrtha was drained in the 1820s.

In the old days, there was water in the Matsyodarī Tīrtha all year
long, especially during and after the rainy season, when it became a
large lake, reaching up a very steep slope to the south as far as

Kāmeshvara Temple. Kāmeshvara, which formerly sat right on the bank of the *tīrtha,* is now a climb of some two hundred feet above the Macchodarī Road. To the north, the waters of the Matsyodarī used to spread as far as Omkāra. From there, during the rainy season, the waters made quite a significant river, flowing north through the small lakes of Kapālamochana ("Where the Skull Fell"), Rinamochana ("Where Debts Fall"), and Pāpamochana ("Where Sins Fall") to empty into the Varanā River. Omkāra was the most important temple on the banks of this great *tīrtha.*

In an ordinary year, the seasonal Matsyodarī River was a north-flowing tributary of the Varanā River. In a rare year of extremely heavy rains, however, something extraordinary happened: the river would begin to run backwards. (Look at Map 3, showing the pools and lakes of Banāras.) The Ganges, flooding into the course of the Varanā River, would swell the waters of the Varanā so that the Varanā would begin to back up along the course of its tributary, the Matsyodarī. The strength of the floodwaters pushed back the waters of the Matsyodarī River and reversed its direction. Rather than flowing north into the Varanā, the Matsyodarī flowed southward, flooding the Matsyodarī lake, which then drained west into the Mandākinī lake. From there the waters followed the route of rain drainage through the Beniā Tālāb and into the Godauliā stream, which ran into the Ganges at Dashāsh-vamedha.[28]

In such a year of heavy rain, central Banāras became virtually an island, with the Ganges flowing along its east bank as usual and the backward-flowing floodwaters of the Ganges, the Varanā, and the Matsyodarī making another river which circled through the city itself. With the waters of the Ganges flowing on both sides of the city, such times were considered extremely auspicious. Also, during these times the waters of the Matsyodarī, auspicious in their own right, met in confluence *(sangam)* with the waters of the Ganges, and of course the confluence of two rivers is always more auspicious than a single river. The mingling of those sacred waters in such a time was called "Mat-syodarī Sangam" or "Matsyodarī Yoga"—"yoga" here meaning "meeting."

It is in this context, then, that we may understand the words of the *Kāshī Khanda,* which, without this geographical information, would sound puzzling indeed:

Seventy million attendants of Shiva came from Mt. Kailāsa, and there they made a very high mountain in the midst of Kāshī. And they made a delightful moat of muddy waters called the Matsyodarī. That *tīrtha,* which is said to be great, meets with the waters of the Ganges. When the waters of the Ganges reach this place by flowing in the reverse direction, then does the Matsyodarī *tīrtha* receive the full measure of its sanctity. Then it is a billion times more holy than an eclipse of the sun or moon. There at that time are present all the holy days and all the *tīrthas* and all the *lingas,* because the Ganges is the Matsyodarī. Those who bathe anywhere in the Matsyodarī at that time and offer rice-balls [*pindas*] to their ancestors never again enter the womb for birth. The holy land of Avimukta takes on the form of a fish. All around the coursing waters of the Heavenly Ganges are seen.[29]

Commenting on this final stanza, the sixteenth-century scholar Nārāyana Bhatta says: "The Ganges is indeed known as the Matsyo-darī by the etymology: 'in whose interior [*udara*] Kāshī has the form of a fish [*matsya*].' " It would seem that Nārāyana Bhatta and the writer of the Purāna had in mind the image that a modern scholar would discover by studying a map of the city: that, indeed, when the flood-waters of the Ganges and Varanā flow south through the bed of the Matsyodarī, linking it to the drainage route of the Mandākinī and the Beniā Tālāb, the city, surrounded by waters, has the form of a fish-shaped island.

Despite what must have been their many hardships, such times of flood are lavishly praised in the Purānas:

When, O beloved, the Ganges comes to Matsyodarī for the *darshana* of God, taking a bath there bestows liberation. When the Ganges shall come into that place, where the waters are mixed, flooded with the waters of the Varanā, then is the time very auspicious indeed—a rare time, even for the gods.[30]

The persistence of this auspicious watery event, the Matsyodarī San-gam, is recorded in the twelfth century in a Gāhadavāla inscription, which states that it was at Kapālamochana during such a flood that King Govindachandra took his bath in the Ganges and made a land donation to a brahmin.[31] It is likely that this sacred circling of the city by the waters of the Ganges recurred periodically until modern times, when the natural course of the city's drainage system was altered by the growth of urbanization.

"WHERE THE SKULL FELL":
KAPĀLAMOCHANA

This rare time of the Matsyodarī Yoga was, according to the myth, the very time of Shiva's visit to Kāshī as the skull-bearing Bhairava. "In such a time and in that place did I bathe," says Shiva, "and by virtue of that, O Goddess, the skull fell from the palm of my hand in an instant."[32] Kapālamochana was apparently precisely at the confluence of the Matsyodarī and the backward-flowing Ganges. Although the Kapālamochana tank is today over a mile to the north of Matsyodarī, it is clear that in ancient times it was but a very short distance north of Omkāra.[33] Even on the 1863 map made by Mr. Bax, the District Magistrate, this pool very close to Omkāra is still called "Matsyodarī Sangam."

Since the skull of heinous sin dropped off at that rare time of confluence, it is understandable that the Purānas make the same claim for all who bathe in the Matsyodarī at such a time, and, indeed, for all who bathe in Kapālamochana Tīrtha at any time.[34] Release from the burden of sins is one of the great blessings, they say, of visiting a powerful *tīrtha*. Here in Kāshī the place called Kapālamochana comes to symbolize the power to make sins fall away, for here "Where the Skull Fell" the worst of sins was shed.

No doubt Omkāra Temple, on its hillock, also became an island in these times of flood. Significantly, its prototype, the Omkāra *jyotirlinga* of Central India, is also set on an island in the middle of the sacred Narmadā River. The high ridges of the island are said to be shaped like the syllable *Om,* and the path that traces its outline is called the Panchakroshī Road.

In Kāshī, Omkāra Temple was once the central temple of Omkāra Khanda. The entire sector of the city was circumambulated in a pilgrimage that began and ended at Omkāra. Pilgrims who followed that route in the twelfth century would have stopped at many of the greatest and oldest temples in the city: Mahādeva, Trilochana, Krittivāsa, Kāleshvara, Madhyameshvara, and others. (*See* Appendix II for a more detailed description of the Omkāra Khanda Yātrā.) This was clearly the heart of the sacred city until the twelfth century, and it was this part of the city that was dealt the hardest blows during the Muslim centuries. Even though certain temples in the northern sector are flourishing today—Mrityunjaya, the "Death Conqueror" Shiva, and Trilochana, the "Three-Eyed" Shiva—the area as a whole has never really recovered.

Vishvanātha

THE TEMPLE TODAY

FOR AT LEAST a thousand years, Vishvanātha has been the pre-eminent Shiva *linga* in Kāshī. In Sanskrit literature, Vishvanātha is also called Vishveshvara. Both names mean the "Lord" *(nātha; īshvara)* of "All" *(vishva)*. It is appropriate that Shiva reigns in Kāshī under this all-encompassing name. This particular Shiva *linga* is one of the most important in all of India and serves as the archetype and namesake for hundreds of temples that local worshippers proudly call "Kāshī Vishvanātha."

Despite its fame, today's Vishvanātha Temple has none of the magnificence, architectural splendor, or antiquity of India's great classical temples in Orissa or South India. It was built as recently as the late eighteenth century under the patronage of Queen Ahalyabāī Holkar of Indore. The history of the previous temples that housed the *linga* of Vishveshvara is, in a nutshell, the history of Vārānasī over the past thousand years: a tale of repeated destruction and desecration. Today, atop the ruins of old Vishveshvara temples, sit two different mosques, one built in the thirteenth century by Razia and one in the seventeenth century by Aurangzeb.

The present Vishvanātha Temple is crowded into the interior of this tightly woven city, and its architectural features are hidden from proper perspective behind the compound wall. One approach to the temple is from the Vishvanātha Lane *(galī)*, the narrow, winding, busy shopping lane which has brought millions of pilgrims to Vishvanātha throughout the centuries. Silks and brasswares, cosmetics and betel nut are for sale here, in addition to every kind of religious paraphernalia: *lingas,* oil lamps, rosaries, incense, sealed vessels of Ganges water, and sweets to offer in the temple. As one approaches Vishvanātha, there

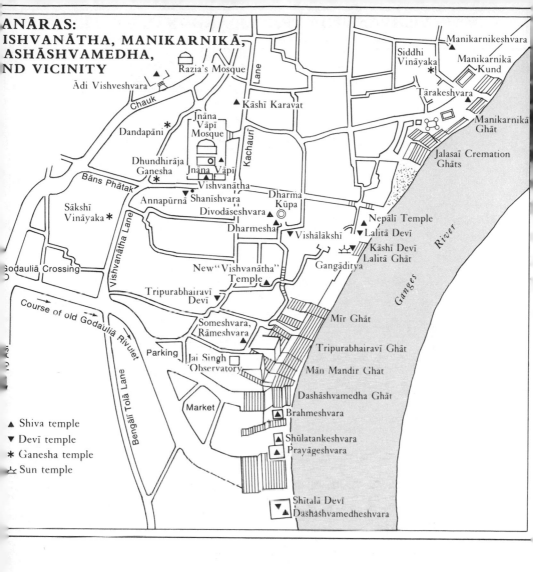

**ANĀRAS:
ISHVANĀTHA, MANIKARNIKĀ,
ASHĀSHVAMEDHA,
ND VICINITY**

Ādi Vishveshvara

Chauk

Razia's Mosque

Manikarnikeshvara

Siddhi
Vināyaka

Manikarnikā
Kund

Tārakeshvara

Kāshī Karavat

Dandapāni

Jnāna
Vāpī
Mosque

Manikarnikā
Ghāt

Dhundhirāja
Ganesha

Jalasaī Cremation
Ghāts

Bāns Phātak

Jnāna Vāpī

Vishvanātha

Sākshī
Vināyaka

Annapūrnā

Shanīshvara

Dharma
Kūpa

Divodāseshvara

Nepālī Temple

Godaulīā Crossing

Dharmesha

Vishālākshī

Lalitā Devī

Kāshī Devī
Lalitā Ghāt

New "Vishvanātha"
Temple

Gangāditya

Course of old Godaulīā Rivulet

Tripurabhairavī
Devī

Someshvara,
Rāmeshvara

Mīr Ghāt

Parking

Jai Singh
Observatory

Tripurabhairavī Ghāt

Mān Mandir Ghāt

Dashāshvamedha Ghāt

Market

Brahmeshvara

Bengālī Tolā Lane

Shūlatankeshvara
Prayāgeshvara

▲ Shiva temple
▼ Devī temple
* Ganesha temple
�>- Sun temple

Shītalā Devī
Dashāshvamedheshvara

Ganges River

are flower merchants whose baskets are heaped with garlands of marigolds and jasmine.

Only Hindus are permitted into the temple of Vishvanātha. Entering through the doorway from Vishvanātha lane with their offerings of
flowers, sweets, and Ganges water, they come into a large rectangular
courtyard in the center of which stands the temple itself. They will
make the rounds of some of the subsidiary shrines in the courtyard and
then enter the sanctum for the *darshana* of Shiva Vishvanātha. The
linga is set into the floor of the temple in a square solid-silver recessed
altar. The seat of the *linga* is also silver, and the shaft of the *linga* is a
smooth black stone. Shiva is worshipped at five principal *āratīs* during

Jnāna Vāpī Mosque

Vyāsa Seat

Tāra-keshvara

Gaurī Shankar

Nandin Bull

Jnāna Vāpī "Wisdom Well"

▲ Shiva linga
▼ Devī
o Vishnu
* Ganesha

JNĀNA VĀPĪ

Gananātha Vināyaka

tree

Sāvitrī

The Court of Vishvanā-tha

▼ Saubhāgya Gaurī
* Vighneshvara Ganesha
▲ Nikumbheshvara
▲ Kapileshvara

Kubereshvara

Shringāra Gaurī

Vyāseshvara

VISHVESHVARA

Mahākāla

Dandapānīshvara

Vaikuntheshvara

Vishveshvara or Vishvanātha

Kāla Bhairava

alleyway

Shanaishchara Virupāksha

Nīlakantheshvara

Avimukta Vināyaka
Virupākshī Gaurī
o Vishnu

Avimukteshvara

Entry

Map courtesy of Rām Shankar Tripāthī and Kuber Nāth Sukul

Vishvanātha Lane

the day, from early in the morning until late at night. In the evening *shringāra āratī*, the *linga* is elaborately decked with flowers. At any time of day, however, worshippers will come, chanting "Jaya, Jaya, Vishvanātha Shambho!" "Victory, Victory to Vishvanātha Shiva!" or

"Om Namah Shivāya!" "Om, Praise Be to Shiva!" They drench the *linga* with water, cover it with flowers and *bilva* leaves, and bend down to touch it with their hands. They will leave with their offerings of sweets, now the consecrated "grace" *(prasāda)* of the Lord.*

Although the interior of this important temple is neither very large nor very elaborate, the atmosphere of worship and devotion is power-fully impressive. The hushed silence which, in other traditions, may be associated with the sanctuary is not at all a Hindu mode of reverence.†
To the Hindu who has come here for *darshana,* the sights and sounds and smells of the temple, the shouting and chanting and clanging of bells, even the jostling of the crowds, all contribute to the aura of sanctity.

Not only does Hindu worship make use of the senses in directing them toward the Divine, but the Hindu sensibility appreciates the intensity of devotion brought *to* a place by the crowds of worshippers. As Rām Shankar Tripāthi, one of the governing priests of Vishvanātha today, explained, "Countless people have come here with worshipful hearts and have centered their devotion here at Vishveshvara for hundreds of years. By virtue of that history, this place is special. There is a saying, 'Pilgrims make the *tīrtha.*' So this *linga* is significant partly because so many people have centered their devotion here for so long."

In addition to the *linga* of Vishvanātha there is an array of other subsidiary shrines in the courtyard of the temple. To the left as one enters is an image of Vishnu, who must be worshipped here along with Vishvanatha.³³ Near Vishnu is the image of Avimukta Vināyaka, the

---

* The food presented to the deity is called *naivedya.* When the blessed food is returned to the worshipper as the remainder of the Lord's feast, it is called *prasāda,* the "bless-ing" or "grace" of God. In general, it is said that there is more reluctance to eat the food that has been offered to Shiva, no doubt because of its holiness and simultaneous danger. This is not the case with the *prasāda* of Vishvanātha, however.

† The Reverend James Kennedy wrote, for example, "The whole scene is repulsive. The place is sloppy with the water poured out by the worshippers, and is littered by the flowers they present. The ear is assailed with harsh sounds" (*Life and Work in Benares and Kumaon,* p. 66). We should note, however, that this peculiarly Protestant sensibil-ity would have been nearly as horrified by Catholic and Orthodox Christian piety. And, of course, the Hindu would certainly be shocked at the Protestant irreverence of entering the sanctuary empty-handed—with no flowers or water offerings—and with one's shoes on.

Ganesha of the old Avimukteshvara Temple. And in a shrine to the far right as one enters is the *linga* of Avimukteshvara, whose antiquity and significance will be discussed later. Elsewhere in this courtyard are the images of Nikumbha, Mahākāla, Dandapāni, and Virupāksha—all *lingas* bearing the names of former *yakshas* who are said to have come to Kāshī long ago in the entourage of Shiva.

Worshippers coming to Vishvanātha after bathing in the Ganges might also approach the temple from the north side, through the open area in which the Jnāna Vāpī, the "Wisdom Well," is located. They pass around the back of the temple through a dark exterior corridor where scores of Shiva *lingas* are arrayed in an area called "Shiva's Court." They enter the temple through the west door. The open area near the Jnāna Vāpī offers some perspective on the temple itself. It has

"View of the Gyan Bapee Well" by James Prinsep,
Benares Illustrated, 1831. The well itself is in the stone
enclosure at the center. To the right is the seated Vyāsa,
ministering to the ritual needs of the pilgrims. The seat
on which he sits is still there in the Jnāna Vāpī pavilion,
and the priestly family in charge of it today has held
religious jurisdiction over Jnāna Vāpī for over three
hundred years. To the left of the well is a pīpal tree,
today much larger (see page 126), still honored with rites
appropriate to the most ancient yaksha layer of Kāshī's
religious history. Behind the tree, the
shikaras of Vishvanātha.

a central dome and two spires called *shikharas*. The one that rises over the Vishveshvara *linga* was plated with gold by King Ranjit Singh of Lahore in 1839; thus this temple is called the Golden Temple by today's tourists.

THE "WELL OF WISDOM"
—JNĀNA VĀPĪ

The "Wisdom Well," a deep well about ten feet in diameter, is set today in a spacious columned arcade which was built to house it in 1828. Here pilgrims come to sip the waters and take a vow of intention

*Jnāna Vāpī pavilion. Entry to Vishvanātha Temple to the left
of the great pīpal tree.*

(*sankalpa*) at the outset of many a pilgrimage in and around Banāras,
and here they return at the end of the pilgrimage to sip the waters
again and to relax in the cool shade of the colonnade.

This is one of Kāshī's most famous wells, said to have been dug by
Shiva himself in order to cool the *linga* of Vishveshvara with water.
This took place "in the beginning," when there was no water on
earth. The waters that emerged here when Shiva dug the earth with
his trident were the first pure waters.[36] The water is said to be a liquid
form of *jñāna*, enlightening wisdom. This well of liquid wisdom is said
to have been here in Kāshī long before the Ganges came to earth.

Today the well has been equipped with iron bars across the top
which, according to the brahmin who has Jnāna Vāpī in his charge,
were installed to prevent the occasional suicides of liberation seekers
who would plunge into the well, happy to die in Kāshī. In addition, a
cloth has been spread over the iron grill to prevent the coins of pilgrims from plunging into the well. Thus, one cannot see the sacred
waters today, but they are drawn up daily and ladled out to worship-

pers who sip these waters before entering Vishvanātha Temple for *darshana.*

On the far side of the well from the temple is the great mosque of Aurangzeb, built upon the ruins of the grand sixteenth-century Vishveshvara Temple. The mosque is a Muslim transformation of the old Hindu edifice. One wall of the old temple is still standing, set like a Hindu ornament in the matrix of the mosque. Viewed from the back of the mosque, the dramatic contrast of the two traditions is evident: the ornate stone wall of the old temple, magnificent even in its ruined condition, topped by the simple white stucco dome of today's mosque. Ironically, the mosque is popularly known in Vārānasī as the Jnāna Vāpī Mosque, taking on the very name of the Hindu sacred precinct on which it stands. In modern times this area has been the site of periodic communal tension. For example, in 1809, one of the worst Hindu-Muslim clashes in the city's modern history broke out when Hindus attempted to erect a small shrine on the narrow strip of neutral ground between the mosque and the Vishvanātha Temple. This

The Jnāna Vāpī Mosque today.

"Temple Vishveshwur" drawn by James Prinsep, Benares Illustrated, *1831. The ruins of the seventeenth-century temple have been transformed into a mosque, the minaret of which can be seen to the right. In the broken remains of one of the eight ancillary pavilions that surrounded Vishveshvara are two Muslim graves.*

sparked widespread desecration of sacred sites on both sides. The Hindus must have come out the better, however, for Prinsep's drawing of the area in 1831 shows that the Hindus had erected a platform for the Jnāna Vāpī on that contested ground. Today the entire area around the mosque is filled with Hindu activity. There are a number of shrines. Pilgrims rest with their bundles, and merchants spread their wares: bright red and orange piles of *kunkum* powder, religious book- lets and maps, *rudrāksha* rosaries, sandalwood, and flower garlands. Yet there are still police guards posted here, a continuing reminder that Hindu-Muslim tension is not entirely a thing of the past.

THE TWO LINGAS

While Vishveshvara has been supreme in Kāshī for a millennium, it has not always enjoyed such a reputation, at least in the Purānic liter- ature. In the twelfth century, for example, Vishveshvara merits but a line or two of mention in the many Purānic *māhātmyas* collected by Lakshmīdhara. Indeed, it seems that over the centuries Vishveshvara has usurped the position of another *linga*, Avimukteshvara, which was of supreme importance in Kashi from Gupta times until the twelfth century and which today occupies only a small corner of the temple of Vishvanātha.

The story of the two *lingas* is a complicated but important strand of Kāshī's religious history. The two are clearly closely related. As the *mahant* of Vishvanātha Temple wrote, "Avimukteshwar is the first name by which Lord Vishwanāth was known."[37] He is right in a religious sense, for each in its own day has been the pre-eminent Shiva *linga* of Vārānasī. Historically speaking, however, there was not sim- ply a change of name involved. There were clearly two temples: Avi- mukteshvara, which was famous in the Purānas, and Vishveshvara, which was a popular local temple. The confusion began during the long centuries of Muslim raids on the city when a number of temples were destroyed. Vishveshvara, one of the first to be razed, must have been an important temple, even if it did not have the sanction of a Purānic pedigree. Vishveshvara was moved to a location near Avi- mukteshvara. It gradually overshadowed Avimukteshvara and finally came to include it within its own walls. While both are very old temples, the point at which Vishveshvara breaks into the Purānic lit- erature in the late twelfth and thirteenth centuries is so clear that the appearance of its name is one of the most useful guides for the dating of Purānic *māhātmyas* of Kāshī.

ANCIENT AVIMUKTESHVARA

The city's name, Avimukta, dates from the very early centuries of our era. Today it has fallen into disuse, but in earlier times this name seems to have been used more frequently than either Kāshī or Vārānasī. Some Purānic *māhātmyas* use the name Avimukta exclusively.[38] This name for the city occurs in such sources as the *Mahābhārata*, the *Jābāla Upanishad*, and in inscriptions from the eighth to the twelfth centuries.[39]

Avimukteshvara, the "Lord of Avimukta," is mentioned as the reigning deity in Kāshī in the sixth-century *Dashakumāracharita*, which mentions the pilgrimage of a young man to Kāshī, where he bathes at Manikarnikā and worships Avimukteshvara.[40] The name Avimukteshvara also occurs on as many as eight separate sealings from the Rājghāt excavations in Banāras, dating from Gupta times to the tenth or eleventh centuries.[41]

In the *Linga Purāna* quoted by Lakshmīdhara, Avimukteshvara is said to be located just to the north of the sacred well, Jnāna Vāpī,[42] precisely where the mosque sits today and where Vishveshvara was previously located. According to that Purāna, around Avimukteshvara stood the shrines of Dandapāni, Tāraka, and Mahākāla—all of which still have their places today near the Jnāna Vāpī and the Vishvanātha Temple. Clearly Avimukteshvara occupied the spot that Vishveshvara later came to dominate.

The Purānic *māhātmyas* of Avimukteshvara claim that this is the primordial *linga* of the beginnings, so no one knows just how it came into being.[43] The *Kāshī Khanda* states that this *linga* was established here by Shiva himself when he left Kāshī for exile on Mt. Mandara during the reign of King Divodāsa (Chapter 4). Since Shiva established his emblem here, he did not really leave the sacred zone of Kāshī, which then became known as the "Never Forsaken."

A mysterious and intriguing explanation offered for the origin of this great *linga* is that of the *Linga Purāna:* In ancient days, a *linga* of Shiva was being pulled along through the night sky by flying goblins called *rākshasas*. When they were just over the area of Kāshī, Shiva thought, "Why shouldn't they drop me in Avimukta?" Just then the sound of the cock's crowing arose from the land. When they heard this sound, the *rākshasas,* who move only by night and hide during the day, let go of the *linga* and flew off in fear. Thus was the *linga* established in Avimukta. It literally dropped out of the sky one day at dawn.[44]

The relationship of this Avimukteshvara *linga* to Vishveshvara is made clearer in both the *Linga Purāna* and *Kāshī Khanda:* "Everyone worships Vishveshvara, the 'Lord of All.' But Vishveshvara, creator of all, worships Avimukteshvara *linga,* which bestows earthly pleasures [*bhukti*] and final liberation [*mukti*]."[45] Even in modern Banāras, Avimukteshvara is sometimes referred to as the *guru* of Vishveshvara, indicating, as is suggested here, that Avimukteshvara is the teacher and respected elder. Today, however, the respected elder has left only a trace: an ancient fragment of stone hidden amidst three Muslim graves on the north side of the Jnāna Vāpī Mosque, sprinkled with flowers once a year on the day of Shivarātri. More recently a *linga* of Avimukteshvara has been established in the southeast corner of the present Vishvanātha temple.

THE ''LORD OF ALL''–

VISHVESHVARA; VISHVANĀTHA

When the great scholar Lakshmīdhara collected materials for his *Tīrthavivechana Kānda* in the twelfth century, his Purānic sources were filled with praise for such Shiva temples as Ātmavīreshvara, Krittivāseshvara, and Avimukteshvara. Vishveshvara, however, is mentioned only in passing. But one can be certain that Lakshmīdhara, who lived in the very heart of Banāras culture during its golden age, knew Vishveshvara far better than did the sources he was compiling. It was during this golden age that much of what was to become the *Kāshī Khanda*—its hymns, stories, and *māhātmyas*—was generated. And when the *Kāshī Khanda* emerged in its present form a little over a century later, Vishveshvara was clearly the presiding Lord of the city. By the time Vāchaspati Mishra collected Purānic selections for the *Tīrtha Chintāmani* in 1460, Vishveshvara had so eclipsed its neighbor, Avimukteshvara, that this scholar was able to think, mistakenly, that the two were different names for the same *linga.*[46] Nārāyana Bhatta made the same mistake in writing the *Tristhalīsetu* in the sixteenth century.[47] Of the digest makers, only Mitra Mishra, who wrote the *Tīrtha Prakāsha* in the early 1600s, pointed out that the two names

referred to distinct temples, which had separate *māhātmyas* and separate days for worship.[48]

In the time of Lakshmīdhara and the Gāhadavāla kings, Vishveshvara was a famous temple locally. We may speculate that it was a
popular temple, a temple of the commonfolk, as the name "Lord of
All" suggests. It sat on a high hill, right in the middle of the city. The
long eighth-century poem, the *Kuttanīmata* ("The Advice of the Procuress"), does not mention Vishveshvara, but describes a city in which
a single temple stands out as impressive: a great temple upon a hill, its
temple-top flags fluttering in the breeze. The city around it is alive
with beautiful dancing girls and courtesans, the red *lāc* on whose carefully painted feet colors the very earth.[49] Was this perhaps old Vishveshvara, the ruins of which are located, even today, in the city's
red-light district, Dāl Mandī? And was its image, perhaps, the "majestic" Deva Maheshvara described by the Chinese traveler Hiuen
Tsiang as being nearly one hundred feet high?[50]

Despite the obscurity of its early history, we know that by the
twelfth century Vishveshvara attracted the worship of King Govindachandra, for he left an inscription to say so.[51] In the same century,
an inscription from South India records that a certain King of
Karnātaka set up a fund to help the pilgrims of his area pay the Mus-
lim-imposed tax so that they could visit Vishveshvara in Vārānasī.[52]

Perhaps the strongest, if ironic, indication of Vishveshvara's importance in the twelfth century is that it was singled out for destruction
by Muhammad Ghūri's captain Qutb-ud-din Aibak in 1194. Rebuilding
on that site was pre-empted by the construction of a mosque there by
the famous ruling princess of the Delhi Sultanate, Raziyyat-ud-din
(Razia) during her short reign (1236–40). Known as Razia's Mosque, it
still stands today.

Where was this hilltop of Vishvanātha? It was the middle hill of the
three hills on which old Vārānasī was said to be built. The three were
likened to the three prongs of Shiva's trident. The Rājghāt Plateau was
in the north, the Kedāra highlands in the south, and the hill of Vishvanātha in the middle. The central hill today is so completely covered
with buildings that it is almost impossible to imagine how spectacular
this landscape once was.

One is always aware of this particular hill in Banāras today, for
even the sturdiest of rickshaw-wallas will have to dismount and pull the
rickshaw up the steepest part of the long hill from Godauliā to the

Chauk Bazaar. Partway up the hill on the left one passes the well-known modern temple of Satyanārāyan, housed in a large building of intricate yellow grillwork with a graceful arcade over the sidewalk. Behind it, one sees the seventeenth-century Ādi Vishveshvara, the "Original Vishveshvara." But it is not really the "original" Vishveshvara. Rather, this temple was built by the patronage of a Rājput from Jaipur as close to the site of the original Vishveshvara as possible. To find that original site, one must go further up the street. Just where the hill is steepest, there is a tiny street on the left. It ascends up a steep staircase between a suitcase shop and a stationer. In India such a climb would normally lead to the open roof. But here, one is surprised to come out upon solid ground: the hilltop of Vishveshvara. Looking down upon the busy streets two stories below, it is amazing to see how completely the city has hidden this hilltop. Here, on the highest ground in all central Banāras, is Razia's Mosque. It nestles amidst trees whose roots are imbedded in ground that is level with the rooftops across the way. At the height of the golden Gāhadavāla era, before the catastrophe of 1194, this was the site of Vishvanātha.

M. A. Sherring, writing in the mid-nineteenth century, notes that just east of the compound of the Ādi Vishveshvara Temple, on considerably elevated ground, stood "a mosque built of very old materials, the pillars of which date as far back as the Gupta period, and possibly earlier." He speculates, quite correctly, "May not these stones and pillars be remains of the original Bisheswar?"[53] Whether or not the structural members are as old as Sherring conjectures cannot be determined, for today the mosque has been whitewashed so many times that the contours of the original stone are invisible.

From the lofty perspective of Vishvanātha's hill, one can look across the way to the domes and minarets of the Jnāna Vapī Mosque, built upon yet a later site of Vishvanātha, and behind it a keen eye can discern the golden *shikhara* of today's Vishvanātha Temple. Here the imagination can glimpse what a glorious temple site this hilltop once was, and one can see in the counterpoint of temple and mosque the stubborn persistence of that glory.

In the years that followed the building of Razia's Mosque on Vishvanātha's hilltop, Vishvanātha was rebuilt in another location, probably a short distance down the hill in the vicinity of Avimukteshvara Temple, an area it soon came to dominate. By the fourteenth century, religious life seems to have regained its vitality in Kāshī. A 1353 inscription records the establishment of a large temple called Padmesh-vara near Vishveshvara, which indicates that by that time the Vishveshvara Temple had been re-established.[54]

In the late fourteenth and fifteenth centuries, however, Banāras temples were destroyed several times, under the reigns of Firūz Shāh Tughluq of Delhi, Mahmud Shāh Sharqī of Jaunpur, and Sikandar Lodī of Delhi.[55] When the great scholar and religious leader Nārāyana Bhatta began his career in the sixteenth century, Vishveshvara again lay in ruins.

Nārāyana Bhatta, who compiled a digest of Purānic verses on Kāshī, Gayā, and Prayāga in his *Tristhalīsetu,* comments on some of the passages that concern Vishveshvara in a manner that tells a great deal about the times:

Even if the *linga* of Vishveshvara here is taken off somewhere and another is brought in and established by human hands, on account of the difficulty of the times, whatever is established in that place should be worshipped. . . . And if, owing to the power of foreign rulers, there is no *linga* at all in that place, even so, the *dharma* of the place itself should be observed, with rites of circumambulation, salutation, etc., and in this way the daily pilgrimage [*ni-tyayātrā*] shall be performed.[56]

Apparently Vishveshvara was hauled away, for in the same passage he also remarks, ". . . even in the absence of the foremost *linga* of light, Vishveshvara, worship should be offered to another *linga* put there in its place."

The reconstruction of the Vishveshvara Temple, perhaps on the most magnificent scale ever, was undertaken by Nārāyana Bhatta in 1585. The mood of the age improved with the reign of Akbar. Indeed it was with the patronage of one of Akbar's courtiers, Todar Māl, whose son ruled the Jaunpur area for the Emperor, that the reconstruction proceeded. The temple was grand in scale and execution, consisting of a central sanctum, the *garbha griha,* surrounded by eight pavilions, or *mandapas.*

The glorious day of this new Vishvanātha Temple, which included the smaller shrine of Avimukteshvara, was very brief indeed. In less than a century, in 1669, it was torn down at the command of the Mughal Emperor Aurangzeb. Half-dismantled, it became the foundation for the present Jnāna Vāpī Mosque. According to legend, the *linga* of Vishveshvara was saved from the temple before it was desecrated by the armies of Aurangzeb. It was thrown by a provident priest into the deep waters of the Jnāna Vāpī. In 1777 the Queen of Indore sponsored the construction of the present temple. Her royal inscription makes no mention of her having established another *linga*.

In addition to this chief temple, there are three other temples in Vārānasī today bearing the name of Vishveshvara/Vishvanātha. First, there is Ādi Vishveshvara, mentioned earlier, built under the patronage of the Rājputs in the late seventeenth or early eighteenth century. While it is a small temple, Ādi Vishveshvara is today in the hands of a very intelligent young priest and it has a dedicated following of worshippers. Second, there is the New Kāshī Vishvanātha Temple at Mīr Ghāt, containing a Shiva *linga* that was established by very orthodox brahmins when, according to their traditions, the old Vishvanātha *linga* was rendered impure by the entry of Harijans ("untouchables") into the temple after 1956. As one might imagine, the move caused a great furor among those many Hindus, brahmins included, who insisted, following Mahātma Gāndhi, that the temples of the Lord are above the human distinctions of high and low. Finally, there is the Vishvanātha Temple at Banāras Hindu University, built under the patronage of the wealthy Birla family. It is a huge temple with a tall white *shikhara* visible from all over the University. Like the Tulsī Mānas Temple, its splendor makes it a favorite with pilgrims and tourists alike.

VISHVANĀTHA'S MĀHĀTMYA

The praises of Vishveshvara are, fittingly, in continuity with those of its kindred predecessor, Avimukteshvara. Both are said to be the first *linga* on earth, the brilliant hierophany of Shiva which illumines the soul and brings liberation. Both are called *svayambhū*, "self-manifest."

The chapters of the *Kāshī Khanda* that praise Vishveshvara occur at the very end of the work.[57] The context of this *māhātmya* is Shiva's long-awaited return to Kāshī after his absence on Mt. Mandara. Entering into his great sanctum sanctorum, called the Pavilion of Liberation, the Mukti Mandapa, he shows the supreme *linga* to Brahmā and Vishnu in what seems a repetition of that ancient time when Shiva revealed his *linga* of light to the two gods.[58] Shiva tells them, "This light you see blazing before you is known as Vishveshvara, the very embodiment of Being, Consciousness, and Bliss."[59] Here Shiva is not one among the gods, but the One transcending the gods, the One called Brahman.

As the greatest of Kāshī's *lingas*, Vishveshvara is often linked with the greatest of the river *ghāts*, Manikārnikā, and the two of them are said to constitute the axis of Kāshī's religious life:

One who bathes in Manikārnikā bathes in all *tīrthas*. One who sees Vishveshvara makes all pilgrimages. One should always see Vishveshvara and always bathe in Manikārnikā. True, true, over and over. True, true, over and over.[60]

The "daily pilgrimage" *(nitya yātrā)* most popular among pilgrims and Kāshī residents alike focuses on the temple of Vishvanātha and its immediate environs, including the temples of Annapūrnā, Dandapāni, and Dhundhirāja, as well as the Jnāna Vāpī. A somewhat longer trip is the circumambulation of Vishveshvara's Inner Sanctum *(Antargriha)*, which includes many of the city's most important temples and *ghāts*. (*See* Appendix II and Map 7 for the boundaries of this area, Vishveshvara Khanda.) One thing is certain: whatever else pilgrims may do in Kāshī, whether they stay here for a week or for an hour, they will come for the *darshana* of Vishvanātha.

Kedāra

THE "FIELD" OF LIBERATION

"IT IS KNOWN as the 'field' [*kedāra*] where the crop of liberation grows. Therefore, that place became famous as Kedāra, both in Kāshī and in the mountains."[61]

The original Kedāra (or Kedāreshvara) is high in the Himalayas in the area called Uttara Khanda, the "North Country." There, at an altitude of some 12,000 feet, is the namesake of Kāshī's Kedāra, called Kedārnāth. It sits on the bank of the Mandākinī, one of the high tributaries of the Ganges, named for the River of Heaven.

The Himalayan Kedāra is one of India's twelve *lingas* of light. There Shiva agreed to dwell with permanent brilliance, at the request

of the ancient divine sages, Nara and Nārāyana. In a later era, the
Pāndava brothers are said to have come to Kedāra in the course of their
search for purification from the sin of killing their kin in the
Mahābhārata War. On seeing them, Shiva turned into a bull and ran
away. When the Pāndavas gave chase, he disappeared into the earth,
leaving only his hindquarters protruding. The temples called the "Five
Kedāras" are the places in Uttara Khanda where the various parts of
Shiva's body emerged from the earth. The Pāndavas gratefully worshipped the portion of Shiva still visible at Kedāra, and pilgrims like
them have done so ever since. In the Purānas, Kedāra is the most
important of the Himālayan shrines and is duplicated in other parts of
India. According to the Purānas, Ujjain, Mt. Abu, and Somnāth—all
sacred sites in Western India—have Kedāra temples and *tīrthas*.[67] Like
Kāshī, Kedāra serves as a prototype for other *tīrthas*.

THE TEMPLE TODAY

Kāshī's Kedāra is the anchoring temple of the southern sector of the
city, called Kedāra Khanda. It is one of the most popular and venerable
temples of southern Kāshī. Unlike Omkāra and Vishvanātha, Kedāra is
a river temple, sitting at the top of an impressive *ghāt* high above the
water's edge on the long hill which is supported by the third prong of
Shiva's imaginary trident. From the river, the temple is distinguished
by its vertical red and white stripes, which indicate the South Indian
hand in the temple's management, and by the many morning bathers
who give this *ghāt* a bustling ambience in contrast with the quieter
ghāts flanking it up and down the river. After bathing in the Ganges,
they climb the broad and steep steps to the riverside door of the
temple, carrying the brass pots of Ganges water which they will offer
in worship to Kedāreshvara. Next to this doorway, inlaid in marble,
is the passage from the *Kāshī Kedāra Māhātmya* quoted earlier: Kedāra is so called because it is the "field" where the crop of liberation
grows.

On the city side of the temple is a busy, narrow lane that parallels
the river from Harishchandra Ghāt to Dashāshvamedha. The lane runs
through both the South Indian and the Bengālī sections of Vārānasī,
and the Kedāra Temple is important to both communities. From that
lane the temple doorway is ordinary and inconspicuous. Only the few

Kedāra Temple from the Ganges.

white-clad widows squatting for alms, or the women selling flower garlands, or the echo of *mantras* from the temple's dark interior would attract one's attention to it.

It is clear from the morning activity of Kedāra that it is the religious focal point of this section of the city. There is a quiet and deep piety almost palpable here. And it is uninterrupted by the noisy throngs of pilgrims who hurry from Dashāshvamedha Ghāt to Vishvanātha and its surrounding temples. "The pilgrims from outside don't generally come here," explained one of the temple's *pūjārīs.* "They don't know about it and their guides don't bring them here. We don't give guides any payment for bringing pilgrims here." Kedāra remains primarily a temple for the devoted residents of this area, and for pilgrims from Bengāl or the South who stay in the pilgrim hostels of this area.

Mondays are always special to the worship of Shiva, here and else-where in Kāshī. Especially during the sacred monsoon month of Shrāvana (July/August), the *ghāt* is thronged with bathers on Monday mornings, and the doorways of the temple are jammed with those who seek the *darshana* of Kedāra. After bathing, the women, with their spouted brass pots of Ganges water, take special care to offer water, flowers, and Shiva's sacred *bilva* leaves to each of the subsidiary *lingas* in the tiny shrines which flank the steps of the wide *ghāt*. The men's special observances are more dramatic: Hoisting huge brass pots of Ganges water to their shoulders, they mount the steps shouting Shiva's names—"Hara Hara Mahādeva! Hara Hara Mahādeva!"—and enter the sanctuary to pour their lavish offerings on the *linga*.

Entering Kedāra Temple by either the street or river entrance, one comes into a dark interior court. Around the outer walls is a multitude of tiny shrines, most of them separately established Shiva *lingas*. In the center of the court is the interior temple, within which are still more subsidiary shrines: those of Shiva's goddess consort and his retainers. Finally one reaches the door of the inner sanctum, guarded by Shiva's bull, Nandin. The *linga* of Kedāra contained within this dark chamber is not an ordinary *linga,* but rather a lumpish outcropping of rock with a white line through it. According to tradition, this was not established by human hands, but was an unusual "self-manifest" appearance of Lord Shiva. The temple *pujārīs* affirm that this *linga* was a jewel in the

The entry to Kedāra Temple from the city-side lane. The pillars and flower sellers to the right mark the entry. To the left are widows, waiting for alms.

untarnished Age of Perfection; in the Third Age, it became gold; in the Second Age, it turned to silver; and, finally, in the present decadent Kali Age, the *linga* has become stone.

FROM THE HIMĀLAYAS TO KĀSHĪ

There are a number of stories that explain how it is that Kedāra came from its Himālayan abode to dwell in Kāshī. One story from the *Kāshī Kedāra Māhātmya* reminds us of the Himālayan Shiva's head-first dive into the earth and also of the eternally popular theme of Brahmā's submission to Shiva. In brief, it is said that, in its Himālayan location, the Kedāra *linga* was so powerful it liberated all who beheld it and who sipped the waters of the nearby Retodaka *tīrtha*. Brahmā, usually contemptuous of Shiva, also wanted to behold this *linga* and be liberated. But Shiva refused to let Brahmā see him. Shiva turned into a bull and ran off. But Brahmā caught him from behind, just as he disappeared into the earth. So it is that only Shiva's backside is seen in the Himālayas today. His *linga,* however, emerged from the earth in Kāshī. At length, Shiva agreed to let Brahmā behold his *linga* here. Brahmā first performed ten *ashvamedhas,* hence the name of the place called Dashāshvamedha, the "Ten Horse Sacrifice." At last, Brahmā had the *darshana* of Kedāra.[63] "From that time on," the *māhātyma* explains, "Shiva has taken the bull-form in Kedāra, but in Kāshī he pushed up the earth and revealed himself as a *linga,* which is his forepart and which gives liberation to sinners who but behold it."[64]

By far the most popular story that accounts for the presence of Kedāra in Kāshī, however, is that of the great legendary king of ancient India, Māndhātri:

The world-ruler Māndhātri gave up his kingdom and repaired to the Himālayas for the *darshana* of Kedāra. After years of worship there, Māndhātri was told by Shiva that only in Kāshī was the *darshana* of his *linga* possible. Māndhātri then made the journey to Kāshī and renewed his worship of Shiva, yearning for *darshana.*

By virtue of a boon from Shiva, the pious king maintained one strict daily observance [*niyama*]: he returned every day, before taking his meal, to the Himālayan Kedāra where he had dwelt for so long, traveling with the swift-

ness of thought by virtue of his yogic powers. There he would worship Shiva
and travel back to Kāshī.

When he became white with age, it was very hard for him to make this
daily pilgrimage. Again Shiva spoke to Māndhātri and told him this time that
he should eat his meal first each day and then commence the journey,
strengthened with food. Reluctantly, Māndhātri gave up the strictness of his
practice and prepared some *khichaṛī*, a dish made of simple lentils and rice
cooked together. But when he went out to find a guest with whom to share
his food, as was proper, Māndhātri could find no one. Unwilling to eat
without serving a guest first, he worried that he would not be able to commence his pilgrimage that day at all.

At last, Shiva himself appeared in the guise of a mendicant and became
Māndhātri's guest. Māndhātri happily cut the *khichaṛī* in two, but when he
went to offer half to his guest, he found that the whole plate of *khichaṛī* had
turned to stone. Shiva appeared to him, right out of the *khichaṛī*, and revealed
his *linga* form.[65]

This brief summary of the Lord's appearance in a plate of lentils is
commonly known by those who worship at Kedāra. After all, the *linga*
of Kedāra is not a smooth-surfaced shaft set into a *pītha*, but a rough
mound with a line through the middle of it, like a mound of *khichaṛī* cut
in half. It is said that the lentils of the *khichaṛī* are actually visible in
this *linga* mound. Thinking about such a divine appearance, we can at
least conclude that in the Hindu view of a cosmos alive with divine
vitality, the possibilities for God's appearances in "name and form"
are infinite. It is a wonder of the Hindu imagination, and especially
that of the Shaivas, that God often appears precisely where one least
expects it—whether in the hindquarters of a bull or in a lumpy plate of
khichaṛī.

A very similar and popular story of Kedāra's immigration to Kāshī
concerns the sage Vasishtha, who went to the Himālayan Kedāra as a
young student in the company of his guru.[66] On the way, his guru died
and was escorted to heaven immediately by Shiva's heavenly charío-
teers. Vasishtha concluded that if such great blessings come even to
one who is only on the way to Kedāra, the power of the place must be
great indeed. So he took up a vow to visit Kedāra on a pilgrimage once
a year. For sixty-one years Vasishtha made the pilgrimage from Kāshī
to the Himālayan Kedāra, even when he became so old that the journey seemed impossible. Finally, Kedāreshvara Shiva appeared to him

and agreed to abide in Kāshī as well as in Kedāra. Shiva said, "What fruit one gets from climbing the snowy mountains and seeing Kedāra, that one obtains seven-fold by seeing Kedāra in Kāshī."[67]

In the stories of Māndhātri and Vasishtha, the pilgrimage place finally came to the pilgrim. The long journey to the high Himālayas could now be made by staying right in Kāshī. According to the *Kāshī Kedāra Māhātmya,* the presence of Kedāra in Kāshī is not just a token, but a primary presence. "This Lord of Kedāra, with fifteen parts of himself, became a *linga* in Kāshī. With one part of himself does he dwell in the Himālayas."[68] The notion that there are sixteen parts in a whole is common in India, and here fifteen of those are said to be present in Kāshī. Thus, from the point of view of Kāshī's *māhātmya,* it would be more accurate to say that Shiva Kedāreshvara, abiding in Kāshī, which is an eternal place, dwells in part in the Himālayas as well, which is a place of this transient world.

Not only is this *linga* of Kedāra present in Kāshī, but several other *tīrthas* of this Himālayan tier are present here as well. In the Kedāra Temple is the famous shrine of Vishnu, Badrīnāth, the Vaishnava counterpart to Kedārnāth in the Uttara Khanda section of the mountains. Outside the Kedāra Temple, near the bottom of the great steps down to the Ganges, the *ghāt* levels out for some fifteen feet, where there is a rectangular bathing tank called Gaurī Kund, also an important Himālayan *tīrtha* near Kedāra. Also in the vicinity are Kāshī's locations of the Retodaka Kund, the lake Mānasarovara, and the Hamsa Tīrtha.

KEDĀRA'S MĀHĀTMYA

Kedāra is one of the first of Kāshī's temples mentioned in the Purānic *māhātmyas.* Even in those sources where only a few of the city's temples are mentioned by name, Kedāra is usually among them.[69] In the *Kāshī Khanda,* Kedāra has a full chapter of praises.[70] Kāshī's Kedāra also has a major Sanskrit work devoted to its praises alone: the *Kāshī Kedāra Māhātmya,* alleged to be a "supplement" to the *Brahmavaivarta Purāna.*[71] While this work may be as late as the sixteenth or seventeenth century, it undoubtedly contains very old traditions about Kedāra in Kāshī.

According to this literature of praise, the Himālayan Kedāra liberated anyone who saw it, but of course that was only a few hardy pilgrims. In Kāshī, however, many could see Kedāreshvara, and soon the gods began to protest that the whole world would be liberated if the sight of Kedāra were sufficient for liberation. The gods, after all, depend for their sustenance upon the offerings of human beings, and they always worry when the heavens become too crowded or when liberation becomes too easy.[72] Shiva agreed, therefore, that Kāshī Kedāra would bestow liberation upon all who die there, not merely upon all who see it. It was further agreed that those who die in the Kedāra sector of the city would not even have to reap the results of their past *karma* at the hand of Kāla Bhairava before gaining *moksha*. They would obtain liberation directly and unconditionally.[73] Therefore, the people who live in this section of Banāras and know its *māhātmya* affirm that this is the best part of the city in which to die. The sector of the city included in Kedāra is carefully mapped in the *Kāshī Kedāra Māhātmya*, and the circumambulation of this area is still a popular pilgrimage today. (*See* Appendix II and Map 7 for the boundaries of Kedāra Khanda.)

Those who love Kedāra claim this as the city's pre-eminent seat of Shiva. For them, Kedāra is the respected elder of Vishveshvara and is the oldest Shiva *linga* in all Kāshī. As one *sādhu* who lives near the temple put it, "Kedāra is the most important of the three sectors of the city and Kedārnatha is the most ancient *linga*. But Kedarnātha gave his position to Vishvanātha, as the elder brother turns over his position to the younger."

That Kedāra is somehow older than Vishveshvara is confirmed to some extent by the Purānas, since Kedāra is mentioned very early in the Purānic corpus and Vishveshvara is mentioned quite late. In addition, it is said locally that Kedāra survived the great destruction of Aurangzeb in the seventeenth century, which makes the present temple of Kedāra older than the present temple of Vishvanātha. According to legend, when Aurangzeb's troops approached the vicinity of the Kedāra Temple, they were met by a Muslim holy man who warned them not to touch Kedāra. The commander would not listen, but stormed into the Kedāra Temple and slashed with his sword at the image of the bull Nandin, kneeling before the doorway to the sanctum. Real blood, it is said, began to flow from the neck of the stone Nandin, and the Muslim assailants backed away in awe and fear.[74]

Kedāra, as a temple and as a symbol, intensifies and gathers together the whole sacred structure of Kāshī. Just as Kāshī is a microcosm of the whole of India's sacred geography, so is Kedāra a microcosm of Kāshī. The Kedāra *māhātmyas* fix the "original" site of Manikarnikā Ghāt here, for example, and call Gaurī Kund on the *ghāt* steps "Ādi Mani-karnikā," the "first" Manikarnikā, thus claiming the greatest of Kāshī's bathing *tīrthas* as its own. Similarly, as we have seen, the origin of the Dashāshvamedha Tīrtha has been associated with Kedāra. In addition, within the temple complex are all of Kāshī's divine dignitaries, whom we shall meet in the next chapter. Dandapāni Bhairava and Kāla Bhairava guard the door to the interior temple. Gaurī or Annapūrnā, Ganesha, Skanda, and others have places in the ancillary shrines there.

So powerful is Kedāra with its many shrines that, according to the *Kāshī Khanda,* merely deciding to go there destroys all of the sins one has accumulated since birth. Leaving the house to go to Kedāra destroys the sins of two lifetimes; getting halfway there destroys the sins of three. Seeing the *shikhara* of the temple destroys the sins of seven lifetimes. Finally, worshipping Kedāra and bathing in the *tīrtha* called "Sin Destroyer" *(Harapāpa)* destroys the sins of 10 million lifetimes![75]

There are many other important Shiva temples and *lingas* in Kāshī. While we cannot begin to list and locate them all, a partial listing can be found in Appendix III. Some are linked to important events in Shiva mythology. Krittivāseshvara, for instance, is the "Lord Who Wears the Elephant Hide," referring to Shiva's victory in battle over an elephant demon, in which Shiva took the hide of his conquered foe for a garment. Some *lingas,* such as the famous Trilochana, the "Three-Eyed" Shiva, are said to be self-manifest, and while they have inspired many stories of their miraculous power, there is no story of their origin. Among the most prominent self-manifest *lingas* are the twelve *lingas* of light, including not only Kāshī's Vishveshvara, but the other eleven from elsewhere in India as well. Mahākāla from Ujjain, located in what is now called Vriddhakāleshvara Temple, is one such *linga* of light. In addition to these, there are many other Kāshī *lingas* which are said to have their primary location elsewhere in India but which have appeared here in Kāshī as well. Shūlatankeshvara at Dashāshvamedha Ghāt, for instance, is said to have come from Prayāga, a short distance up the Ganges from Banāras. There are some sixty-five such transposed *lingas* in the sacred complex of Kāshī. Finally, we might distinguish some of the *lingas* according to how they were established. Some have been established by the gods, such as Brahmā's *linga,* Brahmeshvara, at Dashāshvamedha Ghāt. Others have been established, they say, by Shiva's henchmen or *ganas,* such as the *linga* of Gokarna or "Cow-Ears," which marks the western boundary of Vishveshvara's Inner Sanctum. There are also *lingas* said to have been established by the sages, such as Agastya's *linga* to the south of Godauliā, and Jaigishavya's *linga* in the northwestern part of the city. Finally, of course, there are *lingas* established by ordinary people.

Today people may not know the ancient names of many of Kāshī's *lingas.* The worshippers who pass by daily and sprinkle them with water from the Ganges and leave fresh flowers or *bilva* leaves may simply call them by the name Bābā or, more formally, Mahādeva. A surprising number of these *lingas,* however, do have names and *māhātmyas,* however brief, in the Sanskrit Purānas. Taking into account only those *lingas* that have Purānic names and can be located in the city today, they still number in the hundreds. Walking the streets of Banāras and seeing a temple and *linga* at every turn, one cannot forget that this is the city of Shiva, the Great Lord.

4

THE
SACRED CIRCLE OF
ALL THE GODS

Three Hundred Thirty Million Gods

K Ā S H Ī is not the city of Shiva alone. He shares this city with the whole pantheon of Hindu gods, of which there are said to be 330 million. The gods of Kāshī include the great lords, Brahmā and Vishnu; the Goddess under a multitude of names; seven concentric circles of protective Ganeshas; Shiva's ruling deputies, Kāla Bhairava and Dandapāni; the lords of the eight directions; the governors of the days of the week; the twelve suns; and hundreds of local *ganas, nāgas,* and *yakshas.*

The city with its divine inhabitants may be likened to the symbolic structure of the *mandala.* In a religious or ritual sense, a *mandala* is a sacred circle that represents the entire universe, its powers, its inter-relations, and its grounding center. A *mandala* may be painted on canvas, like the vibrant, teeming *mandalas* of the Tibetan Buddhist tradition. It may be drawn in the dust of the earth, as are the ritual circles of the Tantric tradition. A *mandala* may be constructed in architecture, as in the symbolic worlds of the Buddhist *stūpa* or the Hindu temple. And a *mandala* may be envisioned in the divine plan of a city, as in Kāshī. All such *mandalas* share a common symbolic structure. They show the plan of the entire universe, with its galaxies and its gods. The borders of the universe are guarded by fearsome and protective deities. The orientation of the world is emphasized by the presence of the four or the eight directions, who stake out its farthest limits. And at the center of the *mandala* is a particular god or a particular Buddha who, like the still centering-point of the architect's compass, grounds the ever-turning, ever-changing multiple worlds of the periphery.

The city of Kāshī, with all its divine inhabitants, is such a *mandala*. The radius of its sacred circle is a distance of five *kroshas,* about ten miles, and around its borders are a multitude of guardian deities. Within this outermost circle are increasingly smaller concentric circles, having Shiva as their common center, especially Shiva as he abides in the city's inner sanctum, Vishvanātha Temple. The orientation of the city is emphasized by the presence of the eight directional deities, who are said to have become directional guardians here, at the source and center of all space. All the sages, all the *tīrthas* of India, and all the gods have taken their positions here, within the sacred circle of Shiva.

In the lanes of Kāshī and along its riverfront, the many gods of the city are readily visible. Ganesha guards the doorways of temples and homes and, as we shall see, the "doorways" of the city itself. A jet-black image of the Goddess stares from a streetside shrine. Vishnu reclines on the serpent called "Endless." Rāma and Sītā receive the gifts of evening worshippers chanting, "Sītārām Sītārām Jai Jai Sītārām!" Innumerable stones with names known only to a few are smeared with bright vermilion by the wayside, and broken images from temples long since destroyed are worshipped where they lie, beneath a tree or at the side of the road.

To an outsider and, indeed, to most Hindus, the city may appear as a disordered, crowded jungle of temples. But to those Hindus whose vision is recorded in the *māhātmyas* of Kāshī—those who see the city as a *mandala*—these temples are all part of an ordered whole, a structured universe with its own divine functionaries and its own constellations of deities. And their vision is embodied in the sacred geography of the city.

How did Kāshī become the city of so many gods? One very long myth cycle in the *Kāshī Khanda* tells of the habitation of Kāshī by all the various ranks of deities.[1] The story is an important one, both for the *Kāshī Khanda* and for the vision of Kāshī as shaped by its compilers. And it is important as a key to the sacred order of Banāras as we see it today.

SHIVA'S DEPARTURE FROM HIS CITY

_Long ago the world was tormented by a drought which lasted for sixty
years. The very existence of the earth and its people was threatened, and in
the crisis of the times, all social order broke down. The creator, Brahmā,
worried about what to do. He saw, by virtue of his divine vision, that
there was only one sage-king left on earth who was capable of re-estab-
lishing order. His name was Ripunjaya, and he had retired from his
kingdom to practice_ tapas _in the city of Vārānasī._

    _Brahmā begged Ripunjaya to assume the kingship of the earth and to
restore order. Ripunjaya accepted this responsibility with great reluctance
and upon one condition: that the gods would all retire from the earth and
return to their proper places in heaven. Ripunjaya would consent to rule
only without the interference of the gods. Brahmā accepted his terms and
sent criers out into the town, beating their drums and shouting, "The gods
must all go back to heaven!" Ripunjaya prepared to take the throne, and
he took the ironic name Divodāsa, "Servant of Heaven."_[2]

    _Divodāsa's reign, of course, meant that Shiva would have to leave the
city, and Brahmā was filled with dread as he approached Shiva with the
news. However, in the meantime Shiva had granted a boon to Mt. Mandara, who had been practicing austerities in Kāshī for a long time. Mt.
Mandara requested the very deepest desire of his heart: that his own
mountain peaks be the equal of Vārānasī and that Shiva dwell on this
mountain and make it his home. Thus, Shiva agreed to leave his beloved
city in order to please his devotee and to keep Brahmā's pledge to
Divodāsa._

    Before he left Kāshī, however, Shiva established the linga _there, as a
form and an emblem of himself. This, they say, was the very first_ linga _to
be established on earth. By abiding in this_ linga, _Shiva could depart and
yet remain in sacred Kāshī. When Brahmā and Vishnu saw Shiva's_ linga,
they, together with all the other gods, likewise established Shiva lingas
_there to honor Lord Shiva. Then all the gods departed, as was ordered, each
god going to his own heaven. And Shiva left to dwell on Mt. Mandara._

DIVODĀSA'S RULE IN KĀSHĪ

The new King Divodāsa made Kāshī his capital and ruled his kingdom well. The earth flourished and the people flourished under his leadership. He became the epitome of the dharmarāja, *the just and righteous king. During Divodāsa's glorious rule, Kāshī was a city of flawless harmony and was said to surpass the heavens in excellence. The four castes lived in harmony with one another, each observing its own* dharma *steadfastly. The air was filled with the sacred sounds of the scriptures and the sweet sounds of music.*

Despite the King's adherence to dharma, *the gods, who had been banished from the earth, plotted to bring about his downfall. Their power was increasingly threatened by Divodāsa, and the offerings they received from human rites of worship had ceased. In order to create trouble for Divodāsa, they decided to withdraw their cooperation in the powers of nature. Agni, for example, withdrew his presence as fire, and there were no fires to cook food. Vāyu withdrew the wind, and Indra withdrew the rain. They were sure that this crisis would erode people's confidence in Divodāsa, but this did not happen. Divodāsa himself, by the power of his ascetic "heat"*—tapas—*created his own fire and wind and rain.*

SHIVA'S LONGING LOVE FOR KĀSHĪ

Meanwhile, Shiva suffered greatly on Mt. Mandara. Like a lover separated from his beloved, he burned with the pain of separation from his city. He was on fire with the fever of his longing. Even the coolness of the sandal paste upon his body, even the coolness of the moon and the River Ganges which he wore in his hair, could not calm his aching heart. Only returning to Kāshī would bring relief.

Pārvatī also longed for Kāshī. She said to Shiva,

> *Even in the time of the* pralaya, *when the waters of the earth rise to meet the sky, the two of us dwell in Kāshī, which is beautiful as a lotus, held high on the trident of Shiva. Even this lovely mountain land does not delight me, O Shiva, as much as your excellent city, Kāshī, which sits upon*

*the earth, but is not an earthly city. Kāshī—where people are not afraid of
this degenerate age, or afraid of death. Kāshī!—where death is not followed
by rebirth. Kāshī—where there is no fear of sin. How may we see her again?
Are there not thousands of cities full of treasures at every step? But Shiva, I
swear to you, I have nowhere laid eyes upon a city such as Kāshī. Are there
not hundreds of cities in the heavens, cities which are the very source of
wonders? But they are all like grass, compared to your city, Kāshī, Shiva.
This fever of separation not only oppresses you, it oppresses me too. The city
alone will calm this fever heat, for that city is my birthplace!*[3]

SHIVA SENDS THE YOGINĪS

*Yearning for Kāshī, Shiva and Pārvatī sought a way to create a flaw in
the dharma of the King so that he would fall from power. A king such as
Divodāsa could not be defeated by ordinary plagues of disease, old age, and
death, so Shiva decided upon a subtle plan to corrupt the King. He sent a
group of female goddesses, called yoginīs, to tempt the King. Commanding both the power of yoga and the magic of māyā, they were delighted to
go to Kāshī to practice their arts upon the King. They considered it a great
blessing to serve Lord Shiva and, at the same time, to behold the city of
Kāshī. The yoginīs entered the city and were thrilled with the darshana
of this sacred place.*

*In Kāshī, the yoginīs, sixty-four of them, assumed a variety of forms
by the power of their māyā. They became dancers and female ascetics;
garland-makers, hairdressers, and fortune-tellers; tightrope walkers,
palmists, and magicians. For an entire year, they worked in the city, in
disguise, but they were unable to create trouble, and, for all their deceits,
they could find no way to deceive the King.*

*Having failed in their mission, the yoginīs did not want to return to
Mandara, where Shiva waited. How could they return, leaving the Lord's
work unaccomplished? How could they confess their failure? And, of
course, they loved Kāshī and wanted to stay. From that time on, the
sixty-four yoginīs stayed in Kāshī and never left.* They said, "What
foolish person, having reached Kāshī—the very vessel in which the trea-*

---

* Their temple of Chaumsathī Devī, the "Sixty-Four Goddesses," will be discussed
later.

sure of liberation is stored—would wish to go elsewhere in search of some trifling wealth?"[4]

SHIVA SENDS THE SUN

When the yoginīs *did not return, Lord Shiva called in the Sun, Sūrya, and commissioned him to go to Kāshī and to find some fault with the King. The Sun, like the* yoginīs *before him, trembled with excitement at the prospect of beholding Kāshī at last.*

Taking on disguises, the Sun lived in Kāshī for an entire year, but he was not able to find any flaw in the King or in his city. He appeared sometimes as a beggar, sometimes as a rich man, sometimes as a heretic, and sometimes as a naked ascetic. He appeared as a brahmin, a business-man, and a student. Although he tried in many ways to sow doubt and confusion, he was unsuccessful.

Like the yoginīs, *the Sun too decided to take refuge in Kāshī and he took a vow of* kshetra sannyāsa, *a special vow never to leave the city limits. He reasoned to himself, "Dharma is really living in Kāshī. And that will undoubtedly protect me, even from the angry Rudra. Who in his right mind would leave Kāshī, which is so difficult to reach? Who would want to grab some piece of glass, while throwing away the jewel in his hand? Even if Shiva becomes angry with me and reduces my radiance, I will still receive, in Kāshī, that kind of brilliance that is produced by the knowledge of the soul.*[5]

Thus, the Sun took up residence in Kāshī, dividing himself into twelve parts, called ādityas.*

BRAHMĀ GOES TO KĀSHĪ

Shiva, waiting on Mt. Mandara, still yearned for his city. He who with the fire of his ascetic eye had burned Kāma, the god of passion, was now himself being burned with passion—the passion of his longing love for the enchanting Kāshī.

Shiva then sent Lord Brahmā to Kāshī. Brahmā took on the form of a

---

* The places of the twelve *ādityas*, including the famous Lolārka, the "Trembling Sun," will be discussed later.

brahmin and went to the court of Divodāsa with a scheme in mind. He asked the King for aid in a great religious enterprise: the performance of ten simultaneous horse-sacrifices (ashvamedhas). As patron, the King would have to provide not only wealth, but a long list of accoutrements. And the sacrifice itself would be a complicated and exacting ritual event. Surely somewhere the King would make a mistake, and his perfect dharma would become flawed.

Divodāsa agreed to the sacrifices, and he flawlessly provided everything that was required. When Brahmā performed the ten ashvamedha sacrifices, the place of that rite became known as Dashāshvamedha.* Since that day, it has been one of the earth's most celebrated tīrthas, where one receives the fruit of ten ashvamedhas merely by bathing. There Brahmā established a linga, Brahmeshvara.

Brahmā, finding no fault with the King, did not return to Mt. Mandara, but stayed in Kāshī at Dashāshvamedha. He thought to himself, "Formerly this Kāshī was the very body of Vishvesha Shiva, and that is certain. By serving her, I will not anger Shiva. What low-minded man, once he has arrived in Kāshī, which is able to uproot the karma accumulated in many births, would wish to leave her again?"[6]

SHIVA SENDS HIS GANAS TO KĀSHĪ

When Brahmā did not come back, Shiva was very disturbed, for none of his emissaries had returned. He called in his faithful ganas. Shiva beckoned them all by name, and he commissioned two of the best ganas to go to Kāshī and bring back news. Shankukarna ("Spike-Ears") and Mahākāla ("Great-Death") set out enthusiastically, but as soon as they arrived, they forgot Shiva's orders, for they were distracted by the magic of Kāshī. They said to each other, "Kāshī is a place where an ordinary dip in the river is as holy as a post-sacrificial bath, where placing a mere flower on a Shiva linga is as great as a gift of gold, where offering food to one brahmin is as holy as a great sacrifice, where establishing a single linga is like creating the three worlds. Why should one ever leave Kāshī, where

---

* Dashāshvamedha is the most famous of bathing *ghāts* along the river today. See the discussion following and in Chapter 5 on the Ganges.

liberation is in the very palm of one's hand?"[7] *Thinking thus, the two* ganas *established* lingas *in their own names and stayed there.*

When the two did not return, Shiva sent two more ganas, *Mahodara* *("Big-Belly") and Ghantakarna ("Bell-Ears"). But they too were captivated by the city and did not return. They too established* lingas *in Kāshī and took up residence there.*

Finally, Shiva began to smile to himself, knowing now that Kāshī would captivate anyone he might send. He sent the rest of the ganas he had called, knowing full well that they would not return. With all his attendants dwelling in Kāshī, he thought, it would be a simple matter for him to return as well. All the ganas established Shiva lingas in Kāshī, and none returned to Mandara. (See page 186 for images of these ganas as they guard the Panchakroshī Road around Kāshī.)

THE MISSION OF GANESHA IN KĀSHĪ

Finally, Shiva called in his chief gana, *Ganesha, and sent him to Kāshī. When Ganesha arrived, he took the form of a brahmin fortune-teller. As such, he charmed the citizens of Kāshī and one of Divodāsa's queens, Līlāvatī, told the King of this unusual man.*

The King invited the fortune-teller to the palace and was at once impressed with his wisdom and good character. He called him back again the next day in order to seek his advice. "I have ruled the world as no other king has," said Divodāsa. "I have protected my subjects as if they were my own children. I have honored the feet of brahmins and I have maintained order. But now, even though the kingdom flourishes, I feel a certain indifference toward all this. What is the fruit of all this good work?"

Ganesha said to the King, "Indeed, the power you have assumed is very great. You have become the sun and the moon, the eight directions, all in one. You have assumed the powers of the ocean, the fire, and the wind. But what is the final result of all the energy you have devoted to the service of your people? I cannot answer that question, but I can tell you that exactly eighteen days from today a certain wise brahmin will arrive in Kāshī. He will give you your answer."

Ganesha had Vishnu in mind to complete the task, and in this way he prepared the King for Vishnu's arrival. But Ganesha, like the others, did not wish to return to Mandara, even to report his success to Shiva. He *divided himself into many Ganeshas, fifty-six in all, to await the eventual arrival of Shiva. (See page 188 for an image of one such Ganesha. As we shall see later, the fifty-six are located in concentric circles around Kāshī.)*

VISHNU GOES TO KĀSHI

When it became clear to Shiva that Ganesha too was tarrying in Kāshī, the Lord called upon Vishnu. When he arrived in Kāshī, Vishnu bathed first at the confluence of the Varanā and the Ganges Rivers, a place that later became known as the Pādodaka ("Foot-Water") Tīrtha, where Vishnu washed his blessed feet. His image at that place became known as Ādi Keshava, the "First Keshava."* Many other places also became tīrthas because Vishnu sanctified them by his presence as he made his way from Padodaka toward the center of Kāshī.

Then Vishnu transformed himself into a Buddhist monk, Punyakīrti. A short distance to the north of the city, he established a place called Dharmakshetra, near Sārnāth. Garuda, Vishnu's famous bird-mount, took the form of Punyakīrti's student, and Shrī, Vishnu's consort, took the form of a Buddhist nun named Vijnānakaumudī.

The three of them preached throughout the city and its suburbs, spreading the Buddhist message: Samsāra, this whole universe, is not the work of a creator. It appears and is dissolved of its own accord, and there are no gods. All embodied creatures are enlivened by the ātman alone, so all are equal. Therefore, all violence is forbidden. The sacrifice of animals, even that enjoined by the scriptures, is forbidden. And the discrimination of high and low castes is forbidden.

Hearing these teachings, which were contrary to the dharma of castes, the citizens began to go astray. It is said that women abandoned service to their husbands, and men satisfied themselves with other women. Soon everything was awry; the breakdown of order and of caste had begun. In this chaos, the Buddhist nun began to interest the people in spells and incantations and magic.

---

* Keshava is another name for Vishnu. Ādi Keshava, as we shall see later as well as in Chapter 5, is one of the five great *tīrthas* along the Ganges today.

DIVODĀSA'S DEPARTURE

These Buddhists had successfully cracked the perfect dharma *of the king-dom. Divodāsa's power began to fade and his dissatisfaction with king-ship began to increase. He waited for the eighteenth day, for the coming of the wise brahmin as foretold by Ganesha. On the eighteenth day, Vishnu took on the form of a brahmin and came to the court of Divodāsa, where he was received with great honor.*

The King spoke of his fatigue with the burden of his kingdom and his apathy for the affairs of the world. He asked, "How may I uproot the process of karma *and find final rest?"*
Vishnu replied,

It is excellent that you have ruled so well, O King, and it is excellent that you now yearn to be free. While you have obstructed the gods, still you have upheld dharma. *Your only sin, however, is expelling Shiva from this city. I will tell you how you may expunge that sin: establish a* linga *for Shiva here, and by virtue of that act alone, a chariot will take you to the highest heaven. In one way you are very lucky in this sin, for Shiva has been thinking of you day and night. True, he thinks of how he may dislodge you from his city, but nonetheless you are in his thoughts and in his heart.*

When Vishnu left the court, the King made ready for his departure by passing the mantle of kingship to his son. He established in Kāshī a linga *called Divodāseshvara, and he worshipped Shiva with all proper rites. Finally, Divodāsa was flown in a chariot to Shiva's highest heaven. Even though he was victorious, Vishnu, like the other gods, did not wish to leave Kāshī. Instead, he sent the divine bird Garuda to inform Shiva of the news, while he himself sought out a good dwelling place in Kāshī. He found the pool of the "Five Rivers," Panchanada, bathed there, and settled down to stay. (Panchanada is known today as Panchagangā, one of the five great Ganges* tīrthas. *See later and in Chapter 5.)*

The Well of Dharma, Dharma Kūpa, ringed with small shrines. The temple of Divodāseshvara, the linga *established by Divodāsa, is behind the well in the center rear.*

SHIVA RETURNS TO KĀSHĪ

Shiva rejoiced on Mt. Mandara when he heard the news of Vishnu's success. With the entire retinue of heaven, he set out for Kāshī. All the gods who had preceded him gathered at the northern border of the city at a place which later became known as Vrishabhadhvaja, the "Bull-Emblemed Flag." It was from that place that they first saw, flying in the distance, the flag of the approaching Shiva.

The entire cosmos joined together to form the great chariot on which Shiva made his entry into the city. The Ganges and Yamunā Rivers became the shafts of the chariot; the two winds, together with the morning and the evening, became the chariot's wheels; the sky was the chariot's umbrella; the stars of the heaven were the nails that held the chariot together; dakshinā, *the ritual gift to one's guru, became the axle;* pranava, *the mystical syllable, became the seat;* gāyatrī, *the Vedic chant, became the footrest. The sun and the moon guarded the door of this cosmic chariot, and*

Mt. Meru became the flagpole for Shiva's banner. All of the gods participated in the ārātī, worshipping Shiva with the light of a thousand oil lamps. Accompanied by the seven seas and by all the rivers and mountains and trees of the earth, Shiva entered Kāshī.

Ironically, Divodāsa, who sent the gods back to heaven, ended up ruling a city infiltrated by all the 330 million gods. For them all, Kāshī was truly Avimukta, the "Never Forsaken." But Kāshī is more than the sum of its gods. Here the whole pantheon comes to populate a city that was splendid even before they came. Kāshī is not such a great *tīrtha* because all the gods are there; all the gods are there because it is such a great *tīrtha*. For even when Kāshī was ruled by a godless king, it was the most splendid place on earth and it beguiled even the gods of heaven. When Shiva rode into Kāshī to take his place again at the center of this city, the "sacred circle" of the gods was already in place.

Mythology becomes geography. Having met the gods as they came to Kāshī, we shall now turn to the living myth of the city and examine more closely the sacred dwelling places of the gods in the geography of Kāshī and their ongoing life in its religious traditions.

The Goddesses

T H E R E are many goddess shrines in Banāras, ranging from the lone silver face embedded in the knothole of an ancient tree to the spacious compound of the goddess Durgā. Some, like Durgā, are known by names that are recognized throughout India. Others, like Vishālākshī, the "Wide-Eyed" goddess, are known primarily for their association with this city. Still others, like the knothole goddess, are known simply as Mā or Mātā—"Mother."

The *yoginīs*, sent to Kāshī by Shiva, represent this whole range of female deities. Appropriately, the *yoginīs* were the first to be sent, for they are surely among India's oldest deities, and they have always been linked to place—to some particular hill or grove, to some particular village or crossroads, to some particular river or cave. These goddesses unquestionably occupied their "benches" *(pīthas)* in the Forest of Bliss long before that mythical time when Shiva chose the city to be his home.

Several temples in Kāshī still claim to have been the "benches" of those original sixty-four *yoginīs* that Shiva sent. There is Vārāhī at Mīr Ghāt, Mayūrī at Lakshmī Kund, and Kāmākhyā in the southwest part of the city named Kamacchā in her honor. Although at one time there may have been many *yoginī* temples, the *yoginīs,* as such, are worshipped together today in a single temple, the Chaumsathī Devī Temple, named for the "Sixty-Four Goddesses." The temple is small, located in a tiny lane in the Bengālī Tolā area of the city, high above Chaumsathī Ghāt, also called Rānā Mahal Ghāt. Despite the wide variety of *devīs* included among the sixty-four *yoginīs,* the images in the sanctum of this temple today are called by the names of the great goddesses of the tradition, Kālī and Durgā. While Chaumsathī Devī, affectionately called Chaumsathī Māī—"Mother Chaumsathī"—is a refuge for the many destitute widows of Banāras and is frequented by the people of the Bengālī Tolā district, it is not one of the two or three most popular *devī* temples in Banāras today.

It is difficult to say just who these *yoginīs* were, for among India's many local goddesses, most of them place-specific or task-specific, the lines are not clearly drawn. There are *yoginīs* ("sorceresses"), *yakshīs* ("tree spirits"), *mātrikās* ("mothers"), *vetālas* ("vampires"), *shaktis* ("powers"), and *gaurīs* ("white goddesses"). It is often impossible to list a goddess in one of these categories rather than another. Some of the names that appear among the *yoginīs* sent to Kāshī refer to phantasmic and fearsome goddesses: Elephant-Face, Lion-Face, Bloody-Eyes, and Lolling-Tongue! Others are not such ogresses, but are some of India's most famous goddesses, such as Bhavānī, Shivā, and Vārāhī. Such goddesses, whose names are feminine forms of the names of the male gods, seem to represent an effort to bring these powerful female deities into the range and control of the brahminical tradition.[8] Such goddesses as Brahmī, Maheshvarī, Vaishnavī, and Indrānī are sometimes called *yoginīs,* sometimes *shaktis,* and sometimes *mātrikās.* But however neatly paired they may be with their male counterparts, they have much more in common with their sisters Bloody-Eyes and Lion-Face.

It is clear to scholars who have studied the emergence of the Great Goddess, that the primary source of her worship was non-Vedic and

non-brahminical.[9] In the *Kāshī Khanda,* the worship of these *yoginīs* is
certainly consistent with what is known of non-brahminical folk worship. They are to be honored with offerings of incense and oil lamps,
and with offerings of *bali,* which may include meat and wine. They are
especially to be celebrated during the festival of Navarātra, the "Nine
Nights" of the Goddess that occurs in the fall and again in the spring.[10]

The sixty-four *yoginīs,* like many groupings of goddesses, seem to
represent a stage in the emergence of the Great Goddess when long
lists of *devīs* were drawn together and said to be one. Here they are
even worshipped on one place. Nonetheless, despite the notion that
there is one Great Goddess of whom all the many *devīs* are local
manifestations, these *devīs* came from and are still a part of an essentially "locative" religious tradition—one linked strongly to place. Even
today, most Hindus do not worship Devī in general, but in particular,
be she Vaishnavī Devī, Vindhyavāsinī Devī, or Sankatā Devī. Each
goddess sits on her own geographically particular bench in a village or
on a hilltop. Sometimes she sits alone, and sometimes she is paired with
a local male deity. Her orbit of power is quite specific.

Sometimes goddesses are known not for their geographical sphere of
influence, but for the sphere of life over which they have jurisdiction.
They wield power for good or ill within that sphere. Shītalā, for
example, rules over fever diseases, such as smallpox. Various *mātrikās*
have jurisdiction over childbirth and childhood diseases. These are
formidable *devīs,* who may be benign or malevolent, and who are both
praised and feared

In Kāshī there is a city-goddess, like the *grāma devatās* or *nagara
devatās* found all over India. She is Vārānasī Devī, honored in a shrine
in Trilochana Temple. It is often said, however, that the city as a
whole is a goddess, the very embodiment of Shiva's *shakti.*[11] Remember that the exiled Shiva's longing love *(viraha)* for Kāshī is explicitly
likened to that of a lover separated from his beloved. Kāshī, like the
River Ganges, is, in a sense, Shiva's loved one. She is Shakti, Shiva's
consort and his active power, manifest in this world, on "this shore."
Kāshī is the Goddess, embodied.

On the level of popular piety today, one often hears that Shiva has
turned Kāshī over to the Goddess for governance during the Kali Age,
the worst of the four *yugas,* or ages, and the one in which we now live.
Thus, Annapūrnā Bhavānī, one of the names of Shiva's Queen, is now
the real ruler of Kāshī. Similarly, it is sometimes said that during the

Kali Age the great gods, Vishnu and Shiva, are asleep and do not hear human supplications. But a few deities are wakeful in this dark time, and among them are the goddesses. Significantly, many of the city's Shiva temples have begun to experience the encroachment of the wakeful goddesses in the Kali Age. The famous Purānic temple of Shiva, Chandreshvara, is now better known for its shrine of Siddhesh-varī Devī, and the great temple of Shiva Vīreshvara now shares its popularity with the new goddess cult of Santoshī Mātā.[12]

There has been a great effort made, both by Hindus and by scholars of Hinduism, to classify the goddesses of India. Goddesses may be either gracious or terrible, or, as Charlotte Vaudeville has put it, they may be either luminous or tenebrous, light or dark, corresponding to the fortnight in which they are worshipped—waxing or waning.[13] The luminous goddesses, such as Lakshmī, Gangā, Annapūrnā, and even Durgā, are those whose dangerous side has been mitigated by their association with a male deity. Just as married women are auspicious and unmarried virgins considered dangerous, so is the goddess-consort most often luminous and the independent goddess both powerful and dangerous. Some, like Annapūrnā and Gangā, seem to be always gracious. Others, such as the dark Kālī and Shītalā, are terrible as well as gracious. All may be called "Mother."

We will look now at a few of Kāshī's most prominent goddesses: Annapūrnā, Durgā, Sankatā Devī, and Vishālākshī, who have all become identified to some extent as consorts of Shiva, and Shītalā, who has still managed to retain her fierce independence.

A N N A P Ū R N Ā   B H A V Ā N Ī

For pilgrims to Kāshī, the *darshana* of Annapūrnā always accompanies the *darshana* of Shiva Vishvanātha. The two are close neighbors in the city's Inner Sanctum, their entrances from the Vishvanātha Lane separated by only a few yards. Annapūrnā is Kāshī's queen, reigning alongside the king, Vishveshvara, as the city's governing goddess. She is known in the *Kāshī Khanda* as Bhavānī, the female *shakti* of Bhava, "Being," one of the names of Shiva.[14] Today she is often called by both names: Annapūrnā Bhavānī. "For happiness," the scriptures say, "there is no home like Kāshī; there is no father like Vishveshvara;

there is no mother like Bhavānī, destroyer of rebirth; and there is
no household like the people of Kāshī, who are Vishnu incarnate!"[15]

The name Annapūrnā means "She of Plenteous Food." As such, she
is the one who fills her devotees with food. She is called the "Mother
of the Three Worlds," and she promises to those who come to her
what only a mother can give, naturally and freely: food. In the popular
pamphlets for sale outside the temple door, worshippers of Mother
Annapūrnā are reminded that there may be good and bad children, but
there are not good and bad mothers. Annapūrnā is a completely gracious and luminous goddess. She bears no weapons in her hands, but
carries, rather, a cooking pot and a spoon. As Mother, she will always
provide the nourishment that sustains life in abundance. That nourishment is *anna*, literally "food," but more broadly, the essence of life,
the support of life. As giver of food, Annapūrnā is giver of life. It is
said in Kāshī that Shiva and Annapūrnā made an agreement: she would
provide food and abundance in life, and he would provide *moksha* at the
time of death. Shiva himself depends upon Annapūrnā for life and
sustenance, and he is popularly depicted in penny posters and post-
cards, standing before her as a supplicant for her alms.

There is a popular Purānic story that once in the distant past the
sage Vyāsa had a hard time getting alms in Kāshī. In anger, Vyāsa put
a curse on the city: it would be without knowledge, wealth, or liberation for three generations. Still steaming with rage, Vyāsa begged for
alms at a house where Shiva and Pārvatī had taken human form as
householders. Pārvatī invited the great sage and his entire entourage to
receive her alms. So delicious were they that Vyāsa forgot his curse.
"Who would not live in Kāshī," he said, "where one can get both
delicious food and liberation!" However, because of the sage's bad
temper, Shiva banished Vyāsa from Kāshī, permitting him to visit only
on the eighth and fourteenth days of the fortnight, which are days
sacred respectively to the Goddess and Shiva. In order to be near at
hand, Vyāsa took up residence on the other side of the River Ganges,
where his temple may still be seen at Rāmnagar.[16]

The giving and receiving of alms play an important part in Hindu
society. By their alms, householders support those in other stages of
life, especially elderly *sannyāsins* and widows. On the eleventh day of
each fortnight, when the giving of alms is especially prescribed, one
will hear these *sannyāsins* at the doors of Banāras households, calling to
the mother of the house, *"Mā, anna do!"*—"Mother, give me food!" It

is in just this posture of supplication and dependence that everyone comes before Mother Annapūrnā. In the repeated refrain of a well-known hymn to Annapūrnā, the people chant, "O Goddess, Mother Annapūrnā, Presiding Deity of Kāshī, Reservoir of Mercy, Give me alms!" In the Purānas, she is called Vishveshvara's "housewife." Since the distribution of food would be a twenty-four-hour job for such a wealthy queen, she is said to have two door-guardians to help her in providing for the welfare of those who live in Kāshī: Kāla Bhairava ("Black Bhairava") and Dandapāni ("Club Carrier"). As we shall see, these two have other important duties in Kāshī as well.

Because of the generosity of Annapūrnā and, by extension, the generosity of thousands of pious Banāras householders, it is widely alleged that no one ever starves to death in Kāshī. Here, as at Vishvanātha, the noontime food offerings to the deity are distributed to elderly and disabled pilgrims. During the autumn Annakūta ("Food Mountain") festival, food is distributed on a larger scale. For the most part, however, the temple does not serve as a charitable institution. If no one starves to death in Kāshī, it is because householders and pilgrims give alms, following the example of Mother Annapūrnā.

The story of Annapūrnā's establishment in Kāshī is told in the popular Hindi pamphlet, the *Annapūrnā Vrat Kathā*. A *vrata* (Hindi, *vrat*) is a "ritual observance" which one undertakes for a certain amount of time, usually a number of weeks or months. The *vrata* may include fasting, abstentions, and special observances; it usually includes the recitation of stories *(kathā)* which demonstrate the effectiveness of the *vrata*. In the case of Annapūrnā, one of the stories told is of a poor brahmin, Dhananjaya, who eventually became rich and had plenty to feed his family by virtue of observing the *vrata* of Annapūrnā. According to the story, Dhananjaya first appealed to Vishvanātha and slept overnight at the Jnāna Vāpī. In a dream, Annapūrnā came to him and told him to observe her *vrata*. Dhananjaya was eager to do so, but she had not told him how it was to be done. How was he to make this observance? He inquired among the brahmins of Kāshī to no avail. Finally, he traveled to the great *pītha* of the goddess Kāmākhyā in far-off Assam. There the goddess, seeing his devotion, appeared to him again. She instructed him to return to Kāshī and to establish her image there as Annapūrnā, just to the south of Vishvanātha. She promised that she would grant the deepest wishes of those people who would worship her there during her yearly seventeen-day *vrata,* beginning on the fifth day of the waning fortnight of the winter month of Mārgashīrsha. It was this poor brahmin, then, who is said to have established the first image of Annapūrnā here. It is of significance that the goddess is said to have come to Kāshī directly from Kāmākhyā *pītha*—the most venerable of *pīthas* in all India.

The present compound of Annapūrnā is located near Vishvanātha on the opposite side of the lane. Standing in the court of the compound is the temple itself, a small sanctum with a large pillared porch, where worshippers may stand for the *darshana* of the goddess, or sit down to read the *Devī Māhātmya* or the *Annapūrnā Vrat Kathā.* Around this inner temple there is ample room for circumambulation, and on the eighth day of the autumn and spring Navarātra ("Nine Nights") festival, there are thousands who come especially to circumambulate the goddess. Some make a point of circling this sanctum an auspicious 108 times. The image of Annapūrnā within the sanctum is a new one, established and consecrated in January 1977 in a series of *pratishthā* rites conducted by the Shankarāchārya of Shringeri.*

In the compound of the Annapūrnā Temple is a *matha* where several Dashanāmī *sannyāsins* live under the leadership of the *mahant.* In this respect, the temple organization differs from that of Vishvanātha, where the several *mahants* of the temple are not renouncers but householders.

There are a number of shrines to other deities within the compound of Annapūrnā, but the most important subsidiary shrine contains another image of Annapūrnā herself. This shrine is open for the *darshana* of the goddess only three days during the year: the day of the Annakūta festival in the fall and the two days preceding it. It contains an image of solid gold.

The great festival days of Annapūrnā dramatize her role as sustainer of life. Annakūta, the "Food Mountain" festival, falls on the first day of the waxing fortnight of the autumn month of Kārttika. This feast day follows the fall harvest, and on this day a real mountain of food fills the temple. Sweets of all kinds, purchased by the advance-subscription of patrons, are arranged elaborately in the temple porch, and around the compound are huge mounds of rice, lentils, and other staples. All the food is distributed as *prasāda* to those who come to Annapūrnā on

---

* In the rite of *pratishthā,* literally "establishing," the *prāna,* "breath" or "life," is established in the icon.

this day and the next. The temple is crowded with worshippers who have come to see the display, and who have come, above all, for the *darshana* of the golden image of Annapūrnā. This festival day is so popular that it is observed at nearby Vishvanātha Temple as well, with the same abundance of foods. It is important to note, however, that throughout North India this festival day is primarily associated with the cowherd-god, Krishna-Gopāla. The overall coincidence of the festival days and sacred times of Krishna and Devī points to a very ancient relationship between the two.[17]

The second of Annapūrnā's festivals is during the time prescribed for her *vrata* in Mārgashīrsha in celebration of the sprouted rice crop. On one special day during this season, the temple and the image of the goddess are decorated with green sprouts of rice paddy, and those who come to the temple receive paddy as *prasāda*.

While these two days, with their agricultural associations, reveal the essential elements of Annapūrnā's popularity today, they are not mentioned in the Sanskrit *māhātmyas* of Kāshī. In fact, as popular as she is in Banāras, Annapūrnā has a meager *māhātmya* in the *Kāshī Khanda* and the *Kāshī Rahasya*. As Bhavānī she is mentioned in tandem with Shiva, as his housewife and as the generous almsgiver who satisfied the appetite of Vyāsa. In the *Kāshī Rahasya* she is called Annadātrī, "Giver of Food." As with many other goddesses of Kāshī, however, we may presume she has a history far more complex and extensive than what can be learned from the Sanskrit textual sources.

The temple of this goddess probably met the same fate as other Kāshī temples during the late Muslim period. It was destroyed and lay in ruins for many decades. According to Kuber Nāth Sukul, the confusion of these times was so great that when the present temple of Annapūrnā was reconsecrated in the early eighteenth century, it was actually the image of Bhuvaneshvarī Devī that was installed, while the old Bhavānī lay neglected nearby.[18] This image of Bhavānī may now be seen in the Rāma Temple adjacent to Annapūrnā.

DURGĀ

One of the city's busiest temples is that of the goddess Durgā, which sits on the large rectangular tank called Durgā Kund in the southern sector of the city. The Purānas locate Durgā at her present site, and

she has kept this place for many centuries. She is said to protect
Vārānasī on the south, as one of the fierce goddess guardians *(chandikās)* of the sacred zone.[19] Durgā's temple is built in a common North
Indian style: a free-standing temple set within a walled temple compound. Both the porch of this temple and its *shikhara* are especially
ornate in sculptural detail. It is an impressive temple, when seen from
across the *kund* and compared with the many smaller shrines in
more cramped quarters throughout the city. The temple of Durgā
has long been known to Western tourists as the "Monkey Temple"
because of the scores of temperamental monkeys who make their home
in the *shikhara* and porticoes of the temple, peeping and snarling at
visitors.

In contrast with Mother Annapūrnā, the goddess Durgā is famous
for her weapons and her strength in battle. In her hands the sword
replaces the cooking spoon. In the front courtyard of the temple are
two large painted images of the goddess, guarding the doorway to the
sanctuary. She wears a red *sārī*, rides a tiger, and holds divine weapons

Durgā's image painted by the door at the Durgā Temple.

in her hands, including Vishnu's discus and Shiva's trident. In this front courtyard is further evidence that the goddess within is quite different from the mild and generous Annapūrṇā—a forked sacrificial stake, designed especially to hold the neck of the goats slaughtered here on great ritual occasions. Here Durgā, like many of her powerful goddess sisters, continues to receive offerings not unlike the *bali* offered to such goddesses centuries ago. On a daily basis, however, it is more common for her to receive the "sacrifice" of a coconut than that of a goat.

The story of how the goddess took the name Durgā when she killed the demon Durga is related at length in the *Kāshī Khanda*.[20] The story is a form of the classical myth of Devī's destruction of the demons as told in the famous *Devī Māhātmya*. The *Kāshī Khanda* version of this myth is as follows:

A demon [daitya] named Durga, the "Unassailable," practiced asceticism so fiercely that he was able to usurp the powers of the gods. The whole earth trembled in fear of him. The gods finally went to the Great Lord, Shiva, for refuge, and he commissioned Devī to kill the demon. Devī first sent her messenger Kālarātri, the "Black Night," to warn the demon and ask for his surrender. Scoffing, the demon Durga ordered his attendants to catch her as an ornament to his harem, but Kālarātrī burned them to ashes with the fire of her breath. She returned to the great Devī, who dwelt in the Vindhya Mountains, and they made ready for war. When the hoards of demons attacked, Devī produced thousands of shaktis from her body. The shaktis instantly overwhelmed the demon armies, and Durga, seeing his impotent army, assailed the Devī with his own mighty weapons. But she reduced each weapon he used to powder. He uprooted a mountain and hurled it at her, but she shattered it with a hundred blows of her sword. He became an elephant and charged her, but she cut off his trunk. Finally, he became a bull, pounding the earth with his horns and hoofs, but she wounded him with her trident, and pierced him in the heart with her arrows. When he died, the whole world rejoiced and gathered to praise the Devī. She took the name Durgā from the "Unassailable" demon.

Standing for the darshana *of Durgā.*

It is evident from the *Kāshī Khanda* that this Durgā is the great Durgā of southern Kāshī. In that neighborhood, the living legend is that the goddess rested at Durgā Kund after slaying the demon, and when she let her giant sword fall from her hand, it sliced the River Asi ("The Sword") into the earth. It is also clear from the text that this great Devī resided originally in the Vindhya Mountains as Vindhyavāsinī Devī. The shrine of this ancient *devī* is located in a hilly area about fifty miles from Banāras. Today she is still one of the most important and popular goddesses in North India, and it is common for Banāras devotees to make frequent pilgrimages to her shrine.

The image of Durgā visible to those who come for her *darshana* at Durgā Temple is a silver mask, from which is draped a tinseled red cloth. There is no story of the establishment of this image here, and according to some who serve this temple, it was never established by human hands, but is a self-manifest image. It appeared here of its own accord.

Durgā's special days are Tuesdays and Saturdays, and on those evenings her temple is crowded with those who have come for *darshana.* In the shops around the temple, worshippers may purchase sweets, cloth, coconuts, and flower garlands to be offered to the Devī. On Tuesdays during the monsoon month of Shrāvana, one of Kāshī's greatest fairs *(melās)* takes place in and around Durgā's precincts, with amusements, makeshift shops, and carnival rides for the thousands who make their pilgrimage to Durgā at this time.

Throughout most of the temple's long history, it has been located in the country, in the midst of the groves and fields of southern Kāshī. This part of the Forest of Bliss was settled with occasional temples and ashrams, but it was not part of the city itself until the last several decades. Ryder's map of 1920, for example, still shows Durgā Kund and its temple completely surrounded with trees, and Conchman's 1930 map shows only a little urban encroachment. The residential colonies that surround Durgā Kund today are the modern suburbs of middle- and upper-class Vārānasī.

SANKATĀ DEVĪ

Pilgrims to Banāras will undoubtedly visit the Annapūrnā Temple because it is next to Vishvanātha, and the Durgā Temple because it is easily reached by bus or rickshaw. Few will find their way to Sankatā Devī, however, even though this seat of the Goddess is known in Kāshī as one of the most powerful temples in the entire city. Sankatā-jī, as she is called, is located high above Sankatā Ghāt in the labyrinthine lanes of the city where only Banārsīs can find their way.* Her name means "Goddess of Dangers," for she is the one who vanquishes dangers for her devotees.

This goddess was originally a *mātrikā*, one of the "mothers" of the folk tradition who were known as both seizers *(grahas)* of children in sickness and death and protectors of children in life. In the Purānic stories she is called Vikatā Mātrikā, the "Fierce Mother." She and the nine heavenly *mātrikās* are said to have been the foster mothers of a young prince of Kāshī who was born under an unlucky star and aban- doned to their care.[21] The prince established a *linga* near Vikatā Mātrikā's abode and practiced asceticism until Shiva appeared to him in person. The prince was given the name Vīra, the "Hero," and his temple was known as Vīreshvara.

The story of the prince with multiple foster mothers is also, of

---

* The use of "jī" after the name of a person or deity adds a note of respect to the name. Interestingly, it adds a sense of familiarity and affection as well.

course, the story of Skanda, Shiva's son, who is well known to be a foster child of the *mātrikās* or the *krittikās*. Perhaps the "Hero" child of this Fierce Mother is indeed Skanda, whose portrait is very prominently placed within the sanctum of Vīreshvara. If so, this is one of the only remnants of Skanda's presence in his father's city.

As one of the "mothers," the goddess Sankatā was originally unassociated with any male deity. These *mātrikās* seemed to have a generative power all their own. In time, however, some of these mothers came to bear the names of the great male deities—Brahmī, Vaishnavī, Indrānī, etc. At Sankatā Devī there is some evidence of this wider attempt to appropriate the power of the *mātrikās*, for this *devī* is sometimes assimilated to the Great Goddess. One of her hymns, for example, has the refrain, "Victory! Victory! to the Slayer of the Bull Demon, Woman of Beautiful Wild Hair, Daughter of the Mountain!" She is thus praised as both Durgā, the demon slayer, and Pārvatī, the mountain woman. Another hymnic refrain is "Praise Sankatā who is Bhavānī, Destroyer of Distress!"[22] Here she is identified with Shiva's consort, Bhavānī. Her temple icon confirms this identity with the Great Goddess: she is shown with her foot on the vanquished demon, his bull's head severed from his body. Not only is the slayer of the bull demon known to be the great Devī, but the bull is known to be a multiform of Shiva.[23] Nonetheless, most of the worshippers of Sankatā-jī still readily claim that this goddess has no husband.

The shops outside Sankatā's temple carry copies of the *Sankatā Vrat Kathā*, containing the ritual observances appropriate to Sankata and stories about those faithful ones who practiced them. There are three sequential stories in Sankatā's *vrata*. The first is representative: an old woman whose son was absent in another land was being abused by her daughter-in-law. By worshipping Sankatā Devī and preparing food for married women (the counterpart of preparing food for brahmins, both groups being the most auspicious of their sex), she was blessed with her son's safe return.

The observance of Sankatā's *vrata*, like that of many popular goddesses, takes place on Fridays and is sometimes called the "Friday *vrata*." It involves the usual bathing and putting on of clean clothes, preparing special food and offering this, together with incense, flowers, and oil lamps, to Sankatā. The women who participate in this *vrata* gather in the temple on Friday mornings, and when they have made their offerings, they sing devotional songs together and listen to the stories of those whose troubles have vanished after observing this *vrata,* such as the story of the abused old woman. The author of the *Sankatā Vrat Kathā* states that the *vrata* may be observed by married women to secure the long life of their husbands, by unmarried women to obtain good husbands, or by boys and girls, men and women alike to pass examinations or to keep away sickness and accident. For the most part, these observances are women's rites and the leaders of these Friday morning circles are women. It is also clear that the meteoric rise of the "new" goddess Santoshī Mātā, the "Mother of Satisfaction," whose *vrata* is the most popular Friday *vrata* in North India, has had some positive influence on the performance of the very similar Friday *vrata* at Sankatā Devī.

Entering the compound of Sankatā Devī, one finds a large courtyard in the center of which is an old *pīpal* tree, with a number of shrines tangled in its mass of roots. On Friday mornings, the courtyard is filled with small groups of women observing the *vrata*. In the far corner of the compound is the entrance to the sanctuary of the goddess. The great doors are flanked on either side by the auspicious symbols of the *svastika* and the *shrī yantra*. The sanctuary is dark, but for the oil lamps on the altar. The silver-masked image of the goddess is separated from the crowd of worshippers by a single altar rail. While worshippers are kept at a distance from an image of the goddess and do not touch it as they might a Shiva *linga,* the altar rail in this temple permits a greater proximity to the *devī* and a greater sense of the immediacy of her *darshana* than is possible in either of the other goddess temples discussed earlier.

This goddess Sankatā, under the name of Vikatā Mātrikā, is praised in the *Kāshī Khanda,* but there are no stories of her origin there. One local tradition, however, is that the goddess here is self-manifest. The first to have *darshana* of her, it is said, were the five Pāndavas and their wife, Draupadī, who came to Vārānasī during their forest exile before the great war of the *Mahābhārata.* A locally published collection of her hymns cites verses attributed to the *Padma Purāna* in which the sage Mārkandeya instructs Yudhisthira, the eldest of the Pāndavas, to seek out Sankatā Devī in the Forest of Bliss.[24]

SHĪTALĀ

She is the "Cool Goddess," and yet her area of jurisdiction is fever diseases, especially smallpox. She manifests herself in both the outbreak and the "cooling" of fever diseases. In this, Shītalā is like many *devīs* and *mātrikās:* potentially malevolent and benevolent within her domain, propitiated both from fear and gratitude.

Shītalā, who has emerged from the local traditions of village India, has an important and central location in Kāshī, right at Dashāshvamedha Ghāt, the central bathing *ghāt* of the entire city today. Each year, after the season of rains, the words "Shītalā Mā" are painted afresh on the riverside wall of her temple. Even when the floodwaters of the river are high and worshippers have to wade through deep waters or take a boat to reach Shītalā's temple, she receives a steady stream of supplicants. According to Kuber Nāth Sukul, her site there at Dashāshvamedha was once that of a very significant *mātrikā*. The place was known in the Purānas as Mātritīrtha, the "*Tīrtha* of the Mother."[25] It is perhaps this *mātrikā* whose domain Shītalā has inherited.

The attendants of Shītalā's temple speak of her as one of the nine "sisters," the names of which seem to be colloquial versions of the nine celestial *mātrikās*, among whom they include Shītalā. This *devī*, like Sankatā Devī, is said to have no consort. She is, rather, an independent female power. Her danger, of course, is obvious. But her benevolent and gracious side is sufficient for some to consider themselves her *bhaktas*, or devotees.

The worship of Shītalā has been tenacious in Kāshī as in North India generally. Of course, she receives no mention in the Sanskrit *māhātmyas* of the city, for her origins are elsewhere, in the hinterlands of village India. Nonetheless, the popularity of Shītalā is such that today many neglected shrines of Durgā or Lakshmī and many broken old fragments of female sculpture have been reconsecrated as Shītalā and are worshipped as such. There are hundreds of Shītalā shrines in Banāras, many of them consecrated in just such a fashion.

The temple of Shītalā is certainly the dominant temple of the Dashāshvamedha Ghāt area. None of the many venerable Shiva *lingas*

Shītalā's Dashāshvamedha temple in the rainy season. The ghāt steps are flooded and worshippers approach by boat.

of this vicinity rivals her popularity. Indeed, the most honored *linga* here—Dashāshvamedheshvara—is located within the very precincts of Shītalā's own temple.

VISHĀLĀKSHĪ

Not far from Vishvanātha toward the River Ganges is the "Wide-Eyed" goddess, Vishālākshī, who is mentioned by Lakshmīdhara in his twelfth-century digest and who is included in most of the standard lists of the *pīthas* of the Goddess in India. These *pīthas* are the places where the various parts of the body of Shiva's wife, Satī, fell, when the grieving Shiva danced wildly through the country carrying her dead body. In her next life, Satī was reborn as the goddess Pārvatī. Taken as a whole, these *pīthas* comprise the full body of the Goddess. Individually, they have been sanctified by some part of her. According to tradition, it was her eye, or some say her earring, that fell here.

The *pīthas* are the seats of local goddesses who have often been paired with male counterparts called *bhairavas*. At Kāshī's *pītha*, the goddess Vishālākshī is matched with Kāla Bhairava, whom we shall soon meet, or sometimes with Shiva Vishvanātha. The entire development of the fastidious pairing of *shaktis* and *bhairavas* is certainly a medieval product of Tantrism.

The temple of Vishālākshī is interesting not only for its fame as a *pītha*, but for its strong connections with two other goddesses: Kāmākshī, the "Love-Eyed" goddess from Kānchī in the South and also from Assam in the Northeast, and Mīnākshī, the "Fish-Eyed" goddess from Madurai in the South. The three, with names so similar, are often linked together as a triad of related goddesses. South Indians have had a particularly strong connection with Vishālākshī, and it was with the patronage of people from the Tamil South that the temple was renovated in 1971.

A popular Shītalā shrine in the streets near Dashāshvamedha. An old rock is
surmounted by a new image of Shītalā, four-armed and three eyed, riding her
donkey mount. The prominence of her eyes enhances the powerful exchange of
contact with the worshipper through darshana. *So popular is this shrine that*
brahmins have wasted no time in placing an array of lingas *here as well.*

CYCLES OF GODDESSES

During the "Nine Nights" *(Navarātra)* of the Goddess, celebrated twice-yearly, Kāshī's goddesses are especially honored. The fall festival is in the month of Āshvina, from the first to the tenth day—nine nights in all—of the waxing fortnight. This festival of the Goddess ends on the morning of the tenth day (Dashaharā), which is called Vijaya Lakshmī by those who celebrate the goddess Durgā's victory over the bull demon. The spring Navarātra festival occurs during the same fortnight period of the month of Chaitra.

In each festival cycle there are various groups of nine goddesses to be visited. (*See* Appendix IV for a listing of the Durgās, Shaktis, and Gaurīs specified for the Nine Nights.) The most important are the nine Durgās, one of whom is specified for each day and night. Every evening, people will seek the *darshana* of the Durgā of that day. These cycles of *devīs* are well known in the Kāshī *mahatmyas*,[26] and the Navarātra festival is mentioned in Gāhadavāla inscriptions as one of the most popular in twelfth-century Banāras. It is still of great importance today.

The goddesses have a long history in Vārānasī. Their history, however, is but partially glimpsed in the Purānic literature, where they are undoubtedly not given attention in proportion to their prominence. Here the artistic tradition greatly enhances what can be learned from the literary tradition. As we have seen, these visual texts tell us that from at least the Mauryan period in the fourth century B.C. to the present, the goddesses have been prominent in the sacred circle of Kāshī's deities. From the eighth to the twelfth centuries, their presence was especially strong, as attested to by dozens of Banāras images of the goddesses of this period. In Kāshī today, the Goddess in her supreme forms and the many goddesses of the popular tradition are still of great importance. One sees her image at every turn, as the benign mother Annapūrnā, the giver of life, or as the fearsome Kālī, the wielder of death, garlanded with skulls and standing upon the inert body of Shiva. Without the power and energy of the Shakti, Shiva, they say, is a *shava,* a corpse. It is she who embodies the vibrance of both life and death.

The Goddess Kālī standing upon the body of Shiva. Shiva is small and inert here, for he depends upon Shakti to extend his spiritual presence in the world. Kālī holds a severed head and wields a bone as a club. Her necklace is of skulls and her skirt of severed arms. She is alive and powerful in death, as well as in life.

The Sun and the Adityas

Arise! The breath of life hath come back to us,
The darkness is gone, the light approacheth!
Dawn hath opened a path for the Sun to travel;
Now our days will be lengthened.

Singing the praises of the brightening morn,
The priest, the poet, ariseth with the web of his hymn.
Bounteous maiden, shine upon him who praiseth thee;
Spread upon us the gift of life and children.

Rig Veda I.113.16-17[27]

DAWN is the sacred hour in the City of Light. The devout rise while it is still dark and make their way to the Ganges. As the sky lightens, they bathe and begin their morning worship, called *sandhyā*, "the dawn." By the hundreds, the bathers and worshippers assembled at the great *ghāts* along the river greet the rising sun with a crescendo of drums and bells, prayers and salutations. Nowhere in the world is the sun received daily with such celebration as in Kāshī.

The awakening of the Banāras riverfront at dawn has unfailingly impressed the city's pilgrims and visitors. The British art historian E. B. Havell, for instance, recalling the above verses from the *Rig Veda,* wrote effusively of the sun's daily victory over the forces of the night in Kāshī:

The light brightens as Ushas, the lovely dawn-maiden, beloved of the Vedic poets, clad in robes of saffron and rose-colour, throws open the doors of the sky. . . . At last, Surya, the Sun, appears, glowing with opal fire above the cloudy bars of night. The miasmatic mists, like evil spirits—the wicked Asuras—shrink and shrivel and vanish into thin air, as he pierces them through and through and flings his victorious rays across the river, lighting up the recesses of the cave-like shrines, flashing on the brass and copper vessels of the bathers and on the gilded metal flags and crescents which surmount the temples of Shiva. It seems, at first, as if the whole amphitheatre, about two miles in circuit, glittering in the sunlight, were one vast sun-temple. . . .[28]

From that mythic time when Shiva sent Sūrya, the Sun, as his emissary to Kāshī, the Sun has had an important place in the life of the sacred city.[29] The twelve parts into which he divided himself were the *ādityas,* the "suns" who were the mythical offspring of Aditi and Prajāpati, who fashioned the universe as its mother and father. The notion of multiple suns occurs in the Vedic hymns, and by the time of the *Shatapatha Brāhmana,* the number of *ādityas* seems to be fixed at twelve, identified with the twelve solar months.[30] The *ādityas* of the Vedas and Brāhmanas have well-known mythological names, such as Mitra, Aryamān, Bhaga, Daksha, and even Vishnu. The twelve as they are manifest in Kāshī, however, have local names, except for a few which have names shared by the *ādityas* of other Indian *tīrthas.* In the *Kāshī Khanda,* the individual tales of these *ādityas* are told, their *māhātmyas* are recited, and their locations are specified. (*See* Appendix V.) Although in the larger myth, the Sun is said simply to divide himself into twelve, nonetheless each individual *āditya* has its own particular story of origin. We will take note of three of these *ādityas* here.

Of the twelve, the most important *āditya* in both ancient and modern times is Lolārka. It is said, "Because the Sun's heart trembled when he beheld Kāshī, his name became Lolārka, 'The Trembling Sun.' "[31] The name Lolārka refers today both to the image of the Sun and to the deep *kund* in which that image is located. Stone steps descend steeply on three sides of the *kund* to the rectangular bathing pool, some fifty feet below ground level. The Sun's disc is set into the wall, near the water's edge.

Lolārka is located in the extreme south of Vārānasī, near the Asi *sangam,* the "confluence" of the Asi River and the River Ganges. So great are the antiquity and importance of Lolārka, that the Asi *sangam* is sometimes called the Lolārka *sangam* in the early literature. It is likely that Lolārka was famous long before Asi became known. In the *Kāshī Khanda,* the two are linked as the keepers of the southern gate of Vārānasī: Asi, "The Sword," slashes down the sins of those who enter the sacred city, and Lolārka, "The Trembling Sun," burns them up.

Lolārka is not only the oldest and most famous of Kāshī's *ādityas,* but it is perhaps one of the oldest of all sacred sites in Kāshī. It is named in some of the earliest Purānic *māhātmyas* of the city, at a time when only a few sites are explicitly named.[32] So important is this place that, in the *Kāshī Khanda,* the Purānic author steps back from his *māhātmya* to emphasize that his praises of Lolārka are not just exaggeration and panegyric, but are really true. Historical witnesses to the fame of Lolārka are two copper-plate inscriptions which record the patronage of the Gāhadavāla kings, who bathed here, worshipped, and made charitable donations.[33]

Its brahminical heritage aside, it is likely that Lolārka has an even longer history as a pilgrimage center for the non-brahminical folk tradition. One can well imagine that Lolārka, as a place of Sun worship and perhaps, with its deep *kund,* as a place of *nāga* worship as well, was attracting bathers and worshippers in the Buddha's day, centuries before the great deities of Hinduism, such as Vishnu and Shiva, had captured the popular imagination.

The extraordinary popularity of Lolārka's yearly *melā,* or "religious fair," is a convincing testimony to the significance of this place among the people of the village districts around Banāras. Throughout most of

Lolārka Kund. On the landing above the pool are the many round squashes, offered into the waters by couples wishing fertility.

the year Lolārka does not attract people for daily worship, although a few come on the Day of the Sun, Ravivāra, or Sunday, and on the "sixth" *(shashthī)* of each fortnight, the day appropriate for the worship of the Sun. On one day a year, however, ten thousand people swarm to Lolārka from the country villages around Kāshī. On this day, called Lolārka Shashthī in the autumn month of Bhādrapada (August/September), the ancient folk traditions of Lolārka are clearly evident.

The motive of most who come to the Lolārka *mela* is the birth of sons. Throughout the day, the *kund* and the steps leading down to it are filled with the throng of bathers. To conceive a son, the wife and husband bathe together, her *sārī* tied to his *dhotī*. It is customary for the woman to release some vegetables into the water when she bathes, usually the round variety of squash, signifying, perhaps, the fertility for which she hopes. Those who claim to have had a son in consequence of a previous ritual bath on Lolārka Shashthī return with the child for thanksgiving and for tonsure. Lolārka Shashthī is one of Kāshī's largest yearly *melās,* and witnessing the spectacle of the crowds on this day leaves one certain that this place has been a powerful focus of popular attention for a very long time, probably for as long as has Kāshī itself.

At least two of the other Sun-sites of Kāshī must have been very impressive in their day. One is Uttarārka, the "Northern Sun," which was situated in the great Gupta temple complex at Bakariā Kund, formerly called Uttararka Kund, just south of what is today the Grand Trunk Road in northern Varanasī. Bakariā Kund is really a small lake, which was once rimmed with many temples and perhaps, according to M. A. Sherring, with Buddhist monastic buildings as well. Archeological evidence indicates that at least some of the structures here were Vaishnava, for it was here that the image of Krishna lifting the mountain was found, and the literary tradition of the Purānas holds that this was the location within Kāshī of the sacred city of Mathurā, the birthplace and homeland of Krishna. The Hindu site was demolished sometime during the Muslim centuries of sovereignty, and its ruins were transformed into Muslim structures. The temple of the Northern Sun, however, has vanished. But Sherring, who was fascinated by the ruins of Bakariā Kund, records having found a Sun-disc there, with relief carvings of Suns and other lotiform shapes.[34]

Whereas at Lolārka there is no evidence of a great temple, at Sūrya Kund, the "Sun Pool," another of the great Sun-sites of Kāshī, there was apparently a very large and impressive temple, traces of which still remain in the locale. The temple housed the image of Sāmbāditya. It was evidently of enough significance that it was completely destroyed.

Sūrya Kund, today called Sūraj Kund, is located near Godauliā crossing in the heart of the city. It is clear from the ruins evident around the *kund* that the temple compound once located on the banks of this pond was quite extensive. Part of the plinth of the temple, estimated to have been a fifth- or sixth-century structure, is still visible in the compound of a private home at the edge of the pond.[35] In the grounds of several adjacent homes, images and building stones have been discovered, usually by accident while digging foundations for new construction. Sāmbāditya is today worshipped in a small shrine near the *kund*. However, the most visible remains of the glorious temple of the Sun that once stood here are two very large lotiform Sun-discs, lying beneath a tree in a rubble of less distinguished stone fragments, by the water's edge.

The worship of the Sun-symbol in India is probably as old as Indian culture. Those who have studied this matter have seen evidence of a Sun-cult in the seals and *svastikas* of pre-Vedic India, as well as in the hymns of the Vedic Indo-Aryans.[36] In the context of Kāshī, however, the phase of the Sun-cult's long history that is most relevant is the millennium of its greatest ascendancy, from the fourth to the thirteenth centuries, the "classical age of Sun-worship in India."[37]

For this thousand-year period, the Sun was the center of a developed cult and was one of the major figures of the Hindu pantheon. In the *Saura Upapurānas,* which give a central place to the Sun, it is clear that the Sun is supreme. In one mythological reversal, for instance, it is the Sun who grants Shiva purification from the sin of killing a brahmin, and it is the Sun who advises Shiva to dwell in Avimukta. Indeed, it is the Sun who confers the name Avimukta upon Banāras.[38]

In Vārānasī, the substantial literary evidence of Sun-worship is supplemented by the evidence of the arts. In the limited collection of art located at the Bhārat Kalā Bhavan alone, there is an eighth-century Sūrya, a twelfth-century Sūrya, and an eleventh-century female Sun-image, Chakreshvarī, from Lolārka. Elsewhere, throughout the city and its environs, Sun-symbols may be seen. Lotiform Sun-stones, such as the one at Sūrya Kund, may be found in fragments here and there, and sometimes the full image of Sūrya may be seen, such as the fine

Sun discs at Sūrya Kund.

tenth to twelfth-century Sūrya, mistakenly consecrated as Viru-pāksha, at Kardameshvara along the Panchakroshī Road.

As a group, the twelve Suns are said to be protectors of Kāshī, circling the city with their light. Some of the twelve are located today within the precincts of major Kāshī temples, such as Arunāditya, the "Dawn-Sun" in Trilochana Temple, and Keshavāditya, the "Keshava-Sun" in the temple of Vishnu called Ādi Keshava. While a pilgrimage to all twelve is outlined even today in pilgrim guidebooks, it is not a common or popular pilgrimage.

In India, as in other parts of the world, the Sun-symbol has inspired a grand monotheistic vision. It has been an especially important symbol for both the Vaishnava and the Buddhist traditions. In addition to its singular majesty, however, the Sun is considered to be compassionate, healing, and friendly. The stories of the *ādityas* as told in the *Kāshī Khanda* repeatedly emphasize the relationship of the Sun to the healing of diseases and the restoration of crippled limbs. The afflicted, the orphaned, the childless may also appeal to the Sun. The Sun has to do with important matters of "this shore"—comfort, warmth, and

health—and even in the absence of the devotional "cult" of the Sun
which flourished for a millennium, the prayers of appeal to the Sun
have not ceased. Despite the structural importance of the twelve Suns
in the sacred *mandala* of Kāshī, it has long been true and is true today
that the real focus of the Hindu *darshana* of the Sun is not the Sun-
stone, set in the wall of a temple and colored with vermilion. It is the
Sun itself—in its rising, its zenith, and its setting. These are the day's
"three dawns," and are the proper times for worship. Havell described
the dawning riverfront as "one vast sun-temple," and yet it is not the
Sun alone which is honored. It is the Divine, of many names and
forms, here physically manifest, present in warmth and light.

Ganesha and the Ganas

APPROACHING Vishvanātha Temple through the thread-narrow
passageway of Vishvanātha Lane, one comes upon a small shrine,
bulging with the great orange image of Ganesha. The elephant-headed
Ganesha, plump to begin with, appears in this shrine as an indistinct
corpulent mass, his features blurred by the vermilion *sindūr* with
which he has been smeared in worship for centuries. Garlanded with
chaplets of flowers, he stares into the busy lane with solid silver eyes.
The temple attendant sits by on a narrow ledge, ever attentive to the
continual procession of worshippers and passersby. This Ganesha,
called Dhundhirāja or Dhundhi Vināyaka, sits virtually at the center of
the *mandala* of Kāshī. Around him, throughout the entire city and far
into the countryside, are arrayed fifty-six other Ganeshas in a protective formation. They sit at the eight compass points, spreading out
from the center in seven concentric circles.

THE NATURE OF GANAS AND
GANESHAS

The worship of Ganesha is very old in Kāshī, as in India generally.
Ganesha has his origins among the thick-set, fat-bellied, beneficent
yaksha deities, whose worship in India was prevalent long before the
theistic worship of either Vishnu or Shiva came to the fore.

The honoring of Ganesha, or deities like him, is surely much older than explicit textual and sculptural evidence would indicate. Although the full-fledged worship of Ganesha cannot be definitely dated until about the fifth century, its sources are incalculable centuries earlier. As M. Foucher wrote in his introduction to Alice Getty's monograph on Ganesha:

One must be as short-sighted as a bookworm to deduce from the lack of any mention of Ganeśa in the early epics, that the god did not exist before the fourth or fifth century of our era, and it would require a certain amount of naïveté to believe that this divinity could have suddenly been conceived *ex nihilo,* and his worship established throughout the whole of India at such a comparatively recent date. Whoever is experienced in the ways of that country knows well that by then the Elephant-god had already behind him century upon century, if not thousands of years, of silent waiting at the foot of the sacred tree of the pre-Aryan village. . . . [39]

To explore the emergence of Ganesha would lead too far afield here. Briefly, however, the one called Ganesha (or Ganeshvara, Vināyaka) emerged as a single deity from a whole class of godlings, variously called *yakshas, rākshasas, ganas,* and *ganeshas.* As with the various *devīs,* it is very difficult to draw firm lines between these categories of ancient tutelary deities. Despite their differences, they often refer to a particular type of deity: stout and strong, sometimes pot-bellied, often part-animal, potentially both beneficent and fierce.

Many of these deities, most of whom have a strictly local sphere of jurisdiction, were drawn into the entourage of Shiva as he rose to prominence. They were his *ganas,* "attendants." The term *ganesha* or *ganeshvara* first referred to Shiva himself, as the lord *(īsha* or *īshvara)* of this host of *ganas.* Only later did the name belong specifically to the stout, elephant-headed deity who became the chief of the troop of *ganas.* While Ganesha emerged as a particular deity and became known as Shiva's son, other *ganas,* some with individual names but few with distinct personalities, remained part of the general group. Still others, however, must have resisted the canopy of Shaivism, for they are still worshipped today as independent local tutelary deities.

Like the *mātrikās* and *yoginīs,* most of these *gana/ganeshas* are ambiguous in nature. As place-specific deities they may protect or harm, and they are sometimes linked with similar female deities as partners in the locative folk tradition of the village and countryside. In the ancient tradition, there is some attempt to separate the *yakshas* from the *rāk-shasas,* the former being primarily beneficent and led by the wealthy Kubera, and the latter being primarily malicious and led by the fright-ful Rāvana. But the distinction does not hold in more than a general way. It is not often clear that the deities called *yakshas* are very dif-ferent from those called *rākshasas.* Both can accept the blood offerings of *bali,* both can befriend, and both can be fearsome.

THE LORD OF THE THRESHOLD

The two-faced, Janus-like nature of many of these gods makes them the perfect doorkeepers of the universe, able both to welcome and to turn away those who approach. In the *Mahābhārata,* the *yakshas* are the ones most often cast as the gatekeepers, who must be saluted on en-tering the precincts of the various *tīrthas.*[40] The *ganas* also sometimes assume the role of door-guardian, but it is especially Ganesha who becomes the doorkeeper *par excellence.*

Ganesha is sometimes mistakenly thought of as the "remover" of obstacles. While it is true that he is most often supplicated to remove obstacles, it is more accurate to recognize him as Vighnesha, the "Lord of Obstacles." He may remove them, or he may pose them. He may open the door or close it. Ganesha may be chubby, good-humored, always carrying a radish in one hand and a plate of sweetmeats in the other. But he may also be the stern doorkeeper of the universe, with his elephant goad, his noose, and his hatchet.

As the Lord of Obstacles, Ganesha sits at the threshold, especially at the threshold of the sacred. Ganesha may sit at the gateway of a city, as did Nikumbha in ancient Kāshī, or he may sit at the doorway of a temple. Throughout North India, his image is also painted over the doorways of homes. In addition, Ganesha sits at the thresholds of time and is propitiated at the commencement of worship, at the beginning of a wedding, or at the outset of a pilgrimage. Thus Ganesha holds the key to the success of any venture.

It is significant that this guardian of the *limens,* the "threshold," is himself what might be called a "liminal" deity.[41] He stands betwixt and between the human and the divine spheres. And he stands betwixt and between the human and the animal form, part prince and part elephant. With his elephant head, Ganesha is perhaps a direct descendant of an ancient theriomorphic elephant deity. The elephant, like the *yaksha,* has long been seen in India as a supporter, a guardian, and a directional regent of the world. Like the *yaksha,* the elephant form often appeared in stone carvings at the base of a column or a building, as if bearing it up. And, like the *yaksha,* the elephant was a directional guardian, and eight of these great elephants were imagined to support the entire earth on their backs.

In time Ganesha came to be seen as the son of Shiva and Pārvatī. His creation and adoption into the "holy family" is told in a variety of myths. Perhaps the most commonly known is the story in which Pārvatī creates a son from the rubbings of her own body to guard her door while she is bathing. When Shiva returns home and demands entrance, the loyal Ganesha refuses him. After a terrible fight, Shiva beheads Ganesha. Pārvatī is inconsolable until her son is revived, by attaching the head of another creature to the body of her son. So it is that Ganesha has the head of an elephant.[42] And Ganesha, created by Pārvatī and re-created by Shiva, thus became the child of Shiva and Pārvatī. In a sense, the myth states the accomplished fact of religious history: that from the *ganas* and *yakshas* there emerged a singular deity who became part of the most intimate entourage of Shiva Maheshvara.

THE GANAS AND GANESHA IN KĀSHĪ

In the religious history of Kāshī, Kshemaka and Nikumbha appear as two deities who occupied Kāshī long ago. As already described, according to the brief myth-history of the Purānic accounts, King Divodāsa propitiated Nikumbha, whose popular shrine was at the city gate, for a son. When he did not secure a son for his devotion, the King had Nikumbha's shrine destroyed. In turn, Nikumbha cursed Kāshī to stand empty, and King Divodāsa was forced to leave the city.[43]

What little is known from such an account of the worship of this Nikumbha Ganesha in ancient Kāshī corresponds with the worship of Ganesha even today. Then, as now, his shrine was at the city gate, and then, as now, he was approached by people with requests for earthly boons, such as the bestowal of sons.

The variations of the Nikumbha and Kshemaka story, as we have seen in discussing the early history of Kāshī, show these godlings in the process of being brought under the canopy of Shiva. In two accounts, for example, the two are envoys of Shiva, enlisted by the Great Lord as part of his plan to retrieve the city from Divodāsa and occupy it himself. By the time of the extended Divodāsa myth cycle of the *Kāshī Khanda*, Kshemaka and Nikumbha appear as but two of a great number of *ganas* and *ganeshas* who were sent to Kāshī, who were entranced by the magic of the city, and who settled there and established *lingas* under their own names. Kshemaka *gana* and Kshemeshvara *linga* are both located in a small riverside temple at Kshemeshvara Ghāt, south of Dashāshvamedha. Nikumbheshvara is located within the Vishvanātha Temple compound. Many of the *lingas* established by other *ganas* are also still present in the city's *mandala* of temples,[44] and some of their names correspond with the names of prominent *yakshas* found in the third-century roster of *yakshas*, the *Mahāmāyūrī*.[45]

These *ganas* are also designated as protectors and patrollers of the borders of the sacred zone of Kāshī. In the *Kāshī Khanda*, one *gana* is assigned to each of the eight directions, and from that grouping several are still recognizable today: Ghantakarna ("Bell Ears") in the north;

Ganas posted along the Panchakroshī Road, between Kardameshvara and Bhīmachandī. Left: Nandikeshvara. Right: Kutagana.

Gokarna ("Cow Ears") in the west; and Cchāgavaktra ("Goat Face") in the northeast, for example. In addition, sixteen other *ganas* are posted along the borders of the sacred city: four along the Ganges River in the east; four along the Asi River in the south; four along the western boundary, and four along the Varaṇā River in the north. The names of these *ganas* have changed over the centuries, but the *ganas* standing guard with their clubs in the small shrines of the Panchakroshī Road are clearly evident to anyone who travels the circuit around the city.

When Shiva had sent all his *ganas* to Kāshī and none had returned, he called in Ganesha, the "Lord of the Ganas," and sent him to the city. The Lord of Obstacles was the one who removed the obstacles to Shiva's return. Having accomplished his mission, he divided himself into many parts and waited for Shiva to come. When Shiva arrived in Kāshī, he was very pleased with Ganesha, to whom he gave the name Dhundhirāja.[46] Ganesha, as Dhundhirāja, would have a prime position, right at the center of Kashi, and would be worshipped by all who would gain entrance to the sacred city.

THE FIFTY-SIX GANESHAS

In addition to his central position as Dhundhirāja, Ganesha has multiple forms in Kāshī. In the *Kāshī Khanda,* fifty-six Ganeshas are enumerated within and around the "sacred circle." They are arrayed at the eight directional points in seven concentric circles, centering around Dhundhirāja near the Vishvanātha Temple. These are called the fifty-six Vināyakas.[47]

On the outermost circle there is Arka Vināyaka, located near Lolārka Kund and situated in the southeastern direction. Next comes Durgā Vināyaka, located at Durgā Kund in the southern direction. To the southwest is Bhīmachanda Vināyaka, located in the town of Bhīmachandī, the second night's stop on the Panchakroshī Road. To the west is Dehalī Vināyaka, also along the Panchakroshī Road, and one of the most famous of all the Ganeshas, since it marks the western boundary of the sacred zone. To the northwest and to the north are Uddanda Vināyaka and Pāshapāni Vināyaka. To the northeast is Kharva Vināyaka, near Ādi Keshava Temple at the confluence of the Varaṇā and the Ganges Rivers. Finally, on the east is Siddhi Vināyaka

*Ganesha shrine. In Brahma
Nāla, Vārānasī.*

in the Manikarnikā Ghāt area. The cycles of eight Ganeshas continue in this manner, until the final eight are crowded right around the immediate vicinity of the Vishvanātha Temple.

Five of the innermost circle are known as the Moda Vināyakas, the "Vināyakas of Delight," and they, along with Dhundhirāja, are to be visited at the commencement and completion of many pilgrimages. Nearby in Vishvanātha Lane is yet another important Ganesha who is not among the fifty-six: Sākshī Vināyaka, the "Witness," who is especially visited at the conclusion of pilgrimages to witness the completion of the full pilgrimage rite.

The most celebrated Ganesha in Kāshī today is Bare Ganesha, the "Big Ganesha," known to the Purānas as Mahārāja Vināyaka. His temple in the Saptasāgara, "Seven Seas," area of the city is very spacious indeed, compared to the streetside niches where Ganesha ordinarily dwells. The fourth day of every fortnight, and especially of the waning fortnight, is special to Ganesha and brings a crowd of worshippers to the temple of Bare Ganesha. In Kāshī, the most festive "fourth" is during the waning fortnight of the winter month of Māgha (January/February), the day considered to be Ganesha's birthday. For weeks beforehand, the city's artisans are busy making thousands of painted clay Ganeshas of all sizes, which will be sold to worshippers during the festival. On the day of Ganesha Chaturthī, people come by the thousands from all over Banāras for the *darshana* of Bare Ganesha, and the streets in front of this temple are filled with festivity.

Kāla Bhairava and Dandapāni

KĀLA BHAIRAVA, the "Black Terror," is widely known as the *kotwāl*, the "police chief," of Kāshī, and the section of the city in which his temple stands is known as Kotwālpurī. Dandapāni, the "Club Carrier," is Kāshī's sheriff. In addition to the gods and goddesses sent to Kāshī during the reign of Divodāsa, these two, whose myths occur elsewhere in the *Kāshī Khanda*, are very important functionaries of the sacred city.[48] Here we discuss them in sequence with the *ganas* and *ganeshas*, for they share the same origins in the extensive root-system of the Hindu folk tradition. Kāla Bhairava is from a class of deities called *bhairavas* or, popularly, *bhairons*, the "terrible ones," the "frightful ones," who wield clubs, display fanglike teeth, and ride the despicable dog as a vehicle. These deities became known as Shiva's *ganas* and, in the service of the Lord, were often set as guardians to scare away demons and evil spirits, a task which they no doubt performed with ease. Dandapāni, sometimes said to be a *bhairava* himself, is also depicted in Kāshī mythology as a former *yaksha*, who left the *yaksha* ranks to become a devotee of Lord Shiva. Kāla Bhairava and Dandapāni are closely related, and both are considered to have great power in the sacred circle of Kāshī.

THE BHAIRAVAS OF KĀSHĪ

Bhairava is considered a fearsome manifestation of Shiva. In a streetside image in Brahma Nāla, he wears a garland of skulls and carries a club of peacock feathers, suggesting that his power is not entirely physical and that his original home is in the forest wild-country where the peacocks live.[49] In other Banāras images, we see only the face of Bhairava, the rest of his body being hidden by a cloth apron. His face, usually shown with a mustache, may be a gleaming silver mask, as at the Kāla Bhairava Temple, or a ruddy vermilion sphere, betraying its years of worship with *sindūr,* as at the Bhūta Bhairava shrine.

There are sometimes said to be sixty-four *bhairavas,* corresponding to the sixty-four *yoginīs,* and these male deities also came to be seen as the counterparts of the goddesses at the various *shakti pīthas* throughout India.[50] While many of their Sanskrit names are of relatively recent origin, dating from the upsurge of Tantra in the early medieval period, these *bhairavas* are undoubtedly of great antiquity. Eight of the *bhairavas* are especially counted as leaders: Kapālī ("Skull-Bearer"), Asitānga ("Black-Limbs"), Rūrū ("The Dog"), Chanda ("The Fierce"), Krodhana ("Wrath"), Unmatta ("The Wild"), Bhīshana ("The Horrific"), and Samhāra ("Destruction"). These formidable eight are all present in Banāras shrines, and there is a recognized tour of pilgrimage around to all of them. (*See* Appendix V.)

KĀLA BHAIRAVA

The most important of the Bhairavas stands outside these eight, however. This is Kāla Bhairava, whose name, Kāla, means both Death and Fate, in addition to meaning Black. He is the Black One, who has also assumed the duties of the God of Death in Kāshī. Even Death, it is said, is afraid of Kāla Bhairava.[51]

The story of the origin of Kāla Bhairava has already been told in the myth of the appearance of the fiery *linga* (Chapter 3). Shiva revealed himself out of the column of light and, when Brahmā blasphemed him, Shiva created, out of the substance of his Anger, the fierce Bhairava, who sliced off Brahmā's fifth head. Here Bhairava is none other than a form of Shiva, the manifestation of Shiva's terrible aspect. Occasionally Bhairava, like Ganesha and Skanda, is called the son of Shiva, as in the frequent name Batuk Bhairava, the "Boy Bhairava." However, for the most part Bhairava is said to be an aspect of Shiva himself, even though he is worshipped as a distinct deity.

In the myth, the head of Brahmā, decapitated by Bhairava, stuck fast to Bhairava's hand. In order to get rid of this skull, Bhairava followed

*Kāla Bhairava, who has jurisdiction
over Death in Kāshī.*

the *kapāla vrata,* the "vow of the skull," which demonstrated to the world the only atonement for killing a brahmin. As he wandered through the land, Bhairava used this skull as a begging bowl for his food, thus defying all the strict Hindu ordinances of purity and impurity. When he entered Kāshī the skull fell, and Shiva "danced with joy for all the world to see."[52]

The wandering of Bhairava is clearly intended as a demonstration of atonement. In charging Bhairava with the penance of wandering, Shiva said to him, "Go forth, asking always for alms, observing the 'vow of the skull,' and showing it to the world, in order to destroy the sin of killing a brahmin."[53] As early as the *Yājnavalkya Smriti* (A.D. 100–300), the bearing of a skull in this fashion is said to be a fit penance for the killing of a brahmin: "With a skull and a staff [in his hands], living on alms, announcing his deed [as he begs], and eating little food, the killer of a Brāhmana may be purified after twelve years."[54]

This penance for the worst of sins also became the supreme religious discipline for one of the most ascetic sects, the Kāpālikas—"Skull Bearers." For them, however, the "great vow" *(mahāvrata)* of penance is undertaken not to expunge sin, but to accumulate spiritual power by this ritual identification with the asceticism of Shiva. Thus, the Skull-Bearing Bhairava is a model not only for the most miserable of sinners, but also for the most ambitious of saints, who freely undertake this most severe penance. Strictly speaking, the adhesions of Death dissolved when Bhairava entered Kāshī and bathed at Kapāla-mochana. But Bhairava did not make straight for Kāshī. Clearly the discipline of the road and the way of homeless begging, with that most scandalous of begging bowls, was as much a part of the "great vow" of expiation as the cleansing *tīrtha* itself.

Bhairava is the hero who overcame the worst of sins and who conquered the grotesque, ever-present skull of death. In his pilgrimage to Kāshī, Bhairava achieves that for which all pilgrims hope: freedom from sins and from the fear of death.

Shiva appointed Bhairava to be the chief officer of justice within the sacred city. As one of the temple officiants put it, "In Kāshī, Vishvanātha is the King, Annapūrnā is the Queen, and Kāla Bhairava is the Governor." The authority of Kāla Bhairava as the superintendent of justice in Kāshī is threefold. First, he is said to devour sins, thus earning the name "Sin-Eater" *(Pāpabhakshana)*. In the *Kāshī Khanda* he is vividly described as stationed by the bank of the Kapālamochana Tīrtha, consuming the sins that people shed there.[55] The one freed from the worst sin now devours the sins of others.

Second, Kāla Bhairava is the one who keeps the record of people's deeds in Kāshī. Those who dwell elsewhere on earth are watched by Chitragupta, the mythical scribe who takes notes on their doings. But Chitragupta keeps no records on those who dwell in Kāshī. Kāla Bhairava takes care of that.[56] Therefore it is of great importance to keep in Kāla Bhairava's favor. According to tradition, he should be honored by all who visit Vārānasī: "Even devotees of Vishvanātha, who are not devotees of Bhairava, encounter a multitude of obstacles in Kāshī at every single step."[57] It is said that whoever lives in Vārānasī and does not worship Bhairava accumulates a heap of sins that grows like the waxing moon.[58]

Finally, Bhairava not only scrutinizes the activities of the living, he also administers justice to those who have died. Here Bhairava assumes the duties of Yama, the God of Death, who is not allowed to enter Kāshī to fetch and punish souls. While all who die in Kāshī are promised liberation, they must first experience, in an intensified time frame, all the results—good and bad—of their accumulated *karma*. This is called the "punishment of Bhairava" *(bhairavī yātanā)*, and its dispensation is an important part of Bhairava's function in the city.[59] We shall have more to say of *bhairavī yātanā* in our discussion of the understanding of death in Kāshī later on. For now, we shall say only that this punishment meted out by Bhairava is said to last but a split second and to be a kind of time machine in which one experiences all the rewards and punishments that might otherwise be lived out over the course of many lifetimes. It is the experience of purgatory, run through in an instant, and Kāla Bhairava is in charge of it.

The temple of Kāla Bhairava, who is fondly called Bhaironāth, is located in the maze of lanes between Chaukhambā Lane, the "Main Street" of pre-modern Banāras, and Maidāgin Park. In the *Kāshī Khanda*, however, it is said to be located on the banks of the Kapālamochana Tīrtha, in the Omkāreshvara area north of Maidāgin. "Bhairava stands right there," says the text, "facing Kapālamochana Tīrtha, devouring the accumulated sins of devotees."[60] According to Kuber Nāth Sukul, Kāla Bhairava was reconsecrated in its present location in the thirteenth century, when the shrines in the Omkāreshvara area were destroyed. Here it was established in a humble structure, with a thatched roof, so as to attract little attention in the ensuing centuries. Both locations are mentioned in the *Kāshī Khanda*.[61] In the grand sixteenth-century temple of Vishvanātha, Kāla Bhairava was honored in one of the eight subsidiary pavilions of the temple. It was not until the early nineteenth century, however, that the present temple of Kāla Bhairava was constructed.

Kāla Bhairava's temple today is one of the most interesting in all Banāras. Entering from the street, through a door guarded by Bhairava's mount, the dog, one finds a fine courtyard, in the center of which is the main shrine of Bhairava—a small temple, with a pillared and diamond-tiled porch on which to stand for *darshana*. Only the silver face of Kāla Bhairava, garlanded with flowers, is visible through the doorway of the inner sanctum. The rest of Bhairava's image—said to be pot-bellied, seated upon a dog, holding a trident—is hidden behind a cloth drapery.

Bhairava's lieutenants, the priests of the temple, act on his behalf to bestow Bhairava's protection upon worshippers. The club of peacock feathers, carried by Bhairava in his sculptural representations, is wielded by one of these priests. For the worshipper, being struck or dusted off with this club is considered a blessing *(āshīrvāda)* which is said to keep away bodily sickness and pain. The same is said to be true of the ash *(bhabhūt)* which is applied to the forehead and pitched into the open mouth of the worshipper, who might also take a small envelope of this ash home again to apply daily until returning to the temple. Finally, the worshipper is girded with a necklace *(mālā)* of twisted and braided black threads, which have been blessed by Bhairava before being tied around the neck or wrist as an amulet against illness or evil spirits.

Making a circumambulatory round of the temple compound, one finds an array of subsidiary shrines—to Devī, to Hanumān, to Krishna and Rādhā, to Pārvatī and Ganesha. Most interesting is a large slab of the "Nine Houses" *(navagraha)* upon which each of the planetary houses of the zodiac has its individual representation and altar. The worship of the times and seasons of the zodiac is a reminder that Bhairava, like all his *yaksha* cousins, is a divinity of "this shore" not the "far shore." He is honored for protection, health, and well-being—not for liberation.

The story of Bhairava—his origin, his assault upon Brahmā, and his penance for killing a brahmin—is well known by those who officiate in this temple. One priest, whose station is by the temple door, has the *Shiva Purāna* and the *Kāshī Khanda* in his stack of books and turns quickly to those well-worn pages where Bhairava's story is told. He and his colleagues know by heart the hymns and *māhātmyas* of this temple, as told in the Purānas. In several places around the temple, verses of the Purānas are inscribed in Hindi in marble slabs. One tells the story from the *Kāshī Khanda* of how Kāla Bhairava was created at the time of the argument between Brahmā and Vishnu, and how he received his name and commission from Lord Shiva:

He said, "O Kāla Bhairava, you should punish this head of Brahmā. Because you look like Death *(kāla)* itself, you shall be 'Kālarāja,' the King of Death.

"You are able to bear [*bhartum*] everything. Because of this bearing, you will be known as Bhairava. Even Death will fear you. Therefore you will be 'Kāla Bhairava.' Because you will gladly crush evildoers, you will be known everywhere as Āmardaka, the 'Crusher.'

"Since you will eat up the sins of devotees, your name will be Pāpabhak-shana, 'Sin-Eater.'

"O Kālarāja, you will always be the Governor of that city of liberation, my Kāshī, the most excellent of all places."[62]

At the doorway of the temple, another Purānic inscription reads: "This is Vārānasī's Lord Bhairava, who destroys the terror of *samsāra*. The very sight of him removes the sins of many lifetimes."

For many centuries, this temple was a spiritual center in Kāshī for the most severe of Shaiva ascetics, the Kāpālikas or "Skull-Bearers," and their later descendants, the Gorakhnāthīs and the Kanphata yogis. These ascetic groups take as their model the ascetic and fearsome Shiva, whose ways run counter to the conventions of ordinary caste society. For them, Bhairava epitomizes this counter-conventional aspect of Shiva, the great yogi. Bhairava is famous for the bestowing of great yogic achievements, called *siddhis*—"accomplishments." Today, however, the temple is no longer the exclusive domain of such extremist yogis and is, rather, patronized by ordinary householders for his protective blessings.

Although this temple is popular and beloved among those who live under its influence in the surrounding Kotwālpurī section of the city, it is not a mandatory stop for pilgrims today. "Only a few pilgrims come," said one of the temple officiants. "It is a long way. Generally, people have the *darshana* of Vishvanatha and Annapūrnā, and then they leave. Their guides do not take them into these narrow lanes. Those who know what one ought to do in Kāshī come here. But those who don't know just follow the guides."

Bhairava's special day during each fortnight is the eighth day *(ash-tamī)*. In this, Bhairava is related to some of the other dark deities, such as Krishna and the Devī, who are also worshipped on the eighth. One day a year, on the eighth of the waning fortnight of the winter month of Mārgashīrsha (November/December), the time of Bhairava's first appearance is celebrated, and thousands flock to this and the other temples of Bhairava for *darshana*.

LĀT BHAIRAVA

Among the other Bhairava shrines in Banāras, Lāt Bhairava, known to
the Purānas as Kapālī Bhairava, is of particular interest. This image of
Bhairava is a pillar, encased in copper, and smeared with vermilion.
Thus, it has the name Lāt, the "staff" of Bhairava. This is especially
appropriate, since Bhairava is popularly known as the police chief of
sacred Kāshī, and policemen are armed with staves called *lāthīs*. In the
popular imagination, this huge pillar is thought of as Bhairava's staff.

Lāt Bhairava, located on the northern fringe of Banāras where the
road to Sārnāth intersects the Grand Trunk Road, has a complicated
history and a complex identity. In this it is like many of Kāshī's
northern *tīrthas*, which have been destroyed or partially destroyed,
which have been moved and yet have not been forgotten in their old
locations. Kapālī Bhairava, it seems, was originally in the Serpent Well
or Nāg Kuān area of northern Kāshī, and has only recently been
identified with this present site. Kapālamochana Tīrtha, on which it
sits today, was also originally farther south. And Lāt Bhairava, of
course, while it may well be an ancient folk name, is not known to the
Purānas at all. Nothing here—neither the name of the pool nor the
name of the Bhairava—seems to be in its proper Purānic place, and yet
something of this site must be very old, for Hindus have clung to this
site despite the fact that for over four hundred years their Bhairava has
been located right in the middle of a Muslim mosque and sacred tomb
site.

What is very old here and very sacred is the pillar itself, perhaps the
Purānic Mahāshmashāna Stambha, the "Pillar of the Great Cremation
Ground," or the Kula Stambha, the "Pillar of the Race."[63] It was here,
they said, that Bhairava would administer his punishment, the *bhairavī
yātanā*, as a moment's prelude to liberation. This pillar once stood in a
Hindu temple complex, but in the time of Aurangzeb the temple was
destroyed and the site became a Muslim tomb site. The pillar, however, was wisely left intact, as Sherring put it, "either as an ornament
to the grounds, or under a wholesome dread of provoking to too great a
pitch the indignation of his Hindu subjects."[64] Muslims continued to
permit some access to the pillar and received part of the offerings in
return.

The pillar was once much taller than it is today. The French traveler Tavernier saw Lāt Bhairava in 1665, during the reign of Aurangzeb, and described it as being thirty-two to thirty-five feet high. He was also told that it had sunk into the ground more than thirty feet in the previous fifty years. On the capital of the pillar, he reported, was a round ball encircled below with a row of beads.[65] When Sherring examined the site in the 1860s, he was convinced that the most ancient remains there were not those of the Hindu temple, but of a much earlier Buddhist complex, and that the Lāt itself was really an Ashokan pillar, with just the dimensions of the Ashokan pillar found at Sārnāth a few miles to the north.[66]

According to the prevailing legend, which evidently reached Tavernier's ear, Lāt Bhairava was gradually sinking. When its top became level with the ground, they said, all castes would be one, *dharma* would be completely eroded, and chaos would prevail. The leveling of Lāt Bhairava, however, happened more quickly and more violently than the perpetrators of the legend had ever imagined. In 1809, it was toppled during a spate of Hindu-Muslim rioting. In that year, communal tensions had already been exacerbated when the Hindus had attempted to construct a shrine on the neutral ground between the Jnāna Vāpī Mosque and the Vishvanātha Temple. Then, by an unfortunate coincidence of the Hindu and Muslim calendars, the Muslim Muharram rites and the Hindu Holī festival occurred at the same time. When the mournful processions of Muharram collided with the mobs of Holī revelers, the tensions erupted in a period of communal confrontation and violence. There were incidents of desecration on both sides. The Muslims slaughtered a cow on one of the great *ghāts* and its blood ran into the holy Ganges.[67] The Hindus destroyed a mosque and threatened to destroy all the mosques in the city. But the most stinging incident, which continued to cause tension for many years, was the destruction of Lāt Bhairava. The Lāt was pulled down early in the controversy and its broken pieces hauled away. Only a stub remained, and it is that remainder, now capped in metal and covered on special occasions with a cloth sleeve, that is honored today. One hundred and seventy years after this violent communal disturbance, the Lāt Bhairava area is still vulnerable to communal conflict, and a police guard is permanently stationed there, armed with their own tall *lāthī* sticks, to patrol the area of Bhairava's *lāt*.

DANDAPĀNI

Dandapāni is related to Kāla Bhairava, for he too is the "Club Carrier," armed with a staff to keep order. In fact, a pillar fragment from the Mahāshmashāna pillar at Lāt Bhairava is still worshipped today as Dandapāni's *danda*, his "club," in a small shrine near Kāla Bhairava known popularly by the conglomerate name Dandapāni Bhairava. The capital of this pillar fragment appears to be carved with eight figures seated round it in meditation, although the details are obscured by many layers of *sindūr*.

Dandapāni's primary shrine is elsewhere in Kāshī, however. In the *Kāshī Khanda*, this guardian deity is said to be stationed to the south of Vishveshvara.[68] In the great sixteenth-century temple of Vishveshvara, his shrine, like Kāla Bhairava's, was incorporated into the Vishveshvara Temple as one of the satellite pavilions. Today, the small shrine of Dandapāni is located in the Vishvanātha Lane, just west of the ruined sixteenth-century temple where the Jnāna Vāpī Mosque now stands.

Like Ganesha and Bhairava, Dandapāni is another major figure of the Banāras pantheon who has risen to prominence out of the common ranks of folk deities. Unlike Ganesha and Bhairava, however, Dandapāni is a functionary of Kāshī alone.[69] In the city's mythology, Dandapāni was formerly a *yaksha* who was so devoted to Shiva that Shiva made him a *ganesha* and gave him important guardian duties in Kāshī. Although Dandapāni may be a *ganesha*, he is not ordinarily thought of as such, and he is not one of the traditional fifty-six *ganeshas* of Kāshī. He more often has the name Bhairava.

Dandapāni has two specific jobs in the sacred order of Kāshī. First, he is the sheriff who, with his two deputies, Sambhrama ("Confusion") and Udbhrama ("Doubt"), runs the unworthy out of the city. In addition to this rather fierce role, however, Dandapāni has a beneficent role as the provider of food to those who dwell in Kāshī. Both Dandapāni and Kāla Bhairava are said to be the aides of the goddess Annapūrnā in the distribution of alms. Thus, Dandapāni retains the dual nature of his *yaksha/rākshasa* ancestors. He permits people to settle and thrive in Vārānasī, and he drives them out if they are unfit.

Dandapāni's role as the one who drives the unfit out of the sacred district is particularly noteworthy. Because it is a great blessing to live and die in Vārānasī, it would seem reasonable that all would wish to become residents of the sacred city. Why doesn't everybody live in Kāshī? Does justice prevail in determining who shall live here and die here? Dandapāni is the judge in this matter. Unlike the merely human sheriff, whose judgment of a person's conduct is confined to the limited assessment of a single lifetime, Dandapāni, as a divine sheriff, sees into the many lifetimes through which a person has traveled. From Dandapāni's divinely advantaged point of view, the learned brahmin may be no better than the poor beggar. Those who succeed in settling in Kāshī—rich or poor, high or low—do so with the permission and favor of Dandapāni.

Even the gods do not have the privilege of dwelling in Kāshī unless they have the favor of Dandapāni. The god Skanda, for example, who narrates the *Kāshī Khanda* to the sage Agastya, lives in exile on Shrī Shaila mountain in the South, precisely because he failed to honor Dandapāni. He confesses to Agastya that, because he wants to return to Kāshī, he continually worships Dandapāni from afar.[70] Honoring Dandapāni, therefore, should be the first priority of anyone who wants to live in Kāshī.

The story of how Dandapāni received such an important position in the sacred order of Kāshī is told in two Purānas, in slightly different versions. In the *Matsya Purāna,* young Harikesha *yaksha* was a devotee of Lord Shiva. His father, Pūrnabhadra, scorned Harikesha for not behaving like a real *yaksha. Yakshas* were supposed to be fierce flesh-eaters, not lovers of the Lord. Thus rejected by his own people, Harikesha repaired to the Forest of Bliss to pursue a life of ascetic devotion to Shiva. After years of severe ascetic practice, Harikesha was blessed by Shiva and made the chief of all his *ganas*—Ganeshvara.[71]

The *Kāshī Khanda* version of this story comes from a later time in the city's mythic history. In the *Kāshī Khanda,* yakshas are not portrayed as fierce deities who receive flesh offerings, but are portrayed as Shiva's attendants. Their incorporation into the entourage of Shiva is already complete, so the story has a different tone and emphasis: The child Harikesha was born to Pūrnabhadra and his *yakshī* wife as a boon from Lord Shiva. As a boy, Harikesha was so filled with devotion for Shiva that he made small toy *lingas* out of mud and called all his playmates affectionately by Shiva's names. Pūrnabhadra became disgusted with his son's excess of devotion. It was inappropriate for one so young to care so little for worldly things, he thought. Seeing his father's anger, Harikesha left home and went to Vārānasī to find refuge in the city of Shiva. He grew old there, practicing austerities for many years, until he became a mere skeleton. Then Shiva and Pārvatī, pleased with his great devotion, appeared to the *yaksha* in person and made Harikesha the chief *gana* of the city. They gave him the name Dandapāni and provided him with his two helpers, Confusion and Doubt, to aid in ruling Vārānasī.[72]

These two Dandapāni stories are especially important for understanding the history of *yaksha* deities in Vārānasī. In the first story, the *yakshas* are still an independent group of deities not associated with Shiva. In fact, Harikesha's devotion to Shiva is considered by these *yakshas* to be blasphemous. Dandapāni, in the first story, is the *yaksha* who is "out of character," and who is raised into the family of Shiva by virtue of his great devotion. In the second story, the *yakshas* are already Shiva's devotees, and it was only Harikesha's excessive devotion to religious practices as a child, before passing into the householder stage of life, that roused his father's disapproval. Here Pūrnabhadra *yaksha* is hardly the fierce flesh-eater, but the upholder of the *varnāshrama dharma*. The *yakshas* have been assimilated into the sacred order of the Hindu pantheon of Kāshī, and Dandapāni has been promoted to the chief guardian of that order.

The assimilation of the *yakshas* and other folk deities, however, was never fully complete. While many such deities came into the retinue of Shiva or Vishnu or Krishna, many did not. They continued to be worshipped independently, not as functionaries or attendants of the Great Lord, but in their own right. Today in Kāshī and its environs there are a number of shrines in which just such deities are worshipped. These are, for the most part, called *bīr, bhairon,* or *barahm.* Their image is often a conical or cylindrical shape, but it is not a *linga.* It is commonly smeared with vermilion *sindūr* in worship, an honor reserved only for such folk deities or for those who have risen from their ranks. While deities of this type are worshipped all over India, some of the most important in Vārānasī are Lahurā Bīr and Daitra Bīr, both located near the Lahurā Bīr intersection; Karaman Bīr, located on the Banāras Hindu University campus; and Harasū Barahm in Bhabhua village on the outskirts of the city.[73]

The story of Dandapāni recalls that time in the history of Kāshī

The image of Lahurā Bīr: a vermilioned stone, next to which is a trident. While the trident today has been appropriated by Shiva, its most ancient association is with devīs. Here the trident is the devī *paired with this* bīr.

when the area was not primarily Shiva's Forest of Bliss, but was the domain of *yakshas* and *rākshasas, ganas* and *ganeshas, bhairavas* and *vīras,* and a multitude of *devīs.* The difficulty of distinguishing these groups from one another is notably clear in the case of Dandapāni. He is from a group of fierce meat-eating deities often called *rākshasas,* and yet he is explicitly called a *yaksha.* He is made the lord of *ganas* or Ganeshvara. And he is also referred to as a *bhairava* and shares many duties with his co-worker, Kāla Bhairava.

Brahmā and Vishnu

BRAHMĀ and Vishnu are the two great gods who join with Shiva to form the well-known triad of Hindu deities: Brahmā, the creator; Vishnu, the sustainer; and Shiva, the destroyer. Their names are all familiar in Hindu mythology, but in Hindu devotion Brahmā has no following at all. The great gods are Vishnu and Shiva, and, of course, for those who are their devotees, each of these gods contains the full power of the Godhead to create, uphold, and destroy. There are many stories told to account for the fact that Brahmā has no cult, one of them being the story of Brahmā's slander against Shiva, which occasioned Shiva's angry manifestation as Bhairava to cut off Brahmā's fifth head. In one version of the fiery *linga* story, Brahmā lies and claims to have seen the top of the *linga,* when in fact he could not find it after flying up into the sky for thousands of years.[74] It is Brahmā's braggadocio that earns him the curse of Shiva never to have a cult of his own.

Both Brahmā and Vishnu were sent as Shiva's emissaries to help him regain Vārānasī from Divodāsa. Although Brahmā failed, Vishnu finally succeeded in the mission. As was his fate elsewhere in India, Brahmā came to be of little significance in Kāshī; Vishnu gained a prominent place among the city's divine inhabitants.

BRAHMĀ

In addition to being the creator, Brahmā is also the archetype of the brahmin. His specialties are ritual and liturgy, so it is not surprising that he attempted to fault Divodāsa by means of the power of ritual. Properly performed, ritual has tremendous creative power. But when it is performed with a flaw or mistake, that power may backlash to make everything wrong. Interestingly, it is not the brahmin priest who benefits from ritual, for he is a mere technician. It is the sponsor of the ritual, and in this case that sponsor was King Divodāsa. Brahmā persuaded Divodāsa to sponsor ten *ashvamedha* sacrifices. In this way, according to legend, the most popular of bathing *ghāts* along the Ganges today got its name.[75] After the sacrifice, Brahmā is said to have established two *lingas* there at Dashāshvamedha Ghāt: Dashāshvame-dheshvara and Brahmeshvara. Both may be found there today, the former in the compound of the goddess Shītalā's temple, and the latter in its own small shrine which is flooded every year during the rainy season. By establishing these *lingas,* Brahmā honored Shiva, and then decided to stay in Kāshī forever.

There are several other *lingas* in Vārānasī that are also said to have been established by Brahmā. Two are near the confluence of the Varanā and the Ganges Rivers: the Hiranyagarbha *linga,* named for Brahmā as the "Golden Embryo" from which creation began to evolve, and the Sangameshvara *linga,* which celebrates the joining of the two rivers and is located within the precincts of the Ādi Keshava Temple.[76] Recalling our discussion of Omkāra *linga* and its mythol-ogy, we should note again that it was Brahmā whose austerities and devotion elicited the eruption of that *linga* of light in Kāshī. There, indeed, Brahmā was rewarded for his devotion by being made Brahmā, the Grandfather of the Universe.[77] Thus, while Brahmā has no living cult in Banāras, he is given his due in some of the major myths of the city. He had a hand in shaping the sacred landscape of the city, and he is included in the *mandala* of the city's gods.

VISHNU

Vishnu's association with the City of Shiva is very interesting and very complex. He has a key role, not only in the Divodāsa myth cycle, but in the rest of the city's mythology and sacred structure as well. At times the astounding claim is made that this is really Vishnu's city.

One instance of Vishnu's significance here takes us back to the beginning of time. In the beginning, it is said, Shiva and Shakti created Kāshī as the very first place in the whole universe. Then they created Vishnu and set him to work in Kāshī, where he was to practice aus-terities and to create the cosmos. It was Vishnu who dug with his discus the famous well called Manikarnikā and filled it with the per-spiration generated by his own austerities. And when Shiva granted Vishnu a boon for his labors, it was Vishnu who asked, as a boon, that Kāshī have the great powers of granting liberation that have made the city so famous.[78] We will return to his story in our discussion of Manikarnikā Ghāt.

In the myth of the pilgrimage of the gods to Kāshī, it was Vishnu who finally succeeded where the others had failed in regaining Kāshī for Shiva. As a reward, Shiva again granted Vishnu a boon. Vishnu said, "If you are pleased with me, O Shiva, then may I never be far from your feet." So Shiva granted to Vishnu a prominent place in the Vishveshvara Temple and proclaimed that all who wish to have the favor of Shiva must worship Vishnu there as well.[79]

In addition to his place in Shiva's central sanctum, Vishnu has two great temples of his own in Kāshī—Ādi Keshava and Bindu Mādhava, both of which Vishnu is said to have established when he first came to Vārānasī on his mission for Shiva.

Vishnu, seated upon the serpent called Ananta, the "Endless." He carries the auspicious symbols of the lotus and the conch as well as his two weapons, the discus and the club. Banāras folk art. Wall painting.

ĀDI KESHAVA

This is the "First Vishnu," located, they say, at the place where Vishnu, also called Keshava, first set foot when he arrived in Vārānasī. It is at the confluence of the Varanā and the Ganges Rivers on the northern border of Vārānasī. Here "Vishnu, with pure mind, proceeded to bathe with all his clothes on, washing his hands and his feet in the confluence of the Gangā and Varanā. From that day on, this *tīrtha* has been called Pādodaka ['Foot-Water'] because, in the beginning, Vishnu washed his sacred feet here."[80]

The water in which a holy person or a teacher, to say nothing of a god, washes his feet is considered sanctified water. Touching the feet of a holy one is a sign of humility and, at the same time, a great blessing. So also is touching or sipping the water sanctified by those feet. The waters of this *tīrtha* have been touched by Vishnu himself. According to the *māhātmya* of this place, "Drinking the footwater in Vishnu's Pādodaka Tīrtha, a person will never again drink at a mother's breast, and that is certain."[81] In other words, a person will be liberated from the round of birth and rebirth.

After he bathed, Vishnu established an image of himself, which he made with his own hands. This became the image of Vishnu in the Ādi Keshava Temple, a jet black four-armed image. Ādi Keshava, one of Kāshī's most peaceful temples today, sits in a grove of trees on the high bank of the Rājghāt Plateau, overlooking the two rivers.

As Vishnu moved about the environs of Ādi Keshava, he consecrated many other *tīrthas* by his presence there. There were *tīrthas* named for each of Vishnu's characteristic emblems, such as Chakra Tīrtha, named for his discus, and Shankha Tīrtha, named for his conch. There was a *tīrtha* named for Garuda, Vishnu's divine bird-mount, and one for Prahlāda, Vishnu's famous devotee. And there were *tīrthas* named for Vishnu's various *avatāras*, such as Vāmana, the "Dwarf," and Varāha, the "Boar." Many of the scores of *tīrthas* placed in this area by the *Kāshī Khanda*[82] are located in the landscape of the imagination alone. A few of them, however, such as Prahlāda Tīrtha, are known to be geographical *tīrthas* which can be located today. The point of this extensive listing of Vaishnava *tīrthas* is that Vishnu and his entire mythological retinue are securely ensconced in Kāshī.

BINDU MĀDHAVA

Vishnu's second great temple in Banāras is the place where he lives under the name of Bindu Mādhava. Of this image of Vishnu, the poet Tulsī Dās wrote:

> *You dwell on the bank of the gods' river in a choice temple,*
> *Blessed are the eyes of those men who have the sight of you!*[83]

The choice temple, which existed in the sixteenth century when Tulsī wrote, sat at the top of the Panchagangā Ghāt, one of the highest and finest temple sites along the Ganges. It is clear from Tavernier's account that this "great pagoda," as he called it, was the most impressive building along the Banāras riverfront.[84] Not long after Tavernier saw it, the temple was destroyed at the command of Aurangzeb and replaced by a mosque with towering minarets, which has dominated the riverfront from that same lofty perch ever since.

Bindu Mādhava's temple was built at the place called "Five Rivers," Panchanada or Panchagangā. According to the myth, Vishnu sent his divine bird, Garuda, as a messenger to Shiva. "Then Vishnu . . . looked all around him at Kāshī and thought to himself, 'Which is the purest place where I might dwell here, and where I might lead all my devotees to the highest heaven by means of Shiva Vishveshvara's grace?' Thinking this, Vishnu saw the pool of the Five Rivers, and he bathed there according to proper rites, and he stayed there."[85]

So it was that Vishnu settled at Panchagangā. Another story tells how he came to be called Bindu Mādhava. Mādhava is a name of Vishnu as Krishna. Bindu Mādhava is, literally, "Drop of Krishna." According to the story, there was a sage named Agni Bindu, "Fire Drop," who practiced austerities for a very long time at Panchagangā. Vishnu finally granted this sage a boon, and Agni Bindu said, "O Lord, even though you are present everywhere, stay here especially at this place of the Five Rivers for the benefit of all who desire *moksha.*" Vishnu granted the boon, pledging, "O great sage Agni Bindu, I will stay right here, teaching the way of liberation to people who are devoted to Kāshī. I will stay here as long as Kāshī exists, O sage, for even in the time of universal destruction, Kāshī is not destroyed and stands on the tip of Shiva's trident."[86]

In addition to his pledge to stay at Panchaganga forever, Vishnu gave yet another boon to the sage: this place would be known by the sage's name, Bindu, as well as by his own, Mādhava. Thus, it became Bindu Mādhava. Especially during the autumn month of Kārttika, said Vishnu, this place will be very auspicious. At that time of year, coming to the temple and bathing here in the Ganges will destroy countless sins. And lighting oil lamps here during the month of Kārttika will bring endless blessings.[87]

Today the temple that bears the name Bindu Mādhava is located in an inconspicuous building in the shadow of the great mosque of Aurangzeb. There the traditions of this site continue. During the month of Kārttika (October/November), people come for the *darshana* of Bindu Mādhava and take their morning bath at Panchaganga Ghāt. As the Purāna promises, "What fruit was obtained in the Perfect Age [*Krita Yuga*] by doing austerities for one hundred years, all that is obtained by a bath in the Five Rivers during the month of Kārttika."[88] The oil lamps, called *dīpas,* prescribed by the Purānas as a special offering to the ancestors during this month, are placed each evening in small woven baskets and hung from the tops of tall, slender bamboo poles. During this month, Panchaganga Ghāt is graced with a multitude of these hanging lamps which, along with the hundreds of lighted wicks held in its great stone lamp-stand, brighten the way for the deceased.

BAKARIĀ KUND

There is other striking evidence of Vishnu's presence and prominence in Kāshī: the intriguing site of Bakariā Kund in northern Banāras. There, in a plot of ruins which has become a Muslim graveyard, the huge Gupta period image of Krishna lifting Mt. Govardhana was unearthed (page 67). The image is larger than life-size, and the temple that would have housed it must have been very impressive. Such a temple could well have been supported by the massive stone breast-work that still stands on the west side of Bakariā Kund. A mosque sits on this extensive foundation today.

When M. A. Sherring examined this site long before the image of Krishna had been discovered, he found elevated mounds and great foundation stones on the north and east sides of the *kund* as well. Among the stones on the eastern side was a segment of the circular fluted *āmalaka,* which is the ring-stone supporting the spherical *kalasha* at the top of the temple spire. That ring-stone was nine feet in diameter.[89] As Sherring emphasizes, it "must have belonged to a temple of superior strength and dimensions." The large foundations, the enormous capping stone of the spire, and the great image of Krishna all indicate that here there was a temple, and possibly a whole complex of temples, of very impressive size.

At the time Sherring studied the ruins of Bakariā Kund, he found a number of buildings in the immediate vicinity in which the stones, columns, and other structural elements of the ruined temples had been used, and he found one ancient building that was virtually intact, although it had been capped by a Muslim dome. On the basis of this architectural evidence, Sherring concluded that some of the buildings around Bakariā Kund were once part of an extensive Buddhist monastic and temple complex.[90] This certainly seems likely, recalling that, in the seventh century, Hiuen Tsiang reported that there were some thirty monasteries in the Vārānasī area.

While there is no reason to doubt that this may have been a Buddhist site, we must add a note of caution, for Sherring attributed a Buddhist origin to a great many of the ruined structures of Banāras on the basis of little but speculation. And, of course, the discovery of the great Krishna image here makes it clear that Bakariā Kund was also a prominent Vaishnava site. It is not unusual to find the two traditions together, for in the early centuries A.D. both Vaishnava and Buddhist theism grew up together and flourished in the common milieu of the area around Mathurā, some three hundred miles northwest of Kāshī. In addition to being an important Buddhist center, Mathurā was the birthplace of Krishna and became known as one of the seven sacred cities of the Hindu tradition. Of these seven cities, all present in the *mandala* of Kāshī, the Bakariā Kund area is well known to be the site of Mathurā-in-Kāshī.[91]

THE CITY OF VISHNU

The prominence of Vishnu in Kāshī, which is strongly suggested by the great temple sites of Ādi Keshava, Bindu Mādhava, and Bakariā Kund, is also supported by the Purānic and popular mythology of Kāshī. Occasionally, in my interviews in Banāras temples or along the *ghāts*, I would find a brahmin or a temple *pūjārī* who would volunteer the view that Kāshī was originally the city of Vishnu, or that Vishnu and Shiva share it equally. Along these lines, the temple *pūjārī* at Ādi Keshava told me his brief but revealing version of the story of Divodāsa:

Long ago, Divodāsa was King of Kāshī, and he practiced great austerities. Shiva granted him a boon, and the King chose to have Kāshī for his boon. All the gods had to leave Kāshī, and Shiva also left to live on Mt. Mandara. Pilgrims did not come to Kāshī for a long time, because then it was man's city, and not god's city. Finally, Vishnu came here and instructed the King. He told him that this city really belonged to Shiva, and he persuaded the King to leave. Divodāsa left Kāshī and went to the South. Shiva was very pleased to have his city back, and he told Vishnu that the city would now belong to both of them. It was really Vishnu who gave the city back to Shiva.

It is noteworthy that, at least in the *Kashi Khanda*, the way Vishnu captured the city of Vārānasī was by masquerading as a Buddhist. He corrupted the people by engendering a disregard for Hindu *dharma*, and he evicted the King by engendering a dispassion for the world. There are many ways, of course, in which Buddhist and Vaishnava symbolism, theology, and history overlap and merge. The common emblems and bodily markings of the Buddha and Vishnu distinguish them as the divine "great men" *(mahāpurushas)*. The notion of the divine descents *(avatāras)* is shared by both Buddhists and Vaishnavas. What the two traditions did not share was the Hindu notion of the "gods" and the Hindu notion of the *varnāshrama dharma*. The Buddhists, like the good King Divodāsa, sent the gods back to heaven where they belonged. And the Buddhist teachings, like those that corrupted the people of Divodāsa's kingdom, were contrary to Hindu caste *dharma*. Ultimately, the Vaishnava tradition incorporated the Buddha by considering him an *avatāra* of Vishnu, but in almost all the

stories of the Buddha *avatāra*, Vishnu takes the Buddhist form as a ruse
to bring about the downfall of a kingdom or a demon and to restore the
proper position of the gods. In the Divodāsa story, Vishnu takes the
form of a Buddhist so that he can retrieve the city from the pious, but
godless, King and deliver it over to Shiva and the gods.

The *pūjārī* at Ādi Keshava has a point: it was really Vishnu who
won Kāshī back. And even though the *Kāshī Khanda* tends to see
Vishnu as a mere servant of Shiva, there are other Purānic *māhātmyas*
that emphasize Vishnu's priority, or at least equality, in Kāshī. In the
Nārada Purāna, for example, we hear of the "Vaishnava city of Kāshī."
And it is said that, although Shiva lives in Kāshī, he originally begged
his dwelling place from Vishnu.[92] After all, even when Shiva was
wandering with the skull, Vishnu was the one who told him to go to
Vārānasī. The intimate connection of Vishnu and Kāshī is most clearly
stated in those passages where Kāshī is called the very embodiment
(svarūpa) of Vishnu: "Vishnu dwells partially in other cities, but he
dwells fully in Kāshī. Kāshī is the very embodiment of Vishnu, where
he himself shines forth."[93]

Most often, however, it is the balanced equality of Vishnu and Shiva
in Kāshī that late Purānic authors are eager to stress. The trans-sectarian and eclectic spirit that pervades some of the later *māhātmyas* has
certainly shaped the image of Kāshī as a pilgrimage place. Of course,
pilgrims readily identify Kāshī as the City of Shiva Vishvanātha. But
they do not come to Kāshī as sectarian Shaivas. Both Vaishnavas and
Shaivas come to Kāshī, and Shāktas as well. They come to Kāshī
because it is Kāshī, and it is famous in its own right. There is no room
for narrow sectarianism in such a *tīrtha.* It is a place which Shiva shares
not only with Vishnu, but with the entire *mandala* of the gods.

5

THE RIVER GANGES
AND THE
GREAT GHATS

I am Vishvanātha, the Lord.
Kāshī is the light of liberation.
The waves of the River of Heaven are the wine of immortality.
What can these three not provide?[1]

THE GANGES is called the River of Heaven, flowing across the sky, white as the Milky Way. Long ago, she agreed to flow upon the earth as well. In her great mercy, she came to the aid of a king named Bhagīratha, who appealed to Lord Brahmā to let the Ganges fall from heaven.[2] Bhagīratha's ancestors, sixty thousand of them, had been burned to ash by the fierce glance of an angry ascetic, and only the funerary waters of the Ganges would raise them up again to dwell in peace in heaven. Having won from Brahmā the boon of her descent, Bhagīratha persuaded Shiva to catch the Ganges in his hair as she fell, so that the earth would not be shattered by her torrential force. And so she plummeted down from heaven to the Himālayas, where she meandered in the tangled ascetic locks of Shiva before flowing out upon the plains of India. The Ganges followed Bhagīratha from the Himālayas to the sea where, at the place called Gangā Sāgara, she entered the netherworld and restored the dead ancestors of Bhagīratha. Thus she is called the Triple-Pathed River, flowing in the three worlds—in heaven, on the earth, and in the netherworld.

Kāshī's mythological tradition remembers the time before the Ganges came and tells the story of Bhagīratha's arrival. He came across the plains, they say, leading the Ganges behind him. And when the great *tīrthas* of Kāshī, such as Dashāshvamedha and Manikarnikā, were skirted by the River of Heaven, they became infinitely more powerful and lustrous than before.[3] Even today, a Banārsī, speaking of ancient Kāshī, will refer to the time before the Ganges came, or in discussing the antiquity of a temple or pool, a priest will say, "It was here even before Bhagīratha brought the Ganges to earth."

The multiplication of *tīrthas* in a single place, adding power to power, is well known in Hindu sacred geography. If one river is excellent for bathing, then better still is the confluence of two rivers as at Ādi Keshava, or five rivers as at Panchagangā. So it is with this great triumvirate of holiness: the city of Kāshī, the Lord Shiva Vishveshvara, and the River Ganges. The three together are the triple blessing found nowhere else on earth:

> *This we know for certain: Where the River of Heaven*
> *Flows in the Forest of Bliss of Shiva,*
> *There is moksha guaranteed!*[4]

Archetype of Sacred Waters

A L O N G her entire course the Ganges is sacred: from her source at Gangotrī, high in the Himālayas; to Hardvār, also known as Gangādvāra, "Gate of the Ganges," where she breaks out of the mountains and into the plains; to Prayāga, where she joins the Yamunā River and the mythical Sarasvatī River; to Kāshī, where she makes a long sweep to the north as if pointing toward her Himālayan source; and, finally, to Gangā Sāgara, where the river meets the sea in the Bay of Bengāl.

The Ganges is revered as goddess and mother.* All along the river, and especially at the great *tīrthas,* Hindus bathe in the Ganges. They take up her water cupped in their hands and pour it back into the river as an offering to ancestors and the gods.[5] They present to the river, as to a deity, offerings of flowers and small clay oilwick lamps. On great festival occasions Hindus ford the river in boats, shouting "Gangā Mātā ki Jai!" ("Victory to Mother Gangā!") and trailing garlands of flowers hundreds of feet long to adorn this goddess river. They return to their homes, perhaps many miles away, carrying brass vessels of her

---

* The proper name for the Ganges is the Gangā, a name used for both the river and the goddess. Here we will occasionally retain this name in speaking of the goddess.

Offering the waters of the Ganges to the ancestors.

water. And they will come that distance again to bring the ashes of their dead to her care.

It is said that when the Ganges fell from heaven, she split into several streams. One account speaks of four streams, watering the four quarters of the earth.[6] Another speaks of seven streams, three flowing to the east, three to the west, and the Bhāgīrathī, India's Ganges named for the king who brought her to earth, to the south.[7] In short, the Ganges waters the entire earth with the springs of heaven.

As early as the *Rig Veda,* India's seven divine mother-rivers, flowing with nectar from heaven, are mentioned: the Sindhu (Indus), the Sarasvatī, and the "Five-Rivers" of the Punjab. Later on, as the Aryans moved farther south, the Ganges is mentioned among the great rivers.[8] By the time of the Purānas, the seven sacred rivers are no longer concentrated in the northwest, but extend throughout India: the ancient Sindhu and Sarasvatī, the Ganges and the Yamunā in the North, the Narmadā and Godāvarī in Central India, and the Kāverī farther south. Sometimes the seven are called the Seven Gangās.

Just as Kāshī is the archetype of the *tīrtha,* to which others are compared in sanctity, so is the Ganges the archetype of sacred waters. Other rivers are said to be like the Ganges. Others are said even to *be* the Ganges. The Kāverī River in Tamilnādu is known as the Ganges of the South, and the Godāvarī River is said to be the Ganges diverted into Central India by the sage Gautama.

The land where the Ganges does not flow is likened in one hymn to the sky without the sun, a home without a lamp, a brahmin without the Vedas.[9] Significantly, the Ganges is seen to flow in many lands, not only through the plains of North India, but symbolically in the sacred waters of all India. For example, a Tamil woman, unable to go to the Ganges, might go to the Kāverī River. If even that is too far, she might go to a nearby stream or temple tank. In her home, the Ganges is regularly called to be present in all the waters used in ritual, either by mixing those waters with a few drops of Ganges water or by uttering the name and prayers of the Ganges to invoke her presence. The Ganges is the essence and the source of all sacred waters. So widely is her presence perceived that an Indian visiting professor, having arrived in Boston, is said to have exclaimed on first sight of the Charles, "Ah! So the Ganges is here in Cambridge too!"

Not only is the Ganges said to be present in other rivers, but other rivers are present in her. A modern Hindu author writes, "When a pilgrim dives into the sacred waters of the Ganges, he feels the thrill of plunging into the waters of all the rivers of India."[10] This one river concentrates the sanctity of all India's sacred rivers. Each wave of the Ganges, they say, is a *tīrtha*.

The Ganges is important in both its particular and symbolic existence. However, its symbolic significance as a prototype of all sacred waters does not at all diffuse the significance of bathing in the Ganges itself. For Hindu pilgrims nothing can compare with bathing in the Ganges, especially at a great *tīrtha* such as Kāshī. There are few things on which Hindu India, diverse as it is, might agree. But of the Ganges, India speaks with one voice. The Ganges carries an immense cultural and religious meaning for Hindus of every region and every sectarian persuasion. Even Jawaharlal Nehru, as Westernized and avowedly secular as he was, expressed the deep desire to have a handful of his ashes thrown into the Ganges when he died. He said, "The Gangā, especially, is the river of India, beloved of her people, round which are intertwined her racial memories, her hopes and fears, her songs of triumph, her victories and her defeats. She has been a symbol of India's age-long culture and civilization, ever-changing, ever-flowing, and yet ever the same Gangā."[11]

The Salvation of the Dead

THE ANCESTORS of Bhagīratha, burned to ashes, needed the waters of the Ganges for their *shrāddha* funeral rites, which would enable them to reach Pitriloka, the World of the Ancestors, and then make a smooth transition to another life. Without such rites the dead would not only continue to exist in a limbo of suffering, but would be troublesome spirits to those living still on earth. The waters of the Ganges are called *amrita,* the "nectar of immortality," and as they brought life to the ancestors of Bhagīratha, so will they bring life to all the dead.

Those who die in Kāshī, assured of liberation, will be cremated on the banks of the River of Heaven at this most sacred of *tīrthas.* If one cannot die in Kāshī, then cremation by the Ganges anywhere along her banks is desirable. If even this is impossible, then relatives might later bring the ashes of the deceased to the Ganges at Kāshī, or even send them to Kashī parcel post. And if the ashes have been dispersed elsewhere, a relative might come to Kāshī to perform the yearly *shrāddha* rites, preferably during the "fortnight of the ancestors" *(pitripaksha)* set aside during the autumn month of Āshvina (September–October) for remembering the dead.

Pilgrimage to Kāshī, whether in this special fortnight or at some other time, will invariably include rites for the dead. This may be either the *shrāddha* rites, performed immediately after the death and on particular occasions during the year, or the *pinda pradāna,* a more abbreviated rite that may be performed at any time. In both rites, balls of rice or other grains, called *pindas,* are offered to the ancestors while the litany of their names is recited. In addition, of course, the ordinary rite of bathing in the Ganges will usually include simple water libations with which this nectar of immortality is offered to the departed ancestors. The *Kāshī Khanda's māhātmya* of the Ganges lists the many great benefits that accrue to the dead when a descendant bathes in the

Ganges and makes proper offerings on their behalf. The ancestors
attain the bliss of heaven by virtue of these rites and, it is said, they
dwell in heaven for a thousand years for every single sesame seed in
the traditional *pinda* offerings.[12] Indeed, the ancestors are said to sing
for joy when they see someone in their family bathing in the Ganges
and offering *pindas* on her bank.[13]

An often-quoted verse of the *Mahābhārata* promises, "If only the
bone of a person should touch the water of the Ganges, that person
shall dwell, honored, in heaven."[14] The dramatic story of Vāhīka in
the *Kāshī Khanda* bears this out.[15] Vāhīka, they say, was an utterly
unrefined and despicable character. He was addicted to gambling; he
had killed a cow; he had even kicked his own mother. One day Vāhīka
was killed by a tiger in the forest and his soul was brought promptly
before the Lord of Death, Yama, for judgment. His sins were read off
by Chitragupta, Yama's scribe, and not a single virtue was found to
balance them. He was condemned to hell. In the meantime, Vāhīka's
body was torn up by vultures, and one vulture flew off with his footbone. In flight, it fought with another vulture over the morsel and the
footbone was dropped. It fell, by chance, into the Ganges below, and
just as Vāhīka was being sent off to hell, a divine chariot arrived to take
him, fortunate and blessed, to heaven. As Mother Ganges, the river is
ever the dispenser of grace. No child is too dirty, they say, to be
embraced by its mother.

The Purification of the Living

ACCORDING TO Hindus, the waters of the Ganges are pure and
cleansing waters. Indian skeptics and Western visitors alike have been
astounded by this claim. Surveying the river at Banāras, brown and
muddy in the rainy season and the receptacle of the pollution of the
city, the ashes of the dead, and the diseases of its million bathers, they
see a very dirty river indeed.

At question here, of course, is not really the purity of the Ganges,
but the cultural understanding of what it means for something to be
pure or impure, clean or dirty. In *Purity and Danger,* the British
anthropologist Mary Douglas has exposed the many ways in which
these terms are cultural constructs.[16] "Dirt" is disorder, "matter out of

place," and what is considered out of place depends upon one's notion of order. The bacterial understanding of "purity" which is part of the scientific view of order, may contrast markedly with social and religious understandings of "purity," even in the modern cultures of the West. Quite apart from the issue of whether the Ganges is bacterially pure (and there are countless studies supporting both sides on this matter!) is the issue of its ritual purity and its symbolic purity. Hindus have affirmed for centuries that there is nothing quite as cleansing as the living waters of the River of Heaven.

Ritual purification by water is one of the great themes running through the history of Indian religious life. Even the pre-Aryan Indus civilization was a river culture, and the large ceremonial tank excavated in the ruins of Mohenjo Dāro suggests the significance of cleansing waters in the ritual life of its people. Later on, the Vedic hymns of the Aryan people praise the great rivers of Northwest India as purifying goddesses.

Running water especially is an agent of purification, for it both absorbs pollution and carries it away. The traditional etymology of the word "Gangā" is from the root *gam*, "to go." The Ganges is the "Swift-Goer," and her hymns constantly emphasize the running, flowing, energetic movement of her waters, which are living waters. So great is the power of the Ganges to destroy sins that, it is said, even a droplet of Ganges water carried one's way by the breeze will erase the sins of many lifetimes in an instant.[17]

One of the most powerful and beloved eulogies of the River Ganges is the *Gangā Laharī*, "The Waves of the Ganges." Its author, the seventeenth-century poet Jagannātha, was patronized by the Mughal Emperor Shāh Jahān and his son the scholarly prince, Dārā Shikoh. According to legend, the poet was expelled from his brahmin caste for a love affair with a Muslim woman at court. Jagannātha went to Banāras to try to restore his status by proving himself acceptable to the brahmins there. Unsuccessful, he called upon the Ganges herself to purify and claim him. As the story goes, the poet sat with his beloved atop the fifty-two steps of the great Panchagangā Ghāt and, with each of the fifty-two verses of the hymn he composed there, the river rose one step. Finally, the waters touched the very feet of the lovers, purified them, and carried them away.[18]

In his hymn, the poet addresses the river as mother, comforter, and supporter:

> *I come to you as a child to his mother.*
> *I come as an orphan to you, moist with love.*
> *I come without refuge to you, giver of sacred rest.*
> *I come a fallen man to you, uplifter of all.*
> *I come undone by disease to you, the perfect physician.*
> *I come, my heart dry with thirst, to you, ocean of sweet wine.*
> *Do with me whatever you will.* [19]

The poet portrays himself as the worst of sinners, rejected even by outcastes, even by madmen, and he challenges the Ganges to purify the likes of him. There are plenty of gods who will care for the good, he tells her. But who will care for the wicked, if not the Ganges. The goddess will take on the emblems of Shiva and fight for the salvation of the sinner:

> *Now bind on your strong and lovely girdle of battle,*
> *And anchor the new moon in your crown with ropes of snakes.*
> *Do not take me lightly, thinking me an ordinary sinner.*
> *Behold, O River of Heaven,*
> *This is the hour of Jagannātha's salvation!* [20]

Liquid Shakti

S H A K T I means "power" or "energy." As the female life-energy of Shiva, Shakti is his consort and his enabling power in the world. Here that power runs as a river.

The energy of the Ganges is tremendous as the river rushes out of the mountains at Hardvār, the current so swift that pilgrims must hold on to chains fastened in the concrete embankment when they bathe. The creative power of the river is vast, fertilizing and bringing to life the entire Ganges basin, which today supports some 300 million people. Although the river restlessly changes course and frequently floods in the rainy season, she is invariably thought of as a mother, "Gangā Mātā," and her hymns contain not the slightest suggestion of her destructive power. Even those who have lived along her banks and experienced the river's ravages as well as her blessings have not ascribed to the Ganges the wrathful aspect that so frequently attends India's other goddesses. While she may arm herself for battle, she

[handwritten annotation: if this mother concept is so powerful it lets them rationalize floods and destruction, why not pollution — not a leap]

takes up weapons only to defend and protect her children. It is sometimes said that even the floods of the Ganges are counted as blessings
by those whose fields and homes are inundated.

As a goddess, Gangā is perhaps the only deity claimed as consort by
all three of the great gods of Hinduism. She travels as Brahmā's com-
panion in his brass water pot. She is also said to flow originally from
the foot of Vishnu in the highest heaven and is associated with both
Lakshmī and Sarasvatī as one of Vishnu's wives. It is Shiva, however,
whose relationship with Gangā is most intimate. Having caught the
river as she fell to earth, he tamed her in the tangles of his hair before
releasing her to flow out smoothly upon the earth. She is referred to as
the co-wife of Pārvatī, and Pārvatī is often jealous of the goddess
Gangā's close contact with Shiva.[21]

The Ganges is seen as the active energy through which the lofty and
indescribable Supreme Shiva is present and moving in the world.
While the supreme face of the Transcendent cannot be seen and
described, Shakti can indeed be seen, and praised, and loved. She can
even be touched and sipped in this, her liquid form. Skanda explains it
to Agastya in the "Gangā Māhātmya" of the *Kāshī Khanda:*

O Agastya, One should not be amazed at the notion that this Ganges is
really Power, for is she not the Supreme Shakti of the Eternal Shiva, taken
the form of water?

This Ganges, filled with the sweet wine of compassion, was sent out for
the salvation of the world by Shiva, the Lord of Lords.

Good people should not think this Triple-Pathed River to be like the
thousand other earthly rivers, filled with water.[22]

The Ganges is the liquid essence of the scriptures, the gods, and the
wisdom of the Hindu tradition. She is the liquid essence, in sum, of
Shakti—the energy and power of the Supreme, flowing in the life of
the world. Because she is already overflowing with the sacred, there is
no need for the usual rites of invitation *(āvāhana)* and dismissal *(visarjana)* which invite the gods to be present at the beginning of worship and give them their leave to go at the end.[23] The Ganges is every
drop a goddess, just as she is.

The wakefulness and saving energy of the Ganges are especially
important, they say, in this Kali Age, the Age of Strife. Now the gods

are distant from the earth, and the Ganges alone is here to provide relief from sins and hope for liberation. It is said, for example, that in the Perfect Age, the Krita Yuga, meditation was the way to liberation. In the Third Age, Tretā Yuga, austerity was the way to liberation. In the Second Age, Dvāpara Yuga, meditation, austerity, and sacrifice were viable paths. But now, in this Kali Yuga, only the Ganges can bring the blessing of liberation.[24]

The Panchatīrthī Pilgrimage

There, O Prince, is the very excellent "Five Tīrthas," the Panchatīrthī, having bathed in which a person shall never again be born.

First is the Asi confluence, the foremost and supreme of *tīrthas*. Then there is Dashāshvamedha, honored by all the *tīrthas*. Next comes the "Foot Water" *tīrtha* at Ādi Keshava. Then there is the holy "Five Rivers" of Panchanada, which destroys one's sins by simply bathing there. Beyond these four *tīrthas* is the fifth, O excellent one. It is called Manikarnikā, which bestows purity on the mind and senses.

Having bathed in the five *tīrthas* a person never again receives a body of five-elements. Rather, he becomes the five-faced Shiva in Kāshī.[25]

The Panchatīrthī pilgrimage to the "Five *Tīrthas*" along the riverfront is one of the most popular in Kāshī. Along this route, pilgrims travel the entire length of the city by the banks of the Ganges. Some pilgrims make the journey by boat, but as is the case with all pilgrimages, it is better to practice the *tapas* of walking. Beginning at the southern end of the city where the Asi River meets the Ganges, the Panchatīrthī pilgrims walk to Dashāshvamedha Ghāt, and from there all the way to the northern end of the city where the Varanā River flows into the Ganges. Then, retracing their steps, they stop at Panchagangā Ghāt and, finally, at the pre-eminently sacred Manikarnikā Ghāt. At each stop, they bathe in the Ganges and have the *darshana* of the most prominent deities. Having taken a final ritual bath at Manikarnikā, they proceed to the heart of the city for the *darshana* of Vishvanātha, Annapūrnā, and the "Witnessing Ganesha," Sākshī Vināyaka, who vouches for the completion of their pilgrimage.

At each stage of the journey, the pilgrims make a statement of intention called *sankalpa,* the explicit profession of intent to worship that accompanies every important ritual act. Learned brahmin pilgrims may recite the *sankalpa* for themselves, but ordinary pilgrims hear the words of their *sankalpa* from the *pandā,* the pilgrim-priest whom they employ. Cupping the right hand over the left and holding some grains of rice, perhaps some betel nut, some Ganges water, and a few coins, they listen to the words as they are recited: "I, of this family and this village, am here in Kāshī in this year, in this month, on this day, in this place, making the pilgrimage to the Five *Tīrthas.*" If the pilgrim is journeying in fulfillment of some vow or in the hope of some particular end, that end will be stated. This is a *sakāma* pilgrimage, made "with desires" in mind: to bear a son, to live a long time, to recover from disease. Often, however, pilgrimage is made "without desires," *nishkāma,* without any specific personal goal in mind. It is done, in the traditional words of the *sankalpa,* "to please Shiva Vishvanātha." As a devout housewife explained, "Rewards are in accordance with our good deeds and actions. We should just do these things, like the Pan-chatīrthī pilgrimage, and good will naturally result."

This grouping of five *tīrthas* is mentioned in the "Avimukta Māhātmya" of the *Matsya Purāna,* one of the earliest *māhātmyas* of Kāshī and one which does not mention many specific sites. In its closing verses, the five places are listed: Dashāshvamedha, Lolārka, Keshava, Bindu Mādhava, and Manikarnikā.[26] Lolārka is the oldest of the Asi Ghāt *tīrthas,* Keshava is the temple Ādi Keshava at the Varanā confluence, and Bindu Mādhava is the temple at Panchagangā.

Sometimes only two or three great river *tīrthas* are mentioned as the most prominent in Kāshī. In the *Kāshī Khanda,* for example, the city is compared to a woman "whose two eyes are Lolārka and Keshava, whose two arms are the Varanā and the Asi."[27] The *Vāmana Purāna* describes Shiva's own pilgrimage to Vārānasī to expunge the sin of killing a brahmin, and says that he visited three places—Lolārka, Dashāshvamedha, and Keshava—before coming to the tank "Where the Skull Fell."[28] Whether two, three, or five, the same point is made: the holy territory is stretched out along the Ganges from Asi to Varanā, or from Lolārka to Keshava, and it includes all the *tīrthas* in between.

Each of the great *tīrthas* of the Panchatīrthī also marks a confluence of some stream or rivulet with the Ganges, although at Dashāshva-medha, Manikarnikā, and Panchagangā the stream beds are no longer water bearing.

Asi

THE PANCHATĪRTHĪ pilgrimage begins at Asi Ghāt, where the pilgrims bathe in the confluence of the Asi and the Ganges Rivers. Asi is the only one of the major bathing *ghāts* of the city that is still a clay bank *(kachcha)* without the great concrete steps that descend into the river at the finished *(pakka) ghāts* along most of the riverfront.* The slippery clay bank of Asi Ghāt reminds us that the great stone and concrete *ghāts* of the Banāras riverfront are an innovation of the last three centuries, built primarily by Marāthā patronage in the eighteenth and nineteenth centuries. Throughout most of its history, the entire riverfront was similar to what we see at Asi.

Despite its slippery bank, Asi is one of the busiest of *ghāts,* attracting morning bathers from the entire southern end of the city. Asi is significant as the southernmost bathing *ghāt* in the sacred zone. Fields stretch out beyond it to the south. After bathing in the Ganges here, the Panchatīrthī pilgrims are directed to visit the Shiva *linga* at Asi *sangam,* Asisangameshvara, the "Lord of the Confluence at Asi." Located a few steps into the lane at the head of the *ghāt,* this is a small, well-kept temple, marked with a marble plaque establishing the Purānic heritage of the site with some verses from the *Kāshī Khanda.* There the pilgrims might read: "All the other *tīrthas* that girdle the earth are not equal to a sixteenth part of the *tīrtha* at Asi *sangam.*"[29]

The *linga* most revered at Asi, however, is the big open-air *linga* located under a *pīpal* tree right on the muddy bank of the *ghāt* itself. This *linga,* with its ranks of smaller *lingas* nearby, is the focal point of worship at Asi, receiving the flower and water offerings of a constant procession of morning bathers. This is, in the popular eye, the real "Lord of the Confluence at Asi."

According to the traditional guidebooks, the pilgrims' worship at Asi should also include a visit to nearby Lolārka Kund. This is located above Tulsī Ghāt, formerly Lolārka Ghāt, just north of Asi and now

---

* The words *kachcha* and *pakka* are opposites, *kachcha* meaning "raw, unripe, crude, unfinished, etc.," and *pakka* meaning "cooked, ripe, well-made, finished, etc."

named for the poet-saint Tulsī Dās, whose house and temple still stand at the head of the *ghāt* steps. Lolārka, as we have seen in discussing the Suns of Kāshī, is the "Trembling Sun," and is one of the most ancient sacred sites in Kāshī. Some listings of the great river *tīrthas* even give Lolārka the place now occupied by Asi as the primary sacred center of southern Vārānasī.[30] Indeed, the verses that praise Asi in the *Kāshī Khanda* seem to confirm this, for they are set in the context of the larger Lolārka *māhātmya*. While they are in the Lolārka area, the pilgrims are also advised to visit Arka Vināyaka, one of the fifty-six Ganeshas, who sits overlooking the Ganges here.

Asi to Dashāshvamedha

A s t h e pilgrims walk down the river from Asi and Tulsī Ghāts, they pass the ashram of the contemporary woman saint, Ānandamayī Mā, and then the seventeenth-century palace of the Maharaja Chet Singh, which occupies the riverfront *ghāt* known as Shivālā. Next is Hanumān Ghāt, known to these pilgrims as the birthplace of the great devotional teacher Vallabha, who lived in the late fifteenth and early sixteenth centuries and laid the philosophical foundations for a great resurgence of Krishna *bhakti*. As for its temples, this *ghāt* is known not only for its namesake, Rāma's monkey servant, Hanumān, but also for its image of Rūrū "The Dog" Bhairava, one of the eight Banāras Bhairavas who assist Kāla Bhairava. In this Hanumān Ghāt area today lives a substantial South India community, which has constructed an elaborate new temple in the South Indian style.

The next *ghāt* is Harishchandra Ghāt, named for a legendary king, the truthful Harishchandra, who once worked the cremation grounds in Kāshī. Every one of the pilgrims on the Panchatīrthī pilgrimage knows the story of how the brahmin Vishvāmitra asked King Harishchandra for a ritual fee called the *rājasūya dakshinā*. Harishchandra, in his generosity, gave Vishvāmitra his entire kingdom and all he owned. Having accepted, Vishvāmitra still pressed the King for the token *rājasūya dakshinā,* but Harishchandra had nothing left to give. Rather than break his promise, the King came destitute to Kāshī, where he sold his wife and son into slavery and sold himself into bondage to work the cremation grounds in order to pay the fee. He did not see his loved ones again until the day his wife, worn with hardship, came to the cremation ground carrying her son's body. He had died of snake bite, and she had not even a blanket to cover his corpse. The testing of Harishchandra, like that of the biblical Job, proved the strength of his character, even in the worst of times. In the end, the gods rewarded him and restored his throne and his son to him.[31]

Harishchandra Ghāt is one of the two burning *ghāts* of Banāras, the

The great steps of Chaumsathī Ghāt, above which sits the temple of the Sixty-Four Yoginīs.

other being Manikarnikā. People in this part of the city believe that Harishchandra is the oldest Kāshī cremation ground, surpassing even Manikarnikā in its sanctity. It is sometimes referred to as Ādi Manikarnikā, the "Original Manikarnikā."[32] The brahmins of Tulsī Ghāt and the pandits of Asi will definitely choose to be cremated here.

The next major *ghāt* is Kedāra, the anchor of Kedāra Khanda and the home of the Kedāreshvara *linga*. Like Asi, this is a busy *ghāt*, but the Panchatīrthī pilgrims do not stop here to bathe. Continuing down

the river, they pass Chaukī Ghāt, famous for the huge tree at the top of the steps which shelters a great array of stone *nāgas,* the aquatic serpent deities for which ancient Kāshī, with its streams and pools, must have been famous (page 265). Along with Nāga Kūpa, today called Nāg Kuan, in northern Kāshī, this is a place where the *nāgas* are still honored, especially on the festival day of Nāga Panchamī in the rainy season month of Shrāvana (July/August).

Next the pilgrims walk a quiet section of the riverfront, given over to the laundry work of the *dhobīs,* rhythmically slapping wet clothes on their stone wash slabs. The part of the city they are skirting now is called Bengālī Tolā, settled by Bengālīs, many of whom have come here for Kāshīvāsa, living out one's days in Kāshī until death. Along the riverfront here are Mānasarovara Ghāt, named after the holy lake Mānasa in the Himālayas; Nārada Ghāt, named for the divine sage; Amareshvara Temple, named for Lord Amarnāth in the Kashmīr Himālayas; and, finally, Chaumsathī Ghāt, named for the Sixty-Four Goddesses whose temple is in the city above the *ghāt.*

Dashāshvamedha Ghāt

THE PILGRIMS now reach the second of the five *tīrthas,* Dashāshvamedha, the most popular *ghāt* along the Ganges, drawing large crowds of bathers each morning at dawn. It is the bustling hub of the pilgrim business along the riverfront. Rows of pilgrim-priests, variously called *pandās, ghātiās,* or *tīrtha purohitas,* sit on their low wooden *chaukīs* under bamboo umbrellas, eager to minister to the priestly and practical needs of pilgrims. They tend the clothing and effects of the bathers, utter the words of the *sankalpa,* accept the ritual gifts *(dāna)* of the pilgrims, as well as the traditional fee *(dakshinā)* for their sanctioning services as brahmins. Pilgrims still offer the traditional "gift of a cow" *(godāna)* to brahmins, but today the cow has become a reasonable two or three rupees. When all is completed, these pilgrim-priests daub the bather's forehead with a bright spot of *tilaka.* Here at Dashāshvamedha the Panchatīrthī pilgrims will bathe in the Ganges for a second time.

We have discussed Dashāshvamedha in the context of the Divodāsa myth cycle, for it was here that Lord Brahmā performed the "ten

ashvamedha" sacrifices, the requisites for which were flawlessly sup-
plied by King Divodāsa. The historian Jayaswal suggests, however,
that the name Dashāshvamedha refers, rather, to the "ten *ashvamedha"*
sacrifices said to have been performed here by the revivalist Hindu
dynasty of the second century, the Bhāra Shiva Nāgas.[33] Whatever the
source of its name, the *ghāt* has long been said to confer the lavish
benefits of ten *ashvamedhas* upon all who bathe here.

There are two adjacent *ghāts* that today bear the name Dashāshvamedha. The main road leading from Godauliā crossing to the river
forks to either side of the Dashāshvamedha market, one of the city's
largest produce markets. The two forks reach the river a short distance
apart and turn into long stairways, broadening out as the steps descend
into the river.

The road that approaches the river from Godauliā is a recent im-
provement, little more than a century old. The easy access it affords to
Dashāshvamedha Ghāt is unquestionably an important reason for the
ghāt's popularity today. The pilgrimage buses, which have become a
common way for pilgrims to travel, may park with ease near the
Dashāshvamedha market. Pilgrims may conveniently walk the short
distance to the river and then make a circuit into the city for the
darshana of Vishvanātha before returning to their buses. The prestige
of Dashāshvamedha has grown accordingly.

Before the road was built, however, its course from Godauliā crossing and around the south side of the Dashāshvamedha market was
actually the course of a stream, which provided the drainage for one of
Vārānasī's inland lakes, the Beniā Tālāb. The stream existed all year
round, but it was in full flood during the rainy season. Its former
course is still very vulnerable to floods, and during a flood year one
may still see boats plying the street along the old stream bed. It was
called the Godauliā Nala, and it appears as such on Prinsep's map of
1822. According to the learned traditions of the city, however, Godauliā was simply the scrambled corruption of the stream's real name:
the Godāvarī, named after the sacred river of Central India. Thus,
Dashāshvamedha was at one time the confluence of the Ganges and the
Godāvarī Rivers, an auspicious place indeed!

Approaching the Dashāshvamedha area along the river from the
south, the pilgrims come first to the southern branch of the *ghāt*, the
old Dashāshvamedha, known once by the ancient names Rudrasāra,
"Nectar of Rudra," or Rudrasārovara, "Lake of Rudra." The words

"Dashāshvamedha Ghāt: Old Rudrasārovara" are painted even today on the building rising above the *ghāt*. The most prominent temple on this sector of the *ghāt* is the flat-roofed building that houses the popular shrine of the goddess Shītalā, whom we have met before.

The northern sector of Dashāshvamedha Ghāt, about two hundred feet north of Rudrasārovara, was formerly called Prayāga Ghāt, which the Purānic literature affirms to be north of Dashāshvamedha.[34] Prayāga is the proper name of the modern Allahabad at the confluence of the Ganges, Yamunā, and Sarasvatī Rivers. It is called Tīrtharāja, "King of *Tīrthas*." This is Prayāga-in-Kāshī, and its powers and benefits are said to be exactly those of the great Prayāga some fifty miles away. Today, however, the name Prayāga Ghāt, while it is painted boldly on a temple that sits between the two branches of Dashāshvamedha, is not commonly used. And even the temple there is utterly defunct, used only by boatmen who store their gear in its sanctum.

At Dashāshvamedha there are three Purānic *lingas* that the Panchatīrthī pilgrims are advised to visit. First is that of Shulatankeshvara, "Shiva of the Spear and Hatchet," which marks the southeastern boundary of the Antargriha and the northeastern boundary of Kedāra Khanda. (*See* Appendix II and Map 7.) Second is Brahmeshvara, said to have been established by Lord Brahmā during his sojourn here. Both of these are located in low-lying, unassuming buildings which are under water when the river rises each rainy season and must be reclaimed from a mountain of silt and mud each fall. The third is Dashāshvamedheshvara, located in the compound of the famous Shītalā Temple.

Dashāshvamedha to Ādi Keshava

W H I L E daily bathers climb the steps of Dashāshvamedha and make their way into the city for the *darshana* of Vishvanātha, the Panchatīrthī pilgrims continue northward along the river. They immediately pass Mān Mandir Ghāt, known primarily for the magnificent building with exquisite, ornately carved window casings, towering above it, which housed the eighteenth-century observatory of the Rājput, Jai Singh. Nearby another old Purānic *linga* has its home: Someshvara, the Shiva *linga* established by the Moon, Soma, a recommended stop on this riverfront pilgrimage. Passing Tripurabhairavī

Bathers at Dashāshvamedha Ghāt, the "Old Rudrasārovara." The Shītalā Temple is the low-lying white building on the left. The temple to the right bears the name Prayāga Ghāt.

Ghāt, they come to Mīr Ghāt, above which and slightly into the city they find the famous goddess temple of the "Wide-Eyed" Vishālākshī, one of India's 108 benches of the Goddess. Nearby is the Dharma Kūpa, the "Well of Dharma," surrounded by shrines and shaded by tall banyan trees. There is the Shiva temple of Dharmesha, where the Lord of Death, called Yamarāja or Dharmarāja, received his jurisdiction over the fate of the dead, a power he wields everywhere on earth except in Kāshī.[35] Here also is the *linga* established by Divodāsa before he finally left Kāshī. Also at Mīr Ghāt is the New Vishvanātha Temple, established by some very conservative Banāras brahmins when the old Vishvanātha was polluted, so they said, by the entrance of untouchables, or Harijans, into the temple after Independence.

The next *ghāt*, Lalitā Ghāt, has long been famous for its Vishnu shrine called Gangā Keshava, and its shrine to the Ganges called Bhāgīrathī Devī. The *ghāt's* namesake, Lalitā Devī, is an important goddess in both Kāshī and nearby Prayāga. The pilgrims would be well advised to have her *darshana,* for it is said that the *darshana* of

Lalitā Devī brings the same rewards as circumambulating the whole world! Also at Lalitā Ghāt is the Nepālī Temple, its style and wood carving typical of Nepāl. The temple, although not of Purānic antiquity, contains an image said to be that of Pashupateshvara, Nepāl's most famous manifestation of Shiva.

The pilgrims are now halfway down the river from Asi, but they will not stop at Manikarnikā Ghāt to bathe yet. A dip in these waters is reserved for the end of the journey.

Walking north from Manikarnikā along the river, the pilgrims now skirt a section of the city that stands particularly high above the water's edge, an area dense with very important temples. It is called Siddha Kshetra, the "Field of Fulfillment," and its temples house some of the most powerful and wakeful deities in Kāshī. Above Sindhiā Ghāt is the famous Vīreshvara, the "Hero's Lord," today called Ātmavīreshvara. It was here that the sage Vishvānara, they say, did *tapas* and received as a boon from Shiva the son for which he had yearned. The son—Vaishvānara—bore his father's name, and later became the Lord of Fire, Agni, by doing *tapas* nearby. Even today Vīreshvara is especially propitiated for the birth of a son.[36] Agnīshvara is slightly farther north, and has also given its name to one of the *ghāts*. Here, it is said, Shiva appeared to Vaishvānara and gave him the position of Agni, the fire.[37] Agni is both the sacrificial fire that mediates between heaven and earth and the lord of the southeastern direction. All the directional regents are established in Banāras, and interestingly the temple established by the lord of the southwest, Nirriti, is right next to the shrine of Agni. Next door to them is the popular and ancient temple of Upashānteshvara, the "Peace-Giving Lord," known for the pacifying of diseases.

In the Field of Fulfillment there are also some mighty goddesses. Sankatā Devī is there, above Sankatā Ghāt. Nearby are Kātyāyanī Devī, Siddheshvarī Devī, and a prominent new image of Santoshī Mātā. These temples, like all the temples of this area, are very well known to those who live in Kāshī, but they are seldom visited by pilgrims from the outside. They are hard to find, except by coming along the river as the Panchatīrthī pilgrims do. Especially the Panchatīrthī pilgrims from the districts surrounding Kāshī will make a point of climbing the steep bank for the *darshana* of Ātmavīreshvara and Sankatā Devī before proceeding north along the river.

North of Agnīshvara is Rāma Ghāt, another popular bathing *ghāt*, although today the headland above the *ghāt* is dominated by the massive new Sangaveda Vidyālaya Hospital. Adjacent to it is Lakshmanbālā Ghāt, named for Lakshmana the brother of Rāma. The Lakshmanbālā Temple above the *ghāt* contains a pavilioned hall of beautifully carved heavy wooden pillars and commands a sweeping overlook of the entire riverfront. A short distance away from Lakshmanbālā is the Mangalā Gaurī Temple, another very popular goddess shrine. Her temple also contains one of Kāshī's twelve Suns, Mayūkhāditya, the "Sun of Intense Rays." Here, they say, the Sun did *tapas* and intensified his heat so much that he nearly burned up the whole world. In his great devotion, the Sun established a Shiva *linga* here, still worshipped today as Gabhastīshvara, the "Lord of the Rays."

The Panchatīrthī pilgrims may stop at these temples, although the climb up the *ghāt* steps is very steep here, but they will pass up the next great *ghāt*, Panchagangā, in order to visit its temples and bathe in its waters on the return journey.

There are fewer *ghāts* of modern significance as the pilgrims continue their course northward. Brahmā Ghāt and Durgā Ghāt, immediately north of Panchagangā, fall into the orbit of activity of Panchagangā. Very fine staircases lead from these *ghāts* into the city above. Prinsep's illustration of Brahma Ghat from the early 1800s shows a very busy *ghāt* for bathing and washing. Sārīs hang from the lofty turrets to dry, and wood is stacked high on the *ghāt*, suggesting that perhaps cremations took place on this section of the riverfront too.

The next *ghāt* of importance is Gāya Ghāt, some distance to the north. Here, as at a number of these great *ghāts*, the goddesses dominate, now in the form of Nāgeshvarī Devī, the "Snake Goddess" (whom many call Shītalā here), and Mukhanirmālikā Devī, the "Pure-Faced Goddess." Until about the twelfth century, Gāya Ghāt was on the southern fringes of the urban part of Kāshī. All of the *ghāts* we have discussed to this point were in a much more rural and forested part of the sacred city, the Forest of Bliss. The great Pātan Darvāzā, one of the city's southern gates, still stands in the Gāya Ghāt area.

Trilochana is the next notable *ghāt*. Hidden in the alleyways above the *ghāt* is Trilochana Temple, dedicated to the "Three-Eyed Shiva."[38] The pilgrims may make a detour from their riverside journey to have the *darshana* of Shiva here, for this is one of Kāshī's oldest and most famous *lingas,* said to be *svayambhū.* Near Trilochana is a temple housing the *linga* of Mahādeva, the "Great God."[39] In the *Kāshī Khanda* this is said to be the "first *tīrtha*" in Kāshī, splitting the earth as a great *svayambhū linga*. Mahādeva is called the "establishing deity of Vārānasī," and in his temple was also located Vārānasī Devī, the female city-deity. Despite its impressive Purānic heritage, Mahādeva is a small and dilapidated shrine today, and the goddess Vārānasī Devī is now located within the precincts of the Trilochana Temple.

Beyond Trilochana, the procession of *ghāts* becomes much less elegant. Many of the *ghāts* are still clay-banked, *kachcha ghāts*. They front the river in an area of the city that is largely Muslim and lack the patronage that would produce finer *pakka ghāts*. As the pilgrims walk this section of the riverfront, Prahlāda Ghāt, named for the great devotee of Vishnu, is perhaps the only one of which they will take note.

A thousand years ago, however, this section of the river was surely one of the most popular. On the bank and in the lanes above it were some of the city's most important temples, which were destroyed with the invasion of 1194. Many of these same temples, such as Vīreshvara and Sankatā Devī, were then re-established farther south, where they are found today.

Approaching the northern end of the city, the pilgrims come to Rājghāt, where in ancient times the river was most easily forded and where ferries would carry cargo and passengers back and forth. Just beyond the *ghāt* itself, the embankment becomes much higher, rising to the lofty Rājghāt Plateau, where the ancient center of urban Vārānasī was located throughout most of its long history. On the far end of the Rājghāt Plateau, where the bank pitches sharply down to the River Ganges on the east and the River Varanā on the north, sits the Ādi Keshava Temple, at last, the farthest destination of the Panchatīrthī pilgrims and the third of the five *tīrthas*.

Ādi Keshava

Ā D I K E S H A V A, the "Original Vishnu," has been discussed in connection with the role of Vishnu in Kāshī, for this was the place where Vishnu first came when he arrived in Kāshī as Shiva's emissary. The temple dedicated to Vishnu has a pleasant pastoral setting on the bank above the confluence of the Varanā and the Ganges Rivers. Despite its high position on the plateau, the *ghāt* below the temple is completely flooded during the rainy season and the temple is unapproachable from the river side.

Ādi Keshava, like its southern counterpart Lolārka, is unquestionably an ancient site. It is mentioned in the oldest Purānic listings of Kāshī *tīrthas,* where it is simply called Keshava.[40] It retained its importance until at least the twelfth century, when it was clearly the favorite *tīrtha* of the Gāhadavāla kings of Kāshī. From their inscriptions it is evident that a great number of regal ritual occasions in Kāshī included the worship of Ādi Keshava or a dip in the Ganges at the Varanā *sangam.*[41] Since the ancient city was centered on this plateau, it is little wonder that Ādi Keshava had such prominence.

The elderly priest of the temple today describes the city of Kāshī, stretched out along the river, as having five bodily parts: Asi is the head; Dashāshvamedha is the chest; Manikarnikā is the navel; Panchagangā is the thighs; and Ādi Keshava is the feet. Here it was, he reminds us, that Vishnu first placed his holy feet in Kāshī.

Although the *tīrtha* of Ādi Keshava is visited by Panchatīrthī pilgrims, the *pūjārī* of the temple laments that other pilgrims do not often come. Local people from Rājghāt visit the temple regularly, but pilgrims from elsewhere are rare. As with other ancient temples of north Vārānasī, people do not know its greatness anymore.

Ādi Keshava, however, is not the only goal of the Panchatīrthī pilgrims here. Bathing in the confluence is of great importance, as is the *darshana* of Shiva as the "Lord of the Confluence," Sangameshvara. The *Linga Purāna* takes special note of this place:

... This river Varuna is holy. It liberates one from sins. It embellishes this holy centre and becomes united with the Ganges. An excellent *linga* has been installed by Brahmā at this confluence. It is known in the world as Sangameshvara. If a man shall become pure taking his bath at the confluence of the divine river and then worship Sangamesha, whence need he fear rebirth?[42]

The *linga* of Sangameshvara is located in a temple immediately adjacent to Ādi Keshava. From the pavilion of Ādi Keshava, one can look down into its courtyard. The sanctuary of this temple is occupied by the Sangameshvara *linga,* and in a side shrine is the other *linga* established by Brahmā, Brahmeshvara. It is a four-faced *linga.*

In the area of Ādi Keshava are located two of the fifty-six Ganeshas of Banāras: Kharva "The Dwarf" Vināyaka, and Rājaputra "The Prince" Vināyaka. The pilgrims will visit at least the nearest, Kharva Vināyaka, before retracing their steps up the riverbank again to Panchagangā Ghāt.

Panchagangā Ghāt

T H I S is surely the most dramatic and magnificent of Kāshī's riverfront *ghāts*. Its broad stone staircases march straight up the high bank, becoming narrower, and finally disappearing into the dense city above. This steeply rising escarpment was formerly crowned with the great temple of Bindu Mādhava, which we have encountered in our discussion of Vishnu's great temples. Bindu Mādhava was probably destroyed several times between the twelfth and the sixteenth centuries and was rebuilt for the last time by the Rājasthānī Mahārāja Mān Singh of Amber in the late sixteenth century.[43] It was this grand temple that Tavernier saw on his trip to Banāras shortly thereafter and described as the "great pagoda" of Banāras.[44] It must have been impressive, for it is the one temple in the entire city Tavernier described in some detail. It was built in a cross shape with great towers on each of the four arms and a lofty *shikhara* rising up over the central sanctum. According to this account the temple extended from Panchagangā Ghāt to what is now Rāma Ghāt, and it included within it the present temple of the goddess Mangalā Gaurī. It was an enormous and magnificent edifice.

Tavernier describes the "idol" in this temple as five to six feet in height, garlanded with a chain of such riches as gold, rubies, pearls, and emeralds. "This idol has been made in honour and after the likeness of Bainmadou," he wrote, "who was formerly a great and holy personage among them, whose name they often have on their lips."[45] He did not know this to be an image of Vishnu, but he describes clearly the marking of the worshippers with the marks of Vishnu:

Under the principal entrance of the pagoda one of the chief Brahmins is to be seen seated, close to whom is a large dish full of yellow pigment mixed with water. All the poor idolaters come one after the other to present themselves to him, and he anoints their foreheads with some of this colour, which is continued down between the eyes and on to the end of the nose, then on the arms and in front of the chest; and it is by these marks that those who have bathed in the Ganges are distinguished.[46]

There are many Banāras traditions associated with Bindu Mādhava and Panchagangā. Some of them the pilgrims will recall as they rest on the giant staircases of the *ghāt*. It was here, they say, that Kabīr received his initiatory *mantra* from the teacher Rāmānanda. Being unqualified for initiation by the guru on account of his low birth as a Muslim weaver's son, Kabīr is said to have extracted the sacred blessing from Rāmānanda by lying on the steps of Panchagangā Ghāt before dawn and waiting for the guru to trip over him when he came for a bath early in the morning. When Rāmānanda came down the steep steps and fell over Kabīr, he shouted, "Rām! Rām!" in surprise, and Kabīr considered himself blessed with the name of God spoken from the mouth of the guru. Nearly a century later, but still during the epoch of the grand Bindu Mādhava Temple, the poet Tulsī Dās wrote in praise of Bindu Mādhava. About this same time, in the first part of the seventeenth century, the outcasted brahmin poet Jagannātha is said to have sat with his Muslim lover atop the splendid *ghāt* of Panchagangā and composed the verses of the *Gangā Laharī*.

During the reign of Aurangzeb, the Bindu Mādhava Temple was pulled down and a mosque was built upon its site. The mosque was also constructed on a scale to match the grandeur of its high location on the river ridge. Originally, it had two very tall minarets, which can be seen in a sketch made by Captain Robert Elliott in the 1830s as well as in Prinsep's drawings. By the time Sherring wrote in 1868, the minarets had already been shortened some fifty feet because of their instability. Finally, one of these did fall, and the other was shortened still further, giving the building the somewhat truncated appearance it has today. Nonetheless, it was and remains such a fine building in such a commanding location that, since its construction three centuries ago, it has completely dominated the riverfront skyline, even in this Hindu city.

The riverfront at Panchagangā is notable for the dozens of three-sided cubicle shrine rooms that open out onto the river. Some contain a *linga* or an image, such as the lanky reclining image of Vishnu sleeping upon the serpent Shesha. Others are nearly bare and used primarily for yogic exercises and meditation. For much of the year, this row of cells

The great mosque at Panchagangā Ghāt, as drawn from the north near Trilochana Ghāt by Captain Robert Elliott, Views in India, *Vol. I, 1835.*

along the riverbank is under water. Not for three or four months after the rains cease in September does the river fall enough to reveal these shrines.

One such cubicle shrine honors the "Five Rivers" of Panchanada Tīrtha. The name stems from the old tradition that there are five rivers whose confluence is here. The first two are small rivulets, depicted here in bodily form in two side altars: the Dhūtapāpā ("Cleansed of Sin") and the Kiranā ("Sun's Ray"), whose waters are said to join in a stream called the Dharmanada ("River of Dharma"). The other three rivers are the Ganges, shown standing on her crocodile, the Yamunā, standing on her tortoise, and the Sarasvatī, riding her peacock. The three joined together at Prayāga, one hundred miles upstream, and they arrived together in Kāshī long ago, when Bhagīratha led the Ganges across North India.[47]

It is not hard to imagine from the more forested nature of the riverfront glimpsed in late eighteenth- and early nineteenth-century drawings that these two small streams once flowed into the Ganges here. Today the Dhūtapāpā and the Kiranā are present symbolically on the great stone *ghāt*. Just to the north of the bathing area is a mere trickle of a stream, said to be the Dhūtapāpā. Slightly to the south on what is properly Lakshmanbālā Ghāt is a small rectangular pool about two feet deep, set inside one of the three-sided chambers opening out upon the river. This is affirmed to be the Kiranā River.

Bathing in these five rivers is said to be auspicious beyond measure, particularly during the month of Kārttika when all the gods, including Shiva Vishvanātha, are said to bathe here daily. In addition to bathing,

Panchagangā Ghāt, with its myriad riverfront shrines. Note the minarets of the mosque have been considerably shortened.

the Panchatīrthī pilgrims are instructed to have the *darshana* of Bindu Mādhava, now housed in a building next to the great mosque, and to visit the temple of the goddess Mangalā Gaurī, with its attendant Sun-shrines of Mayūkhāditya and Gabhastīshvara.

Manikarnikā

A R R I V I N G at their last stop, the Panchatīrthī pilgrims might see the bright blue-lettered inscription of a local poet, painted on the white-washed wall above the *ghāt:*

> *This is Manikarnikā, where death is auspicious,*
> *Where life is fruitful,*
> *Where one grazes the pastures of heaven.*
> *There is no tīrtha like Manikarnikā,*
> *There is no city like Kāshī,*
> *There is no linga like Vishveshvara,*
> *Not in the whole universe.*

At last, the pilgrims return to Manikarnikā Ghāt, at the center of the three-mile-long sweep of the city's riverfront. This is the most important of the river *ghāts* and the fifth of the five *tīrthas*. As with many groupings of five in Hindu symbolism, the fifth is the center, the supreme anchor of the quadrant of four; so it is with Manikarnikā. It is said to be the place of the earth's creation as well as its destruction, containing both the sacred well, dug out by Vishnu at the beginning of time, and the cremation ground, where the created order burns at the end of time. Both the waters of creation and the fires of destruction join in the aura of sanctity that pervades Manikarnikā.

Here the Panchatīrthī pilgrims are advised to bathe at Manikarnikā Ghāt as well as in the sacred tank Manikarnikā Kund. Bathing at Manikarnikā and having the *darshana* of Vishvanātha have long been the center of religious life in Kāshī, both for the daily worshipper and the pilgrim. The common saying is "Every day one should see Vish-veshvara and bathe in Manikarnikā" *(Drishyo Vishveshvaro nityam, snātavyā Manikarnikā)*. Many of the city's pilgrimages, such as the Panchakroshī pilgrimage around the city, include a ritual bath at

Manikarnikā and the *darshana* of Vishvanātha at both the beginning
and the end.

MANIKARNIKĀ KUND

Although the name Manikarnikā is today most frequently associated
with the cremation ground, its oldest and most important association is
with the sacred well, called Manikarnikā or Chakrapushkarinī Kund,
the "Discus Lotus-Pool." The pilgrims will surely hear of the antiquity of this site from the priests who make their living here. This well
or tank, according to the *Kāshī Khanda,* is so ancient that it is said to
have been present in Kāshī long before the River Ganges arrived at the
heels of Bhagīratha: "For the benefit of the three worlds," they say,
"King Bhagīratha brought the Ganges to the place where Manikarnikā
is—to Shiva's Forest of Bliss, to Vishnu's Lotus Pool."[48]

The *kund* was originally a very large lake, said by tradition to have
extended from a place called Harishchandra Mandapa near Sankatā
Ghāt in the north, to Gangā Keshava at Lalitā Ghāt in the south, to
Svargadvāra, the "Door of Heaven" located in the city on Brahma
Nāla lane in the west, and to the middle of the Ganges in the east.[49]
The lake of Manikarnikā was, by tradition, quite large and around its
banks were the cremation grounds. On its northern bank, indeed, is
one of the cremation grounds said to have been worked by the legendary King Harishchandra. When the Ganges arrived, it is said to
have inundated this long lagoonlike lake, leaving only a part of it
visible as a spring-fed *kund.*

Manikarnikā Kund is located today right in the middle of Manikarnikā Ghāt proper, to the north of the cremation grounds. Ascending
the flight of steps from the river's edge, the pilgrims reach a broad, flat
landing, from which the city again rises steeply and dramatically,
penetrated by the narrowest of stair-step lanes. It is on this landing
where the city meets the *ghāt* that the pilgrims find Manikarnikā
Kund. The *kund,* surrounded by a cast-iron railing, is some sixty feet
square at the top, narrowing to about twenty feet square at the water's
edge. As the word *kund* implies, this is a tank with stairs—full-length,
broad steps that descend to water level on all four sides. The well is
said to spring from a source independent of the Ganges—an under-

Manikarnikā Ghāt. The Tārakeshvara temple is to the left. A goddess temple built by the Rāja of Ahmety dominates the center. To the right is the temple that caved in with the construction of Sindhiā Ghāt. Directly behind the shikhara of that temple is the broad landing on which Manikarnikā Kund is located.

ground river that flows directly from Gomukha, the "Cow's Mouth" in the Himālayas, the place where the River Ganges emerges from a mountain glacier.

VISHNU'S LOTUS POOL: THE ORIGIN OF MANIKARNIKĀ

At the north end of the *kund* at water level, the pilgrims will find a small shrine dedicated to Lord Vishnu, who carved out this lake with his discus and filled it with the perspiration of his austerities, back in the time of the beginnings. Vishnu has a central role in Manikarnikā's story, as it is told in the *Kāshī Khanda*.

During the great flood of dissolution, there was nothing at all, either moving or non-moving. It was dark everywhere. There was no sun. There were no planets, nor stars, nor moon. There was no day nor night. There was no sound, touch, smell, form, nor taste. There were no directions. There was only Pure Reality, Brahman, not graspable by mind or senses or speech, without form, without change.

Then that One desired to create a second, and it took on the pure form called Īshvara, the Lord. Shiva was the form of that Formless One, and with him was the goddess Shakti, called Prakriti ["Matter"] as well as Māyā ["Illusion"]. And the two of them, Shiva and Shakti, created this place.

That Shakti is Matter, and Shiva is Spirit. The two of them, Shiva and Shakti, both bliss incarnate, delight in this place, which is also bliss incarnate, this place measuring five kroshas, *created to be the very ground under their feet. O.Agastya, they do not leave this place, even in the time of dissolution. Therefore it is called Avimukta, "Never-Forsaken."*

One day, Shiva and Shakti, living in the Forest of Bliss, began to think how fine it would be to have another being who would create the world, bear its burdens, and protect it. The two of them would not have to worry about such matters and could devote themselves to the granting of liberation. Thus, they created Vishnu, beautiful and worthy, the very epitome of all good qualities. They instructed him to create everything on earth, according to the plan of the sacred Vedas.

Receiving this command, Vishnu immediately set himself on the path of severe austerities. Digging there with his discus, called a chakra, *Hari made a beautiful lotus pond, called a* pushkarinī, *and he filled it up with water from the sweat of his own limbs. Like a stone, he sat there, on the banks of the Chakrapushkarinī Pool and performed fierce austerities for 500,000 years.*

One day, Shiva and Shakti came that way and saw him there, aflame with the heat of his austerities. Shiva hailed him, and told him to choose a boon. Vishnu's only wish was to live forever in the presence of the Supreme Shiva. Shiva shook with sheer delight at the great devotion of Vishnu, and his "jeweled-earring"—manikarnikā—fell from his ear into the waters of the pool. Shiva granted Vishnu's request and added another boon of his own: This place, the Chakrapushkarinī, would now be known as Manikarnikā, the "Jeweled-Earring."[50]

Manikarnikā was the world's first pool and first *tīrtha*, dug out and filled with water by Vishnu himself at a time when the only *terra firma* in the entire universe was Kāshī. Kāshī was the very ground under the feet of Shiva and Pārvatī. Nothing else had yet been created. Here the first laboring ascetic, Vishnu, encountered Lord Shiva.

A variation of this myth of the origin of Kāshī and Manikarnikā is found in the *Shiva Purāna:*

*The unmanifest, attributeless One, Brahman, produced a second being,
called Shiva and possessing attributes. Shiva then split into two, becoming
male and female, Shiva and Shakti. They, in turn, created Purusha, who
was Vishnu, and Prakriti, his consort. These two, Purusha and Prakriti,
were commanded to perform austerities in order to create the universe. But
where should they practice their disciplines? As yet there was no place in
the void. The Supreme Shiva then created a beautiful city, radiant and
auspicious, five kroshas in extent. Vishnu, the Purusha, then sat in that
place, laboring and heating himself in austerities. From his labor, water
began to flow from his body and out over the face of the void. When
Vishnu saw the water, he shook his head in wonder, and his earring fell
into the water. Thus, it became known as the "Jeweled Earring," Manikarnikā. Finally, the water became so extensive that the city of the five
kroshas began to float, supported by the trident of the attributeless Shiva.
Vishnu slept there on the waters, and brought forth Brahmā and the
Cosmic Egg from his navel in order to produce creation. Shiva then took
Kāshī down from his trident and released it into the mortal world, but
when that world dissolves again Shiva upholds the radiant Kāshī on his
trident.*[51]

The myth of Manikarnikā's origin at the dawn of creation is well
known in the city today, and is related by Hindus in much the same
form as it is found in the Purānas. The pilgrims who bathe here at the
end of the Panchatīrthī pilgrimage will know some version of this
story and repeat the tale to one another.

The *pūjārī* of the Tārakeshvara Temple on Manikarnikā Ghāt tells
it this way:

*At Chakrapushkarinī, where Vishnu's footprints are seen today, Vishnu
did tapas for 7,000 years. Then one day Shiva and Pārvatī both bathed in
the beautiful* kund *made by Vishnu's discus. Shiva's crest-jewel* [mani]
and Pārvatī's earring [karnikā] *fell off into the* kund *while they were
bathing, and so it is called Manikarnikā.*

The myth, a well-known part of Kāshī lore, is even painted in folk verse in a mixed Hindi and Braj dialect on the wall of the building adjacent to the *kund,* where the scene of Vishnu's *tapas* is also depicted in the brilliant blue-on-whitewash style of Banāras folk art. In hearing the various derivations of Manikarnikā, we should bear in mind, however, that a great many *nāgas* and *yakshas* have names beginning with the word *mani,* a jewel. Especially the *nāgas,* serpents, are known to be the guardians of the treasures that lie below the earth.[52] It is likely that Manikarnikā in its earliest days had some association with the *nāgas.*

In the *Kāshī Khanda,* the story of Manikarnikā continues with a very interesting boon-choosing episode. Pleased with Vishnu, Shiva asked him to choose one boon after another. The things Vishnu successively chose were the very things that made Kāshī famous. First, he asked Shiva to let Kāshī be a place of liberation:

O Shiva, because your earring "let go" [*mukta*] of your ear and fell here, so may this supreme *tīrtha* of all *tīrthas* be a place where people are "let go."
And because light "shines" [*kāshate*] here, that inexpressible light which is the Lord, may this place be known by its matchless name, Kāshī, O Shiva.
May all creatures, from Lord Brahmā down to a clump of grass, in all the four ranks of living beings, be liberated in Kāshī.[53]

Having requested for Kāshī the power of liberation for which it is now so famous, Vishnu went on to ask for related boons.[54] He asked that this be a place where all the various kinds of worship, charity, and sacrifice yield *moksha* as their fruit. He asked that *moksha* be granted here freely without the difficult spiritual disciplines of the yogis and ascetics. He asked that even the lowest of creatures, such as rabbits and mosquitoes, be blessed with *moksha* here.

When Vishnu had chosen, in essence, that Kāshī be Kāshī, Shiva gladly granted all he asked and added another boon of his own: he made Vishnu Vishnu, instructing him to bring forth the creation and to protect it. Shiva, thus freed from earthly tasks, would become the Lord of this city of liberation: "This place, bounded by the five *kroshas,* is dear to me. My command and none other shall hold sway here. No other, O Vishnu, shall govern these creatures who dwell in Avimukta, even if they are sinners. I myself will be their teacher."[55]

Manikarnikā, where Vishnu encountered Shiva and Pārvatī in the beginning, came to be seen as the *tīrtha's tīrtha*—a place so powerful that all the other *tīrthas* are said to come here at midday to bathe, to dump the loads of sins they have acquired from pilgrims, and to become pure again. It is also the *tīrtha* of the gods. Vishveshvara and Pārvatī are said to bathe here daily at midday. Vishnu and Lakshmī come all the way from the Vaikuntha heaven to do the same. Brahmā comes from his heaven, Satyaloka. Indra and the other directional lords come. All the divine sages and all the various classes of gods and goddesses come to bathe at Manikarnikā.

In the beginning, Manikarnikā Kund was dug out by Vishnu himself. But the digging out of the *kund* is repeated, quite literally, each year when the floodwaters of the Ganges recede, having dumped a mountain of alluvial silt into the well. In the rainy season, when the waters rise high up the steep *ghāts* of Kāshī, the *kund* is completely inundated and often disappears from view, except perhaps for the very tops of the iron fence posts that surround it. When the waters recede, the *kund* is left filled with mud and the entire *ghāt* appears to be a clay-banked *kachcha ghāt* like Asi Ghāt. The excavation and reclamation of the *kund* begins, and gradually the *kund* is emptied of its deposit of dirt and becomes accessible to bathers. The faded walls of the buildings that border the *kund* on three sides are repainted with whitewash and lavishly decorated with folk art. This dramatic change of the riverfront through the seasons reminds us that this Panchatīrthī pilgrimage along the riverbank can be done only in the winter, spring, and summer by foot.

THE DEITIES AND TEMPLES OF
MANIKARNIKĀ

The three greatest deities of the living Hindu pantheon—Vishnu, Shiva, and Devī—are all part of the mythology of Manikarnikā and are especially honored here by the Panchatīrthī pilgrims. It is appropriate that these three seem to share equally in the traditions of sanctity and worship attached to this place, for those who know the city well claim it is the most sacred spot of all.

At Manikarnikā today, Vishnu's image is located in the small shrine inside the *kund* on its northern wall. As the Panchatīrthī pilgrims clamber down into the *kund* to bathe, they will stop to honor him there. On the *ghat* itself, a few yards away, are the revered footprints *(pāduka)* of Vishnu, set in a circular marble slab. No pilgrim will leave Manikarnika without honoring Vishnu's feet here. These footprints are said to mark the place where Vishnu engaged in his years of *tapas*. A plate from Prinsep's 1831 collection of engravings shows these footprints, which the subtitle calls "The holiest Spot in the sacred City." This spot has been sprinkled and flowered and touched by millions of Hindus through the centuries, and it has also been a place reserved for the cremation of a select few. The Mahārājas of Kāshī, for example, who are considered the earthly representatives of Vishvanātha, are traditionally cremated here.

The most important Shiva temple on the *ghat* itself is the one containing the Tārakeshvara *linga*, the form of Shiva that imparts the liberating *tāraka mantra*, the "prayer of the crossing," at the time of death. This *linga* was formerly located in the compound of Vishveshvara in the heart of the city.[56] The Tārakeshvara pavilion was one of the eight side-pavilions of the great sixteenth-century temple of Vishveshvara. It was destroyed along with the rest of the temple and is remembered at its old site today by a mere fragment of stone located underneath the small shrine of Gaurī Shankar by the Jnāna Vāpī pavilion. It is fitting, however, that Tārakeshvara is now here at Manikarnikā, for this is the place where the *tāraka mantra* is said to be whispered into the ears of the dead by Lord Shiva himself. The Panchatīrthī pilgrims will certainly have the *darshana* of the *linga* of Tārakeshvara after they bathe.

The temple of Manikarnikeshvara is also an important abode of Shiva in this area. It is located slightly into the city, and the Panchatīrthī pilgrims will approach it from the *ghat* by taking a steeply ascending lane south of the *kund*. The *linga* of this temple—set dramatically underground at the bottom of a deep shaft—could at one time be reached by a tunnel originating on the *ghat*. In the Purānas, this particular *linga* is mysteriously said to be in the middle of the *kund* itself.[57] On the west side of the *kund* today, Shiva's presence is evident in the row of more than a dozen small niches, each containing a Shiva *linga*.

At the northern end of Manikarnikā Ghāt, bordering Sindhiā Ghāt, is another Shiva temple which lost its footing nearly a century ago and slid into the river, coming to a precarious, tilting rest, half under water, where it remains today. It was probably with the construction of Sindhiā Ghāt, which caused an enormous amount of erosion, that the temple began to tilt. There is a local legend that when the engineers were digging to determine the cause of the instability of the terrain here, they unearthed a yogi seated in an underground cavern. Awakened from his meditation, the yogi was shocked to discover that the golden era of King Rāma and Queen Sītā of Ayodhyā had long passed away, and that the Kali Age had arrived. He leaped up from his long-held seat, plunged into the Ganges, and disappeared.

Finally, the Goddess is worshipped at Manikarnikā. The importance of Pārvatī, the Shakti of Shiva, who bathed in these waters in the beginning, is attested to in the ancient myth. She sanctified these waters and left one of her ornaments behind here. Today, however, the goddess most closely associated with the *kund* goes by the name of Manikarnī Devī, who is probably its most ancient *devī* as well. Like many such ancient *devīs,* she is place-specific: this is her well. Pilgrims may see Manikarnī painted on the wall near the *kund.* In the standard depiction, Manikarnī Devī is seated cross-legged by the *kund,* flanked by Shiva and Pārvatī on one side and Vishnu on the other. Her reputation is well established, for she is mentioned by the old *Linga Purāna* as well as by the *Kāshī Khanda.*[58] At times, Manikarnikā is said to abandon her material form as a *kund* and take on the subtle form of a woman and goddess who visibly appears to those who meditate upon her. Her features are described in some detail, as are the *mantras* to be repeated in evoking her image. The calling forth and envisioning of the deity in this fashion suggest a medieval Tantric layer in the development of her cultus. One thing is clear: the goddess associated with this place and these waters has a very long and continually evolving history. Apparently unattached to any consort, she is one of the many local *devīs* included when the divine feminine is spoken of as "the Goddess."

At the Manikarnikā Kund today, an image of Manikarnī Devī is painted yearly on the freshly whitewashed wall after the rains have ceased. It is she who presides over the twice-yearly decoration *(shringāra)* of the *kund.*[59] On these decoration days, the waters here are especially celebrated by the devout, who sit around the steps of the *kund* waiting for the auspicious moment to bathe. A rectangular wooden frame is positioned over the water and adorned with garlands of marigolds and nosegays of juniper and flowers. The waters are thus decorated and a colorful, festival *pūjā* follows. Although the ritual elements of the *āratī* are presented to the goddess waters, the offering is overseen by Manikarnī Devī herself, whose framed icon has been brought forth for the occasion. When the *pūjā* is over, the priest who has been in charge takes the first dip in the sacred waters, acting as a representative of Vishvanātha.[60] He is followed by a crowd of eager bathers, who now plunge into the *kund* in one of the most festive of all bathing celebrations.

MANIKARNIKĀ CREMATION GROUND

Strictly speaking, the name Manikarnikā applies to the *kund* and its adjoining *ghāt*, but in Banāras today the name also refers to the cremation ground immediately to the south. The Panchatīrthī pilgrims will probably pay little attention to the cremation ground, but it is undoubtedly present in their minds as they linger at this last stop on their river pilgrimage. This is the site of liberation, for which Kāshī is famous.

Manikarnikā is the famed "burning *ghāt*" the tourist sees from the safe distance of a boat, or from the turret of an old riverside temple now fallen into disuse. Manikarnikā combines the awesome with the beautiful. The spires of a cluster of temples pierce the sky. And the smoke of the low-lying cremation pyres curls about the temples and spreads an ethereal white veil over the entire *ghāt* as it rises. Manikarnikā is alive around the clock. By night one can see the flames of its pyres from far-off Asi Ghāt, and by day one can discern this *ghāt* along the crescent of the riverfront by its supernal haze.

From the river, the most prominent temple is a great, hulking, four-postered temple that looms over the cremation grounds. Built by Queen Ahalya Bāī Holkar of Indore at the same time she sponsored the construction of the Vishvanātha Temple in the eighteenth century, it is not in use today as a temple. It is dark, stained with years of smoke, and the spaces between its turrets are stacked with wood. Adjacent to this temple is a high bulkhead for flood-season cremations, when the lower part of the cremation ground is under water.

At any one time there may be half a dozen cremation pyres burning. Newly arrived corpses lie at the water's edge, bound in red or white cloth and strapped into the bamboo litters on which they are carried through the streets to this place. They are dipped in the Ganges for the last time before being hoisted on to the pyre. The eldest son, freshly tonsured and dressed in a seamless white garment, circumambulates the deceased and lights the pyre. Mourning and wailing are said to be bad luck for the dead, and here there is an atmosphere of almost casual solemnity. The funeral party stands or sits nearby, and when the body has been burned, the eldest son, his back to the pyre, throws a clay pot of Ganges water over his shoulder, dousing the embers, and walks away without looking back.

The cremation ground is under the professional organization and exclusive supervision of the Doms, an untouchable caste whose dominance here is said to extend far back to that mythical time when King Harishchandra was purchased in slavery by a Dom to work the cremation grounds. Doms sell the wood, collect a tax for each corpse, and tend the ever-burning sacred fire from which all pyres are lit. They also tend the individual pyres and rake up the ashes. The ashes and embers will be sifted for valuables by the Dom workers before being consigned to the river, where they will float lazily for a time near the shore before being carried slowly downstream.

Kāshī's ancient reputation as a cremation ground is unquestionable. In the *Padma Purāna,* for example, it is said, "This well-known cremation ground is called Avimukta. Having become Time itself, I destroy the world here, O Goddess."[61] The sacred city is, after all, the "Great Cremation Ground." It is not clear, however, that Manikarnikā in particular was the famous cremation ground it is today. The only direct reference to Manikarnikā as a cremation ground is in the *Nārada Purāna,* which is a very late work.[62] For the rest, Manikarnikā is known as a sacred bathing *tīrtha* and, by extension, because of its sanctity, a good place to die. The relationship between death and Manikarnikā may be surmised, for example, in the *Matsya Purāna,* which says, "A man who leaves his body at Manikarnikā reaches the desired goal."[63] In the *Kāshī Khanda* as well, Manikarnikā is said to be a place where people surrender their earthly bodies to death and receive spiritual bodies like that of Shiva himself.[64] While Manikarnikā is not mentioned explicitly as a cremation ground, it is surely a place where one might wish to die.

The cremation ground here at Manikarnikā has traditionally gone by another name: Jalasāī Ghāt, the "Sleeper on the Waters." Appropriately, this is a name of Vishnu, who sleeps between eras upon the waters of the Sea of Milk and who slept here at the dawn of creation, before the golden egg containing the creator god Brahmā emerged from his navel and began to generate the universe. In a touching, but inaccurate interpretive attempt, the Englishman Edwin Greaves, writing in 1901, speculated: "Is it just possible that the name is not here applied to Vishnu, but to the dead? that as we speak of the dead as 'sleeping in the graveyard,' so Hindus speak of theirs as sleeping in the Ganges? One would like to read such an idea into the name."[65] Whatever its proper origin, the name Jalasāī has been associated with the cremation ground for some time, and it is noted as such by both English and Hindi authors and mapmakers. On Prinsep's careful map of 1822, it is called "Jalsayn" Ghāt, with the notation "There Hindoo corpses are burnt."

There were a number of cremation grounds in ancient Banāras, and

A satī stone, showing a married couple marking the site where a woman died on the funeral pyre of her husband. Many of these are today worshipped as images of Shiva and Pārvatī. The feet of the stone shown here have been washed and honored with water.

even this one in the vicinity of Manikarnikā Kund was much large
than it is today. For example, the western boundary of the Manikarnikā Kund area as noted in the Purānas was Svargadvāra, the "Door of
Heaven," which today is a temple set into the city several hundred
yards uphill from the river along the lane called Brahma Nāla, which
was itself formerly a rivulet.[66] The many *satī* stones found in that area,
which are always a rough guide to the presence of an ancient cremation ground, confirm the supposition that this little rainy season rivulet
was once part of the larger cremation ground. These *satī* stones mark
the site on which a "faithful wife" *(satī)* was burned upon her husband's funeral pyre.[67]

In Banāras today, the name Manikarnikā bears with it the double-
edged power of a living and transforming symbol. For the pilgrims, it
calls to mind the sacred *kund* with its life-giving waters of creation,
and at the same time it calls to mind the cremation ground with its
burning fires of destruction and liberation. Here at the heart of the
sacred city is the transformation of life and of death. While the very
word Manikarnikā may bespeak death, it is death in Kāshī, which is
liberation.

Finally, the Panchatīrthī pilgrims leave the River Ganges at Manikarnikā. They salute Siddhi "Fulfillment" Vināyaka, one of the most
popular of the fifty-six Ganeshas, and hasten uphill, through the lanes
into the city for a final round of worship at Vishvanātha, Annapūrnā,
and the Jnāna Vāpī. Then they visit the "Witnessing Ganesha,"
Sākshī Vināyaka, to confirm the completion of their day-long pilgrimage.

transformative

6

SEASONS AND
TIMES

"'E v e r y d a y is a great festival day in Kāshī!"—so says the tradition. In the manuals of the brahmins of Banāras, whose business it is to
observe rites and, as priests, to officiate at rites for others, one finds
elaborate confirmation and documentation of this popular saying.
Every day there are deities to be honored, rites and observances to be
attended to. It is not hard to believe that in traditional India being a
brahmin was said to be a full-time job.

The seeming month of Sundays is a striking fact of Banāras life for
all who come to India from those cultures of the West where the view
of time is considerably more prosaic. In India, all times are not qualitatively equal, but each day comes with its own complexion and
characteristics. India's love of categorization, propensity for classifica-
tion, and thoughtful regard for differences have produced a way of
thinking about time that is as elaborate, as ritually significant, and as
little understood by outsiders as is its highly elaborated social system of
caste. Times are different one from the other. Certain days are good
for weddings, others for travel. Certain days are for Shiva, others for
Vishnu. The textured nature of time makes every day special for
something.

The traditional Hindu calendar for sale in the religious bookstores of
Kachaurī Lane in Banāras is called the *panchānga,* the "five-limbs" of
time. It is produced by the most erudite of Banāras pandits. Printed in
a large rectangular book of newsprint, the *panchānga* is not what most

of us would recognize as a calendar. It looks more like a newspaper. Absent are the simple, numbered days, the empty squares of as yet unlived time. This calendar is completely filled with astrological charts, auspicious dates and hours, instructions for religious performances, and countless other details of the months, fortnights, days, and moments as they lie ahead. Time comes to Hindus not as a series of blank, unwritten days, but fully endowed with differentiating qualities and attributes.

Of the five-limbs of time treated by the *panchānga*, two are most important in this context: the lunar day *(tithi)* and the solar day *(vāra)*. The solar calendar is the common Western calendar, with its cycles of seven twenty-four-hour days and its twelve-month yearly cycles. There are also twelve lunar months in a year, but they are slightly shorter, for they follow with faithful regularity the monthly cycle of the moon. Each month consists of two fifteen-day fortnights, called *pakshas*. A *paksha* is, literally, a "wing," like the wing of a bird. The first is the waning fortnight *(krishna-paksha,* "dark fortnight"), which moves toward the new-moon night *(amāvasyā);* the second is the waxing fortnight *(shukla-paksha,* "bright fortnight"), which moves toward the full-moon night *(pūrnimā).* [1] Whereas a solar day may be described by its name, such as Monday, a lunar day is described by its position in the fortnight, such as the "third day of the waxing fortnight." Auspicious times, seasons, and festivals are calculated by the lunar calendar, and we should note that every two to three years an extra month is added to the lunar calendar in order to square it with the solar calendar. Otherwise the slightly shorter lunar year would fall behind and slowly move through the seasons of the entire year, and its festival days would not keep a fixed seasonal time.

The cycles of lunar days and week days are governed in the Hindu mythological scheme by those heavenly orbs by which time is reckoned. The moon and the various constellations that move in relation to it are the markers of the lunar months and years. Each solar day, as in the Western calendar, has its own heavenly governor. The Sun (Ravi) is in charge of Sunday (Ravivāra); the Moon (Soma) is in charge of Monday (Somavāra); Mars (Mangala) governs Tuesday (Mangala-vāra); Mercury (Budha) rules Wednesday (Budhavāra); Jupiter (Brihaspati) rules Thursday (Brihaspativāra); Venus (Shukra) governs Friday (Shukravāra); and finally Saturn (Shani) rules Saturday (Shanivāra).

"Eve of an Eclipse of the Moon, 23 November, 1823," by James Prinsep, Benares Illustrated, 1831. Of this, Prinsep writes, "Conjunctions of the planets, eclipses, and sankrant, or the Sun's entrance into the zodiacal signs, are accounted the most auspicious moments for bathing in the Ganges. . . . On most occasions of festive and multitudinous assemblage, the distinctions of religion give way, and the scene bears more the character of a fair [melā] than of a religious meeting: booths, whirligigs, pastry cooks, and penny trumpets, are accompaniments . . . indispensable upon such occasions in India. . . . "

In Kāshī's mythology, all these time-rulers received jurisdiction over their various aspects of time by establishing *lingas* in Kāshī and engaging in years of religious austerities. In short, time came into being in Kāshī. The Sun took up residence in twelve places. The moon established a Shiva *linga*, engaged in stark austerities, and was appointed to his station as a boon from Lord Shiva.[2] Likewise, each of the constellations and planets has its particular story, and in each case it was in Kāshī, at the center of the world, that these various regents of time received their jurisdiction.[3]

Kāshī's religious life moves in a rhythmic syncopation of lunar days

and week days, each of which has its own glories, its own deities, and its own rites. Each of the weekdays of the solar calendar has a different beat. Sundays are for the Sun and the *ādityas*. On Mondays, the accent is on Shiva's many temples. Tuesdays and Saturdays are the most dangerous days of the week, and on those days the deities most adept at dealing with the dangers of the world and the fears of the heart are propitiated with special vigor. The Goddess is worshipped, especially the great Durgā of Durgā Kund. Hanumān's nearby temple of Sankat Mochan is also lively and crowded. Bhairava too is honored on Tuesdays. Wednesdays and Thursdays are both generally auspicious days, but the fortunes of Friday, again, are ambiguous and lead many to the temples of the Goddess. Fridays are especially associated with those *devīs* such as Sankatā Devī and Santoshī Mātā, whose religious observances are prescribed for Fridays in their *vrata* stories. Saturdays bring to life a small temple of Saturn—Shani—in Vishvanātha Lane, where people make special propitiatory lamp offerings to mitigate the terrible influence of that deity, who is widely known to bring trouble to those whose fortunes fall beneath his shadow.

The lunar days have their own distinctive rhythm, and during the round of each fortnight the beat changes from day to day. For instance, the third *(tīj)* day of the fortnight is special to such goddesses as Lakshmī and Mangalā Gaurī. The fourth *(chaturthī)* is associated with Ganesha. The eighth *(ashtamī)* day belongs to Bhairava and to the Goddess. In the waning fortnight it is especially associated with the dark *devīs,* such as Shītalā. The two eleventh *(ekādashī)* days are especially holy and are associated with Vishnu. They are days of fasting and are auspicious days for any religious observance. As the fortnight moves toward its end, it becomes increasingly the time of Shiva. The fourteenth *(chaturdashī)* is Shiva's day and, perhaps more significantly, Shiva's night. On the fourteenth of each waning fortnight, the "Night of Shiva" is observed, with a fast and a vigil. The next day, the moonless day, is ordinarily inauspicious and dangerous. In the waxing fortnight, the final day, the full-moon day, is very auspicious.

Every day has the qualities, the color, the texture of both the solar and lunar days. With the turning of the days, the kaleidoscope of the city's religious life falls continually into different patterns. We have said that, in Kāshī, mythology becomes geography. Here we can see that mythology also becomes time itself. During the fortnight, the entire pantheon of deities is properly honored. And the multiple images of a single deity also have their assigned times in the complex patterns of the kaleidoscope. For example, there are forty-two well-known Shiva *lingas* in Kāshī, divided by the *Kāshī Khanda* into three groups of fourteen, the first group consisting of the most prominent Shiva *lingas* in the entire city.[4] On the first day of each fortnight, one should honor Shiva at the first temple in each group, and so on through the next fourteen days of the fortnight until, on the fourteenth day, one completes the cycle with the worship of Vishvanātha and two other less important *lingas.* Obviously only the full-time brahmin could do this every fortnight, so for each cycle of *lingas* there is also a single fortnight in the year set aside for this round of systematic worship.[5] The intricacies of the calendar and its precise relationship to the temples of Kāshī could take a lifetime to master, but the point is clear enough. With its intense concern for the proper time for the worship of each deity, for the performance of each pilgrimage, and for the celebration of each temple and *ghāt,* the tradition of Banāras astrologers and brahmins has made certain that nothing is left out. Each temple or image, however disregarded it may be for most of the year, has its day and its hour of celebration. It is often said that the Hindu tradition leaves nothing behind, forgets nothing, and in Banāras the old stones literally come to life, one by one, as they are sprinkled with Ganges water and garlanded with flowers at least once in the course of each year.

Seasons and Festivals

A s t h e m o n t h s and seasons change, one sees yet another cycle in Kāshī's religious life: the annual cycle of observances and festivals. The yearly cycle has its own pattern and pace; some months move gaily through a dozen major festivals, while others have but one or two. Each deity has its special months as well as days. The Goddess is celebrated in Chaitra and Āshvina, the Ganges in Jyeshtha, Shiva in Shrāvana, Vishnu in Kārttika, Bhairava in Mārgashīrsha, and so on. Each of the great *ghāts* has its months too. For Dashāshvamedha it is Jyeshtha, for Panchagangā it is Kārttika. To keep it all straight, there are manuals such as the *Kāshī Vārshika Yātrā,* the "Year's Pilgrimage in Kāshī," which record the days for the celebration and visitation of each temple and *ghāt* and prescribe the seasons for each pilgrimage.[6]

It would be both presumptuous and impossible to describe the year's full cycle of festival rites in Banāras, for it is very complex and, as any Banārsī will tell us, the rites observed depend upon the community to which one belongs—Bengālī or Gujarātī, high caste or low caste. We can, however, get a general sense of the rhythm of the seasons and festivals and in doing so glimpse something of the city's living religious traditions.

The months of the year are twelve:

Chaitra	MARCH/APRIL
Vaishākha	APRIL/MAY
Jyeshtha	MAY/JUNE
Āshādha	JUNE/JULY
Shrāvana	JULY/AUGUST
Bhādrapada	AUGUST/SEPTEMBER
Āshvina	SEPTEMBER/OCTOBER
Kārttika	OCTOBER/NOVEMBER
Mārgashīrsha	NOVEMBER/DECEMBER
Pausha	DECEMBER/JANUARY
Māgha	JANUARY/FEBRUARY
Phālguna	FEBRUARY/MARCH

BEGINNING IN SPRING: CHAITRA

The year begins in the Banāras calendar in the middle of the month, with the second half, the waxing fortnight, of the month of Chaitra. In this northern version of the Hindu calendar there are no clean breaks; rather the year fits together in a seamless whole. It begins on the upbeat, with the brightening half of Chaitra, and ends with the darkening half of Chaitra. Similarly, whenever an extra month is inserted into the calendar, it is tucked in between two halves of another month, and its anomalous danger is safely contained therein.

The year's first festival takes place on its first nine days and nights. This is Navarātra, the "Nine Nights" of the Goddess, and on each of the nine days and nights particular "Durgās" and "Gaurīs" are designated for decoration and *darshana*. (*See* Appendix IV for these goddesses.) During the nine days, the circuit of these temples of the Goddess will be made by countless worshippers. The "Nine Nights" takes place twice during the year, once in the spring and once in the fall. These are the two great seasons of the Goddess, and it is interesting that these two cycles are immediately followed by the year's two greatest *kshatriya* festivals: Rāma Navamī ("Rāma's Ninth") in the spring, and Vijaya Dashamī ("Victorious Tenth") in the fall, the former celebrating the birthday of Lord Rāma and the latter celebrating Rāma's victory over the demon Rāvana, as well as the victory of Devī over the Bull-Demon.

THE HOT SEASON:
VAISHĀKHA AND JYESHTHA

Vaishākha (April/May) is the beginning of the hottest season of the year. For two months or more the sun will be fierce in its intensity, there will be no rain, the earth will become parched and the roads dusty, and the hot wind called the *lū* will begin to blow. For some, such a season of natural austerity is a time for religious austerities as well. It is a time when many will perform the Panchakroshī pilgrimage around Kāshī, walking some fifty miles over the course of five days. In the middle of each night they rise and walk the distance between one halting place and the next before dawn. In this season the night is the best time of day.

The goddesses of this hot season are cooling goddesses: Shītalā and Gangā. Shītalā, the "Cool One," is praised especially on the eighth day of the waning fortnight of Vaishākha as well as on other waning eighths during the hot season. This is the special season of Shītalā, who rules over fever diseases. This is also the season of the cooling goddess Gangā. As the days get hotter, the early-morning plunge in the river Ganges is especially splendid. There are three great bathing months in Kāshī, when people vow to bathe every morning before dawn, and Vaishākha is one of them. The others are Kārttika in the fall and Māgha in the winter. Keeping such a vow in Vaishākha seems a pleasurable austerity. The river is low and clear; the *ghāts* have been cleaned of all the tons of silt and mud left by the flood of the past monsoon season, and the great stone steps stretch out long from city to river. Not surprisingly, this is a favorite time for the Panchatīrthī pilgrimage along the riverfront.

On the third day of the waxing fortnight, Manikarnikā Kund, whose waters, they say, flow straight from the source of the Ganges, is decorated with garlands of fresh flowers. On the seventh day, "Ganges Seventh" (Gangā Saptamī), the descent of the Ganges from heaven to earth is celebrated. In the following month, Jyeshtha (May/June), the tenth day marks that ancient time when the Ganges, led by

Bhagīratha, reached the plains of India at Hardvār. It is called Gangā
Dashaharā, meaning that it "destroys ten" lifetimes of sins. Throughout the first ten days of this fortnight, and climaxing on the tenth,
people bathe by the thousands at Dashāshvamedha Ghāt, and it is said
that bathing here on all ten days destroys the sins of ten lifetimes. On
the tenth day, some of the most enthusiastic of worshippers will cross
the river in boats trailing long garlands of flowers to decorate the
goddess-waters. In former days, this was also a time of great swimming
competitions, when athletes young and old would swim across the
river and back.

It is said in Banāras that on the day of Gangā Dashaharā in the
hottest month of the year the river begins to rise again, swollen by the
melting snows of the Himālayas. The rains are not far off.

THE RAINY SEASON: ĀSHĀDHA, SHRĀVANA, BHĀDRAPADA

In late June, people begin watching for the rains. For nearly three
months the weather has progressively become hotter and drier. The
wells are low, the land is parched, and the air is filled with the dust of
the *lū*. With the thunder of the first monsoon rains, there is relief and
even festivity in the air. If the rains are good, they will last for three
months. The translucent white sky of the hot season darkens with the
rainstorms that bring some of the year's most dramatic and beautiful
weather. The blue skies of midday suddenly fill with enormous rain-
laden clouds. It may rain for hours, and when the black clouds lift, the
golden light of evening streams across the sky beneath them.

Gradually the thousand streams of North India bring their waters
into the Ganges, and the great river begins to rise again. And gradually the magnificent staircases of the *ghāts* with their hundreds of
riverfront shrines begin to disappear as the Ganges climbs the steps,
one by one, and claims Kāshī's riverfront as her own. By the end of the
month of Shrāvana, if the monsoon is especially strong, the river will
rise to the streets of Dashāshvamedha, leaving not a single one of the
hundred steps in view.

During the rains, the focus of the religious life of Banāras moves
from the river to the city. The monsoon months bring a new influx of

itinerant *sādhus* and *sannyāsins* to Banāras. These world-renouncers, who ordinarily move from place to place, avoiding the attachments of settled life, spend the monsoon months in one place, following the ancient practice common to both the Hindu and Buddhist traditions. The flooded rivers of the monsoon months make travel difficult. In addition, these months bring swarms of small creatures to life, which the itinerant monk, especially the scrupulous Jaina, would not wish to crush underfoot on the path. This is the time to observe the rainy season retreat called the *chaturmāsa,* the "four-months" retreat. On several occasions, the Buddha himself spent the *chaturmāsa* in Kāshī.

Those who settle in Banāras for the four months may well stay in a *matha,* run by the order to which they are attached. There are over two hundred ascetic and monastic institutions in Banāras, the most prominent being the monasteries of the Shaiva Dandī, Nāga, and Paramahāmsa *sannyāsins* and those of the Vaishnava Rāmānandī and Rāmānujī *sannyāsins.* Today, although many *sannyāsins* are no longer itinerant, they may undertake special religious observances and abstinences during this season of retreat.

The presence of so many *sādhus* and *sannyāsins* in the city during these months is important to devout Hindu householders. Some of these renouncers will be dependent upon Banāras householders for alms, an act of generosity that benefits the householders as well. Formerly, this was a time when the *sannyasins,* many of whom were learned, would settle among the people for long enough to teach them. In Banāras today something of this tradition lingers on. While the rains pour down in the early evening, certain temples and *mathas* will be crowded with eager listeners, both lay people and *sādhus,* and one of the learned ones will speak. Kāshī's most famous *sannyāsin,* who often spends *chaturmāsa* here, is the great Karpātrī, whose daily lectures on the *Rāmāyana* or the *Kāshī Khanda* attract hundreds of people to his hall at Kedāra Ghāt. The full moon of the month of Āshādha is called *guru pūrnimā* and is famous in Banāras for devotion to its many teachers.

After the searing hot season, the monsoon season is known for its good sleeping weather. Accordingly, one of the popular notions about the *chaturmāsa* is that this is a season when Vishnu goes to sleep. The season begins with the eleventh day of the waxing fortnight of Āshādha (June/July) called Shayanī, the "Sleeping," and ends with the eleventh day of the waxing fortnight of Kārttika in the fall, called

Prabodhinī, the "Waking." In this season laity and renouncers alike may undertake special observances and abstinences, such as giving up certain foods. Because of the sleep of Vishnu, this is not a season for auspicious rites of the life cycle, such as marriages.

Shrāvana (July/August) is the great month of the rainy season. In Kāshī, it is not as famous for its individual festivals as for its *melās* or religious fairs and its temple observances. Mondays, always sacred to Shiva, are especially important during the month of Shrāvana, when there is a special focus on Shiva. Some people keep Shrāvana Mondays as a fast day. The scriptures prescribe a special tribute to Kedāra *linga* on these days, and this is indeed one of the great seasons of Kedāra. In the early morning groups of vigorous men climb the steep steps again and again with huge brass pots of Ganges water on their shoulders, destined for the Kedāra *linga* in the temple at the head of the *ghāt*. Some of them fill their vessels with milk as well, and pour out these gallons of milk upon the *linga* as an offering to Lord Shiva. While the accent may be at Kedāreshvara on these Shrāvana Mondays, Vishvanātha and the other great Shiva temples of the city are also crowded and count this season as one of the high points of the ritual year.

Both Sundays and Mondays in Shrāvana are the days of a *melā* at the temple complex containing Vriddhakāleshvara, the "Old Lord of Death," and Mrityunjaya, the "Death-Conqueror." Approaching this temple compound through the streets north of Maidāgin, one first sees the small, streetside temple of Mrityunjaya, thronged with worshippers who press toward its doors for *darshana*. In its position and popularity, this temple of Mrityunjaya Shiva is the one that has inherited the ancient mantle of Omkāra as the spiritual anchor of the northern sector of Kāshī. Inside this temple compound, in centuries-old courtyards, are many other important Shiva *lingas,* with Purānic names and reputations. Of these, the most revered are Mahākāla, the "Great Death," named for the great *linga* of light in the sacred city of Ujjain, and Vriddhakāleshvara, the "Old Lord of Death." These, along with Mrityunjaya, are forms of Shiva to be worshipped to ward off the onset of old age and the time of death. In a back courtyard of these sacred precincts is one of Kāshī's most holy wells: Kāla Kūpa, the "Well of Time," filled with life-giving mineral waters. According to the tradition of the *Kāshī Khanda,* those who bathe here and sip these waters and who honor these deities on Sundays during Shrāvana will be free from sickness and fever and will have long and healthy lives.[7] These Sundays, together with the wider worship of Shiva on Shrāvana Mondays, have created a weekly two-day fair, in which the weighty concerns of health and longevity are attended to amidst a carnival atmosphere. In the streets are pushcarts filled with food and hawkers selling balloons and noisemakers. And in the inner courtyards are merchants, whose wares include not only religious pamphlets but the many simple things that appeal to the women who have come here from the outlying villages—hairpins and bright ribbons, combs and nail polish.

Tuesdays in Shrāvana belong to Durgā. Around her spacious red temple in southern Banāras one of the year's great *melās* takes place. The streets are lined with the carts and mats of makeshift merchants, and swarming with worshippers and celebrants, whose numbers increase as the month progresses. This Shrāvana Tuesday fair is attended especially by villagers from the area around Banāras. They visit the Durgā Temple for *darshana,* and then they delight in the foot-powered wooden Ferris wheel and the other amusements in the carnival grounds behind the temple.

Durgā is not their only destination, for in recent years the nearby temples of Tulsī Mānas and Sankat Mochan have become part of the Shrāvana festivities as well. The white marble Tulsī Mānas Temple is awesome to these village folk, for its sanctuary is larger than any they have seen and its floor is shiny marble. They linger in the sanctuary to gaze at Lord Rāma, flanked by his faithful wife, Sītā, and his brother, Lakshmana. The temple's mythological Disneyland is moved outside during the fair, and the crowds delight in the three-dimensional animations of their favorite scenes from the *Rāmāyana*.

A short distance away is the third temple which has now become part of the Shrāvana Tuesday *melā:* the Sankat Mochan Temple, dedicated to the monkey god Hanumān as the "Liberator from Troubles." These villagers will not miss the *darshana* of Hanumān-jī. Many, in fact, have come to the *melā* primarily to make their offerings here, to have his *darshana* and receive his *prasāda.* Sankat Mochan's rise to prominence is not recorded in the Sanskrit Kāshī texts, for Hanumān, like many of the other great deities we have reviewed, is from the people's traditions. Also, his extreme popularity in Kāshī is said to be relatively recent, dating to the time of Tulsī Dās in the sixteenth century.

Today, however, Sankat Mochan is one of Kāshī's three most important temples in the eyes of most Banārsīs, ranking behind only Vishvanātha and Annapūrnā.

In the waxing fortnight of Shrāvana is Nāga Panchamī, "Nāga's Fifth," the year's most important celebration of the ancient serpent deities. These *nāgas* have always been propitiated with special care during the rains, for in this season the floods often force them from their usual habitations in the earth, and they suddenly appear in people's gardens, courtyards, and houses. The *nāgas* are both loved and feared, and on Nāga Panchamī their images are painted on either side of the doorways of houses, and they are propitiated there with offerings of milk and puffed rice. At Nāga Panchamī time one can buy entire sheets of *nāga* images for this purpose, printed in pairs on brightly colored tissue paper, so that they can be affixed to every doorway in the house. There are double *nāgas* intertwined in a double-helix; *nāgas* holding Shiva's *linga* in their coils; and the famous images of Krishna dancing on the five headed hood of the *nāga*. Nāga Panchamī is for all, regardless of sectarian belief.

One of the deepest wells in Kāshī is called Nāg Kuān (Karkotaka Vāpī in the *Kāshī Khanda*).[8] It is in the ancient and now dilapidated part of northern Kāshī, and it is said to have been the home of the great Sanskrit grammarian Patanjali, over two thousand years ago. On Nāga Panchamī this well, in a part of the city not usually frequented by most Hindus, comes to life with a great *melā*. Here thousands of people bathe in the deep well, honor its serpent deities, and watch the daredevil young men from this district plunge from the top of the wall surrounding the well into the waters some thirty feet below. These waters, they say, are very deep because they emerge from the netherworlds, Pātāla, which is the realm of the *nāgas*. In the late afternoon, as the festivities wane, a great crowd will gather under an enormous banyan tree to listen to speeches in honor of Patanjali, who is said to have been an incarnation of Vishnu's serpent, Shesha.

Finally, on the full moon of Shrāvana, the attention of the brahmin community is fixed again upon the river. For them, this is the yearly day of atonement. All along the Ganges bank, muddy and slippery as it is at this time of year, battalions of brahmins sit repeating the lines of the *prāyashchitta* rite which cleanses the sins of the past year. They bathe in the river several times during this ritual sequence, and they change their sacred threads—the symbol of their initiation into Vedic

A nāga *or serpent stone, freshly sprinkled with water.*

learning—for fresh ones. They will consecrate several sacred threads for use during the upcoming year. It is said that each of the castes has its special yearly festival, and this festival of purification is the special day of the brahmin caste.[9]

For all castes, however, the full moon of Shrāvana is anticipated for its more popular custom: the tying of a brightly colored band around the wrist of someone who will be one's protector. It is called Rakshā Bandhana, "Tying the Amulet," and it is celebrated by everyone. Sisters tie *rākhīs* on their brothers' wrists, priests upon their patrons', friends upon their friends'. For over a week beforehand these *rākhīs,* some elaborately decorated with tinsel and ornaments, are for sale in the markets, and if one's protector is far away, the *rākhīs* can be sent by mail.

The pace of Bhādrapada (August/September), the last month of the rainy season, is almost as brisk as that of Shrāvana. The month has two very important "thirds" for the worship of goddesses. The third day *(tīj)* of the waning fortnight is called Kajalī Tīj, the "Black Third," and is celebrated in a dozen different ways. It is named for the amorous rainy season songs *(kajalī)* which women sing at this time of year. In the villages around Banāras, sisters sprout barley and put the young sprouts behind their brothers' ears on this day. As many of the *tīj* rites throughout the year have to do with the health and welfare of husbands, this *tīj* is especially for the well-being of brothers. In the city of Kāshī, this day is the great yearly celebration of the goddess Vishālākshī, the "Wide-Eyed" goddess, and in the hills near Banāras it is known as the birthday of the great Vindhyavāsinī Devī, "Dweller in the Vindhya Mountains."

The third day of the waxing fortnight is called Haritālikā Tīj. Here the luminous goddess, the auspicious Mangalā Gaurī, is especially worshipped, as are some of the other great *devīs* of Kāshī. Women keep this day as a fast in order that their husbands might live long or, if they are single, in order to get good husbands. They tell the story of Pārvatī's persistence in winning the great Shiva as a husband.

On the fourth day of the waning fortnight, Ganesha is honored. This is one of two great Ganesha Chaturthī days during the year, the other being in the winter month of Māgha. Every waning fourth, however, is dedicated to Ganesha and is a day to make a point of worship at Bare Ganesha, the "Big Ganesha" northwest of Maidāgin Park.

The eighth day of the waning fortnight is Krishna's birthday, and while its public celebration is not as vigorous in Kāshī as it is in the heartland of Krishna worship in the Mathurā area, still it is one of India's most beloved festivals and is celebrated with great enthusiasm in the Krishna Gopāla Temple, attached to one of the *mathas* of the Vallabha tradition, in the dense Chaukhambā area of the city. On the night of Krishna's birth, here, as in Mathurā; the faithful keep watch at the temple so that they might have the first *darshana* of baby Krishna. Home altars throughout the city display elaborate scenes of Krishna, with his cowherd and milkmaid friends, with tiny cattle and trees, with toys and swings for his pleasure. As Krishna Janmāshtamī approaches, the decorations and figurines for these home altars are for sale in the bazaars.

In the waxing fortnight of Bhādrapada, the sixth day is the great Sun festival of the year, Lolārka Shashthī. This annual *melā* at Lolārka Kund in southern Kāshī attracts tens of thousands of Hindu villagers from the surrounding countryside. The purpose of the *melā* is clearly focused: the birth of sons. Couples without male progeny bathe in the *kund,* and those who have succeeded in this effort bring their sons back for a celebratory bath.

Two days later, on the eighth day of the waxing fortnight, the goddesses again move into the foreground with the beginning of a sixteen-day *melā* in honor of Lakshmī. It takes place at Lakshmī Kund just west of Godaulia on Luxa Road. Every day for sixteen days, those who observe the *vrata* of Mahālakshmī will bathe in the *kund,* hear the stories of this *vrata,* have the *darshana* of Mahālakshmī, and honor her with sixteen kinds of grains and sixteen kinds of flowers. The sixteen days are called the Sorahiā Melā, and the final day—the eighth day of the waning fortnight of Āshvina—is the great *vrata* of Lakshmī, called Jīvit Putrikā Vrata, to be observed by women for the life of their children.

THE AUTUMN: ĀSHVINA, KĀRTTIKA

The fall month of Āshvina (September/October) begins with a fortnight for remembering the dead: *pitri paksha,* the "fortnight of the ancestors." While it is observed widely in India, this time has a special force in Kāshī and in other *tīrthas,* such as Prayāga and Gayā, which are said to be good places for benefiting the dead. People come to Kāshī at this time especially for these *shrāddha* rites, which they perform at Manikarnikā Kund or at Pishāchamochana tank on the western skirts of the city. Pishāchamochana is for those whose departed loved ones have met an untimely or accidental death and have, thus, become *pishāchas,* "goblins." Pishāchamochana means "Where the Goblins Are Liberated," for by rites at this place they may leave their restless state and become *pitris,* "ancestors." Those who perform *shrāddha* here might add force to their rites by driving a spike into the trunk of an old tree in the temple courtyard, thus assuring that the *pishācha* will

The temple of Pishāchamochana.

be left behind. The trunk of this tree bristles with thousands of such spikes. Before leaving, those who perform these rites will certainly have the *darshana* of Pishāchamochana himself, whose round head occupies the sanctum of the temple. They say he was once a *pishācha* who tried to sneak into Kāshī. He was caught and decapitated by Bhairava and then allowed to remain here at the city limits to liberate other *pishāchas* from their painful condition.

After *pitri paksha,* there begins a fall festival cycle so filled with holidays and observances that schools and universities are ordinarily closed for a month. As the month of Āshvina begins its waxing fortnight, the fall Navarātra, the "Nine Nights" of the Goddess begins. This, the most fervently observed of the two Nine Nights cycles, is called by the general name Durgā Pūjā. Each day the focus is on a different one of the city's nine Durgās and nine Gaurīs. Most of the city's great goddesses are among these eighteen. The great Durgā of Durgā Kund is called Kūshmānda ("Pumpkin Gourd") Durgā and is visited on the third day. Vishālākshī is visited on the fifth, Lalitā on the sixth, and Sankatā Devī and Annapūrnā on the eighth. Mahālakshmī is seen on the ninth. (*See* Appendix IV for the two cycles of goddesses and their locations.) In the home people consecrate a round water pot, called a *ghata* or *kalasha,* which is an emblem of the auspicious presence of the Goddess throughout the Nine Nights. Civic and religious organizations sponsor the construction of elaborate clay images of Durgā shaped on a frame of straw and bamboo and painted with precision. These beautiful images are consecrated at the beginning of the Nine Nights and become the dwelling place of the Goddess for these days. On the tenth day of the month, called Vijaya Lakshmī or Vijaya Dashamī—the day of her victory over the Bull Demon—these images are taken out in procession to the Ganges, where the Goddess is given leave to depart and the image, now lifeless, is committed to the river.

Even as Durgā is being celebrated in Kashi, on the other side of the river in the Mahārāja's city of Rāmnagar, another great *melā* has begun. This is the Rām Līlā, the cycle of plays which tells the epic story of Lord Rāma. The plays, sponsored by the Mahārāja, are performed every evening, beginning at the end of Bhādrapada with the "Endless" fourteenth, named for the infinite coils of Vishnu's serpent, Ananta. By the tenth of Āshvina, Vijaya Dashamī, the victory of Rāma over the demon Rāvana is celebrated. This is the year's great *kshatriya* festival. The very next day, an episode of the Rām Līlā is enacted in the streets of Banāras at Nātī Imlī near the Sanskrit University. The episode is called the Bharat Milāp, the "Reunion with Bharata," and it used to attract the largest crowd of any of Kāshī's yearly *melās.* The 1906 District Gazeteer estimated the crowd at 50,000. With barely room to move, people jam the streets to watch a simple and yet moving moment in the dramatic action of the Rāmāyana: Rāma, victorious over Rāvana, has returned at last to Ayodhyā after fourteen years of exile. He meets his beloved brother Bharata, and the brothers embrace. That is all that happens, but the crowd goes wild, shouting, "Victory to Lord Rāma!" "Victory to Brother Bharata!" For this moment, the players actually become Lord Rāma and Brother Bharata in the eyes of the people, and seeing the play is indeed the *darshana* of the Lord.

The first half of the month of Kārttika (October/November) moves with anticipation toward the great festival of Divālī or Dīpāvalī, the

"Row of Lights" festival which occurs at the end of the fortnight on
the new-moon day. The entire fortnight has an air of New Year's
preparation about it, and, indeed, in some parts of India and in some
communities, the day after Divālī—the first day of the waxing fortnight
of Kārttika—is considered to be the New Year's Day. In this season,
houses and temples that had faded in the wash of the monsoon rains are
freshly whitewashed, inside and out. On Dhanteras, the "Wealthy
Thirteenth," the brass market in Thatherī Bazaar is the busiest place
in the city, as women from every household hasten to obey one of the
injunctions of the day: to purchase a new pot. This is the day of the
rich *yaksha,* Kubera, the "Lord of Wealth." It is the first of the three
days of Divālī celebrations. The markets are filled with the paraphernalia of festivity. There are the small, well-crafted and painted clay
images of Lakshmī and Ganesha for which Banāras is famous. There
are piles of shallow clay dishes for oil lamps, the special sweets of the
season, the strings of colored electric lights for home decorations, and
the fireworks for the dark night of the month. The fourteenth day of
the month calls for cleaning the entire house with a broom. By the
fifteenth day, everything has been readied for the worship of Lakshmī,
for it is believed that the Goddess of Fortune will find the groomed and
decorated house attractive, and will wish to dwell there.

All over Banāras, Divālī is celebrated with enthusiasm. For merchants, this is the day on which they will open new account books and
invite the Goddess of Fortune into their shops to honor her at the
outset of the new year. At the auspicious hour, announced by the
pandits, shops and factories will come to a standstill while Lakshmī
Pūjā is performed. As evening approaches, each household will put out
its row of lights, lining the rooftops and windowsills with the small
single-wick oil lamps for which this festival is famous. Even the
poorest household will have a lamp or two, and the richest may replace
the simple oil lamps with festive, even garish, strands of electric lights.
In this way the darkest night of the month is made brilliant, to welcome Lakshmī for another year. The riverfront is also aglow with
lights, as people come to light lamps in small, clay dishes and float them
out into the river.

With all this emphasis on wealth and fortune, it is not surprising to
find that Lakshmī shares this season with some of India's most ancient
yaksha deities, all of whom had a vested interest in the good things of
life. Kubera, Hanumān, and Ganesha are honored along with Lakshmī.

These deities are from the more beneficent side of the *yaksha* family, and in ancient times this autumn season was their great yearly festival.[10]

The day after Divālī—the first day of the waxing fortnight of Kārttika—is called Annakūta, the "Mountain of Food." Like many Banāras festival days, its interpretations and rites are legion. Throughout North India, this is a day sacred to Krishna, and he is worshipped as the Lord of Govardhana, the mountain he lifted up to protect the cowherd folk from the wrathful rains of Indra. On this day in Vraj, Govardhana itself is worshipped with an unsurpassed feast of foods and sweets. In Kāshī, this day is observed with a "Mountain of Food" at the Gopāla Temple, dedicated to Krishna. In Vaishnava homes, Govardhana Pūjā is observed by making a crude image of Govardhana out of cowdung on the courtyard floor. On this one day, this deity, which looks something like a gingerbread man, is honored with foods as the Lord of Govardhana, increaser of cattle.

Annakuta is also observed in the Vishvanātha and Annapūrnā Temples, and in Banāras this is its greatest significance. The courtyards of these two temples are filled with piles of milk sweets, arranged elaborately in the form of castles and temples. And there are mountains of grain as well, celebrating the newly harvested crops. The crowds that come on this day for the *darshana* of Vishvanātha are some of the biggest of the year. This day commemorates the return of Shiva to Kāshī after the reign of King Divodāsa.[11] In nearby Annapūrnā Temple, this is the one day in the year when the golden image of Annapūrnā is revealed for *darshana*. So dense are the crowds in these temples that there is one-way traffic through Vishvanātha Lane, and people stand in line for a brief glimpse of Shiva and Annapūrnā.

On the next day, the religious attention of the city shifts to the riverfront in the Panchagangā Ghāt area, where it remains fixed for the rest of the month of Kārttika. This, the second day of the fortnight, is called Yama Dvitīyā, "Yama's Second," and is another of the festivals on which brother and sister affirm their bond. Yama, the God of Death, is the brother of the River Yamunā, who is also worshipped on this day. In Banāras, this day is also called "Bhīma's Second," in honor of the Pāndava hero and strongman, Bhīma.[12] Like his half-brother Hanumān, Bhīma is the Son of the Wind. In village India he is often represented in something of the same manner as Govardhana personified. In a reclining, blockish form he may be seen at Rama Ghāt along the Ganges, fashioned from a ton of sand and silt collected from the *ghāt* steps, covered with a final layer of mud, and painted with his clothes, his facial features, and his mustache all complete. He lies flat on his back, pot-bellied and mountainous. He is honored here as a deity, but everyone knows that Bhīma is the most hedonistic of the noble Pāndava heroes, and they say that he is lying here, exhausted by the effort of trying to fast for a single day during Kārttika. Even so, they honor him.

Kārttika is one of the three sacred months for bathing in Kāshī, and Panchagangā is the place prescribed. On the eleventh day of the waxing fortnight of this month the *chaturmāsa,* the "four months" retreat, comes to an end. Vishnu wakes up from his slumber on this day, called Prabodhinī, the "Waking." During the five days from the eleventh to the full moon, the *ghāt* is teeming with morning bathers who make a point of coming every day during this auspicious time. And they stop at Bindu Mādhava at the top of the giant steps for the *darshana* of Vishnu, fresh from his months of sleep. During this time, Panchagangā Ghāt is in its

Panchagangā Ghāt on the full moon
day of Kārttika.

glory. Hundreds of "sky lamps" are hung each evening in little wicker baskets at the tops of tall bamboo poles, and the great conical stone lamp holder, which rises above the *ghāt* and holds hundreds of wicks, is lighted. These lights, they say, brighten the way for the dead as they return to the world of the ancestors after their yearly visit to earth.

THE COLD SEASON: MĀRGASHĪRSHA,
PAUSHA, AND MĀGHA

When Kārttika is over, the pace of festivals that has continued, brisk and unbroken, since the first of Shrāvana, slows considerably. The weather is good, increasingly cool and unfailingly clear, and there is work to be done. Not surprisingly, the Sun is especially honored during these winter months, when his warmth is welcomed. And these are good months for pilgrimage rounds. For example, the circumambulation of Vārānasī city is prescribed for Mārgashīrsha and the circumambulation of Kedāra Khanda for Pausha. (*See* Appendix II and Maps 5 and 6.)

The most important sequence in Mārgashīrsha takes place during its first eight days: the pilgrimage to the eight Bhairavas, a different one each day. (*See* Appendix V.) The climax of this sequence is Bhairavāshtamī, "Bhairava's Eighth," when Kāla Bhairava, the city's guardian magistrate, is celebrated. On this day alone, the cloth apron that covers all but Bhairava's face is removed. He is garlanded with a necklace of solid silver skulls. People crowd in for the *darshana* of his complete image on this day.

Also in Mārgashīrsha the *vrata* of Annapūrnā is observed, beginning on the fifth day of the waning fortnight and lasting for seventeen days. During these days the observer of the *vrata* wears a cord knotted seventeen times, eats only fruits or saltless food, listens to the stories of the Annapūrnā *vrata,* and worships the goddess daily. In so doing, one is said to obtain the wealth one desires.

On the fourteenth of January, either in the month of Pausha or Māgha, occurs the winter solstice in the Indian calendrical reckoning. This is the day when the sun begins its northern course (*uttarāyana),* thus marking the beginning of what one might call the "waxing" half of the year. This half is auspicious for all passages of the life cycle, including the final passage of death. The day is called Makara Sankrānti, which refers to the sun's passage into the sign of the zodiac called Makara, or Capricorn. The primary religious requirement of the day is bathing in the Ganges, and the *ghāts* all along the riverfront are busy with bathers. The popular customs of the day, however, include making sweets with sesame seeds; eating *khichari*, a staple food of rice cooked with lentils; and, above all, flying kites. The appearance of these bright tissue kites in the markets and, before long, in the sky is a sure sign that Makara Sankrānti is at hand.

The month of Māgha (January/February) is the time of the year's largest Ganesha *melā* in Kāshī: the celebration of Ganesha's birthday on Ganesha Chaturthī, the fourth day of the waning fortnight. For weeks ahead of time, the city's craftsmen have been busy making and painting the clay images of Ganesha, large and small, which are sold in the lanes around the temple of Bare Ganesha on this day. It is a day of both public and domestic worship, and those who take the *darshana* of Bare Ganesha in his temple will also purchase an image of the stout orange deity to place on their home altars.

Like Vaishākha and Kārttika, the entire month of Māgha is famous for bathing in the Ganges. This is the coldest of the bathing months, however, and a vow to bathe daily during this season seems possible only for the strong, although many of the frail undertake just such a vow. This month of bathing culminates in the great bathing festival on the Māgha new-moon day, the *amāvasyā*, at Dashāshvamedha.

In the last fortnight of Māgha, there is a signal of spring. The fifth day of this fortnight is Vasanta Panchamī, "Spring's Fifth," which heralds the coming of spring. The city is decked out in yellow. There are yellow *saris,* shirts, and ribbons for sale in the markets, and nose-gays of yellow spring flowers and mango blossoms for sale at the doors of temples. Now the great spring festival of Holī is but forty days away, and young boys in every neighborhood begin thinking of the great bonfires of Holī eve. Beginning on Vasanta Panchamī, they start scavenging wood for the neighborhood Holikā fire.

On the same day as Vasanta Panchamī the city celebrates the goddess Sarasvatī, who has jurisdiction over educational institutions and learning. For this occasion, artisans have made images of Sarasvatī, both of clay and of *papier-mâché*, which are installed in classrooms, colleges, and elaborately decorated makeshift shrines. After a day and night of worship, Sarasvatī's images, like those of Durgā after Navarātra, are deconsecrated and taken out in festive processions to be thrown into the Ganges.

SPRING: PHĀLGUNA AND CHAITRA

Although it is sometimes said that India's spring season begins only in Chaitra, the month of Phālguna (February/March) is definitely a spring month in Banāras. The coldest months are over, and the month of Phālguna brings to the city both its greatest high holy day, Mahā-shivarātri, the "Great Night of Shiva," and its greatest carnival, Holī.

The fourteenth day of every waning fortnight is observed as Shi-varātri, and the pious offer special honor to Shiva on that day. In Phālguna, however, is the Great Shivarātri, and in Banāras this is one of the year's most important festivals, for it is the major yearly cele-bration of Lord Shiva. Some Hindus will observe an all-night vigil during the night before Shivarātri day. In Banāras, people will gather in the Jnāna Vāpī pavilion for the night's vigil, singing *bhajans,* or devotional songs, to keep themselves awake as the night passes. The Purānas contain many stories of the benefits showered upon those who have kept the Shivarātri vigil, even those who have done so inadver-tently, such as theives or hunters.

On Shivarātri, the tradition in Banāras is to have *darshana* in one of the great temples of the city, and preferably in many such temples. Some people spend the better part of the day making a grand circuit of the city's temples. Most important of all is Vishvanātha, which will be thronged with worshippers. Such temples as Mrityunjaya, Trilochana, and Kedāreshvara will also be crowded. It would be safe to say that every visible *linga* in the city is heaped with flowers and drenched with Ganges water on Shivarātri, even those that are broken, name-less, and ill-attended the rest of the year. For certain temples, such as Omkāra, this is the one day of the year when more than a few people come. For others, such as the ancient site of Krittivāsa, this is the one day when worshippers are permitted to come. The once-famous Krit-tivāsa is now contained within a mosque, in the Maidāgin area not far from Mrityunjaya. Although no *linga* remains, on Shivarātri day Hindus are allowed to enter the mosque, where they make their offer-ings in the now-defunct tank used for Muslim ablutions. By the day's end, the tank is heaped high with garlands of marigolds. Similarly, in one corner of the Jnāna Vāpī Mosque, Hindus are allowed to honor the ancient site of Avimukteshvara—now a Muslim gravesite—with flowers.

On the eleventh day of the following fortnight, the last half of Phālguna, the yearly decoration-day *(shringāra)* of Vishvanātha takes place. After Shivarātri, this is the biggest festival day of the year at Vishvanātha. On this day, the special silver four-faced cap which sits upon the *linga* is set in place and decorated with all the proper sandalwood paste, leaves, and flowers. On this day, however, rather than sprinkling the *linga* with Ganges water, worshippers sprinkle it with colored red powder. The day is called the "Colorful Eleventh," Rangabhārī Ekādashī, and it anticipates the riot of color throwing which will break out four days later on Holī.

Holī is the great festival of springtime, a time of gaiety, chaos, and saturnalia. Holī falls on the first day of Chaitra, but for at least a week ahead of time the piles of brightly colored powder with which one "plays" Holī are for sale in each neighborhood bazaar, and for a few days before Holī one travels the city streets in constant risk of being splashed with pink-colored water by zealous schoolboys. On the eve of Holī, the full-moon night of Phālguna, the festivities begin with the burning of the many neighborhood Holikā fires. These are said to consume the witch Holikā, who had tried to burn up Vishnu's devotee, Prahlāda, but was instead burned to death herself, while Prahlāda was saved by his great devotion to the Lord. With the Holikā fire begins the revelry, the license, and the wildness which the boys, young and old, have anticipated since they began scavenging wood and rubbish for the fire on Vasanta Panchamī, forty days before.

The dawn of the day of Holī brings the saturnalia, the ritual reversals, and the social leveling, which are elements of many springtime and New Year's festivals. The usual order of this hierarchical society almost disappears. In the streets and in the courtyards of homes, revelers drench one another with buckets of colored water and smear one another's faces with wet streaks of blue and red, pink and green. In the dense lanes of downtown Banāras, the women, for the most part, play Holī in their own households and immediate neighborhoods, while the men, most of whom have begun the day with a taste of intoxicating *bhāng,* careen through the streets, singing, throwing colors, and shouting obscenities.

The "wet" colors are over at noontime, and the ethos of the after-

noon changes from raucous frivolity to familial amiability. After a
shower or a bath in the Ganges, people put on a fresh change of
clothing, preferably immaculate white, and begin another round of
visiting in one another's homes, bringing sweets, singing, and making
amends for any misunderstandings of the past year. Now they greet
one another with "dry" red powder, rubbing a bit on the foreheads
and faces of those they meet and embracing with a warm "Happy
Holī!" Again, groups of young men, still warm with the blur of *bhāng*,
swagger through the streets singing to the accompaniment of drums
and musical instruments. Many of these groups will eventually make
their way to Chaumsathī Ghāt near Dashāshvamedha, where on the
evening of Holī and throughout the next day there is a *melā* in honor of
the Sixty-Four Yoginīs. Here groups of respectable merchants from
the city and rustic rickshaw pullers from the outlying villages, as
red-faced as clowns, enjoy their madness and their song.

Today the Holī festivities, with all their elements of the return to
chaos and the subsequent restoration of order, seem to launch the new
year. They are New Year rites *par excellence*. Yet the new year does
not officially begin for another fortnight. The waning fortnight of
Chaitra, which immediately follows Holī, is the last fortnight of the
year. In former days, the mood of this fortnight was entirely focused
upon its last four days and the great river festival, the Burhwā Mangal,
which combined boating, festivity, and music and which completed the
year in a style utterly characteristic of high Banārsī culture. Since the
1920s the Burhwā Mangal, an emblem of the great days of Hindu
princely culture, has disappeared.

The Burhwā Mangal was a festival of boats. For weeks ahead of
time, the well-to-do would compete in decorating their boats—with
flags, with carpets, even with chandeliers. Hundreds of boats came out
for the festival, and their patrons would invite musicians and dancers
to provide cultured entertainment for their guests. The riverfront,
from Asi to Panchagangā, became a floating music festival. Between
the larger boats plied hundreds of smaller craft selling flowers and
betel leaves, sweets, and toys. At the outset of the festival, the
Mahārāja's boat, the most lavishly decorated of all, would appear to the
simultaneous greeting of a thousand musicians up and down the river.
And at the end of the festival, the Mahārāja would beckon all to follow,
and his boat would lead the floating procession back to the palace at
Rāmnagar for an entire night of music.

Kāshī in and out of Time

F R O M this look at the movement of the seasons, we can see that time in Kāshī is both rhythmic in its weekly and monthly cycles and highly variegated in its pace and accent as the year passes. The diversity of the gods is played out in the cycles of time, each deity having its own days and months. And the intricate complexity of Kāshī's sacred geography begins to fall into place, not in any scheme of hierarchy, but in the beats and accents of time. The strong currents of the city's religious life move from place to place—from Dashāshvamedha to Kedāra to Panchagangā. Every deity, every temple, every *ghāt* has an important place, in due time.

Kāshī is rich with time, the very source of time, but it is also said to stand aloof from time. In this one place, they say, time—as fascinating and complex as it is—does not fully have its way. All the diversity of time—its auspicious and inauspicious days, its festivals and fasts—is said to be transcended in Kāshī:

Here in the ashram of Vishveshvara it is always the Perfect Age. Here it is always a great festival day, and here one is never troubled by unfavorable conjunctions of the stars. Here where Vishveshvara abides it is always the blessed half of the year, always lucky, always auspicious.[13]

Elsewhere, one must pay special attention to the textures and implications of time, but these ordinary considerations are overshadowed by the glory of Kāshī. In one Purāna it is affirmed:

When sinful people set out for Kāshī, all their sins, even those that have affected the very elements of their bodies, stagger and fall off. For travelers destined for Kāshī, all time is good time. It is wholly auspicious, and one need not think further about it. This means that in going to Kāshī, one need not wait for the right moment or omen.[14]

The time when one sets out for Kāshī *is* the auspicious time, for the sanctity of Kāshī makes time auspicious.

Likewise, the time of death in Kāshī is always auspicious. Here, one need not wonder whether the stars are right for dying. In Indian legend, the importance of dying at the right time is dramatized by the hero Bhīshma, who had a boon to die whenever he chose. Even when mortally wounded, he waited to die until the auspicious half of the year. However, Kāshī is the one place in the world where Bhīshma need not have waited.

The one who dies in Avimukta, even if he has sinned a thousand times and met with grief thereafter, gains the supreme prize. He should not worry about whether it is the half of the year when the sun travels north, or the half of the year when the sun travels south. For one who dies in Avimukta, any time is auspicious. There one should not think about whether time is auspicious or inauspicious. [15]

Kāshī is also said to stand apart from the great cycles of cosmic time called the *yugas,* or "ages." In the Hindu view of the Four Ages, the first age is called the Krita Yuga, the Age of Perfection, when time is golden. In the Age of Perfection, the imaginary cow of *dharma* is four-footed. But in the Tretā Yuga, the Third Age, the cow becomes three-legged; and in the Dvāpara Yuga, the Second Age, it becomes two-legged. Finally, in the Kali Yuga, the Age of Strife, *dharma* has but one leg to stand on. It is a time of corruption and sin, when human abilities and possibilities are so contracted and impoverished that the performance of *dharma* is virtually impossible.[16] This is the age in which we live now, so they say.

The four ages run in cycle over and over again. And after a thousand such cycles, a vast period of time called a *kalpa* or a day in the life of Brahmā, everything here below is destroyed and lies quiescent for the equally long night of Brahmā. This period of dissolution is called the *pralaya,* and after it is over another day of Brahmā begins to dawn, and the universe emerges once again.

In Kāshī the times are different. In Kāshī there is no Kali Yuga.[17] In fact, the running down of time through the course of the four ages does not take place in Kāshī at all. Here it is always the Age of Perfection. It is no wonder, then, that the *māhātmyas* praise the power and effectiveness of rites done and prayers said in Kāshī, for here time has retained the energy and potency of "beginning time." Charity, austerity, fasting, rites for the dead—all these are amplified in their blessings and benefits a thousandfold.

In exhorting people to come to Kāshī, the traditional Hindu writers not only glorified the blessings that could be obtained here by those who performed traditional rites, they also lauded the pilgrimage to

Kāshī as a substitute for these rites. So corrupt is this Age of Strife, with but one leg of righteousness left, that all many people can do is take refuge in Kāshī, rites or no rites.

This notion of Kāshī as a refuge for the afflicted in these dark times is one to which the Purānic writers return repeatedly, almost poignantly, in their hymnic exaltations of the city.[18] In these times when the homeless have no place to go, Vārānasī is the place to go. In these times when there is no relief from the darkness, Kāshī is the light. In these times when there is no shelter for the oppressed, Vārānasī is the shelter. The city of Shiva requires nothing of people but their presence here. The rest is a gift of grace.[19]

The vision of a city which is a refuge from the terror of this Age of Strife is a compelling one. But what does it mean to affirm that the Kali Age does not exist in Kāshī? It is certainly not apparent to the visitor, Hindu or Western, that the times in this crowded and noisy city are different from those of the rest of the world. In some ways, the city seems to have been a magnet for the homeless and suffering, the diseased and deformed—all of whom can make a scanty living in the streets of Banāras. The hardship of these times is often visible with special intensity here.

Even among those who know Kāshī best, some will scoff at the notion that there is no Kali Age here. "Where on earth has the Kali Age not penetrated?" one *sādhu* asks rhetorically, gesturing toward the chaos of a crowded bazaar in a narrow lane. "It is a lie to say that the Kali Age has not entered Kāshī, for it extends everywhere. You must not think that Kali is not here in Kāshī, or that I am a *sādhu* and therefore Kali is not here in my body." He strikes his fist upon his chest. "Kali is here, as everywhere."

The Kali Age is a subtle thing. It is not simply an era of time, but a quality of time, and a quality of heart. As the *Kāshī Rahasya* states:

Kali does not enter in some embodied form and torment people here, but wherever the heart is impure—that is called the Kali Age.

How can the Kali Age, which is experienced outside Kāshī, over the course of thousands of previous births, vanish here when it has influenced people's hearts, O sages?[20]

It is not so easy to claim that the Kali Age has no influence in Kāshī, for people carry the Age of Strife around with them, in their hearts.

And yet Kāshī too is a subtle thing. There are those who ask,

"Where is this Kāshī, where there is no Kali Age?" According to the Purānas, they say, Kāshī exists as the City of Light throughout the first three ages, but in the Kali Age, it disappears. In this age, what meets the eye is quite an earthly city, but those yogis and people of true vision can still see the real Kāshī, the spiritual city.

It is as a spiritual entity, they say, that Kāshī is beyond the reach of the Kali Age. Swāmi Karpātrī, in one of his evening lectures during the monsoon season, explains the presence of the Kali Age in Kāshī this way:

It is a subtle matter to say that Kāshī is situated on Shiva's trident or that there is no Kali Age in Kāshī. The obvious truth is this: just as there is famine outside, so there is famine here; just as there are heat and cold outside, so are there heat and cold here. But Kāshī has a subtle form too. All of us alike can see her obvious form, but only the pure of heart can see this special, subtle form of hers. To them, Kāshī shows her subtle form, and that is the form of Shiva himself, because all of Kāshī is a great *linga* of light.

Karpātrī here is articulating a very old metaphysical position, applied in this instance to the understanding of Kāshī: the two levels of truth, the spiritual and the earthly. While the earthly *(ādhibhautika)* Kāshī no doubt partakes of its portion of the Age of Strife, Hindus affirm that the spiritual *(adhyātmika)* Kāshī is a place that does indeed transcend this world with its cycles of time. And it is for the *darshana* of this luminous Kāshī that pilgrims come.

7

CITY OF
ALL INDIA

"ALL THE *tīrthas* on earth are here in Kāshī," said an elderly
widow from Jhansi, now living in Kāshī in her old age. "If you stay in
Kāshī you never need to go anywhere else on pilgrimage." The notion
she expressed, as we walked by the Ganges late one afternoon, is an
ancient one, voiced over and over in the Sanskrit Purānas and given
geographical expression in the temples and *tīrthas* of Banāras. The
whole world is here in this one place.

Just as the gods are all present in Kāshī, so are all the sacred places
present here. There is no need to go elsewhere.

All *tīrthas*, and all cities, and all sixty abodes of Shiva, rivers, streams, lakes,
and oceans, all the gods and all the sages dwell in Kāshī, desiring their own
liberation, under the great influence of Shiva, who quenches desire. The
mind of those who have beheld Kāshī delights no more in other *tīrthas*.[1]

O sages, I have established all *tīrthas* in this place, a place which I never
leave. It is made of all the *tīrthas;* it is pure, the most secret of the secret,
great, the first-born of all places, the Great Lord.[2]

Spatial transposition is a fascinating fact of India's spiritual geography.
Kāshī, of course, is present in a thousand places in India, each with its
own temple of Kāshī Vishvanātha, some even boasting a Panchakroshī
Road. Kāshī is the paradigm of the sacred place, to which other places
subscribe in their claims to sanctity. At the same time, Kāshī includes

all the other *tīrthas* within it. According to Purānic commentators, these *tīrthas* exist only partially and in gross form in their separate places, but in their fullness and in subtle form, they exist in Kāshī.[3] Kāshī is dense with *tīrthas.*[4]

The presence of all *tīrthas* in Kāshī is more than a matter of literary eulogy, for many *tīrthas* and groups of *tīrthas* are part of Kāshī's sacred geography. The various temples, wells, pools, parks, and streams of the city symbolically embody the whole of India. When we ask the question, "What kind of *place* is Kāshī?" one of the answers we find is that Kāshī is a place that gathers together the whole of India. Kāshī is a cosmopolis—a city that is a world.

The Seven Cities

THE "SEVEN CITIES" *(saptapurī)* are known all over India. In the North, there is Ayodhyā, the capital of Lord Rāma; Mathurā, the birthplace of Krishna; Hardvār, the gate of the Ganges; and Kāshī, the city of Shiva. In Central India is Ujjain, sacred to Shiva. In the West is Dvārakā, the capital of Krishna. And in the South is Kānchī, sacred to both Vishnu and Shiva. All seven are said to bestow *moksha* at the time of death.

Still, as a contemporary Hindu guide to the *tīrthas* puts it: "Among these seven, Kāshī is held to be supreme."[5] In Kāshī, those who think about such questions maintain that the other six cities bestow *moksha* only indirectly, by first bringing the good fortune of rebirth in Kāshī. Only Kāshī leads directly to *moksha,* with no stops on the way. The story of Shiva Sharma, the brahmin from Mathurā, bears this out.[6] According to the *Kāshī Khanda,* Shiva Sharma, when he saw the first gray hair upon his head, renounced home and family for a life of pilgrimage and simplicity—an age-old tradition. He went on a pilgrimage to all the seven cities, intending finally to live out his days in Kāshī. As fate would have it, however, he died in Hardvār. Soma Sharma was fetched by a heavenly chariot, which took him through the various realms of heavens to Vaikuntha, the highest heaven. After enjoying his stay in heaven, Shiva Sharma was reborn in Kāshī, and only at the end of that lifetime did he obtain the liberation of *moksha.* "Other places of liberation cause one to reach Kāshī," it is said; "And having reached Kāshī one will be liberated, and not elsewhere, not even by a million *tīrthas!*"[7]

The other six cities are said to be located in Kāshī, as well as in their native places.

Just as Brahmā, Indra, and the other gods, as well as all the multitude of souls, being parts of Brahman, having their home in Brahman, ultimately go to Brahman and to no other refuge, so do all *tīrthas* and the seven cities take refuge in Kāshī and dwell there in order to increase their own power. . . . All these cities of liberation should be known to have been created in Kāshī at the time of creation. They dwell in Kāshī during the time of abiding, and they dissolve in Kāshī at the time of universal destruction.[8]

Shiva also explains the various locations of the cities of liberation in Kāshī as well as the seasons for visiting each of them.[9] The living religious tradition and the "text" of the sacred geography of Banāras bear him out. First there is Ayodhyā, the capital city of the Sun Dynasty of Lord Rāma. From here Rāma went forth into exile, along with his brother, Lakshmana, and his wife, Sītā. After years of struggle, Rāma finally returned to Ayodhyā, the episode enacted in the famous Bharat Milāp fair in Kāshī. South and west of Dashāshvamedha are parts of the city called Rāma Pura and Lakshmana Pura, for the famous brothers. It is Rāma Kund which is said to be Ayodhyā—a large, clay-banked pond just north of Luxa Road. This place is also famous as Rāmeshvaram, the southern *tīrtha* at the tip of India, where Rāma established a Shiva *linga* when he returned from Lankā after rescuing Sītā. Rāma Kund, with the small Rāmeshvaram Temple on its bank, is a quiet pond today, more attractive to water buffaloes than to bathers. The scriptures prescribe a visit here in the hot season, Jyeshtha and Āshādha.

Mathurā, as we have seen before, is located at Bakariā Kund in Kāshī. In the height of its glory, the atmosphere there must have been as eclectic as that of the other Mathurā to the west, with Buddhist, Vaishnava, and Sūrya traditions intermingling with the tradition of the cowherd hero-god Krishna. According to the text, Mathurā should be visited in the spring months of Chaitra and Vaishākha, but in Kāshī no Hindu visits Mathurā at all today, for its ruins have been turned into mosques.

Hardvār is located at the base of the Himālayan foothills where the Ganges enters the plains of North India. It is one of the several places in India where the Kumbha Melā and the Half-Kumbha Melā bathing fairs take place every six years. In Kāshī, Hardvār is at Asi Ghāt. While there is no particular shrine at Asi Ghāt to indicate the presence of Hardvār there, the Hindu guidebooks affirm it to be so. And the religiously literate people of the Asi neighborhood, such as the brahmin women who bathe here daily before dawn, even through the cold winter months, know that this is Hardvār. Every year in the winter month of Māgha especially large crowds bathe at Asi, as at Hardvār in the North. And when the day of the Half-Kumbha Melā comes around—a time when tens of thousands of pilgrims flock to Hardvār—Asi Ghāt is suddenly inundated with bathers too. And the low wooden *chaukīs* where riverside vendors and priests sit are stacked high with *kumbhas,* the fat clay water pots, representing the famous *kumbha* of old which held the nectar of immortality. This nectar, churned up from the ocean at the beginning of time, is said to have splashed the earth in four places as it was whisked away to heaven by the gods: Prayāga, Hardvār, Nāsik, and Ujjain, the four sites of the Kumbha Melā pilgrimage. One such pilgrimage took place during the first fortnight of Vaishākha in 1974, and the Kāshī *panchānga* prescribed: "In Kāshī, bathe at the confluence of the Asi and the Ganges."

Kānchī in the Tamil south has its abode in Kāshī in the Panchagangā Ghāt area, "at the side of the Bindu Mādhava Temple." Like the other cities of liberation, Kānchī is established in Kāshī in a locale, not in a particular temple. Kānchī in Tamilnādu has two parts, Shiva Kānchī and Vishnu Kānchī. In addition, it is the "bench" of the goddess Kāmākshī, one of the most important goddesses in South India. Like Kāshī, the whole complex of Kānchī has a trans-sectarian significance. In one Purānic *māhātmya,* Kāshī and Kānchī are said to be Shiva's two eyes.[10] The season for pilgrimage to Kāshī's Kānchī is the fall, especially the month of Kārttika.

Ujjain, in Madhya Pradesh, is a very old city, sometimes known by the name of Avantikā, "The Victorious." It is famous for its *linga* of light called Mahākāla Shiva. In Kāshī, Ujjain extends from the area around the Kāleshvara Temple, dedicated to Shiva as "Lord of Death," to the temple of Krittivāsa a short distance away. Since the temple of Krittivāsa is now a mosque, the focus of Ujjain is in the shrines of Kāleshvara, Old Kāleshvara, and Great Kāleshvara in the temple complex now dominated by the "Death-Conquering" Shiva, Mrityunjaya.

The riverfront, looking toward Panchagangā—the location of Kānchī.

The winter months of Mārgashīrsha and Pausha are prescribed for a pilgrimage to this part of Kāshī.

Finally, Dvārakā, the capital city of Krishna in his later princely life, is located in the far West of India on the coast of the Saurāshtra peninsula of Gujarāt. In Kāshī, Dvārakā is situated in the area called Shankhoddhāra in the southwestern outskirts of the city. Here one can glimpse something of the ancient Forest of Bliss. The temple and its adjoining ashram sit on the banks of a large pond, which is the center of a quiet and semi-rural neighborhood. Above the door of the temple is painted "Shrī Dvārakādhīsha Shankudhāra," and the Vaishnavas who live here and teach Sanskrit to young resident boy-students are in the tradition of Rāmānanda, the fifteenth-century devotional leader of Banāras. Although the temple itself is not ancient, the site contains some very old remains, the most notable being the Pāla period Vishnu, at least nine hundred years old, standing in a separate shrine within the walls of the temple compound.

The name Shankhoddhāra means the "Salvation of Shankha." But who is Shankha? In this context, Shankha is said to be the name of a demon, slain and also saved by Krishna. There is, indeed, a shrine and story to this effect in Gujarāt's Dvārakā.[11] In Kāshī, however, Shankha is a very old name attached to one of the great *nāgas* who owns and guards the treasures of the earth. We know him from Buddhist texts, which tell of four great *nāgas* of India, who were said to hold up the four quarters of the earth. Shankha was the *nāga* of Banāras, and there is evidence that Shankha had a significant cultus in Banāras even in the time of the Buddha.[12] Might we imagine that this deity was saved by one of the great gods in the fashion of so many of these autochthonous deities of the life cult—incorporated into the entourage of an ascendant deity? The rainy season months, associated with the *nāga*, are prescribed for pilgrimage to Shankhoddhāra, and there have traditionally been *melās* at this site in the months of Shrāvana and Bhādrapada.

These six cities of liberation are all said to be located within Kāshī, the seventh. Each has its own *māhātmya*, of course, but none of the other cities makes Kāshī's sovereign claim to include and comprehend the rest.[13] The positioning of the cities of liberation in Kāshī must have occurred after the time the *Kāshī Khanda* was complete in the fourteenth century, for this illustrious group is not mentioned in the *Kāshī Khanda*. When the rounds of pilgrimage to the seven are described in pilgrim manuals of the past two centuries, they take their lead from the *Kāshī Rahasya*. The circuit of the cities of liberation is not a common pilgrimage in Kāshī. In most of the cities there are no shrines to visit; they are simply parts of the geography of Kāshī. The important thing is that these others are here and everyone knows they are here. They contribute their lustre to the power of Kāshī, whether anyone visits them or not.

The Four Abodes

K Ā S H Ī also contains the four *dhāmas*, the "abodes" of the gods at the four directional compass points of India. Kāshī is not one of the *dhāmas*, although it is sometimes said to be at the center of the quadrant of the others. These four *dhāmas,* all ancient shrines in their own right, were given further emphasis in the ninth century when, according to tradition, the great philosopher Shankara traveled around India, organizing the Dashanāmī orders of *sannyāsins* and establishing monastic centers at these places. Some say he established a center in Kāshī as well.[14] In any case, it seems certain that Shankara visited Kāshī and perhaps spent several years here in the course of his travels.

The term *dhāma* is very ancient and has a variety of meanings that cluster around "dwelling place" and "light." A *dhāma* is the location of divine power in a place, or as one scholar has put it, a "refraction" and "embodiment" of the Divine.[15] It is the dwelling place that is imbued with the light, the refulgence of the holy. In this sense, Kāshī, the place of divine light, is the *dhāma par excellence.*

The northern refraction of the divine light is called Badrīnāth, a Vaishnava site located high in the Himālayas, set between mountains named for the sage-gods Nara and Nārāyana, along the banks of one of the mountain rivers that comes to form the Ganges. Open only during the summer months, Badrīnāth is one of the most popular of Himālayan pilgrimage places and a favorite retreat for ascetics. When the snows close the shrine a woolen cloth is wrapped around the deity, and the monks and ascetics move down the mountain to Joshimath for the winter. In Kāshī, Badrīnāth is placed at Nara-Nārāyana *tīrtha,* in the northern sector of the city between Gāya and Trilochana Ghāts. There is also an image of Badrīnāth within the compound of the Kedāra Temple.

In the far South, at the tip of India in Tamilnādu, is the *dhāma* of Rāmeshvaram. Here it was that Lord Rāma, with the help of the monkey armies, built the great bridge to the island of Lankā where the wicked Rāvana held Sītā in captivity. When he had slain Rāvana, Rāma returned to Rāmeshvaram and established a *linga* there as a penance for killing Rāvana, who was a brahmin as well as a demon and whose death incurred for Rāma the terrible sin of killing a brahmin. The *linga* Rāma established came to be considered one of the great *lingas* of light, so holy that it destroys the worst sins by merely beholding it. In Banāras, Rāmeshvaram is present by name and reputation in three different places: the temple at Rāma Kund in central Kāshī, the village of Rāmeshvara on the Panchakroshī Road, and the shrine of Rāmeshvara at Mān Mandir Ghāt.[16]

As for the refractions of the Divine in the West and the East of

India, we have already taken note of Dvārakā, the western *dhāma* in Gujarāt. In the East, on the coast of the Bay of Bengal in Orissa, is Purī, where the great Krishnaite temple of Jagannāth is situated. The temple of Jagannāth is one of the largest in India, its sanctum with its various subsidiary pavilions and kitchens covering an entire city block. It houses the blockish, wide-eyed, brightly colored images of Krishna Jagannāth, with his brother, Balarāma, and sister, Subhadrā, images that show the ancient roots of these deities in the folk traditions of Orissa. One of India's most vibrant *melās* takes place in Purī, beginning on the second day of the waxing fortnight of Āshādha, just as the monsoon rains are about to begin. The images of the Jagannāth deities are taken out on their own pilgrimage *(yātrā)* on giant chariots *(ratha)* some forty-five feet high. The *melā* is called the Ratha Yātrā, the "Chariot Pilgrimage," and it attracts tens of thousands of people to Purī each year. In Kāshī, the site of Purī is now near Asi Ghāt, in a large pastoral temple compound. Here, too, the sandalwood images of the deities are taken out for the *darshana* of everyone during the time of the Ratha Yātrā festival. For three days, they remain in their chariots at "Ratha Yātrā" crossing, before being taken back to their temple.

The pilgrimage to the four *dhāmas* of India is quite popular, especially in these days of bus pilgrimage tours. In Kāshī, the presence of the four *dhāmas* is widely known and is an impressive fact of the city's sacred geography. A pilgrimage to the four *dhāmas* is described in the pilgrim manuals, but perhaps more significant is that these refractions of the divine light enhance the many-faceted light of Kāshī.

The Twelve Lingas of Light

H I N D U S love the story of the argument of Brahmā and Vishnu and the sudden appearance of a blinding shaft of light between them, a light so brilliant and so fathomless that both gods were humbled by it. It is not surprising that many places of pilgrimage in India have appropriated the story of the appearance of the fiery *linga* as their own.[17] It applies, in a sense, to every place that people have experienced as a place of hierophany, where the Divine has broken through the earthly. In these places, they say, the *linga* was not established by human hands, but is "self-born." In the beginning, it was a *linga* of light. It is not clear just how, out of all the places that have claimed to be *lingas* of light, a group of twelve came to be recognized. There are many more than twelve, but this group has the imprimatur of the wider Hindu tradition.

All twelve of India's *lingas* of light are located in the sacred geography of Kāshī, and their presence here adds to Kāshī the dignity and weight of some of India's mightiest *tīrthas*. Among them is Someshvara, or Somnāth, the "Moon's Lord," located on the seacoast in the western peninsula of Gujarāt. It is also called Prabhāsa, "Place of Splendor," and indeed until its devastation by Mahmud of Ghazna in the eleventh century, it was one of India's most splendid temples. Today the temple is being restored. In Kāshī, Someshvara is located just north of Dashāshvamedha on the heights of Mān Mandir Ghāt. Also present in Kāshī is Mahākāla, the "Great Lord of Death," whose *linga* of light is located in Ujjain, one of the cities of liberation. Here Mahākāla is found in the compound of the "Old Lord of Death," Vriddhakāleshvara. From eastern Bihār comes the very popular and powerful Vaidyanāth, the "Lord of Physicians," with many miracles to his credit. In Kāshī, Vaidyanāth is located in the Kamacchā area and is the most important *linga* in that part of the city. The *linga* of light called Bhīma Shankar is claimed by two locations, one in Mahārāshtra and the other near Gauhāti in Āssām. In Kāshī, its location is undisputed: in the famous temple of Kāshī Karavat in Kachaurī Lane, one of the busiest lanes in the city, and the *linga* is located some twenty feet below the ground, where it is honored daily by priests who approach it by a tunnel entrance. From the street-level temple, Bhīma Shankar may be seen from above. Among the other *lingas* of light in Kāshī are two great *lingas* we have already discussed: Kedāra from the high Himālayas, and Omkāra located on an island in the Narmadā River in Central India.

Finally, of course, the Vishveshvara *linga* is in Kāshī, at the very center of the city. In its true sense, however, the *linga* of light here is the entire sacred zone of Kāshī, of which the Vishveshvara *linga* is a symbol. Kāshī includes all the other luminous *lingas*, for it is not only the place where a single hierophany of light took place, it *is* that hierophany of light. As we shall discuss later, Kāshī itself is said to be a vast *linga* of light, a light extending five *kroshas* to fill the entire sacred zone.

Other Tīrthas in Kāshī

PRAYĀGA is one of India's most famous *tīrthas*. The name means "The Sacrifice," and it reminds us of the way in which pilgrimage to a sacred place came to be considered the primary substitute for the Vedic sacrificial rites. Known as the "King of *Tīrthas*," Prayāga is located at the confluence of the Yamunā and the Ganges Rivers, about fifty miles as the crow flies from Banāras. (Today it bears the Muslim name Allahabad, City of Allah.) According to the Hindu tradition the mysterious, sacred underground river, the Sarasvatī, is also said to emerge there, at the confluence called the Trivenī, "Where Three Rivers Meet." Bathing at this confluence, it is said, is always auspicious. Sins from countless lives begin to "tremble like a tree struck by a great wind" when one prepares to go to Prayāga.[18] Especially during the month of Māgha people come to Prayāga to bathe, and every twelve years they come by hundreds of thousands to India's greatest *melā*, the Kumbha Melā.

Prayāga is also located in Kāshī, and in two places. The first is Prayāga Ghāt, on the riverfront adjacent to Dashāshvamedha. As Vishnu describes it in the *Kāshī Khanda*, there was once a temple of Vishnu, called Mādhava, there as well:

North of Dashāshvamedha is my Mādhava called Prayāga, having seen which and having bathed in Prayāga *tīrtha*, one is released from all sins. The goodness [*punya*] that comes to those who bathe in Prayāga in the month of Māgha, that goodness is multiplied ten-fold by simply bathing in my presence here.[19]

The second place in Kāshī said to be Prayāga is Panchagangā Ghāt. There are several temples of Mādhava or Vishnu in the original Prayāga, two of the most important being the Bindu Mādhava and the Venī Mādhava Temples. Likewise here at Prayāga-in-Kāshī there is a temple site of Bindu Mādhava atop the great flight of steps at Panchagangā, and many people, conflating the two temples of Prayāga, call this "Benī Mādhava." In addition, it is said that in the month of Māgha all the places of pilgrimage in India become pilgrims themselves and make a journey to Prayāga to bathe, to deposit the load of sins they have accumulated during the year, and to become pure again. In the *Kāshī Khanda,* however, Vishnu says that the *tīrthas* of Kāshī do not need to go to Prayāga for this purpose, but are purified in Kāshī, going first to the "Five Rivers" of the Panchagangā.[20] Moreover, they say that Prayāga itself comes to Kāshī bearing its great burden of sins, accumulated from all the other *tīrthas,* and washes them off at Panchagangā Ghāt during the autumn month of Kārttika.

Along with Prayāga, other *tīrthas* of considerable fame live in Kāshī. There is Kurukshetra, the holy "Field of *Dharma,*" where the war of the *Mahābhārata* was fought, located at a great *kund* in southern Vārānasī. There is Kāmākhyā Devī, whose famous "image" in Āssām—but a depression in stone—is one of the pre-eminent "benches" of the Goddess in India. In Kāshī, she resides in a small temple and lends her name to an entire section of the city, "Kamacchā." And there is Pashupatināth of Nepāl, located in the new Nepālī Temple and also in the narrow lanes between Chauk and the Ganges; the Himālayan Lake Mānasarovara, located on Nārada Ghāt; the Narmadā River, present in Revā or Revarī Tālāb; and the Godāvarī River, flowing through "Godauliā."

Some of the *tīrthas* that have come to Kāshī are among the most sacred sites in the city; others are neglected or covered over now by buildings, streets, or parks. Some, like the Godāvarī, have been incorporated by name into the common topography of the city. The important thing about the location of these many *tīrthas* in Kāshī is not that by being in one place they may be visited more conveniently, but rather, by being in this one place, they need not be visited at all. We have noted that there are pilgrimage rounds, established by the tradition, to visit the cities of liberation and the *lingas* of light, but these are not common pilgrimages, and one doubts they ever were. Here all these *tīrthas* contribute to the glory of Kāshī. Coming to Kāshī, pilgrims come to that one place where, according to tradition, all these sacred places arise, where they all dwell, and where they all, finally, dissolve at the end of time.

It is said that once Lord Brahmā took a balancing pan, the most common equipment in any Indian marketplace, and weighed Kāshī on one side against the heavens and all their gods on the other. Kāshī, being heavier, came down to rest on earth, while the heavens rose up to fill the sky. The weight of Kāshī is the cumulative weight of the city of all India. We have seen that the *tīrtha,* in general, has a cumulative nature. Better than a single river is the place where two rivers meet, as at Asi Sangam; or three, as at Prayāga; or five, as at Panchagangā. The place is the sum of its constituents—the gods and the *tīrthas* that abide there, the rivers that flow there. Kāshī is the place where all gods and *tīrthas* abide, where all sacred waters flow. There is no other place in India that is host to the myriad sacred powers that have gathered in Kāshī. It is no wonder that Kāshī outweighed the heavens.

The old woman from Jhansi, who in her years of widowhood has traveled the pilgrim road from Badrināth in the Himālayas to Rāmesh-varam in the South, who has now come to Kāshī to live out her final years, and who affirms contentedly that this beloved Kāshī contains all the *tīrthas* on earth, has probably never been to Shankhoddhāra or Vaidyanāth in Kāshī, and has certainly never been to Rāma Kund or Bakariā Kund. But that is not the point. She does not need to go, nor would she wish to go to all the company of *tīrthas* in Kāshī, for she has come to Kāshī.

The Eight Directions

IN ANY *mandala* the directions are extremely important, for they guard and frame the sacred universe at its borders. There may be four directional guardians; or eight, counting the intermediate directions; or ten, including a guardian above and below. While Kāshī has a host of other guardian deities, these directions have an additional significance. They represent all space, for all space is included within the embrace of the compass points.

In the vision of Banāras as presented by the *Kāshī Khanda*, this city is said to be the place where the directions originate. It is the center, and all the directions have their starting point here. We have met the notion of Kāshī as the center and origin of the universe before. The *linga* of light, of course, is a fiery *axis mundi*, arising from the nether-worlds, piercing the earth at Kāshī, and rising up through the highest heavens. And in the story of Manikarnikā, we are told that Shiva and Pārvatī created Kāshī, in the beginning, to be the very ground under their feet. It follows, then, that everything else begins in Kāshī, including the directions that mark the bounds of space.

The stories of the directional guardians occur in the *Kāshī Khanda*

in the context of the larger story of Shiva Sharma, the Mathurā brahmin who made the pilgrimage to the cities of liberation, but died in
Hardvār rather than in Kāshī.[21] Remember that Shiva Sharma was
taken in a chariot to the highest heaven, where he enjoyed himself for
many years before being reborn in Kāshī. On the way, however, the
good brahmin passed through all the different heavenly realms, including the kingdoms presided over by the various directional guardians. Shiva Sharma's accommodating charioteers told him the stories of
each of these directional guardians, all with a common plot. Long ago a
certain great devotee practiced austerities in Kāshī for an impressively
long time and was rewarded by Shiva by being appointed the regent of
one of the directions.

Who are these directional regents? Some of them are well known to
us from the ancient Vedic pantheon. There is Indra, for example, the
Vedic war god, who now guards the East. There is Agni, the Vedic
fire, who is in charge of the Southeast. Yama, the God of Death, guards
the South; and Nirriti, a much-feared black-goddess of death and
decay, guards the Southwest. In the West is Varuna, who rules the
waters and who had a very high position as the guardian of the moral
order in Vedic times. In the Northwest is Vāyu, associated with the
wind. In the North is Kubera, the wealthiest of the great *yakshas* of
ancient India, with his capital at Alakā in the Himālayas. Finally, in the
Northeast is Ishāna, one of the forms of Rudra-Shiva. Of these regents,
Indra, Agni, and Varuna were among the greatest of Vedic deities.
The Hindu tradition never forgets such deities, but as the imaginative
myth-making process continued, these deities found their places not in
the center, but in the far reaches of the Hindu *mandala*.

The positioning of the directional guardians around a sacred space is
clearly evident in Hindu temple construction. The temple *is* a cosmos,
and its sanctum is often surrounded by these cosmic guardians.[22] The
Rājarānī Temple at Bhuvaneshvara in Orissa and the sanctum of the
Lakshmana Temple at Khajurāho are good examples of this concep-
tualization in the temple architecture of North India. The various
directional deities are represented in their respective corners of the
temple-cosmos, carved with iconographical detail.

The cosmos of Kāshī is not as clearly visible or organized as that of a
temple, but its elements are schematically the same. The directional
guardians have their posts in the various parts of the city, although in
rather a random fashion. They abide in the very places where each of

them, in the beginning, established and worshipped a Shiva *linga.* While it is not a perfectly circular and well-appointed *mandala,* the presence of these directional regents here serves its symbolic purpose: to locate all of space within the sacred borders of Kāshī.

One may easily find the temples of these directional lords in Kāshī (*see* Appendix V for a listing of the eight), and there is a bona fide "Pilgrimage to the Eight Directional Guardians" prescribed in the pilgrimage manual, the *Kāshī Yātrā Prakāsha,* but again there is little evidence that this is an important modern pilgrimage route. The very presence of these eight lords tells the pilgrims what they want to know: one need not travel the globe in search of the sacred, for one has come to Kāshī.

Above the Earth, on Shiva's Trident

T H E   W H O L E of the cosmos embraced within the eight directions is said to be gathered together within the five *kroshas* of the city of Kāshī. Moreover, Kāshī not only gathers up and condenses everything that is auspicious and blessed in this world into a single place, Kāshī also transcends this world. Kāshī is India's great "crossing place." Here the threshold of the finite is crossed over. Kāshī is as a bridge, beginning on this shore and linking us to the far shore.

Where is Kāshī? According to the *Kāshī Khanda,* this city is in the world, but not limited by it. It is in the middle of the universe, but not in the midst of the universe.[23] Pārvatī, in her admiration for the city, exclaims to Shiva at one point in the *Kāshī Khanda,* "Even though it sits upon the earth, Kāshī is not an earthly city."[24] Similarly, in the *Kāshī Rahasya* it is said that the city is not made of earth. Therefore, when everything else in the universe is submerged in the waters of destruction at the end of time's cycle, Kāshī alone does not sink:

Just as a jewel is inlaid in gold, so is Kāshī inlaid in the earth. This Kāshī, which was never a created thing, made of earth, does not sink repeatedly. When all inert things sink, she, made of consciousness and bliss, does not sink. Were Kāshī herself submerged, how could she rescue others? Both common sense and the Vedas tell us this.[25]

Where is Kāshī? In another common image, Kāshī's true location is described as high above the earth on Shiva's trident. When the waters of the *pralaya* swell to engulf the whole of creation, they do not touch Kāshī.[26] Kāshī is exempt from the *pralaya:*

Just as the Lord lifts up the floodwaters of universal destruction [at the end of the cycles of *yugas*], so does he lift up this place out of the floodwaters of destruction.

This place stands on the tip of Shiva's trident, O twice-born ones. It is in the sky and not on the earth. But those who are ignorant do not see it.[27]

It is often said that Kāshī is simply not attached to the earth. In colloquial Hindi, the city is said to be "separate from the three worlds." In the scriptural traditions of the Purānas, it is called by the lofty term *lokottara,* "above the earth," or "transcendent": "Kāshī should not be considered to be just like the thousands of cities on the earth's surface, for it is above the earth."[28] Those who are of keen vision, such as yogis, are the only ones who truly can "see" Kāshī.

What does it mean to say that Kāshī rests on top of Shiva's trident? It is, after all, an earthly city in the sense that people build houses, buy and sell goods, elect city officials, and use the Vārānasī pin code numbers on their postal addresses, as do the residents of any other city in India. Everyone knows that it sits on Shiva's trident, but people have quite different understandings of what that means. "It is a geographical thing," said one. "If you go to the far side of the Ganges, you will see that Kāshī sits on three hills, like the three points of Shiva's trident." "It means that Shiva protects Kāshī," said another, a priest. "The trident is Shiva's weapon, and with it he protects his devotees. To say that Kāshī is on top of his trident means that Shiva protects all the people who live in Kāshī and gives them liberation." "It just means that Kāshī is different," said a medical doctor. "This is a way of saying that we who live here have a life and culture that are very different from others, and that this place is different from other places." A businessman put it this way: "The three points of Shiva's trident are the three worlds: the netherworld below, this world of birth and death where we live, and the world of heaven above. Kāshī is above all these, and separate from them." The wife of a *pūjārī* explained, "Lord Shiva said that Kāshī cannot be destroyed. Even when the whole world vanishes, Kāshī will not vanish. This is what it means." Finally, the philosophical *sannyāsin* Karpātrī said, "Kāshī has a subtle form that is separate from this earth. That subtle Kāshī sits on Shiva's trident."

In all these interpretations, one hears the same overtone: Kāshī is set apart from the rest of the world. It is different, separate, unique. Even the most casual visitor would agree. As the creator Brahmā said, according to the *Kāshī Khanda:* "Many times have I, who spread out the creation, created the world. But Kāshī is of another sort, created by Shiva himself."[29]

Kāshī, Linga of Light

I N   T H E *Kāshī Rahasya,* the time is recalled when the earth has sunk into the waters of the flood, as it does at the end of each cycle of ages. The great sages, from their vantage point in the heaven of the sages, look out and see that the earth has sunk, and they call upon Vishnu to assume his boar incarnation, to dive into the water and raise the earth up again. Scanning the waters, the sages see something astounding: a great shaft of light, rising and fanning out over the waters like an umbrella. "What is this light which shines above the waters of destruction," they ask, "and why does it not sink when everything else is submerged in the ocean?" Vishnu tells them, "This is the supreme light, famous in the scriptures as Kāshī."[30]

In telling the sages about Kāshī, Vishnu contrasts Kāshī with everything else on earth. Everything else is created, but Kāshī is not. Everything else is, in the end, too dense and heavy to float in the ocean of the *pralaya,* and so it sinks. Kāshī, however, is made of luminous wisdom and does not sink. When the earth sinks, Kāshī floats above the waters of destruction. And when Vishnu retrieves the earth from the bottom of the sea, he brings it up and places it as *terra firma* beneath Kāshī. But Kāshī is not attached to the earth as other places are.

The City of Light transcends the cycles of time and the eternal evolution and dissolution of space. This is the light that Brahmā and Vishnu saw. They tried to discover its source and its top, but they could not. It was called a *linga* of light—the "partless" *(nishkala)* form of the Supreme Shiva, Sadā Shiva, an unfathomable brilliance, transcending the three worlds. "The *linga* Vishnu and Brahmā saw, that very *linga* is known in the world and in the Vedas as Kāshī."[31]

The word *"linga"* ordinarily refers to the image of the Supreme Shiva, either established by human hands or self-manifest, as the focal point of worship in a temple. The word "Kāshī" ordinarily refers to a city, sacred as it is. Here, however, we have an extraordinary statement: the city is a *linga.* The whole of the sacred zone of Kāshī, encompassed by the Panchakroshī Road, is an enormous *linga* of light, the focal point of worship in the sanctum of the entire universe: "This great place, Avimukta, bounded by the five *kroshas,* is to be known as the one *linga* of light, called Vishveshvara."[32] The phrase "the *linga* whose extent is five *kroshas*" is common, both in the Kāshī *māhātmyas* and in the descriptions of the city offered by the priests of the city today.

The city is the embodiment of the Supreme Shiva. The sages ask, innocently, "Why does Kāshī have a feminine name if it is a *linga?*" Shiva tells them that "he" is both Shakti and Shiva, both the manifest and visible energy of life and the unmanifest, invisible spiritual essence. Taking form in the world, active and luminous in the world, is Shakti. Kāshī as Shakti is a goddess, with a *mūrti* or "image" form. She is also a city, with a *kshetra* or geographical form. And she is the embodiment of *chit,* "luminous wisdom," which is always feminine.[33]

Sometimes Kāshī is said to be the very body of Shiva. For instance, "This city is my body—measuring five *kroshas,* with wealth of unfractured magnitude, the very cause of *nirvāna.*"[34] Since the body is a primary symbol of the whole, it is an appropriate image for Kāshī, which is the whole. The Rivers Asi and Varanā are the two great arteries of Shiva's mystical body here. In the language of yogis, they are called *idā* and *pingalā,* and the third artery, *sushumnā,* where duality is transcended and *moksha* achieved, is identified with Matsyodarī River or with Brahma Nāla. The various *tīrthas* and *lingas* here are said to correspond to the parts of the body of God.[35]

Whether Kāshī is spoken of as Shiva's *linga,* Shiva's *shakti,* or Shiva's body, this is a visible and earthly ford for the crossing to the far shore of liberation.

Embodiment of Wisdom

T H E   M O S T persistent image of Kāshī is light. The language of light
is also the language of wisdom—"enlightenment," "illumination,"
"vision." *Chit*, "luminous wisdom," is sometimes said to be "pure
consciousness"—the wisdom of the utterly lucid mind. Another word
for such wisdom is *jnāna*—the deep knowing, the liberating insight for
which all renouncers and yogis aspire. Kāshī is also called *jnāna-
svarūpa*, the "embodiment of liberating insight." It is so called because
this is the place where Shiva reveals such insight to the dying, and we
will discuss this further when we consider the importance of death in
Kāshī in Chapter 9. In this context, however, as we look at the more
mystical interpretations of Kāshī as a place, we ask, "Where *is* that
'place' that embodies *jnāna* and where *jnāna* is revealed?" It is Kāshī,
to be sure, and yet we find that Kāshī is also an interior place; it is
one's very soul.

The word *krosha*, meaning a unit of measurement about two miles
long, might also be considered a *kosha*, a "sheath, layer," says the
Vishvanātha *mahant* Rām Shankar Tripāthī. Just as a person is composed of these five *koshas*, so is Kāshī. Like the sheaths of the tall field
grasses or the layers of an onion, the sheaths or layers of the person
become progressively softer and more subtle, from the outer sheath
made of food *(anna)*, to the inner sheaths made of breath *(prāna)*,
heart *(manas)*, intellect *(vijnāna)*, and bliss *(ānanda)*. The invisible
ātman is here, at the center of these sheaths. The five-*krosha linga* thus
describes the inmost self, the place where wisdom is attained.

The sacred city is also an interior landscape. The *Jābāla Upanishad*
explores its "geography":

"Who is the eternal unmanifest *ātman* and how can I know it?" asks the
seeker Atri.
The sage Yājnavālkya replies, "That which is the eternal, unmanifest
ātman is to be worshipped in Avimukta. It is established in Avimukta."
"In what is Avimukta established?" asks Atri.
"It is established between the Varanā and the Nāsī."
"What exactly is Varanā and what is Nāsī?"

"It is Varanā because it 'obstructs' all sins committed by the senses. It is called Nāsī because it 'destroys' all sins committed by the senses."

"Where is its place?"

"The place where the nose and eyebrows meet—that is the meeting place of heaven and the beyond. This meeting place [*samdhi*] does the knower of Brahman worship at dawn [*samdhyā*]. This Avimukta should be worshipped. This Avimukta is called 'wisdom.' Whoever knows this, knows."[36]

The place where Brahman is realized is called Kāshī. It is Light. It is Wisdom. It is what enables one to see and, therefore, to make the crossing: "Look, dear! Look at Kāshī—a boat set for the crossing, a motionless refuge, set just above the earth, a boat not of wood and nails, but the illuminer of all people, whom she rescues from the sea of being."[37] Kāshī may be located on the plains of North India, on the bank of the Ganges, on the tip of Shiva's trident, or where the nose and the eyebrows meet. Wherever that place is, it is the place where one is able to see into the true nature of things. "In Kāshī," it is said, "one sees one's own soul."[38]

Kāshī as Brahman

FINALLY, Kāshī is described with the most spiritually reverberating term of Sanskrit philosophy: Brahman. This is the Supreme Reality, that which underlies and transcends all. Within the soul, it is called *atman*. It is the least tangible and the most real of everything that exists. Here in Kāshī, Brahman is said to take the tangible form of a place: "What is regarded as the Supreme Brahman, without expansion, without egoity, without change, without form, unmanifest, mighty and subtle—that very One, having filled this place, established itself here, although it goes everywhere."[39] The few philosophical terms used to describe Brahman are also applied to Kāshī: it is *paramātman* (the "supreme soul"); it is *chidānandamayī* ("made of consciousness and bliss"); it is *nishprapancha* ("without expansions"); and it is *anākhyeya* (the "unspeakable").[40]

In the *Kāshī Rahasya*, the student Dīpaka asks his teacher about its nature: "What is Kāshī? Who made it? How does it work wonders? How is this great place, beloved of Shiva and Vishnu, so powerful?

And how did that which is without form, take this great blissful form?"[41] The teacher explains: "Kāshī is said to be Brahman, of which this turning world is an expansion. Knowers of Brahman call that which is without expansion 'Kāshī.' "[42] In interpreting this passage, the commentator quotes the *Garuda Purāna* to similar effect: "Kāshī is said to be Brahman, for here Brahman is revealed."

Kāshī is Brahman. And Brahman not only illumines the world without, it dwells inside the citadel of the five *kroshas,* the world within. To the great Shankara is attributed a hymn entitled the "Five Verses on Kāshī":

> *The repose of the mind is peace supreme,*
> *And that is Manikarnikā, the greatest place of pilgrimage.*
> *The stream of wisdom is the pure, original Ganges.*
> *I am that Kāshī whose essence is self-knowledge.*
>
> *Where the magic of the world is made,*
> *Where the whole world of moving and non-moving things*
>   *seems the dalliance of the mind,*
> *Is the One Place with the nature of the Supreme Soul—*
>   *Truth, Luminous Wisdom, and Bliss.*
> *I am that Kāshī whose essence is self-knowledge.*
>
> *The intellect, Bhavānī, holds sway within the five sheaths*
>   *in the household of each body.*
> *The witness, Shiva, the omnipresent, is the inner-soul.*
> *I am that Kāshī whose essence is self-knowledge.*
>
> *In Kāshī the light shines.*
> *That light illumines everything.*
> *Whoever knows that light, truly reaches Kāshī.*
>
> *The body is the sacred field of Kāshī.*
> *All-pervading wisdom is the Ganges, Mother of the Three Worlds.*
> *Devotion and faith—these are Gayā.*
> *Devout meditation on the feet of one's own guru—*
>   *this is Prayāga.*
> *And the highest state of consciousness, the inner-soul,*
>   *the witness of the hearts of all people—*
>   *this is Vishvesha, the Lord of All.*
> *If all this dwells within my body,*
> *What other place of pilgrimage can there be?*

"I am Kāshī." It is this radical interiorization of the *tīrtha* that has led some to conclude that one need not go on a pilgrimage at all. The truly luminous place is to be found only within oneself. And yet pilgrims continue to come to this place, every day on every train and bus. Arriving, they touch the dust of Kāshī to their foreheads, so tangible is the substance of Kāshī's sanctity. They come to walk these particular streets, to bathe in these waters, to see these divine images, to see the city itself. Even those who know Kāshī to be the luminous *ātman* deep within would not consider staying home. Beginning with the tangible substance of Kāshī's dust, they have seen in this city one dimension of meaning after another. They have finally seen Kāshī as Brahman, the light of all. And yet they do not relinquish the dust.

8

CITY OF THE
GOOD LIFE

T H E R E is a special spirit among people who call themselves Banārsīs, whether they are rickshaw-pullers, merchants in the market, or the old aristocracy. It is an art of living, both passionate and carefree. They call it *mastī* (*"joie de vivre"*), *mauj* ("delight, festivity,"), and *phakkarpan* ("carefreeness"). It is the exhilaration and drunkenness of Holī, the extravagance and culture of Burhwā Mangal, and the glitter of Divālī. It is enjoyment of life without ostentation. Most of its pleasures are simple: a morning bath in the Ganges, clean and plain clothing, simple *dal* and rice, a boat ride to the far sandy bank of the river for a morning walk. A small parcel of delicate milk-sweets, layered with pistachio and covered with thin silver paper; a mouthful of *pān*, betel nuts and other condiments, wrapped in the tenderest and most succulent green *pān* leaves; a tall frothy draft of *thandāī*, laced with intoxicating *bhāng*—these are the finest pleasures of the day. In the evening, there will be the clang of temple bells, and perhaps, later, some music. It is an ambience of urbanity, good living, and culture, all of which comes to be synonymous with the word "Banārsī."

Everyone knows that Banāras is a good place to die. And it is precisely this fact that makes it a good place to live. Banāras is as famous for living as it is for dying. *Moksha,* "liberation," after all, is but the last of the four *purushārthas,* the "aims of life," which together constitute the Hindu sense of the life well lived. One cannot rush headlong toward *moksha,* for there is also pleasure to be enjoyed *(kāma),* wealth and power to be gained *(artha)*, and religious duties to be performed *(dharma)*. Only by the ripening of the fruits of life is one truly ready for the fruits of death.

Kāshī is a city of the good life—famed for its brass shops and its silk palaces as well as its temples. It is known for its courtesans, poets, thugs, and wrestlers as well as its priests and *pūjārīs*. It is famous for its mangoes, its *pān* leaves, its sweets, and its intoxicants. In Kāshī there is a colloquial verse which goes: "Since God affords a few lentils to eat and Ganges water to drink, one should never leave Kāshī, the court of Vishvanātha!" Lentils imply the meager, but adequate, diet of the poor. By the promise of Annapūrnā, everyone will have lentils to eat and Ganges water to drink in Kāshī. And by the promise of Shiva,

Brass merchant in Thatherī Bazaar.

everyone will be blessed with liberation at death. One need not worry about life, or about death. And this is at the very core of Kāshī's *joie de vivre*. The joy of living can become a high art only where the fear of dying has been vanquished.

Of the aims of life, called the *purushārthas,* three have to do with life in this changing world of *samsāra*. These *purushārthas* may be seen as motivations to action as well as the goals of action.[1] One may do something because it is pleasurable, because it is productive or useful, or because it is right or good. By calling them *purushārthas,* the tradition recognizes and, indeed, underlines the importance of the passionate, the acquisitive, and the religious aspects of life. The Hindu tradition itself rejects the mystical and otherworldly caricature that outsiders have sometimes drawn, for three of the four aims are very much concerned with *this* shore, *this* world.

Kāshī is said to bring all the aims to fruition, not *moksha* alone. It is called "the great mine of those jewels called *dharma, artha, kāma,* and *moksha,*" "the one mother of all the *purushārthas.*"[2] It is said, "The four aims of life—*dharma, artha, kāma,* and *moksha*—are complete here in Kāshī as nowhere else on earth."[3] Kāshī is often called *sukhada,* the "bestower of happiness" as well as *mokshada,* the "bestower of liberation." She is said to provide *bhukti,* "enjoyment," as well as *mukti,* "liberation."

> *In Kāshī, there is* dharma *and it stands four-square.*
> *In Kāshī, there is* artha *and it is of many kinds.*
> *In Kāshī, there is* kāma *and it is the one source of all delight.*
> *And in Kāshī, there is* moksha.
> *What is there that is not here?*[4]

The City of Kāma

K Ā M A is passion or desire. It is also the name of India's Cupid, who moves through the world of human hearts, riding on the moonlight and carrying his magical bow, with a string of buzzing bees for a bowstring and flowers for arrows. He wields intoxicating power and is called Madana, the "Intoxicator."

The kind of passion excited by the God of Love is certainly the most universal example of *kāma,* and Hindus have recognized that such passion is something to be affirmed. *Kāma* is more than sexual pleasure, however. It is the attitude that informs all that people do for the sheer love of doing it, all that they enjoy simply because it is enjoyable. It is delight in the beloved; it is the aesthetic enjoyment of music or art.

Kāshī is a place where pleasure is enjoyed to the fullest. The city is famous for its traditions of music and the complementary art of dance. In ancient times, its dancers were also courtesans, and Banāras courtesans had a wide reputation for their beauty and their sophistication in the arts of love. It is said that in the time of the Buddha there was a courtesan, the daughter of a distinguished Banāras family, who was so beautiful and cultured that her fee for the night was exactly what the king of Kāshī received in daily revenues. For those who could not afford that, she charged half as much by day, and thus came to be known by the name Ardha Kāshī, "Half-Kāshī"![5] Other Buddhist Jātaka tales tell of a Banāras courtesan who earned a thousand coins a day, a Banāras courtesan who fell in love with a robber, or a Banāras courtesan with five hundred servant girls in her entourage.[6]

Over a thousand years later the courtesans of Banāras were still famous, and they are known to us through Sanskrit literature. In the eighth century, the Kashmir poet Dāmodara Gupta wrote a long poem entitled the *Kuttanīmata,* the "Advice of the Procuress," which was set in Banāras amidst the society of courtesans.[7] It is the story of Mālatī, a young Banāras courtesan who is extremely beautiful and gifted in the arts, but cannot seem to attract suitable clients. Mālatī visits the old procuress, Vikarālā, who in her day had been very successful as a courtesan. The procuress is to courtesans as a guru is to Sanskrit students. Mālatī bows at her feet, praises her, and then listens to her advice. Vikarālā tells the young courtesan what she needs to know about the arts of love: how to seduce an influential man; how to convince him that she is in love with him, though she be a courtesan; how to extract all his wealth from him; and, finally, how to get rid of him.

The *Kuttanīmata* gives us a glimpse of the City of Shiva in the days when the arts were still very much a part of the life of the temples. At the Shiva temple of Vrishabhadhvaja, "Bull-Bannered Shiva," the famous temple to the north of Kāshī, situated on the Panchakroshī

Road as the last night's stop on the journey, we are told that the prince
Samarabhata worshipped and then was immediately surrounded by a
crowd of courtesans. The association of courtesans with temples is
very old, of course, and has persisted until this century in some temples. These courtesans were called *devadāsīs,* the "servants of the
gods," and were seen as the earthly counterparts of the divine dancing
girls called *apsarases,* who are said to entertain the gods in heaven. Not
only was there dancing in the temples, but drama had its place as well.
The *Kuttanīmata,* for example, mentions the performance of the
Sanskrit drama *Ratnāvalī* within the compound of the Vrishabhadhvaja
Temple.

In its opening verses, the *Kuttanīmata* describes Kāshī as a sensually
captivating city, where the arts of love are highly refined. There, the
earth appears to be carpeted with rose petals because it is reddened
with the decorative *lāc* that is painted on the feet of its many beautiful
women, and left behind in their footprints as they walk the streets.
There, the ornaments of these lovely women tinkle as they walk and
fill the air with such music that Sanskrit teachers cannot even hear
their pupils make mistakes!

It is little wonder that this city which has so cultivated the arts of
pleasure should arouse in people's hearts the intensity of emotion, the
kāma, for which she is famous. The city is fair and beautiful. She
captivated the hearts of the gods the moment they saw her. And she
captivates the hearts of many others as well.

The legendary sage Agastya, for example, had to leave Kāshī ages
ago in order to travel to South India and quell the pride of the Vindhya
Mountains on the way. The Vindhyas, it seems, had tried to match the
great Himālayas and had risen up, puffed with pride, so high as to
block the course of the sun. Agastya was called to the rescue, and as he
approached the Vindhyas, the mountains bowed down to touch the
sage's feet. "Ask anything you wish, sir," the mountains said to him.
And he told them, "Stay bowed down until I return from the South."
He never returned, and the Vindhyas are still bowed down today. But
Agastya was heartbroken to have had to leave Kāshī. He wept as he
left his beloved city, and as he traveled farther and farther south, he
experienced the kind of *kāma* known as *viraha,* "love in separation."
This is the yearning, searing, burning love experienced, like a great
fever, when the loved one is far away. The *Kāshī Khanda* tells us,
"The sage Agastya, even though he wandered the lovely banks of the

Godāvarī River, could not get rid of the fire in his heart, which came from being separated from Kāshī. That sage, spreading wide his arms, embraced the very wind that came from the North, and asked after the well-being of Kāshī."[8]

Agastya's anguish in separation from his beloved is matched only by that of Shiva himself, when he was forced to live apart from Kāshī on Mt. Mandara. Shiva is said to love Kāshī as passionately as he loves his own wife, and the words in which he expressed that love are the words a lover speaks to his beloved. Aflame with *viraha*, Shiva cried, "If the breeze that comes from Kāshī would embrace me, that raging fire would be extinguished, but not by plunging into water will it be extinguished. . . . O sweet Kāshī, when will I again feel the happiness of union with your body, by which my own divine body will become cool again in an instant!"[9]

According to the *Kāshī Khanda,* it was in trying to cool that fever of passion that Shiva acquired some of his characteristic emblems. He rubbed cooling sandalpaste on his limbs to relieve his fever, but the sandalpaste turned to ashes with the heat. He took the moon, hoping to be cooled by its rays, but the moon wasted away to a mere crescent, unable to withstand Shiva's fever. He took snakes for ornaments to replace the lotuses that had been his bracelets, for snakes are said to be cooling. Finally, he took the Ganges and drenched his head with its heavenly waters to bring down the fever of his passion. The gods assembled in the heavens were astonished, for Shiva is the all-powerful Lord of the Three Worlds. He is the very one who, as an ascetic, burned Kāma, the God of Love, to mere ash, with the fire of his powerful third-eye, and it was he who condemned Kāma from that day on to live in spirit, but not in body. And now Shiva, who burned Kāma, was burned by Kāma, aflame with the pain of separation from Kāshī.[10]

The language of love, ordinarily spoken to the beloved, is here directed full force toward the city Shiva loves. Kāshī alone does he desire. In Kāshī alone will he delight.

Neither in the space within the heart of a yogi, nor on Mt. Kailāsa, nor on Mt. Mandara, do I delight to dwell as I delight to dwell in Kāshī. O Goddess, there are two eternal objects of my love: you, fair one, skilled in ascetic arts, and Kāshī, the Forest of Bliss. I have no place but Kāshī. I have no delight but Kāshī. There is no *nirvāna* but Kāshī. I tell you, it is true, it is true.[11]

Kāshī is not only the place Shiva lives. It is, above all, the place Shiva loves. If only Kāshī will satisfy the passion of the Lord, what can be said of its promises for ordinary mortals?

The Forest of Artha

A R T H A means "purpose" or "aim." As a *purushārtha,* it refers to that kind of action undertaken because it is useful, or because it will yield prestige or power, not simply because it is pleasurable. *Artha* is the profit motive; it is what generates power and wealth. The projects, plans, and ambitions of people, when pursued in accordance with *dharma,* are affirmed by Hindus as an important part of the good life. The pursuit of wealth and the relish of the worldly are important, for if some did not work hard to keep the world going, who would support those who have renounced the world?

Kāshī is called the "Forest of *Artha*"—where wealth and prestige grow strong and flourish, like the trees of the forest.[12] Whatever power, wealth, or boons people seek may be found in Kāshī, for this place is the very source of *artha.* In the long drama of the *Kāshī Khanda,* with its dozens of acts and scenes, it becomes clear that every power in the universe has its source in Kāshī. The regents of the directions and the governors of time came to power here. Vishvakarman became the chief architect of the world here. Agni became the fire and chief messenger of the gods here. Brahmā became Brahmā here, and Vishnu became Vishnu.

As for wealth, it is clear that from the time of the Buddha on Banāras has been an important center of business. The city was at the crossroads of great trading routes. The old Jātaka tales speak of merchants from Banāras setting off on their business trips with five hundred cartloads of goods. It is said that in the second century B.C. the merchants nicknamed Kāshī "Jitvarī," the "Victorious," because they reaped such great profits here.[13]

Throughout its long history, Banāras has been famous for its wares. There is the finest muslin, so soft that it was selected in ancient times, they say, to wrap the body of the Buddha for his cremation. There are the most exquisite silks in a rainbow of colors. And there is silk brocaded with gold and silver threads, woven into intricate floral and animal designs, prized by the high culture of the Mughal court as one of the few arts, they thought, in which India excelled even Persia. And there is jewelry—gold and silver ornaments, beads, bangles, and ivory. There is brassware, the highly polished and sometimes elaborated ornamented brass pieces which glitter in the narrow lanes of Thatherī Bazaar. There are the wooden toys, the carefully carved and painted animals and birds, courtiers, and gods, which delight the eye in Vishvanātha Lane. And there are the clay figurines for which Banāras artists are famous throughout North India—painted clay images of Ganesha, Lakshmī, Vishvakarman, Sarasvatī, Shiva, Kālī, Rāma, and all the other gods and godlings that make their appearance in the street markets in the proper season.

From the time the earliest Greek invaders and traders passed this way on their way to Ashoka's capital at Pātaliputra, to the time of the Muslim invaders, the British invaders, and now the tourist invaders, the bazaars of Banāras have dazzled the imagination. Temples and *lingas* they could not understand, but the goods of the bazaars needed no interpretation. In his famous description of Banāras in the late eighteenth century, Macaulay writes:

Commerce had as many pilgrims as religion. All along the shores of the venerable stream lay great fleets of vessels laden with rich merchandise. From the looms of Benares went forth the most delicate silks that adorned the balls of St. James's and of Versailles; and in the bazaars, the muslins of Bengal and the sabres of Oude were mingled with the jewels of Golconda and the shawls of Cashmere.[14]

Nineteenth-century visitors to Banāras were not disappointed in the fabled bazaars described by Macaulay. Miss Emma Roberts, in *Scenes and Characteristics of Hindostan,* speaks of the "celebrated gold and silver brocades which are known in India by the name of *kinkob,*" "splendid webs of silk and silver," "silver and gold lace, of every kind and pattern," "closely-linked gold chain of exquisite workmanship," and "pearls of immense size, and of the finest colour."[15] Edwin Arnold, although his interest in India was primarily spiritual, was nonetheless captured by the wares of Banāras. In *India Revisited,* he describes the "dazzling flood of gold and silk *kincobs,* embroidered cloths and scarves, cashmere shawls of marvellous make, texture, and tints, slippers for princesses, turbans for kings, and *cholīs* glittering with gems and gold laces."*[16]

The romantic vision of Banāras as a city of fabulous wealth has not been perpetrated by its foreign visitors alone. This opulence is part of the city's self-image and is the vision of the city projected by the Purānas and *māhātmyas*. One of the most delightful stories in the *Kāshī Khanda* tells of the journey to Kāshī of Pārvatī's father, Himālaya, well known to be the richest man on earth, since his mountain range is the storehouse of all the earth's jewels and minerals:

~~~~~~~

Some time after the marriage of Shiva and Pārvatī, Pārvatī's mother, Menā, remarked to her husband, Himālaya, "We have not seen Pārvatī since she married that naked god Shiva, who rides a bull, decorates himself with snakes and ashes, and lives in a cremation ground. Why don't you go to their place in Vārānasī and get news of her?"

Himālaya, who missed his daughter very much, agreed to the trip and packed up a great treasury of jewels and clothing to bring to Pārvatī. After all, she had married a god who possessed not so much as a suit of clothes and who dwelt in the cremation ground called Vārānasī. There was no telling what kind of home she had or what she might need. Himālaya set out for Vārānasī with sacks of the most excellent jewels—rubies, emeralds, and sapphires mined from his deep treasury.

Arriving from the North, Himālaya came to the bank of the Varanā River and from there beheld the city of Vārānasī. He could not believe his eyes:

> *Its very earth was completely studded with a multitude of different kinds of jewels, and the brilliance of the rubies of its many palaces filled the sky.*
> *The city illumined the four directions with the many golden pinnacles that topped its mansions. It surpassed even the paradise of the gods with its profusion of flying banners. Marvelous was the pleasure palace of the eight perfections, with its forests which bore all fruits, surpassing even the wishing-trees of heaven.*[17]

---

* A *cholī* is a bodice piece, the upper garment worn with a *sārī*.

Seeing Kāshī, a city that seemed to be made of solid gold and decked with nets of jewels, Himālaya was embarrassed and ashamed. Could this really be the city of his poor son-in-law, Shiva? How trifling was the wealth he had brought compared to the great wealth of Shiva. Amazed and humbled, Himālaya said to himself, "I may be the Lord of Mountains, but Shiva is the Lord of All. The wealth I have can be measured, but Shiva's wealth is immeasurable."

If he could do nothing else, thought Himālaya, he could build a great temple here with the wealth he had brought from his treasury. Having bathed at Panchagangā Ghāt, and having obtained the good favor of Kāla Bhairava, Himālaya established a linga *and had a temple built. It was called Shaileshvara, "The Mountain's Lord," and Shiva was so pleased with this temple that he agreed to dwell there forever, granting both wealth and liberation to all who came to worship.*[18]

The fabulous wealth of Banāras is described by Himalaya in its earthly terms: temple spires of gold and pillared pavilions studded with rubies. It is conventional wealth, and the Hindu tradition, for all its alleged otherworldliness, is not opposed to getting and keeping conventional wealth. It is only one among the aims of the good life, but it deserves its place. A person bent on the pursuit of wealth and power, however, must not do so rapaciously, at the expense of *dharma,* the "right."

Today Banāras continues to flourish as a center of commerce; its economy is primarily based upon pilgrimage and tourism. Its bazaars are still filled with a flood of merchandise, and its second-floor backroom silk dealers and jewelers still display dazzling goods, meant only for the rich. It would be impossible to describe Banāras as a wealthy city, however. And some of what meets the eye is most certainly poor.

Some Hindus, especially those who still consider themselves to stand firmly in the old tradition, might say that the true wealth of Kāshī is not conventional wealth, just as its greatest power has never been conventional political power. According to the scriptures, it is better to be poor, better even to be a bird or a mosquito, in Kāshī than to be a king ruling a vast kingdom elsewhere. And there are countless stories of kings and queens, merchants and thieves, who have left their palaces

and businesses to live simply by the Ganges in Kāshī. This view of
Kāshī is a romantic one, but it is a view popular in the traditional
literature.

For those from the West who visit Banāras, who travel through its
streets by bus or by rickshaw, eyes busy with the seeing of everything
there is to see, the paradox of Kāshī's wealth and power is even more
difficult. There is both wealth and poverty at every turn, opulence and
misery confronted in every hour. The questions that haunt our hearts
are the very questions that the Hindu tradition has raised more boldly
than any other. They are not only our questions. This god, Shiva, is he
rich or penniless? Does he live in poverty in the shelter of a tree, or in
the cremation ground, or in palaces of gold? This place, Kāshī, is it the
Forest of Bliss or the Great Cremation Ground? Is it a city of gold, or
a city of rags? These questions cannot be answered simply, neither by
us nor by the Hindus.

City of Dharma

H I N D U I S M is a tradition of ritual. Ordinary daily activities, such as
bathing and eating, are accompanied by prayers and actions which
make them ritual activities. Going to the temples for the *darshana* of
the gods, listening to the stories of the many *vratas,* making offerings
of money or food to the brahmins—all are daily rites which are a
ceaseless part of the rhythm of Banāras life. When a child is born,
there are rites of birth and name-giving. When a couple is married, the
long marriage rites are followed by a bath together in the Ganges.
When a new house is built, the brahmins are called in to sanctify the
bricks that will form its foundation. When a person dies, there are
cremation rites, followed by twelve days of *shrāddha* rites to help the
soul make its journey to the world of the ancestors. In Banāras, the
elaborate ritual tradition of Hinduism is active and visible as almost
nowhere else in India.

The word *dharma* refers to these many rites. It includes the sac-
raments of the life cycle *(samskāras);* the ancient sacrificial rites *(yajna);* rites for the dead *(shrāddha* and *tarpana);* rites of atonement
(prāyashchitta); giving gifts *(dāna);* observing fasts *(upavāsa* and
vrata); traveling on pilgrimage *(tīrthayātrā);* bathing in sacred waters

(snāna); and all the various acts of ordinary temple worship *(pūjā).*

Kāshī, it is said, brings all such rites to fulfillment. It is a place of such power that it magnifies the fruits of any ritual action. Giving a small offering to a brahmin here is the equivalent of giving a gift of solid gold elsewhere. Bathing once in the Ganges here is the equivalent of bathing every day in the winter before dawn elsewhere. Fasting for a single day here is the equivalent of fasting for a whole month elsewhere. Better yet, fasting for three nights here is the equivalent of performing austerities for many lifetimes elsewhere, "Here, O excellent ones, what is sacrificed, chanted, given in charity, or suffered in penance, even in the smallest amount, yields endless fruit, because of the power of this sacred place."[19]

Dharma is much more than rites, however. It is whatever upholds or sustains the universe.* On a cosmic scale, *dharma* is natural law, which holds the planets in their places and maintains the seasons in their proper time. Within society, *dharma* is the sense of social order and duty, determined in part by one's caste and one's stage of life. One's duties and responsibilities are different for the brahmin and the *shūdra,* different for the man and the woman, different for the householder and the retired person. Some of these duties are precisely the ritual activities mentioned above, for in the Hindu view, the right ordering, the ritual ordering, of the individual life contributes to the upholding of the entire social order and, indeed, the wider ecological order of the world. Finally, *dharma* is the sense of right order and harmony within the individual heart. It is conscience, the sense of what is right.

Dharma is sometimes called law, religion, or ethics. It is all of these, in part. As a *purushārtha, dharma* might best be described as the motivation to do something not because it is pleasurable, not because it is profitable, but simply because it is the right thing to do. *Dharma* is right action, or righteous action, either because it is prescribed by the *shāstras,* the teachings of the tradition, or because it is prescribed by one's conscience. If we are to think of it as "religion," it is not in any transcendent sense. The subject matter of *dharma* is this world and this shore. *Dharma* is that religiousness that has to do with people and their relationships, with families, with health, with prosperity, with politics, and with business. Sometimes the purpose for which a ritual activity is undertaken, as stated in the *sankalpa,* is very worldly indeed: success in

---

* The word *dharma* is from a root that means to hold up, to bear.

business; the conception of a child; the cure of a disease; safety in travel; or success in examinations. In understanding *dharma,* we must understand that it has to do not with some other world and its concerns, but with this very world in which we live. What better place for the gods to be at work?

The Destroyer of Sins

B E I N G released from the sins of the past and making a fresh start in life are things for which religious people have yearned the world over. For Hindus, Kāshī makes this possible. They say: "The sins of one who enters Avimukta, sins which have been heaped up in a thousand lifetimes, all of them are destroyed; they are consumed by the fire of Avimukta as if they were tufts of cotton."[20] So great is the cleansing power of Kāshī, that even remembering Kāshī from afar will free one from the burden of sins; entering Kāshī, even those who are without faith or who know nothing of Kāshī's greatness start afresh.[21]

How do Hindus understand sin? First, it is *adharma,* what is not *dharma.* The more common words for sin, however, are *pāpa* and *pātaka,* both of which are the opposite of *punya,* what is virtuous, good, sanctifying. *Pāpa,* then, is what is defiling and reprehensible. Just as *punya* is the goodness attached to particular actions, such as religious bathing, worship, or fasting, and is not a generalized sense of holiness, so *pāpa* is the sin of particular misdeeds, such as thievery or blasphemy, and is not a generalized condition of sin. There is no sense of "original" sin, for by nature the soul, *ātman,* is pure and divine. By actions, however, one's awareness of this truth becomes clouded with sins. Accumulated over many lifetimes, their weight becomes a burden to the soul.

The tradition has also held that there are ways in which these sins may be put down, or washed away. These "atonements" *(prāyash-chittas)* may be such things as meditational breath control, austerities, chanting the name of God, or fasting. One of the most important atonements is pilgrimage, especially to a place such as Kāshī.

In the praises of all the *tīrthas* it is said that they remove one's sins, perhaps even the sins of many lifetimes. Bathing in the holy waters, having the *darshana* of the divine images, and hearing the words of the wise—all contribute to the refreshment of the *tīrtha*. The journey is important, too. Especially in the days before modern transportation could deliver pilgrims speedily to their destinations, the journey to the *tīrtha* was a kind of asceticism. The long days, perhaps months, of travel by foot to Kāshī were filled with both hardship and anticipation. The life of the road made the fulfillment of reaching Kāshī even sweeter.

In this matter, there is a striking works-grace tension in the Hindu tradition, between the importance of individual faith and effort, on the one hand, and the gracious, saving power of the place itself, on the other. The pilgrims who have walked miles to Kāshī, anticipating the city at every step, are sure to be cleansed of their sins. And yet, they say, the cleansing power of Kāshī is so great that even a bit of her sacred dust, carried off by the wind, will cleanse the lucky, unwitting traveler it chances to touch, no matter what that person's spiritual disposition might be.

Kāshī is not alone among *tīrthas* in destroying sins, but here the power to destroy sins is so highly praised and so carefully elaborated that it gives us a better opportunity to see what this claim means. How do Hindus speak of the destruction of sins in Kashi? We have already met a great number of deities whose job it is to guard the sacred city from the inroads of evil: *ganas* and *ganeshas, devis* and directional deities. The Asi and Varanā Rivers are protectors, halting sinners at the borders and cutting away their impurities. And Kāla Bhairava stands at the gate of the city, gobbling up sins. The imaginative vision of the Purānic literature is quite vivid. Sometimes it is the sinner who is turned back; sometimes the sins themselves take ghoulish forms and fall screaming out of the body of the sinner.

The stories in which Kāshī extends her blessings to even the wickedest of the wicked are among the most popular in Kāshī. The Hindu writers and, presumably, their pious public as well, seem to have taken special delight in describing the worst sinner possible and detailing his deeds before telling the tale of his salvation. For example, there was the nefarious Durdhara, who spent all his money on meat, drink, and women; who raped his foster mother; who took up with a prostitute; who even tried to murder a brahmin. Durdhara's only positive mark on Chitragupta's heavenly record was that once, when apprehended while stealing flowers for his lover, he leaped over the garden wall to escape, dropped the flowers, shouted "For Shiva!", and ran away. But even uttering Shiva's name as a curse must have begun to change his fortunes, for it earned him a few minutes in heaven before being plunged into hell forever. In those few minutes, he met a heavenly damsel named Menakā, and he was filled with remorse for his sins. She helped him to get to Kāshī, though he was stopped at the borders by Shiva's *ganas*. Only after Menakā brought holy water from the city to sprinkle upon wicked Durdhara was he pure enough to enter. As he stepped into the city, the sins which emerged in ghostly and ghoulish forms from his body were burned up by Kāshī's fire, and the smoke, they say, was so dense that it made the sky permanently blue![22]

In another tale, there was a man so wicked that the only hint of *punya* on his heavenly record was that once he seduced a woman in an abandoned Shiva temple in the countryside and threw her clothes upon the *linga,* inadvertently making an offering of cloth—one of the standard "honor offerings" *(upachāras)* of Hindu worship. But that one act was enough to enable Kāshī to extend her grace to him. In another tale, a proud man who had become arrogant in his cultivation of the physical arts of yoga was roasting on the fires of hell. For a split second, he remembered his good brother, who had gone to Kāshī to seek salvation. The name Kāshī passed through his mind, and suddenly the pain of his torture abated and he earned enough *punya* to be reborn in Kāshī.

In a sense, the standards of Kāshī are very high. Much is asked of a person who wishes to reach the holy city. Kāshī is known as "difficult to reach" *(durlabha),* and for the sinful the obstacles are great and the guardians at the gates fearsome. And yet her grace is plentiful. In a sense, very little is asked of the sinner in order to gain entry. Even the smallest, perhaps accidental act of goodness may impart enough sanctity that even the worst may gain access to the City of Light. In all these tales, the worst of sinners heard, spoke, or remembered, quite by chance, the name of Kāshī or of Shiva, and the name brought just enough light to their dark lives that remorse, eagerness for salvation, rebirth in Kāshī, and ultimately salvation itself followed. "This Kāshī, the very embodiment of the fire of Brahman, burns up all sins when it is seen, touched, or even remembered. How much more so shall it burn up the sins of those who live there according to *dharma!*"[23]

Sinners in the City of Light

O NE   MIGHT   ASK , and Hindus have done so, "What about the sins done in Kāshī, after the slate has been wiped clean?" The question has exercised the most scholastic minds of the Purānic writers and the Hindu priestly community. They have given many answers, but here we can look only briefly into this thicket of religious law.

First, they often say that sin done elsewhere may be expunged in Kāshī, but sin done in Kāshī becomes "imperishable" *(akshaya)* or "hard as rock" *(vajralepa)*.[24] Just as righteous acts yield a bountiful harvest of blessings here, so do sinful acts yield an unimaginable store of sufferings. The *Kāshī Khanda* is filled with verses that insist upon the high standard of moral life for all who live in Kāshī:

The person who is prone to deprecate others or who lusts after another's wife should not live in Kāshī. Kāshī is one thing, and hell quite another.

Those who deprecate Shiva or the Vedas, or who live lives that violate the Vedas, should not live in Vārānasī.[25]

One writer draws a vivid analogy: just as a lustful man should avoid seducing his mother, at all costs, so too a sinful man should avoid sinning in Kāshī. The world is a big place: if you must sin, do it elsewhere.[26]

It is also said that Kāshī is one of those few special places on earth where the seeds of *karma* do not grow. It is called an *ūshara,* a place of saline soil which will not support the growth of seeds. What does this mean? For the good citizen, who lives and then dies in Kāshī, the deeds done here will not ripen into the fruits of another lifetime. In a world view in which the vegetative, organic model of birth, growth, death, and rebirth is seen to apply to the growth of the whole universe, as well as to the growth of the individual, Kāshī as an *ūshara* stands apart. It does not participate in the organic growth of the seeds of *karma.* "Of all barren soil," they say, "Kāshī is the most barren. The seed sown by the sower here does not grow."[27] And Shiva says, "I am a flaming forest fire, here in the Forest of Bliss. I burn up people's seeds of *karma* and do not sprout them." For one who lives in Kāshī, *karma* ceases to grow.[28]

For the sinner, however, the fact that *karma* ceases to grow is a disaster. This is why it is impossible to eliminate the sins done in Kāshī. To imagine it in the vivid imagery of the Hindu world, these sins rather than becoming little seeds which will work themselves out in other lives, become hard as rock. They cannot be burned up; they cannot grow.

According to some, these can be destroyed only by the severest punishment, meted out by Kāla Bhairava at death. One becomes a hideous *rudra-pishācha,* a "ghoul of Rudra," and lives a life of pain, hunger, thirst, and torment for many aeons. According to others, there is atonement possible to rid oneself of these rock-hard sins. Interestingly, some of the acts of atonement described in the *Kāshī Rahasya* have quite a practical side to them, when considered in the context of the troubled Vārānasī of the fifteenth and sixteenth centuries: one can repair a ruined Shiva temple, put a roof over a *linga* that has no temple to house it, sponsor the building of a house for a brahmin, or sponsor the construction of a new temple.[29] Despite the gloomy predictions for the Kāshī sinner, a way was found to help him atone for his sin.

The most popular atonement for sin in Kāshī is the Panchakroshī pilgrimage, following the circumambulatory route of some fifty miles around Kāshī. One must be especially careful on this journey, however; for they say that while sins in Kāshī may be expunged by taking the Panchakroshī pilgrimage, sins committed in thought or deed along that sacred route also become hard as rock.

The *Kāshī Rahasya* contains the only extensive account of the Panchakroshī pilgrimage.[30] It tells of the many shrines along the way and relates the story of the young man, Mandapa, who was released from his terrible burden of his sins by making this pilgrimage:

Mandapa, the son of a very pious man, was a wild and wicked boy. He and his bad friends drank liquor and committed crimes. One day they stole gold from the palace of the King, and Mandapa swindled his friends out of their share of the gold and hid in the house of a prostitute. His two friends were furious. They told Mandapa's father of his son's wicked doings. His father disowned him, and when his friends

got hold of him, they beat him up and left him for dead by the river-bank at Asi Ghāt.

When Mandapa came to, he saw a band of pilgrims setting out on the Panchakroshī pilgrimage. Having nothing else to do, wicked Mandapa decided to go with them. Even starting off on a pilgrimage with good people began to have a transforming effect on Mandapa. That first night, when they had reached Kardameshvara, he stayed up all night with the pilgrims, singing and dancing before the image of Shiva. Everyone praised him, for little did they know he had been such a wild young man.

The next night, they reached Bhīmachandī, and again Mandapa sat up all night, this time in the temple of the goddess Chandikā. He listened to brahmins tell stories about the greatness of Kāshī. Vaishnavas and Shaivas alike danced and sang that night, and they were led by none other than Mandapa!

On the third day, he meditated on Shiva at every step as he walked along the path. The party passed the great Ganesha at Dehalī Vināyaka, where Mandapa worshipped with great peace of mind. He did not eat or drink, but meditated upon his sins and burned with remorse. He cried out, "Kāshī! Kāshī! Shiva Shankara! Keshava! Protect me, for I have fallen so low! I have sinned against the gurus and the gods!" Reaching Rāmeshvara, the third night's stop, he bathed and worshipped, but still he did not eat or drink.

The next day, they walked to the final stop at Vrishabhadhvaja, where he worshipped and bathed in the tank of Kapila. After spending the night, they all began the final leg of the trip. They bathed where the Varanā meets the Ganges, and they walked along the river to Manikarnikā and, finally, to Vishvanātha for the darshana of Shiva.

Everyone was amazed at the great transformation in Mandapa. He had been the town scoundrel, and now they said, "You are sinless indeed. You are a devotee of Shiva and of Keshava. You have circumambulated the linga of five kroshas, Kāshī, in the company of good people." Over-whelmed at Mandapa's atonement, his parents claimed him again as their son.

Life Transformed

THE TRUE secret of Kāshī is just this: here one does not have to *do* any special religious act, for the city sanctifies every act. Being here is *dharma* enough, is yoga enough:

> Here sleep is yoga, and going about town is sacrifice.
> O Goddess, eating whatever one pleases is the great sanctified food-offering to the gods.
> One's play, O Goddess, is a holy act of charity.
> Everyday conversation is the repetition of God's name.
> And lying upon one's bed is prostration.[31]

What is yoga in Kāshī? Sleep, the most passive of human activities, is here tantamount to yoga, the most wakeful and demanding of human activities. And what is sacrifice in Kāshī? Wandering about town, which requires no expenditure or elaborate preparation, is here a complex sacrifice, a rite involving infinite care, preparation, and expense. Eating whatever one chooses in Kāshī is as blessed as partaking of *naivedya,* the food offerings made to the gods, so sacred that only in special cases may they be eaten at all. One's play in Kāshī is the giving of a religious gift, and one's ordinary conversation equals the repetition of the name of God. And lying upon one's bed is the equivalent of prostration before the Lord in the temple.

One may practice yoga in Kāshī, of course, and many people do. But according to the Purāṇic *māhātmyas,* such practice is unnecessary here, for the goal of the spiritual adept is easily, even playfully, attained in Kāshī by everyone. The famous "eight-limbed" *(ashtānga)* yoga is described as follows:

Residing in Kāshī, coming in contact with good people, bathing in the Ganges, avoiding sinful deeds, delighting in the good, enjoying things as they come one's way, making gifts according to one's ability, and not accepting handouts—yoga consists of these eight things. What is the use of other yogic practices in Kāshī?[32]

Elsewhere there is a six-limbed yoga described, which consists of visiting six places:

Vishveshvara, Vishālākshī, the Heavenly Ganges, Kāla Bhairava, Dhund-hirāja, and Dandapāni: this is the six-fold yoga.

Whoever always practices this six-fold yoga in Kāshī, having reached the waking-sleep of yoga, long drinks immortality.[33]

Kāshī's sacred geography is itself a spiritual path, which one travels simply by walking its streets, visiting its temples. And to live in Kāshī is to enter upon that spiritual path, as naturally as one breathes. The one who lives in Kāshī is not necessarily the epitome of the devout and pious person. Religious life is not necessarily pursued with greater vigor here than elsewhere. Part of what accounts for the enjoyment of living in Kāshī is that one need not make a point of being pious, for everything one does in this sacred zone is a religious action. This, after all, is what religious life is: living life at that center-place that gives meaning to all one's activities—sleeping and waking, buying and selling, bathing and worshipping. Kāshī is that place at the center.

9

CITY
OF DEATH AND
LIBERATION

No other city on earth is as famous for death as is Banāras. More than for her temples and magnificent *ghāts,* more than for her silks and brocades, Banāras, the Great Cremation Ground, is known for death. At the center of the city along the riverfront is Manikarnikā, the sanctuary of death, with its ceaselessly smoking cremation pyres. The burning *ghāt* extends its influence and the sense of its presence throughout the city. Entering Banāras from the villages to the south, one sees, leaning against the walls of the shops on Lankā Street, stacks of bamboo litters for carrying the dead. Along the main roads of the suburbs or in the dense lanes of the city one suddenly hears the familiar chant of a funeral procession on its way to Manikarnikā: *"Rāma nāma satya hai! Rāma nāma satya hai!"* "God's name is Truth! God's name is Truth!"

In Kāshī, life is lived in the perpetual presence of death. One of the most popular couplets of the poet Kabīr, painted upon the walls of buildings throughout the city, reminds the passerby of death's inevitability:

> *Seeing the grinding stone turning, turning,*
> *Kabīr began to weep.*
> *Between the two stones, not a single grain is saved!*

The verse is often accompanied by a vivid folk art depiction of a woman turning the simple domestic grinding stone, throwing not grains but people into the mill, where they are sure to be crushed between the two stones. Death is as common, as certain, as the grinding of wheat once it is thrown into the mill. Rounding the corner of a narrow lane, or glancing up from a streetside market, one will see this famous couplet, next to the advertisements for the newest movie, or the slogans of the latest political campaign. The rickshaw-pullers and vegetable vendors know it by heart. Kāshī is comfortable with the fact of death.

For death in Kāshī is death transformed. As the saying goes, "Death in Kāshī is Liberation"—*Kāshyām maranam muktih.* It is dying that unleashes the greatest holy power of Kāshī, the power of bestowing liberation, *moksha* or *mukti.* Death, which elsewhere is feared, here is welcomed as a long-expected guest. Death, which elsewhere is under the terrifying jurisdiction of Yama, is free from that terror here, for Yama is not allowed within the city limits of Kāshī. Death, which elsewhere is polluting, is here holy and auspicious. Death, the most natural, unavoidable, and certain of human realities, is here the sure gate to *moksha,* the rarest, most precious, most difficult to achieve of spiritual goals.

"Bound for Moksha"

K ā s h ī' s greatest gift is the bestowing of *moksha*—the final fording of the river of *samsāra* to the far shore, beyond birth and death. Here, as the Purānas put it, "the ferryboat is set for the crossing." But the fare cannot be purchased with any of the other *purushārthas.* No amount of wealth, no accumulation of *punya,* no perfection of *dharma* can qualify one for *moksha.* Only that wisdom that completely floods one's consciousness with light will enable one to make that final crossing.

Moksha is the fourth of the *purushārthas,* but as an aim of life it constitutes a qualitative break from the others. *Kāma, artha,* and *dharma* are pursued by those who still consider this world to be their home—students, householders, even retired people. But *moksha* and the wisdom by which it is gained are pursued only by those who have "left behind" *(sannyāsa)* their worldly home. These renouncers may be seen in the streets of Banāras, dressed in faded orange garments, car-

rying only a wooden staff and a coconut husk water vessel. Although they may belong to an order of *sannyāsins* and live in a *matha*, they are, strictly speaking, homeless in this world. They are called *mumukshus*, those "bound for *moksha*."

Since the era of the Upanishadic sages and the Buddha, Banāras has been a gathering place for those who have renounced the world. They have come to the groves of the Forest of Bliss to practice asceticism,

to pursue disciplines of yoga, and to strive toward wisdom. For them, Banāras is famous as the "Bestower of *Siddhi*"—the spiritual attainments, the perfections, which are the goals of those who devote themselves totally to spiritual disciplines. It is called the "Birthplace of *Siddhi*."[1]

Jaigishavya is one of the ancient legendary yogis in the Hindu tradition, and it is well known in the Purānas that his yogic practice was brought to fulfillment in Kāshī, by the grace of Lord Shiva. His story is taken as a paradigm for the fulfillment of spiritual goals in Kāshī. It is said that when Shiva left Kāshī to dwell on Mt. Mandara, during the reign of Divodāsa, Jaigishavya established a *linga* and vowed that he would neither eat nor drink until Shiva returned. Jaigishavya sat in meditation until his limbs withered. When Shiva returned, entering the city from the north, he went immediately to Jaigishavya's place of meditation and bestowed upon this yogi a much-deserved boon:

"I give you the wisdom called *Yogashāstra*," said Shiva, "which is the means to *nirvāna*. May you be the teacher of yoga to all yogis. O sage, rich in ascetic practice, you will know the whole secret of yogic knowledge, by my grace, and by that knowledge, you will reach *nirvāna*."[2]

Shiva pledged to dwell in the *linga* which Jaigishavya established in order to bestow *siddhi,* "fulfillment," upon all who practice yoga.

The *linga* of Jaigishavya may still be seen today. Its temple is in a small, peaceful monastic compound in the northeastern sector of the city. Here the ancient traditions of the yogi Jaigishavya continue. The *linga* in the temple is striking: an enormous, rounded stone some five feet tall.

There are many renouncers who have emulated Jaigishavya's severe ascetic practice, the most radical being those called the Aghorīs, who not only renounce the world for a life of asceticism, but turn the values of the world upside down and fasten upon the reverse side, so to speak. Their name is euphemistic, meaning "Not Terrible," but in truth they are the most terrible of all from a worldly point of view. They haunt the cremation grounds and sleep upon graves. They drink wine, sever and cure a human skull to use for collecting food, and cook their food on the embers of cremation pyres. Like Shiva, who is also known by the name Aghora, they seem deliberately to adopt the things the world scorns, following a path of spiritual tempering that ensures their liberation from the values of *dharma.* If all, indeed, is Brahman, then one must not spurn any aspect of life or death. It is no coincidence that a modern Aghorī, Bābā Bhagavān Rām, has established the most active center for the treatment of lepers in Banāras.

The goal of the renouncer, whether the ordinary yogi or the radical Aghorī, is to become "liberated-in-life," a *jivan mukta.* Such a person has transcended the tensions, the dualities, the anxieties of life and of death, even while living on "this shore." When he dies, he will make that final crossing, never to return.

Renouncers, of course, are not the only ones bound for *moksha* in Kāshī. In a sense, this city, while it is famous for its ascetics, yogis, and renouncers, constitutes a challenge to their labors, for everyone here is bound for *moksha.* We have already heard that sleep is yoga in Kāshī, and it is said that what is discovered by studying the Vedānta and all the Upanishads may be learned playfully in Kāshī, with no effort at all. The Purānic *māhātmyas* are filled with the radical juxtaposition of the hard path of the ascetics and the easy path of those who do nothing more than meet their death here in Kāshī.

Here why should a man dwell in a solitary place?
And what is the use of turning from the pleasures of sense?
And what is the use of practicing yoga or sacrificing to the gods?
For without these one gets mukti *easily in Kāshī.*[3]

Not only is living in Kāshī as good as the ardent seeking of the professional *mumukshus,* but it is a more certain path. The yogi may not reach his desired goal in this lifetime, perhaps not in many lifetimes. But the rickshaw-puller, haggling over the price of a ride, peddling through the streets all day, waiting for a few late customers at night, is following a spiritual path that leads directly to *moksha.*

People come from all over India to live in Kāshī until they die. They come for *Kāshīvāsa*—"living in Kāshī." Having come to Avimukta, they never leave. For them, this is the final stop on a pilgrimage that has lasted for many lives, through birth and death and birth again. Dying in Kāshī, they make the final crossing which ends the pilgrimage of this life, and of all lives.

Through the ages, Banaras has been colonized in its various sectors by these Kāshīvāsīs. The Madrāsīs have settled at Hanumān Ghāt, the Bengālīs in Bengālī Tolā, the Mahārāshtrians near Rāma Ghāt and Panchagangā Ghāt. Some have come here to retire. Some are widows, who are left without recourse in their old age. They have been the pillars of their family religious life for decades. They have gone barefoot on more pilgrimages, observed more fasts, sung more devotional hymns than either their husbands or their sons. And now, thin and almost invisible in their plain white *sārīs,* they are among the most pious of the Kāshīvāsīs.

In addition to the Kāshīvāsīs, there are others who have come to Kāshī at the eleventh hour. They come for what is colloquially called Kāshī Lābh—"The Benefit of Kāshī." They make it just in time. They are brought to hospices such as Kāshī Lābh Mukti Bhavan, near Godauliā crossing. Here they may die in peace, for dying a good death is as important as living a good life.

Entering the Kāshī Lābh Mukti Bhavan from the street, one passes into a garden compound where the two-story hospice building is located. There are sacred *tulsī* bushes on either side of the path, with little signs set amidst the plants saying "Rām, Rām—Remember the name of Rām." Entering the hospice, there is a *pūjā* room, with an altar and many deities. There are attendants and employees of the

The Kāshīvāsī, "bound for moksha."

hospice who take turns chanting "Hare Krishna! Hare Rāma!" throughout the day and night. And if the attendants are all busy at other duties, there is a record player which carries the sound of sacred *mantras* softly through the quiet building. Around the center courtyard are the small, bare rooms where the dying may be cared for by their families. There is no conventional medicine here, however, for the patients have come, not to recover, but to die in an atmosphere in which their final thoughts may be directed toward God. Every few hours they are given some *tulsī* leaves and Ganges water, the finest medicine there is for the dying. On the wall of the hospice, as one enters, the rules of the house are painted. Here are the first few: (1) Only those sick people who are dying and who believe in liberation in Kāshī and have come especially for "The Benefit of Kāshī" may stay here. The ill who wish to get well by taking medicines should stay elsewhere in a hospital. (2) Those good people who are followers of the Hindu *varnāshrama dharma* may stay in this place. (3) One may stay here for fifteen days. After that, one may stay, if there is special necessity, by the permission of the director.

The praises of dying in Kāshī are well known to those who have come here to die. There are thousands of verses, any two or three of which they may know by heart:

Where else does a creature obtain liberation as he does here, simply by giving up the body, with very little effort at all!

Not by austerities, not by donations, not by lavish sacrifices can liberation be obtained elsewhere as it can be obtained in Kāshī simply by giving up the body!

Even the yogis practicing yoga with minds controlled are not liberated in one lifetime, but they are liberated in Kāshī simply by dying![4]

Shiva, the Teacher at Death's Door

"THE PLACE where Shiva himself, the Great Lord, teaches the *tāraka mantra* at the time of death—that is Avimukta."[5]

When one dies in Kāshī, they say, it is Shiva himself who whispers in one's ear the *tāraka mantra,* the "ferryboat *mantra,*" or the "*mantra* of the crossing.*" In the Hindu tradition, it is the guru who ordinarily bestows the *mantra* upon a qualified student, and the *mantra* is the means of wisdom. The guru mediates the kind of wisdom that cannot be learned from books but is conveyed in personal instruction from one generation to the next. Here in Kāshī, Shiva himself is the guru. The light of wisdom here is shed by no human teacher but communicated directly from God to the human ear and the human heart.

Shiva's personal role as bestower of salvation is one he chose in the beginning. Remember how Shiva and Pārvatī stood in Kāshī, before the world was made, and decided to create Vishnu precisely so that Vishnu could take over the task of sustaining and governing the rest of the universe, freeing Shiva to spend his time doing that in which he most delights: bestowing liberation. Shiva became the ruler of Kāshī, the place of light and wisdom, and he pledged:

This land, bounded by the Panchakroshī, is dear to me. My rule will prevail here, and no other rule will have power. O Vishnu, no other shall teach the creatures who live in Avimukta, even if they are sinners. I alone shall be their teacher.[6]

Hindus have portrayed Shiva, the merciful deathbed teacher, with great tenderness. In his posture of granting liberation, Shiva has a very personal form, bending down to the ear of the dying to whisper the secret of wisdom. It is said that when the great saint Rāmakrishna came to Kāshī in the late nineteenth century, he went into a deep trance of meditation as he passed Manikarnikā by boat. He later described what he had seen in his moments of vision: The goddess Annapūrnā held in her lap the body of a dead man, while Shiva knelt to whisper the *tāraka mantra* in his ear. It is little wonder that death is said to lose its terror in Kāshī, for Shiva will be present and will speak into one's ear all one needs to know.

The Tāraka Mantra

Creatures are released by the knowledge of Brahman, and never in any other way. I am that knowledge of Brahman for those who die in Kāshī. I teach the *tāraka* at the time of death, and they are released at that moment.[7]

W H A T is this "ferryboat" *mantra* which Shiva whispers in the ear of the dying? Our curiosity is aroused as with any whispered secret. The word *tāraka*, like *tīrtha*, comes from the Sanskrit root meaning "to cross over." *Tāraka*, however, is from the causative form of this root, meaning "to carry over" or "to rescue, save." Since a boat carries one across the flood, it is also called a *tāraka*. Like a boat, the *mantra* saves one from the waters of *samsāra*. In one work on this subject, the *Kāshī Moksha Nirnaya* ("The Discussion of Liberation in Kāshī"), the author explains the meaning of *tāraka:* "It is the boat, which carries one over the sea of *samsāra*. And that [boat] is Brahman. Thus it is called the Tāraka Brahman."[8]

In the classical tradition of the Upanishads, the *mantra* that *is* Brahman is *Om*—the verbal symbol of the Supreme Reality. According to some, *Om* is the *mantra* Shiva utters at the time of death. Others claim it is the mantra "Rāma, Rāma" that is spoken. The scholar Nārāyana Bhatta in his sixteenth-century digest, the *Tristhalīsetu,* cites scriptural evidence for both views.[9]

On one level, of course, Rāma is the hero-*avatāra* of the *Rāmāyana.* But over the centuries in North India, the name Rāma has gathered so much weight and significance that it has come to mean God, with no sectarian connotations: the Supreme, and yet personal, Lord. It is Rāma's name they chant as they carry the dead to the burning *ghāt.* And so the poet Tulsī Dās has said, voicing the hope of many Hindus:

> *What instruction does the great lord Shiva give the dying*
> *Upon the banks of [the] Ganges in Kāshī, the land of Dharma?*
> *Hara tells them of the glory of Ram's Name, and he himself recites it,*
> *From age on age this universe has known it and the Vedas too describe it.*[10]

Whatever the uttered word of the *mantra* is, however, is quite beside the point. When Shiva speaks in person it is a revelation of God, from God.

"Death in Kāshī is liberation." This is the great religious claim of the City of Light. But an objection may be raised by those who stand firmly upon *shruti,* the "revealed scriptures." It is this: According to the Upanishads liberation comes only from wisdom—*jnāna.* This is the one prerequisite for release: the deep, transforming knowledge of *ātman,* the soul, and of Brahman, the one Reality. How, then, can liberation come from merely dying? How can this claim be justified in the light of the revealed tradition?

Both Sureshvara, the author of the *Kāshī Moksha Nirnaya,* and Nārāyana Bhatta, the compiler of the *Tristhalīsetu,* have taken on these objections, and many others, in their discussions of liberation in Kāshī. Both authors emphasize that it is not the physical act of dying that occasions liberation, or the word of the *mantra* itself. Rather, it is precisely the wisdom one receives at the time of death, when the *mantra* is imparted. Nārāyana Bhatta explains, "There is no liberation in the absence of wisdom—that is clear from statements in both the revealed and remembered tradition, such as 'From wisdom alone comes liberation.' Therefore, knowledge of the *ātman* arises here from the *tāraka,* which is taught by the guru Vishveshvara." He goes on to quote the *Kāshī Khanda* on the matter: "Creatures are released by knowledge of Brahman and never in any other way. *I am* that knowledge of Brahman for those who die in Kāshī. I teach the *tāraka* at the time of death, and they are released at that moment."[11]

The author of the *Kāshī Moksha Nirnaya* takes the strictly "nondualist" point of view in discussing this matter. The soul, *ātman,* and Brahman truly are "not different" one from the other, but the soul is shrouded with dark veils of ignorance and subject to a mistaken perception of the nature of reality. Death in Kāshī does not "cause" liberation, but is the occasion of liberation. It is the time when the veils of ignorance are lifted, and the light of day shines:

Receiving knowledge from the Great Lord Shiva at the time of death, all creatures, bound by beginningless ignorance, are liberated.

Liberation for them means absolute unity, like the unity of the air that is inside a pot with that that is outside the pot. There remains no cause at all for the creation of another body.

God, the Supreme Lord, destroys ignorance . . . merely by rising, just as the sun destroys darkness, merely by rising![12]

"All Creatures"

"Whatever is known as a 'creature'—from Lord Brahmā down to a blade of grass, in the four categories of beings—gets liberation in Kāshī."[13]

ONE MIGHT ASK, "Who is liberated in Kāshī? What is meant when it is said that all creatures are liberated here?" I posed the question to a number of Banāras pandits, including one very learned man nearly eighty years old.

"There is liberation for all creatures," he replied. "Not only people, you see, but birds and animals reach *moksha* here as well."

"Birds?"

"Yes, *moksha* for birds too." One could tell by the twinkle in his eye that the notion delighted him. "Dying here is sufficient, that is all.

Dying here is sufficient, even for a mosquito," and he added with a mischievous smile, "even for the tiniest germ." There was a long silence. *Moksha* for mosquitoes stretched the imagination. "You see," he went on, "living beings are always *mukta*—liberated, free. When Shiva gives the *tāraka mantra* at the time of death, he tells creatures what has been true all along: they are free, *mukta. Aham Brahmāsmi. Tat tvam asi.* 'I am Brahman. That thou art.' "

"He says this to all creatures?"

"Yes, even donkeys." He smiled again.

"How about Muslims and Christians?" came the foolish question.

"Of course! They are more worthy than donkeys!"

The poignant image of Lord Shiva whispering wisdom into the ear of the dying is here shattered by an even more challenging claim—that Shiva enlightens not only human beings, but all creatures in the "four categories of beings": those born from moisture, such as insects; those born from seeds, such as plants; those born from eggs, such as birds; and those born from the womb, such as humans. The chain of life extends "from Lord Brahmā down to a blade of grass."

A substantial scriptural tradition supports the claims of this pandit. There are dozens of verses in the Purānic texts that take that same apparent delight in confounding the religious imagination with the saving power of Shiva:

Brāhmanas, kshatriyas, vaishyas, shūdras, *and even bastards,*
And others who are worms, or foreigners, who are impure and born to a
sinful estate,
And insects, and ants, and animals, and birds
Hear, O Beloved, when they reach a timely death in Avimukta
They all wear the crescent moon in their hair, have eyes in their foreheads,
and become bull-bannered Shivas![14]

Brahmins to ants all in one breath: this is the continuum of life that animates the universe as perceived by Hindus. All life is qualitatively one. The same life breath unites "mobile creatures" *(jangamas)* like ourselves and the birds, with the "stable ones" *(sthāvaras)* of the plant kingdoms that are unable to move about. For Hindus, life is not "one" in any simple sense. Life is infinitely diversified and stratified. Even human beings are not all born into the present lifetime with the same maturity of spirit and self-awareness, and these human differences are

reflected in the *jātis,* literally "births," which we call castes. Despite
the elaborate stratification, there is an undergirding unity that links all
life together into one coherent whole. The individual life spirit, the
ātman, moves through the various realms of the living until it realizes
its true nature and its true home, in oneness with Brahman.

All the levels of life can therefore be given a common name as
creatures. They are called *jantu,* those "born," or *prānin,* those with
"breath," or *bhūta,* those "existent" ones. All these Sanskrit terms
refer to living beings by their common denominators: they are born,
they have breath, they come into being. When it is said that all "creatures" are liberated in Kāshī at death, these are the creatures included.

Naturally, the stories of the Kāshī literature are filled with examples
of the salvation of great and small creatures. There are stories about
animals or about people who have been reborn as animals in Kāshī. It is
assumed, of course, that to dwell in Kāshī as a donkey or a bird is far
superior to living elsewhere as a king. In one story, a flock of birds
speak of their past lives. Once they were gods, enjoying the delights of
heaven. Once they were heavenly musicians and dancers. In the
earthly realms, they were born in every rank of being from fishes to
kings. They lived in forest and town, they were beggars and donors,
wise and foolish, winners and losers. They had happy births and sad.
From all this they learned one thing: that everything in this world and
in the worlds above and below is forever changing and cannot bring
lasting happiness. Now at last, having lived so many lives, they have
become birds in Kāshī, for the final crossing, from this shore of birth
and death to the far shore of immortality.[15]

Finally, according to most Banāras pandits and priests, "all creatures" means people of all religious persuasions, including Christians,
Muslims, and atheists. Karpātrī, the scholar *sannyāsin,* has written that
just as poison will poison anyone who drinks it, so will the nectar of
immortality, called *amrita,* impart immortality to anyone who drinks
it. "In this same way," he said, "from dying in Kāshī everyone will get
liberation, whether he be Muslim, or Christian, or an unbeliever."
While some pandits would quibble that non-Hindus may live in the
earthly Banāras, but do not truly live in "Kāshī," most would agree
with one priest who exclaimed to me, "God knows that, according to
our faith, you will also get *mukti* if you die in Kāshī!"

If everyone is liberated by death in Kāshī, how can there be justice
among people? What of those who appear to be shameless scoundrels,

and yet they die here? And what of those who have been very pious and yet, perchance, die elsewhere? This issue has perplexed thoughtful Hindus, just as the issue of evil and the apparent prosperity of the wicked has perplexed people the world over. According to some, the scoundrel simply will not die in Kāshī. Something will happen at the last moment, and the scoundrel will die on the road to Allahabad or on a business trip to Calcutta. After all, running the undeserving out of the city is the job of the divine sheriff, Dandapāni, along with his two deputies, Confusion and Doubt. Who dies in Kāshī, then, is not a matter of chance. As one priest put it, "A really great sinner will not die here, but will leave. Not all of the millions of people in India can die in Kāshī. Many will come, but 'accidentally' or through the conspiracy of the Lord, some will leave before they die."

Just as the flock of birds had come to Kāshī at the end of a long pilgrimage through countless lifetimes, so the saints and sinners of Kāshī have come to this city in the course of a journey through many lives. It is also true, then, that from our limited perspective in this lifetime we cannot begin to say who is a saint and who is a sinner. The law of *karma*, operating inexorably as it does through life after life, does not permit us to say that the beggar or the swindler is undeserving of death in Kāshī. Sureshvara addresses just this point when he writes in the *Kāshī Moksha Nirnaya:* "Some people say, 'Such and such a sinner dies in Kāshī while the doer of good dies outside.' People who really understand should not think along these lines. In this lifetime, we are the ones who discriminate our good and evil deeds, but the Great Lord is the one who discriminates what good and evil we have done, by thought, word, and deed, from time immemorial."[16]

The Punishment of Bhairava

T H E R E is another answer to this question of justice, however, and that is that the scoundrel will be severely punished before attaining *moksha* here. This punishment, meted out by Bhairava, is called the *bhairavī yātanā,* the "punishment of Bhairava."

The *bhairavī yātanā* is the product of a religious imagination as complex and legalistic as that which produced the notion of purgatories

in the West. Indeed, *bhairavī yātanā* is a kind of purgatory and serves
something of the same purpose, as a way station between this world
and the bliss of heaven.

The question to which *bhairavī yātanā* is the answer is, in part, the
question of justice: How can the apparent scoundrel get off without
punishment and, what is more, attain liberation here? In part, it is also
the question of *karma:* How can liberation in Kāshī be squared with
the law of *karma,* by which the results of one's previous actions are
experienced? *Karma* in the Hindu view operates as inexorably as the
natural law of gravity, and that portion of *karma* that is in the process
of being worked out cannot be destroyed by wisdom. It is like an
arrow shot from a bow, they say. It cannot be retrieved until it has
reached its destination. Similarly *karma* cannot be destroyed. It must
reach its destination, and this means one must experience its results,
both good and bad.[17]

The mechanism by which all this *karma* is experienced is the
bhairavī yātanā. Because it is called a "punishment" one can only
conclude that it applies especially to the experiencing of bad *karma.*
Bhairava's punishment is brief, lasting but a moment, and very intense.
It is a kind of compression chamber of experience in which the *karmas,*
which might ordinarily land one in hell or in countless difficult births
and rebirths, are experienced completely in a split second. As one of
the *pandās* at Manikarnikā Ghāt put it, "The punishment that Yama,
the God of Death, would deal out in a thousand years is experienced
here in one second of *bhairavī yātanā.* That is how intense it is. After
the punishment one is pure, and then one sees Shiva himself."

Sureshvara compares the experience of this punishment with the
experience of dreaming.[18] Just as in a dream one might experience a
whole lifetime of activity in a very brief moment, so in *bhairavī yātanā*
one might take on many bodies, one after another, and live through
many lives, in one moment. In explaining this time chamber, Sureshvara recalls the famous story of Nārada, a tale used to illustrate the
nature of *māyā:*

———— ∿∿∾∾ ————

Once Brahmā told the sage Nārada to take a dip in a nearby river. When
he did so, Nārada emerged from the water as a lovely woman of a good
family. She was given in marriage by her father and, in time, she had

many sons and grandsons. Ultimately a war broke out between her father and her husband, and in the course of the battle both were killed, along with many of her sons. Mourning, she mounted the funeral pyre that had been laid for her husband, and as she began to burn, engulfed in flames, she suddenly felt cool, as if she were in the water. And indeed she, as the sage Nārada, was still in the water, taking that dip recommended by Lord Brahmā.

〜〜〜〜〜

Sureshvara also tells the tale of King Lavana in which the king, under the influence of a court magician, experienced a lifetime of adventure and anguish, only to wake up and find that but a moment had passed. Commenting on these stories, Sureshvara says, "Remembering stories like this, one should understand that it is after the manner of *māyā* that certain people [who die] in Kāshī enter into other bodies and experience the punishments of Kāla Bhairava."[19]

There is one further mechanism in the Hindu universe for dispatching the sins of the scoundrels who die in Kāshī: they become *pishāchas* of Rudra for a vast number of years and only then will they be granted *moksha*. This fate is apparently worse than the *bhairavī yātanā* and reserved especially for those who have sinned grievously within the bounds of the sacred city.

A *pishācha* is a "fiend" or a "goblin." One scholar describes them as "eaters of raw flesh," "evil elves," "half-fabulous, half-human."[20] *Pishāchas* are also the unsatisfied spirits of the dead, especially the spirits of those who have died violent or unnatural deaths, or whose death rites were improperly performed. Being a *pishācha* is a wretched in-between state of being, neither in this world nor in the world of the ancestors. In a cosmological system in which there are so many "worlds" and "heavens," so many compartments of the universe, there is nothing worse than being neither here nor there. The *pishācha* is doomed to be perpetually thirsty, to eat food mixed with blood, to be roped to Kāla Bhairava's post for punishment, and to roast on Kāla Bhairava's fire. His *mukti* is hard won, for the scriptures agree that the miserable fate of the *pishācha* lasts for 300,000 years.[21]

Yet even the claims of Bhairava's terrible punishments for the sinful are countered in Kāshī by equally strong attestations of Kāshī's grace. After all, Bhairava's punishment is said to endure but one terrible

moment. For those fated to become *pishāchas,* there is Pishāchamochana, "Where *pishāchas* are set free." There one may be released
from that condition. And according to some, if one dies in the Kedāra
Khanda of the city, one cannot be touched by any punishment, and one
reaches *moksha* directly. As quickly, it seems, as the brahminical
imagination could concoct the most fearsome and ferocious of punishments and purgatories, it could invent the means of mercy to avoid
them or to circumvent their effects.

In the last analysis, there are many who believe in no punishment at
all in Kāshī. The City of Light is a place of pure grace. There Shiva
pours the nectar words of immortality into the ear of the dying without asking after their good and bad deeds.[22] There people who die
become pure by the power of the City of Light, just as wine poured
into the Ganges becomes the Ganges.[23] "This Vārānasī is the divine
embodiment of mercy," they say, "where, leaving one's body, one
enters happily into the brilliance of the Universal Lord and, with one's
own form, attains formlessness."[24] "In Kāshī," they say, "the great
tree of *samsāra,* which grows from the seed of desire, is cut down with
the axe of death, and grows no more."[25]

The Last Sacrifice

A T M A N I K A R N I K Ā cremation ground, there is a sacred fire which
is said to have burned constantly for as long as anyone can remember.
It is kept by the Doms, the untouchable caste that cares for the cremation ground and tends the pyres. With the flame of this sacred fire, the
cremation pyres are lighted, although some groups of mourners may
bring embers from home.

The cremation rite is called the "last sacrifice"—*antyeshti.*[26] The rite
is, indeed, a sacrifice, having a certain structural continuity with all
fire sacrifices in India, from the most complex to the most simple.
What is prepared, ornamented, and offered into the fire is, in this case,
the deceased. When the body arrives at the cremation ground, after
the chanting procession through the lanes of Banāras, it is given a final
dip in the River Ganges. It is sprinkled with the oil of sandalwood and
decked with garlands of flowers. The deceased is honored as would

befit a god, and in Kāshī it is said that the dead take on the very form of God.

The word for a dead body is *shava,* and Hindus have often underlined the phonetic relation between *shava* and Shiva. The identification of the dead with Shiva is suggested by the brahmins in their *māhātmyas* of Kāshī. In the great cremation ground, they say, the dead receive the form and emblems of Shiva. They become three-eyed, wearing the crescent moon in their hair, carrying the trident. Little cares Shiva for the pollution usually associated with death, and here in Kāshī he takes up his post on the cremation ground and transforms the dead into his very likeness. In the fire of the "last sacrifice," the *shava* is a holy offering indeed.

It is the chief mourner, usually the eldest son, who takes the twigs of holy *kusha* grass, flaming, from the Doms' eternal fire to the pyre upon which the dead has been laid. He circumambulates the pyre counterclockwise—for everything is backward at the time of death. As he walks round the pyre, his sacred thread, which usually hangs from the left shoulder, has been reversed to hang from the right. He lights the pyre. The dead, now, is an offering to Agni, the fire. Here, as in the most ancient Vedic times, the fire conveys the offering to heaven.

After the corpse is almost completely burned, the chief mourner performs a rite called *kapālakriyā,* the "rite of the skull," cracking the skull with a long bamboo stick, thus releasing the soul from entrapment in the body. Now, truly, nothing but ash remains. The chief mourner takes a large clay pot of Ganges water, throws it backward over his left shoulder upon the dying embers, and walks away without looking back. "These living have turned back, separated from the dead," they say; "this day our invocation of the gods became auspicious. We then went forward for dancing, for laughter, firmly establishing our long life."[27] The members of the funeral party do not grieve openly, for it is said that many tears pain the dead.[28]

The rites for the dead that follow the cremation last for eleven days and consist of daily offerings of rice balls, called *pindas,* which provide a symbolic, transitional body for the dead. During these days, the dead person makes the journey to the heavens, or the world of the ancestors, or the "far shore." As a whole, these rites are called *shrāddha,* or *pindadāna,* the "offering of *pindas.*" The rites also include the providing of feasts for a group of brahmins, who take nourishment on behalf

of the dead. On the twelfth day, the departed soul is said to reach its destination and be joined with its ancestors, a fact expressed symbolically by joining a small *pinda* to a much larger one.

Death is dangerous because it is a time of transition. It is a liminal or marginal time, a space between life and life. In this transitional period, the soul is called a *preta*, literally one who has "gone forth" from the body but has not yet arrived at its new destination.[29] The rites following the cremation enable the *preta* to become a *pitri*, an ancestor, or more precisely, a "father." Without such rites, one might remain a homeless *preta* for a long time. For those who are very great sinners or who have died hideous deaths, this transition from life to new life might be obstructed by becoming a *pishācha.*

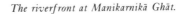

But death is not only a time of danger, for it is also held to be a time of great illumination. At death, they say, the light is very intense, and what separates this shore from the far shore is almost transparent. The time of death, therefore, is a time of clear seeing, of vision, of insight. One's thoughts are to be on God at such a time, for what one thinks and sees at the time of death directs one's first steps toward the next life. Those close to the dying should whisper the name of God in that person's ear. While death may be the final event in one life, it is also, in a sense, the first event in the life beyond. For Hindus, death is not the opposite of life; it is, rather, the opposite of birth.[30] The great transition which death occasions is not from life to death, but from life to life.

In Kāshī, rites for the dead are enacted with great care. One might ask, since such rites are intended to see the soul safely to the heavens or the world of the ancestors from which ultimately the soul will take birth again, "Why are such rites necessary in Kashi?" Here, after all, the dead merit liberation: freedom from this endless journeying through the various compartments of the universe, through life after life. According to the very cautious, the rites do no harm and one can never be too careful. According to the very thoughtful, these rites and the sense of ongoing connection with the loved one that they engender are as much for the living as the dead. For most Hindus, however, the question of this seeming contradiction does not arise. One always does these things, for they are the right things to do, even in Kāshī. It is the *dharma* of the living to perform rites for the dead. It is one of the debts a Hindu man must honor, not only for the sake of his own father and mother recently deceased, but for the sake of all the ancestors who have gone before.

Kāshī promises much more than a good life. This city promises a good death. Here death comes as no surprise. Every day the processions pass, bearing a corpse toward Manikarnikā. Every night the fires burn on the riverbank. The procession of life includes the procession of death. Here death is not denied. Perhaps that is why they can say that death is not feared, but welcomed as a long-awaited guest.

The promise of a good death takes the danger out of the transition, the crossing, death occasions. The very sick or the distressed may lose consciousness as death approaches and be unable to place their thoughts upon the name of God, but Shiva himself will be there, they say, to whisper wisdom into the ear of the dying. Yama, the God of Death, may not approach the dead here, noose in hand. Kāla Bhairava takes charge of the dead, and he is Shiva's own servant, indeed, Shiva's own self. Even if there is some terrible punishment to be meted out, it is guaranteed to be short-lived and to be followed by the bliss of liberation. Here even as one dies, the boats are ready for the crossing.

Kāshī draws into powerful focus the greatest symbols of Hindu culture—its gods, especially the Great Lord, Shiva; its sacred geography, especially the Heavenly River, Gangā; and its vision of transcendence, *moksha*. For over 2,500 years, the people of India have come to this place, which they have described as both the Great Cremation Ground and the Forest of Bliss. Here they have built temples and ashrams, palaces and homes, schools and businesses, transforming the ancient groves and pools of the *yakshas* and *nāgas* into one of the most awesome cities in the world. It is a city of wealth, exuberance, and life. It is also a city of poverty, confusion, suffering, and death. But the City of Light, they say, extends one's vision across the river of life and death to the far shore of immortality. "It is called Kāshī, for here the light shines."

APPENDIXES

NOTE ON TRANSLITERATION
AND PRONUNCIATION

GLOSSARY

NOTES

BIBLIOGRAPHY

ACKNOWLEDGMENTS

ILLUSTRATIONS

INDEX

APPENDIX I

Sanskrit Sources
for the Study of Banāras

I. PURĀNAS

1. *Kāshī Khanda.* One of seven *khandas,* sections, of the *Skanda Purāna.* The structure of the whole *Skanda Purāna* is based on the great *tīrthas* of India. The *Kāshī Khanda* is 100 chapters long and contains myths, *māhātmyas,* ritual prescriptions, and geographical information. In several chapters (83, 84, 97) the temples and *tīrthas* of Kāshī are located in relation to one another. The *Kāshī Khanda* is not quoted by Lakshmīdhara (twelfth century), but certainly describes the ascendant Kāshī of Gahadavala times. Since it cites old and new locations for several temples, its final compilation must have been after the destruction of many of the city's temples in 1194. Sukul dates it in the mid-fourteenth century.

2. *Kāshī Rahasya,* "The Secret Lore of Kāshī." Purported to be an appendix *(parishishta)* to the *Brahmavaivarta Purāna,* but not generally acknowledged as such. The work is both mystical in its identification of the city with Brahman, and ecumenical in its attempt to see the city as belonging to both Shiva and Vishnu. In general, it contains little geographical information, but it does contain the only major *māhātmya* of the Panchakroshī pilgrimage and its stations (KR 9-11). It contains twenty-six chapters, and dates from the fourteenth to the seventeenth century.*

3. *Kāshī Kedāra Māhātmya.* The praise of the Kedāra *linga* in Kāshī. The work also purports to be a supplement *(khila)* to the scriptures, containing secrets held apart. It tells the story of how the Himālayan Kedāra came to Kāshī and praises the *tīrthas*

---

* The centuries cited in this appendix are intended only to give the reader a general time frame. The dating of a literature as fluid as the Purānas is very difficult. The *māhātmyas* of Kāshī must often be dated independently of the Purānas in which they occur or to which they are attached. Any single Purāna contains traditions accumulated through a great number of centuries. I have discussed these sources at greater length in "Sanskrit Sources for the Study of Vārānasī," *Purana* XXII, No. 1 (1980), pp. 81-101.

surrounding Kedāra. It contains thirty-one chapters and dates from the fourteenth to the seventeenth century.

4. *Brahma Purāna* 11; *Brahmānda Purāna* 2.3.67; *Vāyu Purāna* 92. Ancient mytho-historical accounts of the rivalry of the Kāshīs and the Haihaiyas, containing the seed of the story of Divodāsa. These accounts are from the earliest Purānic traditions, fourth to sixth centuries A.D.

5. *Matsya Purāna* 180–5, The "Avimukta Māhātmya." Its final verse mentions the famous five *tīrthas* along the Ganges in Banāras. It contains the myth of the *yaksha* who became Shiva's devotee, the story of Kapālamochana, and the story of Vyāsa's bad temper in Kāshī. It dates from the eighth to the eleventh century.

6. *Kūrma Purāna* I.29–34; II.31. The "Vārānasī Māhātmya" (I.29–34) told by Vyāsa to Arjuna. It mentions the great *lingas* of ancient Kāshī—Omkāreshvara, Krittivāseshvara, Madhyameshvara, etc. The Kapālamochana story, beginning with the fiery *linga* and ending with Kāla Bhairava's expiation of the sin of brahmin-killing, is told in II.31. It dates from the eighth to the eleventh century.

7. *Padma Purāna* I.33–37; V.14; VI.235–236, 278. Diverse myths, *māhātymas,* and diverse dates for its various sections.

8. *Vāmana Purāna* 3. Brahmin-killing destroyed in Vārānasī; eighth to eleventh century.

9. *Linga Purāna* 92. "Vārānasī Māhātmya," in praise of Avimukteshvara; eighth to eleventh century.

10. *Nārada Purāna* II.48–51. Praises various *tīrthas* and *lingas,* especially Krittivāseshvara, Avimukteshvara, Omkāreshvara. It dates from after the twelfth century, for the author plagiarizes from Lakshmīdhara.

11. *Shiva Purāna* IV.22–3. The creation of all, from Manikarnikā. The *māhātmya* of Vishveshvara; twelfth to thirteenth century.

12. *Bhāgavata Purāna* X.66; *Vishnu Purāna* V.34. Account of Krishna's destruction of Kāshī. A story with its seed in the most ancient Purānic traditions.

13. *Mārkandeya Purāna* 7–8. The story of King Harishchandra.

14. *Agni Purāna* 112. Short mention of the measurement of Vārānasī and its several *tīrthas.*

II. NIBANDHAS
Digests or Compendia of Purānic Lore

1. *Tīrthavivechana Kānda ("The Discussion of Tīrthas").* One of the fourteen parts of Lakshmīdhara's "Wishing Tree of Duties," the *Krityakalpataru,* it collects verses on the various *tīrthas,* beginning with over 100 pages on Vārānasī, then treating Prayāga, Gayā, Mathurā, and others. This twelfth-century date provides a watershed for the dating of *tīrtha māhātmyas.*

2. *Tīrtha Chintāmani ("The Wishing Jewel of Tīrthas").* Part of the fifteenth-century digest called the *Smriti Chintāmani,* compiled by Vāchaspati Mishra, a scholar of Mithilā; it deals with Gayā, Purī, Prayāga, Kāshī, and Gangā.

3. *Tristhalīsetu ("Bridge to the Three Sacred Places").* Compiled by Kāshī's Nārayana

Bhatta in the sixteenth century, it consists of four sections: the "General" section on pilgrimage (published separately as the *Sāmānya Praghattaka*), followed by sections on Kāshī, Prayāga, and Gayā.

4. *Tīrtha Prakāsha* ("The Glory of Tīrthas"). Indebted to the TS. Compiled by Mitra Mishra of Gwalior in the seventeenth century as part of the *Vīramitrodaya*.

APPENDIX II

The Zones
of the Sacred City

The names Kāshī, Vārānasī, and Avimukta may sometimes refer to progressively smaller circles of the sacred city. Each zone has its own pilgrimage of circumambulation *(pradakshinā)*, that of Kāshī taking five days, and the others taking but a single day. The smallest unit in this series of concentric circles of sacred geography is called the Antargriha, the "Inner Sanctum" of the city, which is the area immediately around the central temple of Shiva Vishvanātha. Although most pilgrims are unaware of these zones of the sacred city, it is clear from the Sanskrit pilgrimage literature and from the pilgrimage routes which are recorded in popular manuals that the structure of Kāshī as a whole is complex.* Its largest circle—Kāshī—encloses a sacred area which extends far into the countryside to the west of the city. As one approaches the center, each sacred zone becomes increasingly charged with power. In a mystical sense, one might say that just as there are five *koshas* (literally "sheaths," a word interchanged in this context with *krosha*, a unit of measurement) in the human person, layered like the leaf sheaths on a stalk of grass, so are there five *koshas* in Kāshī: Kāshī, Vārānasī, Avimukta, Antargriha, and, finally, the innermost *linga* of Vishvanātha.

KĀSHĪ

The area to which Kāshī refers includes all that is within the circular route around the city, called the Panchakroshī Road. A *krosha* is a unit of measurement equivalent to about two miles, and the term *pancha-krosha*, "five *kroshas*," refers to the radius of the

---

* The Purānic discussion of the measurements and borders of the sacred city is summarized by Lakshmīdhara, *Tīrthavivechana Kānda*, pp. 39–40; Nārāyana Bhatta, *Tristhalīsetu*, pp. 100–4; and Kuber Nāth Sukul, *Vārānasī Vaibhava*, pp. 44–58.

sacred circle of Kāshī. Its geographical center is said to be the Shiva temple of Madhyameshvara, the "Lord of the Center," once an important temple on the north bank of the Mandākinī Tīrtha (now Maidāgin Gardens). Sometimes Krittivāseshvara, also in that immediate vicinity, is cited as the geographical center. According to the *Padma Purāna*, Kāshī is measured as follows:

> Beginning from Madhyameshvara, stretching a string as far as Dehalī Vināyaka, move that string in all directions so as to form a circle. The supreme sacred land [*kshetra*] is what is inside the arc. The Vedas know it as Kāshī. That place is famous for liberation.[1]

A thousand years ago, the temple of Madhyameshvara, and the nearby temples of Krittivāseshvara and Mahākāleshvara, were indeed at the center of the sacred city. The present "Inner Sanctum" around Vishvanātha is a somewhat later development. The old center-temples were destroyed during the Muslim era. Today the grounds of Madhyameshvara are filled with ruined shrines and broken *lingas* set deep into the earth. The temple itself is very small, but it is well kept and known as the "navel" of Kāshī to the people in its immediate locale.

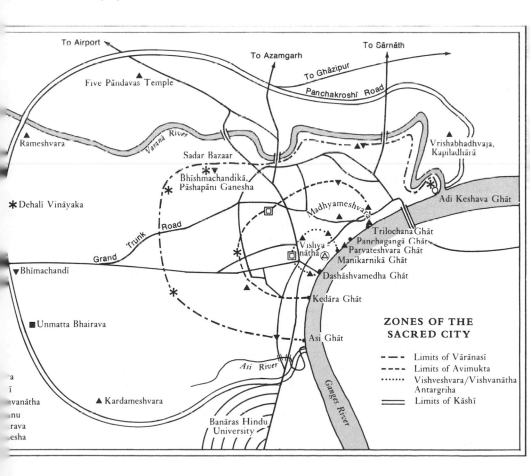

Dehalī Vināyaka is the name of one of the Ganeshas who are guardians of Kāshī. Stretching a string from Madhyameshvara it is, indeed, about five *kroshas* or ten miles due west to Dehalī Vināyaka, which is called the "western door" of Kāshī. It is situated along the Panchakroshī Road.

The circle with the five-*krosha* radius is, of course, a symbolic circle. The sacred zone marked off by the feet of the Panchakroshī pilgrims extends not quite six miles north and south of Madhyameshvara, and hardly a mile to the east, where the circuit follows along the Ganges River. The far bank of the Ganges, which would be included in any geometric circle, is a floodplain and is conspicuously uninhabited compared with the densely populated west bank. It is commonly said that anyone who has the misfortune to die across the river will be reborn as an ass. It is definitely not a part of the sacred circle.

The Panchakroshī Yātrā, the "Pilgrimage of the Five Kroshas," makes the circuit around all of Kāshī. The area, called the "Linga of the Five-Kroshas," is honored by circumambulation, just as one would honor a deity by circumambulating the sanctum of its temple.

The Panchakroshī Road has 108 sacred "stations" along its route, including Shiva and Devī temples and wayside shrines housing *ganeshas, ganas,* and *bhairavas.** The stations where one should stop are today marked with plaques. The pilgrims begin each day long before dawn and reach the day's destination shortly after midday. In each of the four traditional halting places—Kardameshvara, Bhīmachandī, Rāmeshvara, and Kapiladhārā—there are many *dharmashālas,* pilgrim rest houses.

The first day, the pilgrims bathe in the Ganges at Manikarnikā Ghāt; make their statement of intention to undertake the pilgrimage *(sankalpa)* at the Jnāna Vāpī; worship Vishvanātha, Annapūrnā, and Dhundhirāja Ganesha; and then strike out toward the south, following the river to Asi Ghāt. From Asi, they follow the road to the gate of Banāras Hindu University, where the route to Kardameshvara begins. Following this route, they will pass dozens of temples, all on the right side of the road, before reaching their first day's destination at Kardameshvara. The temple at Kardameshvara, set beside a large tank, is especially beautiful. It dates from late Gupta times, as do many of the sculptural fragments found nearby.

From Kardameshvara, the road, which had previously been paved, becomes a dirt road. It takes the pilgrims through the countryside, past several Shiva and Devī shrines, to the village where Unmatta Bhairava, the "Wild One," dwells. This is one of the eight great Bhairavas of Kāshī. Continuing past a number of fierce guardian *ganas,* the pilgrims come to Bhīmachandī, the "Fierce Goddess," located in a domed temple inside a lovely courtyard. Here is the second night's stop.

---

* The *māhātmya* of this pilgrimage route, the *Panchakroshī Māhātmya,* is found in the *Kāshī Rahasya,* pp. 9–11. It is also published separately, for example; *Shrī Kāshī Panchakroshī Māhātmya* (Banāras: Victoria Press, 1906). In English, the description of the 108 stations may be found in Jean Herbert, *Banāras, A Guide to Panch-Kroshī Yātrā.* On Map 6 it should be noted that the Panchakroshī Pilgrimage Route has been truncated to fit the page; the route swings out into the countryside half again as far as it is shown here.

Just past Bhīmachandī, the Panchakroshī Road crosses the Grand Trunk Road and continues across the field to the site of Dehalī Vināyaka, the Ganesha who stands at the western door of the sacred city. There is a large tank there, and in addition to Ganesha's shrine there is a huge *mukha linga*, a *linga* shaft from which the face of Shiva emerges. The pilgrims stop for the third night at the village of Rāmeshvara, a stop sometimes identified with Rāmeshvaram in the far South. According to local traditions, related by informants in the villages along this road, this site was established by Rāma and Lakshmana, heroes of the epic *Rāmāyana,* who visited it long ago when they made this sacred circuit.

From Rāmeshvara the pilgrims cross the Shivapur Road, and near that crossing is the temple of the Five Pāndavas, containing five *lingas* established by these great heroes. The Pāndavas, heroes of the *Mahābhārata,* are also said to have made the circuit around Kāshī during their years of forest exile. The Panchakroshī Road continues, skirting the suburbs of northern Kāshī to its final stop, Kapiladhārā.

Kapiladhārā is one of Kāshī's most ancient temple sites. It is mentioned in the *Mahābhārata* (3.82.69), where only a few *tīrthas* in this area find mention at all. This *tīrtha* also receives considerable attention in the KKh (62), for it was here that Shiva met all the gods upon his triumphant return to Kāshī after the eviction of Divodāsa. At that time, five divine cows gave enough milk to fill a great tank, and all the assembled gods bathed in that *tīrtha* of milk. The *tīrtha* also became known as Vrishabhadhvaja, after the "Bull-Bannered" Shiva, whose emblem flag, flying in Kapiladhārā, was visible from afar in the city itself. Kapiladhārā is, of course, named after the ancient sage Kapila, who is said to have had his ashram there, and to have been visited by Rāma and Sītā. Kapila is often associated with cows and milk.

From Kapiladhārā, the pilgrims cross the fields to the Varanā River. They salute Ādi Keshava, Kharva Vināyaka, and others, and then follow the river back into the city, stopping at Manikarnikā to bathe, and returning to the center at Vishvanātha. They honor the five Moda Vināyakas and the "Witness," Sākshī Vināyaka. Finally, they honor Vishvanātha.

VĀRĀNASĪ

The territory included in Vārānasī is considerably smaller than that of Kāshī. In the first place, it is strictly limited by the course of the Varanā and the Asi Rivers, the latter sometimes referred to as the "Dried-Up River" (Shushkanadī) in the traditional literature. The Purānas cite the other boundaries of Vārānasī as well: it extends from Parvateshvara, the "Mountain's Lord," along the Ganges at Sankatā Ghāt, to Bhīshmachandikā, the *devī* who dwells in the area called Sadar Bazaar in the western part of the city. Near Bhīshmachandikā is Pāshapāni "Noose-in-Hand" Ganesha, who is also said to mark the boundary of Vārānasī.*

---

* The verses that describe Vārānasī's limits include *Matsya Purāna* 183.61–2; 184.40–1; see also *Tīrthavivechana Kānda,* p. 39 and *Tristhalīsetu,* p. 101. Sukul discusses some of the confusion resulting from these verses in *Vārānasī Vaibhava,* pp. 49–51.

The details of the Vārānasī pilgrimage are given in the *Kāshī Yātrā Prakāsha* in its description of the "Pilgrimage Around the City" (Nagara Pradakshinā Yātrā). As usual the pilgrimage begins with a bath in the Ganges at Manikarnikā, the vow of intention at the Jnāna Vāpī, and the worship of Vishvanātha and the surrounding central deities. Returning to the river, the pilgrims proceed from Manikarnikā south along the Ganges to Asi Ghāt. Then they turn inland to Durgā Kund and, having honored Durgā, they swing into the western suburbs of Banāras. Since they do not salute the outermost tier of Ganeshas, many of whom are along the Panchakroshī Road, they stop at the second tier of Ganeshas, such as Shālakatankata Vināyaka (of the southwest) in the village of Maruā Dih and Kūshmānda Vināyaka (of the west) in Phulavariyā village. At one point they do touch the outer tier of Ganeshas—at Pāshapāni Ganesha in Sadar Bazaar. These pilgrims do not cross the Varanā River, so they follow the cityside bank of the Varanā, past Shaileshvara at Marhiyā Ghāt and on to Sangameshvara and Ādi Keshava at the confluence of the Varanā and the Ganges. Again, they return to Manikarnikā and make their final rounds at Vishvanātha.

Those who have taken a vow never to leave the sacred city usually define the limits of the city as those of Vārānasī. For them, and for others unable to make the longer five-day pilgrimage, this circuit of Vārānasī fulfills the same spiritual purposes: it honors the city and all its gods and it destroys all the sins one has committed within the city limits.

AVIMUKTA

The name Avimukta, although it is used to refer to the sacred city in general, also seems to have had specific geographical reference to a zone somewhat smaller than Vārānasī. The Purānas describe it as measuring two hundred bow-lengths from Vishveshvara;[2] however, the area circumambulated in the pilgrimage described by the *Kāshī Yātrā Prakāsha* is somewhat larger.

Following the bath at Manikarnikā and the statement of intention at the Jnāna Vāpī, the pilgrims worship the ancient and revered *linga* of Avimukteshvara in the Vishvanātha compound. Returning to the Ganges at Manikarnikā, they follow the river to Kedāra Ghāt. Turning inland to the west, they pass Kinnarām's ashram where one of the Ganeshas is located and continue to Kamacchā where the famous *linga* of Vaidyanātha is located. From there they travel north, past another of the Ganeshas to Pishāchamochana tank. Continuing their circle, they stop at Vāgīshvarī Devī, ancient Omkāreshvara, Kāmeshvara, and Trilochana. Reaching the river at Trilochana Ghāt, they return to Manikarnikā and then back to the center at Vishvanātha.

ANTARGRIHA

The "Inner Sanctum" of the city extends around Vishvanātha Temple. The circumambulation of this area is perhaps the most popular of all, and it can be done in just an hour or two. The boundaries of this Inner Sanctum are agreed upon: "On the east, Manikarnīsha; in the south, Brahmesha stands. In the west, Gokarna; and in the north

Bhārabhūta. This is the supreme field [*kshetra*] yielding great fruit within Avimukta."[3]

The pilgrimage around this zone is described in the *Kāshī Yātrā Prakāsha* and is so important that it was outlined by James Prinsep in his 1822 map of the city. Leaving Vishvanātha, the pilgrims go to the river at Manikarnikā and follow it south to the temple of Brahmesha at Dashāshvamedha Ghāt. Turning inland, they pass the old ashram and temple of the sage Agastya, in the section of the city named for him, and they proceed to the Sūrya Kund area with its several temples. The small temple of Gokarnesha or Gokarna, "Cow Ears," is prominent on this route as its western boundary, as is the *linga* of Bhārabhūta in the north. Reaching the river near Parvateshvara, the pilgrims honor the important deities of that area, including Agnīshvara and Vīreshvara. Passing Manikarnikā, they enter the city at Mīr Ghāt, honoring Vishālākshī and others before returning to the center. Back at the center, they honor Annapūrnā, the Jnāna Vāpī, and the five Moda Vināyakas. Finally, they return to Vishvanātha.

THE THREE KHANDAS

The Inner Sanctum of Vishveshvara is part of another division of the city into three sectors or *khandas:* the Omkāra Khanda in the north, the Vishveshvara Khanda in the middle, and the Kedāra Khanda in the south. This triple division of the city is not mentioned explicitly until the time of the *Kāshī Kedāra Māhātmya.* Prior to this, only the Vishveshvara Antargriha is mentioned.

Although the mention of the *khandas* is late, the tendency to see the city as three-fold is not. Many Purānic accounts picture the city as raised above the earth on the three points of Shiva's trident. It is also commonly known that the city rests on three hills, taken to be the three trident points. The Rājghāt Plateau in the north is the highest of the three, sloping gradually to the low inland lakes of Mandākinī and Matsyodarī. From the Mandākinī (now Maidāgin) the land begins to rise again toward the south. The hill is steep. It levels in the small square in front of the Chauk Police Station, and then makes a long, winding descent to Godauliā crossing. On the summit of this second great hill the temple of Vishvanātha was once located. Godauliā was another lowland area which once had a rainy season lake and a drainage rivulet linking it with Dashāshvamedha Ghāt. Beyond Godauliā to the south the terrain rises again, gradually this time, to the broad highlands of southern Banāras. This southern sector is named for the great Kedāra Temple.

KEDĀRA KHANDA

Like all the pilgrimages within Kāshī, the circumambulation of Kedāra is complex and includes many temples and shrines. The full pilgrimage may be found in the *Kāshī Kedāra Māhātmya* (which also contains a schematic map), as well as in Sukul's *Kāshī ke Yātrākrama* and the older *Kāshī Yātrā Prakāsha.* Beginning with a dip in the Ganges at "Ādi Manikarnikā," that is, at Kedāra Ghāt, the pilgrims worship Kedāreshvara and all the auxiliary shrines of the temple. Proceeding along the river to the south, they

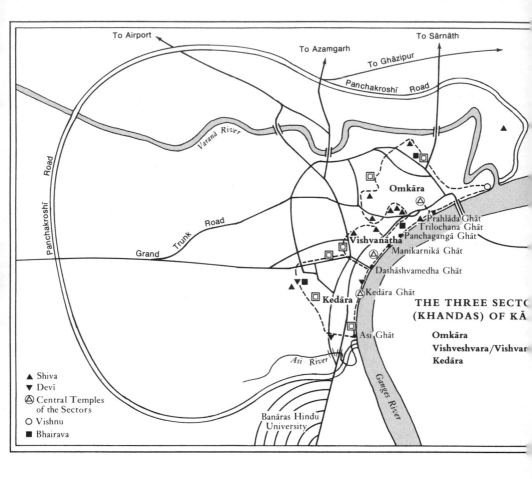

Map legend:

▲ Shiva
▼ Devī
Ⓐ Central Temples of the Sectors
○ Vishnu
■ Bhairava

Map labels:
To Airport
To Azamgarh
To Ghāzipur
To Sārnāth
Panchakroshī Road
Varanā River
Panchakroshī Road
Grand Trunk Road
Omkāra
Prahlāda Ghāt
Trilochana Ghāt
Panchagangā Ghāt
Vishvanātha
Manikarnikā Ghāt
Dashāshvamedha Ghāt
Kedāra Ghāt
Kedāra
Asi Ghāt
Asi River
Ganges River
Banāras Hindū University

THE THREE SECTO
(KHANDAS) OF KĀ
Omkāra
Vishveshvara/Vishvar
Kedāra

acknowledge all the riverfront shrines, stop at Lolārka Kund, and finally reach Asi Ghāt. Turning away from the river at Asi, they proceed to Durgā Kund and then to Shankoddhārā Kund, where the Dvārakā cluster of temples is located. A short distance past Shankoddhārā they come to the locale of Batuk Bhairava, Kāmākshī Devī, and Vaidyanātha Shiva. Then the pilgrims turn back toward the river, stopping at Lakshmī Kund on the way, and reaching the Ganges at Dashāshvamedha Ghāt. The last section of the circular pilgrimage is again along the river, passing Chaumsathī Devī, and finally reaching Kedāra.

OMKĀRA KHANDA

This pilgrimage, rarely made today, traces the outline of Omkāra Khanda, beginning and ending at Omkāreshvara Temple. After an initial dip in the ancient Matsyodarī Tīrtha and the *darshana* of Omkāra *linga* and the subsidiary *lingas* of that complex, the pilgrims would go first to the Ganges at Prahlāda Ghāt. Turning south, they would follow the riverbank, visiting great temples such as Trilochana along the way. Passing Panchagangā Ghāt, they would turn into the city again at Rāma Ghāt and follow the narrow lanes to the Maidāgin area with its many temples: Kāla Bhairava, Kāleshvara, Krittivāseshvara, and Madhyameshvara. From there they would turn briefly to the south again, into the area dominated by the Jyeshtheshvara Temple, and then proceed north to Jaigishavya *linga* and the Nāg Kuān, the "Serpent Well." Still further to the north, they would reach the Varanā River at Marhiyā Ghāt, the location of the "Mountain's Lord," Shaileshvara. Dipping south again, the pilgrims would find the Kapālamochana tank with Lāt Bhairava at its side, and then they would make their way to Rājghāt and the Ādi Keshava Temple at Varanā *sangam*. After following the river-bank again to Prahlāda Ghāt, the pilgrims would return to Omkāreshvara.

APPENDIX III

The Shiva Lingas
of Kāshī

THE FOURTEEN MOST IMPORTANT LINGAS
(KKh 73.32–5)

1. *Omkāreshvara* (KKh 73–4). North of Macchodarī.
2. *Trilochana* (KKh 75–6). Between Macchodarī and the Ganges. Contains a *linga* of the "Three-Eyed" Shiva, considered to be self-manifest.
3. *Mahādeva* (KKh 69.26–35; KKh 97.7–8). Northeast of Trilochana. The "Great Lord," also considered self-manifest. Called the "first *tīrtha*" of Vārānasī.
4. *Krittivāseshvara* (KKh 68; Kurma I.30.15–29; Shiva I.2.5.5; TVK, pp. 76–7). Northeast of Maidāgin. "The Lord who wears the Elephant Hide." One of Kāshī's most famous ancient *lingas*. Temple demolished for the last time during the reign of Aurangzeb. Now a mosque, open to Hindus only on Shivarātri.
5. *Ratneshvara* (KKh 67). In the middle of the road from Maidāgin to Mrityunjaya. "Lord of Jewels." A *linga*, originally of jewels, they say, and established by Pārvatī's father, Himālaya.
6. *Chandreshvara* (KKh 14). West of Sankatā Devī. Temple also contains Chandra Kūpa (a well) and the goddess Siddheshvarī/Santoshī Mātā. "The Moon's Lord," established here by Chandra, the Moon.
7. *Kedāreshvara* (KKh 77). At Kedāra Ghāt.
8. *Dharmeshvara* (KKh 78–9). East of Vishvanātha at Dharma Kūpa. "Dharma's Lord," a *linga* established and honored by Yama, who was then made Dharmarāja, the "King of Dharma."
9. *Vīreshvara* (TVK, pp. 49–51; KKh 82–4). South of Sankatā Devī. The "Hero's Lord," a self-manifest *linga* in which Shiva appeared to a young boy-hero, the foster child of the *mātrikās*. Later, Shiva appeared out of this *linga* as a young boy and granted the devout Vishvānara the boon of a son, who became Vaishvānara, also known as Agni. Known today as Ātmavīreshvara, this *linga* is still worshipped for the boon of sons.
10. *Kāmeshvara* (KKh 85; TS, pp. 169–70). Just east of Macchodarī. "Desire's Lord," established by the great ascetic Durvāsas, who became furious with Shiva for not appearing before him to grant a boon. When Shiva did appear, he vowed to grant all

desires of those who worship "Desire's Lord." Formerly on the bank of Matsyodarī Tīrtha.

11. *Vishvakarmeshvara* (KKh 86). Northeast of Mrityunjaya. "Vishvakarma's Lord," named for the one who established this *linga,* worshipped it, and was rewarded by being appointed the master architect and craftsman of the universe, Vishvakarma, "Maker of Everything."

12. *Manikarnīshvara* or *Manikarnikeshvara* (KKh 61.104–5; TVK, p. 103). Above Manikarnikā Ghāt and just into the city. "Manikarnikā's Lord" has Purānic prominence in connection with Manikarnī Devī. The *linga* is at the bottom of a thirty-foot shaft and is said to have been formerly approachable by a tunnel from the *ghāt.*

13. *Avimukteshvara* (KKh 39.70–80; TVK, pp. 108–9; TS, p. 166). Inside the Vishvanātha Temple.

14. *Vishveshvara* (KKh 98–9). In the center of Kāshī, the "Lord of All," today called Vishvanātha.

SECOND FOURTEEN *(KKh 73.45-7)*	THIRD FOURTEEN *(KKh 73.60-1)*
Amriteshvara	Shaileshvara
Tārakeshvara	Sangameshvara
Jnāneshvara	Svarlīneshvara
Karuneshvara	Madhyameshvara
Moksheshvara	Hiranyagarbha
Svargadvāreshvara	Īshāna
Brahmeshvara	Gopreksha
Lāngalīshvara	Vrishabhadhvaja
Vriddhakāleshvara	Upashānteshvara
Vrisheshvara	Jyeshtheshvara
Chandīshvara	Nivāseshvara
Nandikeshvara	Shukreshvara
Maheshvara	Vyāghreshvara
Jyotirūpeshvara	Jambukeshvara

APPENDIX IV

The Cycles of
Kāshī Goddesses

The Nine Durgās and Nine Gaurīs to be visited on the successive days of the "Nine Nights" of the Goddess are as follows, with their locations:

DURGĀS
(The "Unassailable" Goddesses)

1. Shailaputrī Durgā, "The Mountain's Daughter" (Marhiyā Ghāt, Varanā River).
2. Brahmachārinī Durgā, "The Chaste" (Durgā Ghāt, just north of Panchagangā).
3. Chitraghantā Durgā, "Wonderful Bells" (Lakhīchautara Lane).
4. Kūshmānda Durgā, "Pumpkin Gourd" (Durgā Kund Temple).
5. Skanda Mātā, "Skanda's Mother," also called Vāgīshvarī, "The Eloquent" (in Jaitpurā, east of Nāg Kuān).
6. Kātyāyanī Durgā, "The Middle-Aged Widow" (in Ātmavīreshvara Temple).
7. Kālarātri Durgā, "The Black Night" (in Kālikā Lane).
8. Mahāgaurī, "Great White Goddess" (Annapūrnā; some say Sankatā Devī).
9. Siddhidātrī Durgā "Bestower of Success" (south of Maidāgin; west of Kāla Bhairava; also in Chandreshvara Temple).

GAURĪS
(The "White" or "Fair" Goddesses)

1. Mukhanirmālikā Gaurī, "The Pure-Faced" (Gāya Ghāt).
2. Jyeshthā Gaurī, "The Eldest" (west of Jyeshtheshvara).
3. Saubhāgya Gaurī, "The Auspicious Wife" (in Ādi Vishveshvara Temple).

4. Shringāra Gaurī, "The Elegantly Decked" (in Vishvanātha Temple).
5. Vishālākshī Gaurī, "The Wide-Eyed" (southwest of Vishvanātha at Mīr Ghāt).
6. Lalitā Gaurī, "The Amorous" (Lalitā Ghāt).
7. Bhavānī Gaurī, "Wife of Bhava" (Rāma Temple adjacent to Annapūrnā).
8. Mangalā Gaurī, "The Auspicious" (at Rāma Ghāt).
9. Mahālakshmī Gaurī, "The Great Fortune" (at Lakshmī Kund).

APPENDIX V

Other Deities
of Kāshī

THE TWELVE ĀDITYAS

1. *Lolārka*, "The Trembling Sun" (KKh 46). Near Tulsī Ghāt.
2. *Uttarārka*, "The Northern Sun" (KKh 47). At Bakariā Kund.
3. *Sāmbāditya*, "Sāmba's Sun" (KKh 48). At Sūrya Kund. Sāmba is the son of Krishna, who was here cured of leprosy, according to myth.
4. *Draupadāditya*, "Draupadī's Sun" (KKh 49.1–24). Just west of Vishvanātha Temple, beneath a tree.
5. *Mayūkhāditya*, "Sun of Rays" (KKh 49.25–96). Inside Mangalā Gaurī Temple.
6. *Khakholkhāditya*, "Sky-Meteor Sun" (KKh 50). In Kāmeshvara Temple. Said to have been established by Vinatā, the mother of Vishnu's bird, Garuda.
7. *Arunāditya*, "The Dawn's Sun" (KKh 51.1–26). In Trilochana Temple. Said to have been established by the legless Aruna, another son of Vinatā.
8. *Vriddhāditya*, "The Old Man's Sun" (KKh 51.27–43). South of Vishālākshī Temple at Mīr Ghāt.
9. *Keshavāditya*, "Keshava's Sun" (KKh 51.44–82). In Ādi Keshava Temple.
10. *Vimalāditya*, "Vimala's Sun" (KKh 51.83–100). In Jangambādī area south of Godauliā crossing.
11. *Gangāditya*, "Gangā's Sun" (KKh 51.101–4). At Lalitā Ghāt.
12. *Yamāditya*, "Yama's Sun" (KKh 51.105–15). At Yama *tīrtha* near Vīreshvara.

THE EIGHT BHAIRAVAS

1. *Rūrū Bhairava*, "The Dog." At Hanumān Ghāt.
2. *Chanda Bhairava*, "The Fierce." In the Durgā Temple at Durgā Kund.
3. *Asitānga Bhairava*, "Black Limbs." Now established in Vriddhakāleshvara Temple.
4. *Kapālī Bhairava*, "The Skull-Bearer." Now at Lāt Bhairava.
5. *Krodhana Bhairava*, "The Wrathful." In Kāmākshī Devī Temple.

6. *Unmatta Bhairava*, "The Wild." On the Panchakroshī Road between Kardameshvara and Bhīmachandī.
7. *Samhāra Bhairava*, "The Destructive." Near Pātan Darvāzā.
8. *Bhīshana Bhairava*, "The Horrific." Called Bhūta Bhairava; in the district southwest of Maidāgin called Bhūta Bhairava.

THE EIGHT DIRECTIONAL GUARDIANS

1. *Indra* (E). Indreshvara. Near Tārakeshvara Temple at Manikarnikā.
2. *Agni* (SE). KKh 10–11. Agnīshvara. Northeast of Vīreshvara.
3. *Yama* (S). KKh 78. Yameshvara. At Yama Ghāt near Sankatā Ghāt.
4. *Nirriti* (SW). KKh 12. Nairriteshvara. South of Dashāshvamedha.
5. *Varuna* (W). KKh 12. Varuneshvara. Southwest of Manikarnikā.
6. *Vāyu* (NW). KKh 13. Pavaneshvara. Near Bhūta Bhairava.
7. *Kubera* (N). KKh 13. In Annapūrnā Temple; another in Vishvanātha Temple.
8. *Ishāna* (NE). KKh 33.1–52. Īshāneshvara. In Bāns Phātak.

APPENDIX VI

The Year in Banāras:
A Partial Calendar

CHAITRA *(March/April)*

II. Waxing Fortnight
    1–9   The "Nine Nights" of the Goddess (Navarātra).
    9   Rāma's Ninth (Rāma Navamī).

VAISHĀKHA *(April/May)*

II. Waxing Fortnight
    3   Imperishable Third (Akshaya Tritīyā). Trilochana *darshana*. Decoration of Manikarnikā Kund.
    7   Ganges Seventh (Gangā Saptamī).

JYESHTHA *(May/June)*

I. Waning Fortnight
    1–14   First Fourteen-*Lingas* Pilgrimage.
    8   Shītalā's Eighth (Shītalāshtamī).
II. Waxing Fortnight
    1–10   Dashāshvamedha bathing.
    10   Gangā Dashaharā.

ĀSHĀDHA *(June/July)*

I. Waning Fortnight
    1–14   Second Fourteen-*Lingas* Pilgrimage.
    8   Shītalā's Eighth (Shītalāshtamī).

II. Waxing Fortnight

  2 Chariot Pilgrimage (Ratha Yātrā). From Asi to Sigra crossing.
  11 Vishnu's Sleeping Eleventh (Vishnu Shayanī Ekādashī).

SHRĀVANA *(July/August)*

I. Waning Fortnight

Mondays: Shiva *darshana;* Tuesdays: Durgā Kund *melā.* Throughout the month.

II. Waxing Fortnight

  1-9 Nine Gaurī Pilgrimage.
  5 Serpents' Fifth (Nāga Panchamī).
  15 Full Moon (Shrāvanī). Ganges bank. Also Rakshā Bandhana.

BHĀDRAPADA *(August/September)*

I. Waning Fortnight

  3 Kajalī Third (Kajalī Tīj). Vishālākshī Gaurī Temple.
  4 Ganesha's Fourth (Ganesha Chaturthī). Bare Ganesha Temple.
  8 Krishna's Birthday Eighth (Krishnajanmāshtamī). Gopāl Temple.

II. Waxing Fortnight

  3 Haritālikā Third (Haritālikā Tīj). Mangalā Gaurī Temple.
  6 Lolārka Sixth (Lolārka Shashthī). Lolārka Kund.
  8 Mahālakshmī Pilgrimage begins. Lakshmī Kund, sixteen days.

ĀSHVINA *(September/October)*

I. Waning Fortnight

  1-15 Fortnight of the Ancestors (Pitri Paksha). Manikarnikā Kund, Pitri Kund, Pishāchamochana Kund.

II. Waxing Fortnight

  1-9 Autumn "Nine Nights" of the Goddess (Navarātra). Nine Durgā and Nine Gaurī Temples, Appendix IV.
  10 Victorious Tenth (Vijaya Dashamī).
  11 Reunion with Bharata (Bharat Milāp). Nātī Imlī crossing.

KĀRTTIKA *(October/November)*

I. Waning Fornight

  13 Wealth's Thirteenth (Dhanteras). Thatherī Bazaar.
  14 Hanumān's Birthday (Hanumān Jāyantī). Sankat Mochan Temple.
  15 Row of Lights (Divālī).

II. Waxing Fortnight

  1 The Mountain of Food (Annakūta). Annapūrnā, Vishvanātha Temples.

2   Yama's/Bhīma's Second (Yama/Bhīma Dvitīyā).
11   Vishnu's Waking (Prabodhinī). Panchagangā Ghāt.
14   Vishnu's-Heaven Fourteenth (Vaikuntha Chaturdashī).
        Panchagangā Ghāt.
15   Kārttika Full Moon. Panchagangā Ghāt.

MĀRGASHĪRSHA *(November/December)*

I. Waning Fortnight
   1–8   Eight Bhairava Pilgrimage.
   8   Bhairava's Eighth (Bhairavāshtamī). Kāla Bhairava Temple.

PAUSHA *(December/January)*

II. Waxing Fortnight
   15   Full Moon (Pūrnimā). Four Dhāma Pilgrimage.

MĀGHA *(January/February)*

I. Waning Fortnight
   4   Ganesha's Fourth (Ganesha Chaturthī). Bare Ganesha Temple.
   15   Silent Sages Amāvasyā (Maunī Amāvasyā). Bathing at Dashāshvamedha.
II. Waxing Fortnight
   5   Spring's Fifth (Vasanta Panchamī) and Sarasvatī's Pūjā.

PHĀLGUNA *(February/March)*

I. Waning Fortnight
   14   The Great Night of Shiva (Mahāshivarātri). Twelve *Lingas* of
        Light Pilgrimage.
II. Waxing Fortnight
   11   Colorful Eleventh (Rangabhārī Ekādashī). Vishvanātha Temple.
   15   Holikā Fire.

CHAITRA *(March/April)*

II. Waning Fortnight
   1   Holī.
   1–14   Third Fourteen-*Lingas* Pilgrimage.

Note on Transliteration
and Pronunciation

Sanskrit is "perfectly made" speech, the highly polished language of the gods. For those of us who are mortal, however, I have taken the awesome liberty of simplifying the subtle and complex transliteration of the gods' language so that this text will not be unnecessarily cumbersome to read.

I have kept the use of diacritical marks to a bare minimum: the long mark or macron, which is indispensable for the pronunciation of vowels. Sanskrit vowels are pronounced as follows:

a (as the "u" in but: Banaras)   ā (as in father: Kāshī)

i (as in it: *linga*)   ī (as in magazine. *devī*)

u (as in put: Upanishad)   ū (as in rude: Annapūrnā)

The diphthongs are: e (as in prey: Ganesha); ai (as in aisle: Vaishnava); o (as in blow: *moksha*); and au (as in now: Gaurī). The underdotted ṛ, also a vowel in Sanskrit, has been written "ri" as in rich: Krishna.

As for the consonants, I have departed somewhat from standard scholarly transliteration and written certain Sanskrit phonemes in their closest Roman equivalents. Thus, I have written as "sh" both the retroflex sibilant (ṣ as in Vishnu) and palatal sibilant (ś as in Kāshī, Shiva). The "c" has become "ch" as in *chandra;* the "ch," which occurs rarely here, is "cch." Other distinctions in this precisely articulated language have also been lost in this attempt at simplicity. For example, there are two "t" 's and "d" 's, one dental and the other the underdotted retroflex (ṭ, ḍ) produced by curling the tongue slightly backward toward the roof of the mouth. Here they are written as one—without the dot. The retroflexed phonemes are not common in English, but in the vocabulary of this book we will find this retroflex "ṭ," for example, in the word *ghāṭ.* There are four "n" 's in Sanskrit. In most cases, the tongue tends naturally to make these distinctions when "n" occurs in combination with other consonants. However, the retroflex underdotted "ṇ" is a distinct sound, produced by curling the tongue backward toward the roof of the mouth. The reader should know that this is the "n" sound in such common words as Krishna, Vārānasī, Vishnu, and Ganesha.

Aspirated consonants (those followed by an "h") are pronounced as follows: "bh" (as in clubhouse; Bhagavad Gītā); "dh" (as in roundhouse: *dharma*); "th" (as in hothouse: *tīrtha*); etc.

In the glossary, the full Sanskrit transliteration of each word is provided.

The material for this book poses another problem in transliteration, since it comes from both the classical Sanskrit and modern Hindi contexts. The most noticeable difference between Sanskrit words and names and their Hindi cognates is the presence of a final "a" in the Sanskrit. For example, *darshana* ("seeing" the divine image) would be *darshan* in Hindi. The Vishvanātha Temple would be Vishvanāth; Ganesha would be Ganesh. To avoid the confusion of using both forms, I have spelled almost all such terms in their Sanskrit form. After all, this study begins with Sanskrit textual traditions, and although I discovered Banāras through the Hindi vernacular, the city has a range of pilgrims and residents much wider than the Hindi-speaking world of North India. In referring to places outside Banāras, however, I have for the most part kept the form in which they are most readily recognized today. For example, I write Badrināth, rather than Badarīnātha, and Hardvār, rather than Haridvāra.

In Sanskrit, two-syllable words are accented on the first syllable (Kāshī, Víshnu, Shíva). In words of more than two syllables, the penultimate syllable is accented if it contains a long vowel, a diphthong, or a short vowel followed by two consonants (Vishvanātha, Ganésha). Otherwise, the accent is upon the antipenultimate (third from last) syllable (Himálaya, *mándala*, Vāránasī).

GLOSSARY

Words are spelled here with all of the standard diacritical markings. In those cases where the complete Sanskrit transliteration differs from the modified form I have used in this book, the standard transliteration is given in parenthesis.

āditya	One of the suns or solar deities.
Agni	The Vedic fire god; the sacrificial fire itself.
Akbar	Late sixteenth-century emperor of the Mughal Dynasty.
amāvasyā	The new-moon day in the Hindu lunar calendar.
ānanda	Bliss, happiness. The sublime bliss of oneness with Brahman.
Ānandavana	"Forest of Bliss," a name for Banāras.
Annapūrṇā	"Rich in Food," a name of the goddess who is consort of Shiva.
antyeshti (*antyeṣṭi*)	The "last sacrifice." Cremation rites.
ārati	The circling of oil-lamps before the divine image; used also to describe the entire sequence of honor-offerings made to the deity.
artha	"Wealth, power, purpose"; one of the four *purushārthas*, the pursuit of wealth and power.
āshram (āśrama)	A forest retreat, dwelling place of sages, yogis, and their students.
āshrama (āśrama)	A stage of life, traditionally four: student, householder, forest-dweller, and renouncer.
ashvamedha (*aśvamedha*)	The Vedic horse-sacrifice; a rite of fertility and creation, performed also at the consecration of a king.
Asi	The rivulet that borders Vārāṇasī on the south and enters the Ganges at Asi Ghāt.

ātman	The essence of life, identical with Brahman but used to refer to that essence within the person.
Aurangzeb	Late seventeenth-century emperor of the Mughal Dynasty. Identified with emerging Muslim conservative orthodoxy.
avatāra	The "descent" of a deity; an incarnation, especially of Vishnu.
Avimukta	The "Never-Forsaken," a name of Banāras.
Badrīnāth (*Badarīnātha*)	A place of pilgrimage in the Himālayas, where Vishnu as Badarī Nārāyana is honored.
Balarāma	Name of the elder brother of Krishna, an ancient *nāga*.
bali	The type of worship offered to ancient deities of the *yaksha* clan, including offerings of flowers, water, incense, as well as meat and liquor.
Bhagavad Gītā	The "Song of the Lord," forms part of the sixth book of the *Mahābhārata* and contains Krishna's teaching and revelation to the warrior Arjuna, one of the Pāndavas.
Bhairava	The "terrible, frightful" one; a fearsome form of Lord Shiva as well as the name for a group of ancient deities.
bhakti	"Devotion, honor, love"; from *bhaj* meaning to share, to be devoted, to love. The heart's attitude of devotion and love toward God.
Bhārat (Bhārata)	The land of India, named for an ancient king, Bharata (not to be confused with Bharata, the brother of Rāma).
Bhīma	One of the five Pāndava brothers of *Mahābhārata* fame. Great in size, appetite, and temper.
bilva	The woodapple tree, with clusters of three leaves used in the worship of Shiva.
bīr	A folk deity, descendant of the *yaksha* clan. Perhaps from the term *vīra*, "hero."
bodhisattva	One who has attained enlightenment, but postpones *nirvāna* in order to help others on the way; a "Buddha-to-be."
Brahmā	The Creator God, having four heads, one to look in each direction. Brahmā has no cult.
Brahman	The essence of life; the supreme, transcendent One; the Reality which is the source of all being and knowing; identical with *ātman*.
Brāhmana	The name of the priestly and ritual texts attached to the Veda.
brahmin (*brāhmana*)	The priestly class or a member of the priestly class, charged with the duties of learning, teaching, and performing rites and sacrifices.
chaturmāsa (*caturmāsa*)	The "four months" of the rainy season; a time of retreat for monks and *sannyāsins*.
Chitragupta (*Citragupta*)	The demi-god who keeps the heavenly records.

Daksha *(Dakṣa)*	A creator demi-god who insulted Shiva by not inviting him to a great sacrifice.
dakshinā *(dakṣiṇā)*	Fee paid to brahmins for their ritual service.
dāna	A ritual gift, often a charitable donation.
Daṇḍapāni	The "Club-Carrier," a deity in charge of keeping order in Kāshī.
darshana *(darśana)*	The "auspicious sight" of the deity; also a "point of view," or a philosophical position.
Dashāshvamedha *(Daśāśvamedha)*	The *tīrtha* of the "Ten Horse-Sacrifices," along the Ganges in Banāras.
deva	A god, deity.
devī	A goddess. Used to refer to the thousands of local goddesses as well as to the consorts of the great gods and the Great Goddess, called Devī or Mahādevī.
dhāma	The "abode, dwelling" of God. A sacred place where the Divine is said to dwell.
dharma	Duty, law, righteousness; religious duties, especially rites; in more modern usage, religious tradition.
Divodāsa	An ancient legendary king of Kāshī who expelled the gods.
Durgā	One of the names of the Devī as consort of Shiva.
Dvārakā	The sacred city of Krishna in West India, on the Arabian Sea.
Gāhaḍavāla	The twelfth-century Hindu revivalist dynasty, ruling from Kanauj and from Kāshī.
gaṇa	The "group, troup" of demi-gods who are attendants of Lord Shiva.
Ganesha *(Gaṇeśa)*	"Lord of Gaṇas," the elephant-headed son of Shiva and Pārvatī, keeper of the thresholds of space and time, to be honored at the doorway and at the outset of any venture.
Ganges *(Gaṅgā)*	Sacred river of North India, also personified as a goddess, Gaṅgā.
Gaurī	The "white" goddess, name of Pārvatī.
ghāṭ	The landing places or banks along a river or coast.
ghāṭiā	A brahmin who has jurisdiction over a small section of the *ghāṭ*, upon which he tends to the needs of pilgrims. Also called Gangāputra, the "Son of the Ganges."
Godāvarī	Sacred river of the Deccan in Central India.
Govardhana	The holy hill lifted by Krishna to protect the cowherds; the site of the cultus of an ancient local cowherd deity.
Gupta	The great North Indian empire from the fourth to sixth century A.D.
guru	Teacher, spiritual guide.
Hanumān	The monkey god, famous as the faithful servant of Rāma, who helped Rāma retrieve Sītā from captivity in Lankā; worshipped today in his own right as the focus of a vigorous cult.

Harishchandra (*Hariścandra*)	Legendary king, famous for his righteousness and his suffering.
Hiuen Tsiang	A seventh-century Chinese monk who traveled to India to collect the sacred Buddhist scriptures.
Indra	The Vedic warrior god, wielder of the thunderbolt and drinker of the intoxicating Soma. In later times, a directional regent.
Ishāna (*Īśāna*)	A name of Shiva, the regent of the Northeast.
Ishvara (*Īśvara*)	Lord. Used alone to refer to the personal Lord, generally. Used in compound with other names to refer to particular manifestations of Shiva, such as Vishveshvara, the "Lord of All."
Jagannāth (*Jagannātha*)	"Lord of the Universe," name of Krishna as he dwells in Purī, Orissa. Also, name of a seventeenth-century poet, author of the "Gangā Laharī."
Jātaka	The folk stories that tell about the former lives of the Buddha.
jñāna	Wisdom, transforming knowledge.
Jñāna Vāpī	The Well of Knowledge, next to the Vishvanātha Temple in Banāras.
jyotirliṅga	The "*liṅga* of light," a manifestation of Shiva as a brilliant column of light.
Kabīr	A late fifteenth-, early sixteenth-century Banāras poet, who shunned the religious establishments of both Hinduism and Islam.
Kāla	Time, death, and destiny. The word also means Black.
Kāla Bhairava	A form of Shiva, who is the Lord of Death. The "Black Bhairava," or the "Bhairava of Death."
Kālī	The "Black Goddess" who is both mother of life and destroyer. Sometimes the Shakti of Shiva, and sometimes the supreme being, Mahādevī, unattached to any consort god.
Kāma	The God of Love. Also, one of the four *purushārthas,* the pursuit of passion, pleasure.
Kāmākshī (*Kāmākṣī*)	The "Love-Eyed Goddess" who dwells in Kānchī as well as in the famous *pītha* of Kāmākshī, also called Kāmākhyā, in Āssām.
Kānchī (*Kāñcī*)	One of the seven sacred cities of India, situated in the Tamil South.
Kapālamochana (*Kapālamocana*)	"Where the Skull Fell," a famous pool in Vārānasī where the skull of Brahmā fell from the hand of Shiva.
karma (*karman*)	An act, and its results, which will be manifest in time.
Kārttikeya	"Son of the Krittikās," also known as Skanda, the hero son of Shiva.
Kāshī (*Kāśī*)	The most beloved name for Banāras. From *kash,* to shine. The shining city, the luminous, the City of Light.

Keshava *(Keśava)*	The "long-haired god," a name of Krishna.
khaṇḍa	A section of land (as in Kedāra Khaṇḍa) or of a literary work (as in *Kāshī Khaṇḍa,* a lengthy section of the *Skanda Purāṇa*).
Krishna *(Kṛṣṇa)*	The ancient cowherd god; hero and adviser in the Mahābhārata War; playful lover of the milkmaids in his rural homeland near Mathurā. Called an *avatāra* of Vishnu, but honored and loved in his own right.
krishna paksha *(kṛṣṇa pakṣa)*	The waning fortnight of the lunar month.
Krittikās *(Kṛttikās)*	The Pleiades, the six stars who are the mothers of Kārttikeya.
kshatriya *(kṣatriya)*	The warrior or noble class; more broadly, those who rule the land and protect the people.
kshetra *(kṣetra)*	Field or area of land. In the case of Kāshī *kshetra,* the "sacred zone" of Kāshī.
kumbha	A round water pot, sometimes consecrated to represent the Devī.
Kumbha Melā	A great fair held once every twelve years at Prayāga.
kuṇḍ	A pool, especially a sacred pool for bathing. May be clay-banked *(kaccha)* or improved with steps which descend to the water and make access easier *(pakka).*
Kūrma	The tortoise-incarnation of Vishnu; the name of one of the Purānas.
Kurukshetra *(Kurukṣetra)*	The holy site which was the scene of the great war described in the *Mahābhārata.*
Lakshmana *(Lakṣmaṇa)*	Brother of Rāma who accompanied the hero during his forest exile.
Lakshmī *(Lakṣmī)*	The goddess who embodies auspiciousness, wealth, and fortune.
Lakshmīdhara *(Lakṣmīdhara)*	The chief minister of the Gāhadavāla King Govindachandra in the twelfth century. Great scholar of *dharma;* compiler of the *Tīrthavivechana Kānda.*
liṅga	The "sign" or "emblem" of Shiva and the focus of Shiva worship.
māhātmya	The "glorification, praise" of a deity or a sacred place; eulogistic literature.
Maheshvara *(Maheśvara)*	"Great Lord," Shiva.
Mandākinī	One of the great lakes of ancient Kāshī, named for the Heavenly Ganges. Now Maidāgin Park.
maṇḍala	The "circle" or circular diagram which functions as a schematic map of the sacred universe in symbolic paintings, temples, and even cities.
Mandara	The mythical mountain of riches, used to churn the ocean of

	milk; the place to which Shiva retired when exiled from Kāshī by Divodāsa.
Maṇikarṇikā	One of the great Ganges *tīrthas* in Banāras. More recently, the cremation ground.
mantra	A sacred formula or utterance; a prayer.
maṭha	A monastery.
Mathurā	One of the seven sacred cities of India, located in central North India on the Yamunā River. Early center of the Buddhist tradition; famous as birthplace of Lord Krishna.
mātrikā (*mātṛkā*)	The "divine mothers," female divinities associated with fertility, children, and disease.
Matsya	The fish-incarnation of Vishnu; the name of one of the Purānas.
Matsyodarī	One of the great lakes of ancient Kāshī. Today Macchodarī Park.
Maurya	Fourth to second century B.C. North Indian empire, its most famous emperor being Ashoka (third century B.C.), who became a patron of Buddhism.
māyā	Illusion, the illusory quality of this transitory world of "names and forms"; the mistaken perception of the world as permanent, when in truth it is a "passage," *samsāra*.
melā	A fair, especially a religious fair or festival to which people often come great distances on pilgrimage.
moksha (*mokṣa*)	Liberation, freedom from attachment to the round of birth and death.
mudrā	In artistic representation, a hand gesture to convey particular meanings.
mukti	Liberation, *moksha*.
mūrti	Form, likeness. The divine image of the deity as a focus for *darshana*.
nāga	The ancient serpent deities of India, associated with pools and streams; coopted by all the great deities in their rise to supremacy.
Nārāyaṇa Bhaṭṭa	Sixteenth-century Banāras scholar and civic leader; compiler of the *Tristhalīsetu* and influential in the reconstruction of Vishvanātha Temple.
Navarātra	The "Nine Nights" of the Goddess; a twice-yearly festival of the Goddess, celebrated in Chaitra and in Āshvina.
nirguṇa	Without qualities or attributes; refers to Brahman, to which no qualities, attributes, or adjectives may be ascribed; opposite of saguṇa.
nirvāṇa	The extinguishing of earthly attachments and desires, freedom from rebirth; used by both Hindus and Buddhists to describe the highest spiritual goal.
nivritti (*nivṛtti*)	Returning to oneness, cessation, repose; opposite of *pravritti*.

Om Also *Aum*. The sacred syllable, regarded as the supreme *mantra*, the seed and source of all wisdom.

Panchagangā The "Five Gangās," or the *tīrtha* of the five rivers, one of the
(Pañcagaṅgā) great river *tīrthas* in Banāras.

Panchakroshī The circular pilgrimage route around Kāshī, said to have a ra-
(Pañcakrośī) dius of five *(pancha) kroshas*, or about ten miles. The pilgrimage on this route takes five days.

panchānga The traditional Hindu calendar, setting forth the "five limbs"
(pañcāṅga) of time.

Panchatīrthī The "five-*tīrtha*" pilgrimage along the riverfront at Banāras:
(Pañcatīrthī) Asi, Dashāshvamedha, Ādi Keshava, Panchagangā, and Manikarnikā.

paṇḍā A brahmin who serves the needs of pilgrims. A generic term
describing a great many types of ritual officiants.

Pāṇḍavas The five brothers, including Yudhisthira, Bhīma, and Arjuna,
whose battle with their cousins is described in the
Mahābhārata.

pāpa Sin.

Pārvatī "Daughter of the Mountain." The wife of Shiva who won the
ascetic lord as her husband by austerities.

pinḍa The balls of rice and other grains used ritually in rites for the
dead, usually as offerings to nourish the deceased.

pishācha A goblin or malevolent spirit, sometimes in the entourage of
(piśāca) Shiva as his horrible attendants.

Pishāchamochana The "Liberation of the Pishācha," where *pishāchas* are freed
(Piśācamocana) from their condition; a Banāras *tīrtha*.

pitri Father, in the sense of ancestor, for whose well-being a son
(pitṛ) must perform the rites of *shraddha* and *tarpana* after death.

pīṭha Seat, bench. The locus of goddess worship. There are said to
be as many as 108 such *pīṭhas* all over India.

pradakshinā Circumambulation; honoring something holy by walking
(pradakṣiṇā) around it, keeping it to one's right.

pralaya The universal dissolution after one of the vast aeons of time
called a *kalpa*, or a day of Brahmā.

prāṇa Breath. Both the spiritual breath of a person and the breath of
a deity established in an image.

prasāda Divine grace. In worship, the food offered to the deity and returned, consecrated.

pravritti Flowing forth, active manifestation, rising; opposite of *nivritti*.
(pravṛtti)

Prayāga The "place of sacrifice," a *tīrtha* at the confluence of the
Ganges, Yamunā, and mythical Sarasvatī Rivers.

prāyashchitta Atonement, a rite of expiation.
(prāyaścitta)

pūjā Worship, ordinarily including the presentation of honor-offer-
ings *(upachāras)* to the deity.

pūjārī	The brahmin priest responsible for worship in a temple.
puṇya	Goodness, a good or meritorious act.
Purāṇa	One of the eighteen collections of "ancient stories" which preserve traditions of myth, legend, and rite.
Purī	The sacred city of Krishna-Jagannāth in Orissa, on the Bay of Bengāl.
pūrṇimā	The full-moon day of the Hindu lunar calendar.
purushārtha *(puruṣārtha)*	Aim of human life, of which there are traditionally four: *kāma* (pleasure), *artha* (wealth and power), *dharma* (righteous action), and *moksha* (liberation).
rākshasa (rākṣasa)	Demons who haunt the night.
Rāma	Virtuous king and hero of the epic *Rāmāyaṇa;* an *avatāra* of Vishnu, honored and loved in his own right.
Rāmānanda	A fifteenth-century *bhakta* who gave life to a new wave of devotionalism in North India.
Rāmānuja	An eleventh-century South Indian thinker who gave a philosophical foundation to the Vaishnava devotional movement which became known as Shrī Vaishnavism.
Rāmāyaṇa	The Hindu epic celebrating the legend and deeds of Rāma.
Rāmeshvaram *(Rāmeśvaram)*	Sacred place in the far South, on a small island reaching out toward Srī Lankā.
Ratha Yātrā	The Journey of the Chariot. The yearly festival of Jagannātha's procession in Purī; also celebrated in Banāras.
Rig Veda *(Ṛg Veda)*	The most important collection of Vedic hymns, forming the nucleus of the scriptures considered to be revealed *(shruti).*
Rudra	A Vedic god, later identified with Shiva.
rudrāksha *(rudrākṣa)*	Literally, the "Eye of Shiva." The large, bumpy, brown berries used for rosaries.
sādhu	A "holy man," generally an ascetic as well.
saguṇa	"With qualities," referring to that understanding of God which is describable with qualities, attributes, and adjectives; opposite of *nirguṇa.*
saṁsāra	Passage. The term used to describe the ceaseless round of birth, death, and rebirth. The world of change.
saṅgam	The confluence of rivers.
saṅkalpa	The vow of intent taken at the outset of any ritual activity.
sannyāsin	A renouncer who has "left behind" worldly attachments for a life of contemplation and asceticism.
Sārnāth	A Buddhist site just north of Kāshī where the Buddha is said to have begun his teaching career, setting in motion the wheel of *dharma.*
Satī	The former consort of Shiva who cremated herself because of her father Daksha's insult to Shiva. Thus, the "good wife," who dies on her husband's pyre.
Shaiva *(Śaiva)*	Pertaining to the cultus of Shiva; a worshipper of Shiva.

Shākta *(Śākta)*	Pertaining to the cultus of Shakti, the Goddess; a worshipper of the Devī.
Shakti *(Śakti)*	Energy, power. A term applied to the Goddess, either alone or as the consort of one of the male deities.
Shankara *(Śaṅkara)*	An eighth- to ninth-century teacher *(āchārya)* who is the principal exponent of the non-dualistic philosophy called Advaita. Also a name of Shiva.
shāstra *(śāstra)*	Teaching. A sacred treatise or body of learning, such as the Dharmashāstra, the "Teachings About Dharma."
shikhara *(śikhara)*	The spire of a temple, literally the "peak." Also the word for mountain peak.
Shītalā *(Śītalā)*	The goddess of fever diseases.
Shiva *(Śiva)*	The "Auspicious." The many-powered deity, both creator and destroyer, who, along with Vishnu and Devī, is one of the most widely worshipped deities in India.
Shivarātri *(Śivarātri)*	The "Night of Shiva," the year's greatest Shaiva festival. The fourteenth of the waning fortnight of Phālguna.
shmashāna *(śmaśāna)*	The cremation ground.
shrāddha *(śrāddha)*	Rites for the dead performed after cremation to nourish the deceased for passage to the world of the ancestors.
shukla paksha *(śukla pakṣa)*	The waxing fortnight of the lunar month.
shūdra *(śūdra)*	The fourth of the four classes, traditionally servants.
sindūr	Powder made from red lead, used for anointing the images of particular folk deities.
Sīta	Faithful wife of Rāma, kidnapped by Ravana and recovered by Rāma with the aid of Hanumān.
Skanda	The God of War, son of Shiva and Pārvatī; said to have been raised by six foster mothers, the Krittikās.
stūpa	A Buddhist monument, shaped like a dome, where the earthly relics of the Buddha were honored.
svayambhū	Self-manifest. Used to describe certain *lingas* and images which are said to be uncreated, to have appeared of their own accord.
Tantra	An esoteric religious movement, which emerged after the Gupta period, emphasizing the union of opposites, especially symbolized by male and female.
tapas	Heat; especially the heat generated by ascetic practice, believed to be creative, like the brooding heat of a mother hen.
tāraka mantra	The *mantra* of the "crossing," which Shiva is said to utter to the dying in Kāshī.
tīrtha	Ford, crossing place. A place of pilgrimage.
tīrthayātrā	The journey *(yātrā)* to a sacred place; pilgrimage.

Trilochana (*Trilocana*)	The "Three-Eyed" Shiva, whose third eye is of power and omniscient wisdom.
Tulsī Dās	Late sixteenth-, early seventeenth-century *bhakti* poet, author of the Hindi interpretation of the *Rāmāyana*, the beloved *Rāmcharitmānas*.
Upanishad (*Upaniṣad*)	One of the speculative sacred texts attached to the Vedas.
Vaishnava (*Vaiṣṇava*)	Pertaining to the cultus of Vishnu; a worshipper of Vishnu.
vaishya (*vaiśya*)	The third of the four classes, traditionally merchants and farmers.
Varaṇā	The river that borders Vārānasī on the north, entering the Ganges at Ādi Keshava or Varanā *sangam*.
Vārāṇasī	Banāras, the city between the Varanā and the Asi Rivers.
varṇa	The four classes of Hindu society: brahmin, *kshatriya, vaishya, shūdra*.
Veda	Wisdom, knowing. The sacred literature considered to be "heard" or "revealed" (*shruti*).
viraha	Love in separation. The longing love for an absent lover.
Vishnu (*Viṣṇu*)	The "Pervader," known for the three giant steps with which he claimed the whole universe. Along with Shiva and Devī, one of the three most widely worshipped deities in India.
Vishvanātha (*Viśvanātha*)	Shiva, the "Lord of All," as present in Banāras.
vrata	A vow; religious observances done in fulfillment of a vow.
yajña	Sacrifice, especially the Vedic sacrifice.
yaksha/yakshī (*yakṣa/yakṣī*)	Ancient male and female deities of the "life cult," of non-Aryan India; associated with trees, pools, and vegetative abundance.
yantra	A "device" for harnessing the mind in meditation or worship. A diagram, usually of geometric interlocking triangles and circles.
yoginī	Female divinities, "enchantresses."
yuga	The "ages" of the world, four in number: *krita, tretā, dvāpara*, and *kali*; the first being the perfect age of the beginnings, the last being this age of strife, the Kali Age.

NOTES

ABBREVIATIONS

KKh   *Kāshī Khanda*
KKM   *Kāshī Kedāra Māhātmya*
KR   *Kāshī Rahasya*
TS   *Tristhalīsetu*
TVK   *Tīrthavivechana Kānda*

CHAPTER I

[1] M. A. Sherring, *The Sacred City of the Hindus,* p. 7.
[2] Mark Twain, *Following the Equator,* p. 480.
[3] Lewis Mumford, *The City in History,* p. 570.
[4] Norman Kotker, *The Earthly Jerusalem,* p. 169.
[5] Gustav von Grunebaum, *Muhammadan Festivals,* pp. 20–1.
[6] Paul Wheatley, *The Pivot of the Four Quarters.*
[7] William Foster, ed., *Early Travels in India,* p. 20.
[8] *Ibid.,* pp. 20–1.
[9] Jean Baptiste Tavernier, *Travels in India,* vol. II, p. 236.
[10] Reginald Heber, *Narrative of a Journey Through the Upper Provinces of India,* p. 392.
[11] *Ibid.,* p. 371.
[12] *Ibid.,* pp. 371–2.
[13] Emma Roberts, *Scenes and Characteristics of Hindostan,* p. 177.
[14] Mark Twain, *Following the Equator,* p. 496.
[15] W. S. Caine, *Picturesque India,* p. 302.
[16] Edwin Arnold, *India Revisited,* pp. 218–19.
[17] François Bernier, *Travels in the Mogul Empire,* p. 334; Arnold, *India Revisited,* p. 214.
[18] C. J. C. Davidson, *Diary of Travels and Adventures in Upper India,* vol. II, p. 11.

[19] Norman Macleod, *Days in North India,* p. 20.

[20] James Kennedy, *Life and Work in Benares and Kumaon,* p. 68.

[21] Macleod, *Days in North India,* p. 20.

[22] Count Hermann Keyserling, *India Travel Diary of a Philosopher,* pp. 118–22.

[23] Sherring, *Sacred City of the Hindus,* pp. 16–17.

[24] Foster, *Early Travels in India,* p. 23.

[25] Macleod, *Days in North India,* p. 23.

[26] Sherring, *Sacred City of the Hindus,* p. 37.

[27] Mark Twain, *Following the Equator,* p. 504.

[28] The Shrī Vaishnavas of South India have articulated the understanding of the *archa avatāra,* the "image incarnation" in which the Lord graciously takes the form of the image so that he may be worshipped by his devotees. While the Shrī Vaishnava theologians Rāmānuja and Pillai Lokāchārya state this understanding most dramatically, it is nonetheless true that all image worship in India is based on the faith that the Lord is present, either permanently or temporarily, in the image worshipped.

[29] Kennedy, *Life and Work in Benares and Kumaon,* p. 117.

[30] Martin Haug, trans., *The Aitareya Brāhmanam of the Rig Veda,* 7.15.

[31] The duties of these sacred specialists and the distinctions among them are described in L. P. Vidyarthi, *The Sacred Complex of Kāshī.*

[32] A list of the Kāshī *māhātmyas* is to be found in Appendix I.

[33] *Kāshyām maranam muktih.* This is the most important of Kāshī's praises.

[34] Jātaka Nos. 239 and 283 speak of *Kāshīgrāma.* (The Jātaka tales noted in this text will be numbered according to the accepted numeration of V. Fausbøll's edited Pali text of the Jātakas.) The *Mahābhārata* also mentions *Kāshīpurī* (VI.14.6; XIII.154.23, Critical Edition).

[35] KKh 26.67. Here Vishnu is speaking, choosing a boon granted by Lord Shiva. See the Manikarnikā myths in Chapter 5.

[36] Quoted in Nārāyana Bhatta, TS, p. 102.

[37] When the rivers of India are named in the *Mahābhārata* (VI.10.30), the Varānasī is among them. The *Matsya Purāna* also mentions the Varānasī River as having a confluence with the Ganges (183.73) and as constituting one of the boundaries of Varānasī (183.61–2). See also Vāchaspati Mishra, *Tīrtha Chintāmani,* pp. 351–2, 367, for mention of the Varānasī River. It is also relevant that, according to rules of vowel combination, Varanā and Asi would combine to form Varānasī, but, in fact, the name is never written with a long final a.

[38] Lakshmīdhara, TVK, p. 61, cites the *Matsya Purāna* verses, naming the "Dried-Up River."

[39] KKh 30.17–23.

[40] *The Vāmana Purāna* with English Translation, A. S. Gupta, ed., II.26–9.

[41] *Jābāla Upanishad* 2.

[42] *Matsya Purāna* 180.54.

[43] TS, p. 89. Here a number of etymologies are cited, including the unusual notion that Avimukta means "released" *(mukta)* from "sin" *(avi).*

[44] KKh 46.38; 60.55.

[45] *Kurma Purāna* I.29.35; *Matsya Purāna* 181.23–4.

[46] KR 14.39.

[47] KKh 3. The idyllic location of the sage Agastya's ashram is described. *Matsya Purāna* 180.24–44; *Linga Purāna* 92 Shiva shows Pārvatī the Forest of Bliss.

[48] KR 3.37–8.

[49] KR 14.40–1.

[50] KR 7.21.

[51] KKh 30.96–102. They are also called his "moving *lingas*," KKh 55.34–7.

[52] KKh 53.96; 64.43.

[53] KKh 87.67. Chapters 87–9 tell the Daksha sacrifice story.

[54] *Satī* stones may be found at Gayā Ghāt, Sankatā Ghāt, Tripurabhairavī Ghāt, Dashāshvamedha Ghāt, and others.

[55] KKh 30. 103–4.

[56] See, for example, Rig Veda X.90; *Aitareya Upanishad* 1; and *Matsya Purāna* 167–71 for instances of the spinning forth of creation from the divine body.

[57] *Mahābhārata* XIII.111.16.

[58] TS, p. 131.

[59] See, for example, Mircea Eliade, *The Sacred and the Profane* and *Cosmos and History: The Myth of the Eternal Return.*

[60] For example, Pandharpur is a focus of pilgrimage in Mahārāshtra, Girnār in Gujarāt, and such Skanda sites as Pālnī and Tiruchendur in Tamilnādu.

CHAPTER 2

[1] The *Mahābhārata*, which in legend dates to perhaps the eighth or ninth century B.C., is a long, composite epic, more a library than a single work, dating from the fifth century B.C. to the fifth century A.D. (J. A. B. Van Buitenen, ed. and trans., vol. I, xxiv–xxv). The Jātaka tales, while they may contain popular stories and sayings from earlier centuries, were not composed in their present narratives until about the third century B.C. (Winternitz, *History of Indian Literature*, vol. II, pp. 121 ff.). The composition of the Purānas comes from a later era, ranging from the fourth to the fifteenth centuries A.D., but they too contain materials, especially genealogies, that are very old. See F. Éden Pargiter, *The Ancient Indian Historical Tradition.*

[2] Jātaka No. 5. Bārānasi is the Pali spelling. See also Jātakas Nos. 483, 515, and 543.

[3] Jātaka No. 243.

[4] Jataka No. 23.

[5] Jātaka No. 521.

[6] Jātakas Nos. 1, 2, 54, and others.

[7] Jātakas Nos. 239 and 283.

[8] *Ibid.* This rivalry between "Pasenadi" and "Ajātasattu" is recorded several places in Buddhist literature; *Samyutta Nikaya* I.84–5 and *Dhammapada Commentary*, vol. III, p. 259 (H. C. Norman, ed., Pali Text Society, London: Luzac and Co., 1970 reprint of 1906 edition).

[9] These excavations were begun in the 1940s under the direction of Dr. Krishna Deva and the work was resumed in the early 1960s under the direction of Dr. A. K. Narain. A summary of findings was published by Dr. T. C. Roy, "Archaeological Excavations at Vārānasī," in A. K. Narain and Lallanji Gopal, eds., *Introducing Vārānasī* on

the occasion of the thirty-first meeting of the Indian History Congress in Vārān-asī. Unfortunately, the excavations have not been thoroughly studied and inter-preted, although the artifacts may be found at the Bhārat Kalā Bhavan and in the museum of the Department of Ancient Indian History and Culture, Banāras Hindu University.

[10] R. L. Singh, *Banāras: A Study in Urban Geography*, p. 18.

[11] Samuel Beal, ed. and trans., *Buddhist Records of the Western World*, p. 45.

[12] Motī Chandra, *Kāshī kā Itihās*, pp. 32-4, speaks of the *yakshadharma*, and Ananda Coomaraswamy, *Yaksas*, vol. II, pp. 13-17, speaks of the "life-cult."

[13] The most famous are the early *yakshīs* depicted on the railing posts around the Buddhist *stūpa* at Bhārhut (second century B.C.). These may be seen in the Indian Museum, Calcutta. The *yakshīs* hanging, as if from trees, on the gates of the Bud-dhist *stūpa* at Sānchī date from the first century B.C.

[14] See Pargiter, *Ancient Indian Historical Tradition*. One of the five traditional subjects a Purāna should treat is royal genealogies.

[15] *Brahma Purāna* 11.40-54.

[16] M. N. Dutt, trans., *Harivamsha* I.29, p. 116; *Vāyu Purāna* 92; *Brahmānda Purāna* 2. 3. 67.

[17] In Pali, this phrase is *Atīte Bārānasiyam Brahmadatte rajjam kārente.* . . . It is so common that, in his six-volume edition of the Jātakas, Fausbøll begins his tales with an abbreviation: A. B. Br. r. k. . . .

[18] Motī Chandra, *Kāshī kā Itihās*, p. 40.

[19] B. C. Bhattacharya, *The History of Sārnāth*, pp. 18-21. Jātaka No. 12.

[20] The *Mahāvagga* of the *Vinaya Pitaka* has numerous references to the Buddha's return to Bārānasi (see Oldenberg's Index). Hermann Oldenberg, *The Vinaya Pitaka*, 4 vols., vol. I: *The Mahāvagga* (London: Williams and Norgate, 1879).

[21] *Mahāparinibbāna Sutta* V. 16-22; in T. W. Rhys-Davids, trans., *Sacred Books of the East*, vol. XI, *Buddhist Suttas* (1889, reprint ed., New York: Dover Publications, Inc., 1969).

[22] Jina Prabha Sūri, *Vividha Tīrtha Kalpa*, p. 72.

[23] *Ibid.*, p. 74.

[24] *Shvetāshvatara Upanishad* 1.1. See Robert E. Hume, trans., *The Thirteen Principal Upanishads*.

[25] *Brihadāranyaka Upanishad* 2.1.20.

[26] Kuber Nāth Sukul, *Varanasi Down the Ages*, pp. 19-20. In his Introduction to Motī Chandra's *Kāshī kā Itihās*, V. S. Agrawal, discussing Brahmavārdhana, says that today the city is called Jnānapurī, the City of Wisdom.

[27] See S. Sinha and B. Saraswati, *Ascetics of Kāshī*.

[28] Motī Chandra, *Kāshī kā Itihās*, pp. 66-7, 79-80. The consensus of opinion today is that this is a Buddha, here called a Bodhisattva.

[29] See *Vishnu Purāna* V.34 and *Bhagavāta Purāna* X.66. See also *Harivamsha* 89-115, where the tale is told in the context of the wars between Krishna and Jarāsandha and Krishna's move to Dvārakā.

[30] Charlotte Vaudeville, "The Cowherd God in Ancient India," in L. S. Leshnik and G. D. Sontheimer, eds., *Pastoralists and Nomads in South Asia* (Weisbaden: Otto Harrassowitz, 1975).

[31] K. P. Jayaswal, *History of India, 150 A.D. to 350 A.D.*, p. 7.

[32] *Ibid.*, p. 5.

[33] Kāshīshvara, the "Lord of Kāshī," is named among the gods to be worshipped in the Grihyasutras of Hiranyakeshin (II.7.10.6), dating to about the fifth century B.C.

[34] Julius Eggeling, trans., *Śatapatha Brāhmana* IX.1.1.

[35] *Matsya Purāna* 180.1–9, 80–100.

[36] Samuel Beal, *Buddhist Records of the Western World*, pp. 44–5.

[37] J. N. Tiwari, "Studies in Goddess Cults in North India," pp. 46–52. The female identity of the city is seen in the Kāshī *māhātmyas* (e.g. KKh 45.28; KR 17.29). KR 17 deals with Kāshī's female identity in general. Vārānasī Devī is still worshipped at Trilochana Temple.

[38] *Ibid.*, pp. 14–28.

[39] *Harivamsha* II.3.6.

[40] F. Eden Pargiter, trans., *The Mārkandeya Purāna*. The *Devī Māhātmya* is contained in Chapters 81–93.

[41] J. N. Banerjea, *Development of Hindu Iconography*, pp. 168–73, 489.

[42] The most authoritative work on Skanda in this period is P. K. Agrawala, *Skanda-Kārttikeya: A Study in the Origin and Development*.

[43] KKh 25.22, 32.163 ff.

[44] Alice Boner and Sadā Śiva Rath Śarma, *New Light on the Sun Temple at Konārka*: L. P. Pandey, *Sun Worship in Ancient India*.

[45] Samuel Beal, *Buddhist Records of the Western World*, pp. 44–5.

[46] D. R. Sahni, "Benares Inscription of Pantha," *Epigraphica Indica*, vol. IX, no. 8, pp. 59–62.

[47] Roma Niyogi, *History of the Gāhadavāla Dynasty*, pp. 200–2, 234–6.

[48] *Ibid.*, p. 196. Shiva is referred to as Krittivasa in some inscriptions, indicating that the great temple of Krittivāsa was at its height in this period.

[49] *Ibid.*, pp. 202–3.

[50] *Ibid.*, p 230.

[51] *Ibid.*, p. 193. She cites the work of Taj ul-Ma'athir.

[52] Motī Chandra, *Kāshī kā Itihās*, part 2, Chapters 1, 2, and 3, detail the history of this period.

[53] François Bernier, *Travels in the Mogul Empire A.D. 1656–1668*, p. 334.

[54] Kuber Nath Sukul, *Vārānasī Vaibhava*, pp. 278–9.

[55] Mahāmahopadhyāya Haraprasād Shāstri, "Dakshini Pandits at Benares," *Indian Antiquary* 41 (January 1912), pp. 7–13. Shrī Gopināth Kavirāj in *Kāshī kī Sārasvat Sādhanā*, pp. 14–42, also details the intellectual history of thirteenth- to eighteenth-century Banāras.

[56] Charlotte Vaudeville, *Kabīr*, p. 267.

[57] *Ibid.*, p. 46. I have kept our spelling, "Kāshī," here.

[58] *Ibid.*

[59] W. D. P. Hill, trans., *The Holy Lake of the Acts of Rāma*, p. xvii.

[60] F. R. Allchin, trans., *The Petition to Rām*, pp. 22–3.

[61] F. R. Allchin, trans., *Kavitāvalī*, pp. 197–204.

[62] A. S. Altekar, *Benares and Sarnath: Past and Present*, p. 24.

[63] Motī Chandra, *Kāshī kā Itihās*, pp. 421–7.

[64] Heber, *Narrative of a Journey Through the Upper Provinces of India*, vol. I, p. 390.

[65] Kennedy, *Life and Work in Benares and Kumaon*, pp. 86–7.

CHAPTER 3

[1] *Skanda Purāna* II.2.12.21–40.

[2] S. Sinha and B. Saraswati, *Ascetics of Kashi*, Chapter 4, "The Shaiva Sampradaya," and Chapter 5, "Other Shaiva Ascetic Organizations."

[3] *Vāyu Purāna* 92.27–55. Brief summary.

[4] *Vāyu Purāna* 92.56–9.

[5] Rig Veda I.43, 114; II.33; VII.46. For an English translation, see Ralph T. H. Griffith, *The Hymns of the Rigveda.*

[6] Rudolf Otto, *The Idea of the Holy*, J. W. Harvey, trans., Chapters 4–6.

[7] *Shiva Purāna* II.3.26–8. This episode also occurs in Kalidāsa's play, *Kumārasambhava*, V.

[8] The story of Daksha's sacrifice is popular in the Purānas and takes a number of forms. Here we cite the *Kāshī Khanda* version. KKh 87.28–37.

[9] A *Varāha Purāna* myth contains the story of how the Shaivas became *vedabāhyas*. See T. A. G. Rao, *Elements of Hindu Iconography*, vol. II, part 1, pp. 1–3.

[10] J. Gonda discusses the many aspects of Shiva's fivefold nature in *Visnuism and Śivaism*, pp. 42–8. The five aspects of Shiva are also discussed in *Linga Purāna* I. 11–16.

[11] Ananda Coomaraswamy's title essay in *The Dance of Shiva* (1918; reprint ed., New York: Farrar Straus & Co., 1957) is a readable interpretation of the complexities of Shiva's dance.

[12] Wendy Doniger O'Flaherty's work on Shiva, *Asceticism and Eroticism in the Mythology of Śiva*, explores the tension in Shaiva mythology between Shiva as the ascetic god and Shiva as the phallic and erotic god.

[13] *Yoga chittavritti nirodha*. This is the short definition of yoga given by the sage Patanjali in the *Yoga Sūtras*.

[14] The Abbé J. A. Dubois, *Hindu Manners, Customs and Ceremonies*, p. 631.

[15] The castration motif takes many forms, castration being sometimes the result of Shiva's refusal to procreate, i.e., his excessive asceticism, and sometimes the result of his excessive lust. See O'Flaherty's extensive treatment of this in *Asceticism and Eroticism in the Mythology of Śiva*, pp. 130–6, 172–209.

[16] For example, *Linga Purāna* 17.6–19.7; *Shiva Purāna* I.5.10–13; *Kūrma Purāna* II.31; KKh 31.12–124; *Matsya Purāna* 183.57–62, 81–100.

[17] See, for example, Mircea Eliade, *The Sacred and the Profane*, Chapter 1, and *Cosmos and History, The Myth of the Eternal Return*, pp. 12–21, "The Symbolism of the Center."

[18] KKh 97.5–6.

[19] KKh 58.63.

[20] KKh 97 is the most lengthy enumeration of all the *lingas* of Kāshī. Several hundred *lingas* are mentioned and located in Kāshī. In KKh 69, the sixty-eight great "self-born" *lingas* from all over India are named and their location in the sacred circle of

Kāshī is given. In KKh 73, three groups of fourteen *lingas* each are listed as Kāshī's most prominent icons of Shiva. These *lingas* are listed in Appendix III.

[21] KKh 97.261, 269, 280. The phrase "made of all *lingas*" *(sarvalingamayī)* is a familiar one.

[22] KKh 73.20–1, 24–7.

[23] H. R. Nevill, *Benares: A Gazetteer*, p. 254.

[24] In the eighteenth century, the Marāthās took a leading role in the reconstruction of *tīrthas* and temples in Kāshī. Queen Bhavānī is also said to have had a hand in the construction of the Durgā Kund Temple, the repair of the Panchakroshī Road, and other local projects.

[25] KKh 73.76–151.

[26] The essence of *panchāyatana pūjā* is explained in P. V. Kane, *History of Dharmaśāstra*, vol. II, part II, pp. 716–17.

[27] *Kūrma Purāna* 1.30.4, 5, 8.

[28] It was Kuber Nāth Sukul who first introduced me to this extraordinary phenomenon in the course of our conversations. See his *Varanasi Down the Ages*, pp. 198–9.

[29] TS, pp. 139–40.

[30] The first verse is cited in TVK, p. 58 and TS, p. 141; the second is cited in TS, p. 168.

[31] Sukul, *Varanasi Down the Ages*, p. 199.

[32] TS, p. 168.

[33] The old *Linga Purāna* cited in TVK, p. 55, states that the Rinamochana Pool ("Where One's Debts Fall") is just north of Kapāleshvara, where Brahmā's skull fell from Shiva's hand. Rinamochana is still very much in evidence on Mr. Prinsep's 1822 map of the city, which must mean that the Kapālamochana pool was between Omkāreshvara and Rinamochana.

[34] KKh 73.158–9; TS, p. 141.

[35] KKh 98.30 ff. In this passage, Shiva, standing in the Mukti Mandapa, the "Pavilion of Liberation," grants to Vishnu an important place, right at the center of the sacred world of Kāshī.

[36] The myth occurs in KKh 33.1–52. Ishāna, a form of Shiva, saw the *linga* of light which had burst forth in the argument between Vishnu and Brahmā and wanted to honor and cool the *linga* with pots of water. With his trident, he dug this well and discovered the earth's first springs of water. Sipping this water, they say, causes a *linga* to spring forth in one's own heart.

[37] Shree Rām Sankar Tripātthī, *The Chequered History of the Golden Temple of Kāshī Vishwanāth*, p. 3.

[38] The *Matsya* and *Kūrma Purānas*, for instance, use the name Avimukta throughout.

[39] See *Mahābhārata*, Vana Parva 84.79 (Bombay edition); *Jābāla Upanishad* 2; the eighth-century Pantha inscription which mentioned Avimukta *tīrtha* is cited in full by Motī Chandra, *Kāshī kā Itihās*, pp. 109–10. The twelfth-century Gāhadavāla Inscriptions are cited in Appendix B of Niyogi, *History of the Gāhadavāla Dynasty*. See No. 40.

[40] Dandin, *Dashakumāracharita* ("The Adventures of the Ten Princes"), IV.198–9. Motī Chandra, *Kāshī kā Itihās*, p. 95. Here Avimukteshvara is paired with Manikarnikā, the most important temple with the most important bathing *tīrtha*.

[41] V. S. Phatak, "Religious Sealings from Rājghāt," *Journal of the Numismatic Society of India*, vol. XIX, part II, 1957, pp. 171–5.

[42] TVK, pp. 109–10. The Jnāna Vāpī is not mentioned here by name, but the reference is explicit.

[43] TS, p. 166.

[44] Lakshmīdhara cites this from the *Linga Purāna*, TVK, pp. 108–9. Also cited in *Tīrtha Chintāmani*, p. 358.

[45] KKh 39.77; TS, p. 166.

[46] Vāchaspati Mishra writes, ". . . the Avimukteshvara *linga*, established by Shiva, is famous among the people by the name of Vishvanātha." *Tīrtha Chintāmani*, p. 360.

[47] TS, p. 296. He glosses Avimukta here as Vishvesha.

[48] *Tīrtha Prakāsha*, p. 87. He cites the KKh, the *Brahmavaivarta Purāna*, and the *Padma Purāna* for evidence.

[49] Dāmodara Gupta, *Kuttanīmata*. Verses 3–18 introduce the poem by describing Vārānasī.

[50] Samuel Beal, *Buddhist Records of the Western World*, vol. II, p. 45.

[51] Sukul, *Varanasi Down the Ages*, p. 178.

[52] *Ibid.* He cites *Epigraphica Carnatica*, vol. XV, copper-plate grant No. 298.

[53] Sherring describes the "Ad-Bisheswar" Temple in *Sacred City of the Hindus*, p. 55.

[54] Motī Chandra, *Kāshī kā Itihās*, p. 190.

[55] *Ibid.*, pp. 195 ff.

[56] TS, p. 208.

[57] KKh 97–9.

[58] KKh 99.16b–20.

[59] From the *Padma Purāna*'s story of the *linga* of light. Cited in TS, p. 182.

[60] TS, p. 185. Here Nārāyana Bhatta has collected a whole page of such verses linking Manikarnikā and Vishveshvara. See also KKh 98.49b–51a.

[61] KKM 29.38.

[62] There are also Kedāra *māhātmyas* in the sections of the *Skanda Purāna* that treat these *tīrthas*.

[63] The entire story is told in KKM 1.62–103.

[64] KKM 1.101–2.

[65] KKM 19.32–20.70.

[66] KKh 77.13–55.

[67] KKh 77.46.

[68] KKM 31.67.

[69] Kedāra is mentioned in the *māhātmyas* of the *Agni, Matsya, Kūrma, Padma,* and *Linga Purānas*. See Appendix I.

[70] KKh 77.

[71] See Appendix I. The work, containing thirty-one chapters of *māhātmya* and myth, is in print and in circulation in Kāshī today.

[72] See O'Flaherty, *The Origins of Evil in Hindu Mythology*, Chapter IX on "Crowds in Heaven." KKM 21.

[73] KKM 20.30–5; KKh 77.54–5.

[74] This story, known to those who frequent Kedāra, is also told in Hindi in the introduction to KKM. It is a common story in North India with reference to different

temples and images. Even in Kāshī, the same story is told of the *linga* at Agastya Kund.
[75] KKh 77.4–9.

CHAPTER 4

[1] KKh 39, 43–64. See also Wendy Doniger O' Flaherty's discussion of this myth and related myths in *The Origins of Evil in Hindu Mythology,* Chapter 7, Section 5.

[2] A king named Divodāsa is mentioned in the Rig Veda, but there is no convincing evidence that this is the same figure we meet here. Pargiter has concluded from his genealogical studies in the Purānas *(Ancient Indian Historical Tradition)* that there were two different Divodāsas in the line of Kāshī kings. Traditional genealogies place Divodāsa in the line of descent from Dhanvantari, the legendary father of Indian medicine, and Banāras tradition even today claims Divodāsa as the teacher of Sushruta, the master surgeon who composed one of the famous texts on Ayurvedic medicine. While the common etymology of Divodāsa is. "Servant of Heaven," it would also be possible to construe the name as meaning "Indifferent to Heaven." Here, with the King's blatant disregard of the gods, this might be a more fitting name.

[3] KKh 44.29–34.

[4] KKh 45.28.

[5] KKh 46.37, 38, 42.

[6] KKh 52.74–5.

[7] KKh 53.20–25, summary.

[8] These feminized gods are sometimes called *shaktis,* because they are said to embody the power of the male deity, and sometimes called *mātrikās,* mothers. They are also listed as *yoginīs.* Varahi, the female counterpart to the Varāha *avatāra,* is called a *yoginī* in the *Kāshī Khanda* 45.34 ff. list. V. S. Agrawala in *Ancient Indian Folk Cults* finds such names as Brahmānī, Kumārī, Rudrānī, and Ishānī on the various traditional lists of the sixty-four *yoginīs.*

[9] See Pushpendra Kumar, *Śakti Cult in Ancient India,* and J. N. Tiwari, "Studies in Goddess Cults in Northern India, with Special Reference to the First Seven Centuries A.D."

[10] KKh 45.46 ff.

[11] For example, "This Kāshī is Shiva's Shakti. . . ." KKh 45.28.

[12] Santoshī Mātā, the "Mother of Satisfaction," is the focus of a new goddess cult and has become one of the most popular goddesses in India during the past fifteen years. See Margaret Robinson, "Santoshī Mā: The Development of a Goddess."

[13] Charlotte Vaudeville, "Krsna-Gopāl and the Great Goddess," disscusses the luminous and tenebrous goddesses, in J. S. Hawley and D. Wulff, eds., *The Divine Consort: Rādhā and the Goddesses of India.*

[14] Bhavānī's primary *māhātmya* is in KKh 61.123–38. Here it is said that her *tīrtha* is located south of Dhundhi Ganesha's.

[15] *Annapūrnā Vrat Kathā,* p. 3. The author, Mahant Gosvāmī Shrīvishvanātha Puri, quotes the KR.

16 KKh 65, 66; *Matsya Purāna* 185.

17 See Vaudeville, "Krsna-Gopal and the Great Goddess."

18 Kuber Nāth Sukul, *Varanasi Down the Ages*, p. 189.

19 The *Linga Purāna* locates her "west of Lolārka" (TVK, p. 118) and stations her as the southern guardian *chandikā* (TVK, p. 126).

20 KKh 71, 72.

21 The story is told and the sanctum called Panchamudrā Mahāpītha is praised in KKh 10.100–1; KKh 83.26 ff.; TVK, pp. 49–51.

22 Both hymns may be found in the *Sankatā Vrat Kathā*.

23 See Wendy Doniger O'Flaherty, *Women, Androgynes, and Other Mythical Beasts*, Chapter 4, and David Shulman, *Tamil Temple Myths*, Chapter 4, Section 4.

24 *Sankatā Stuti* is the name of this collection. In *Vārānasī Vaibhava*, Kuber Nāth Sukul cites the *Padma Purāna* as well (pp. 96–7): "In the Forest of Bliss is a famous *devī* named Sankatā, in the vicinity of Vīreshvara, east of Chandreshvara." This is precisely her location.

25 TVK, p. 116. Sukul, *Vārānasī Vaibhava*, p. 94.

26 KKh 72.89 ff. (the nine Shaktis); 72.81 ff. (the nine Durgās); KKh 100.67 ff. (the nine Gaurīs); KKh 45.48 ff. speaks of Navarātra.

27 The translation here is from the work of E. B. Havell, *Benares, the Sacred City*, p. 90.

28 *Ibid.*, p. 93.

29 KKh 46 is the story of the Sun's mission and the *āditya* Lolārka. The other twelve *ādityas* have their stories in KKh 47–51; see Appendix V.

30 Lalta Prasad Pandey, *Sun Worship in Ancient India*, pp. 23–4, 32–3, 112. See *Shatapatha Brāhmana* VI.1.28; XI.6.3.

31 KKh 46.48. KKh 46 contains Lolārka's *māhātmya*.

32 Lolārka, sometimes called Lola Ravi, is mentioned in the *māhātmyas* of the *Matsya* (185.69), *Vāmana* (3.40), and *Kūrma* (1.33.17) *Purānas*.

33 Roma Niyogi, *History of the Gāhadavāla Dynasty*, Appendix B.

34 M. A. Sherring, *The Sacred City of the Hindus*, p. 281. All of Chapter 19 concerns his findings at Bakariā Kund.

35 Dr. Kamala Giri, "Kāshī me Āditya Devasthān," in Sītārām Chaturvedī and V. Mukharjī, eds., *Yaha Banāras Hai*. Dr. Giri's home is one of those in the Sūraj Kund area that contains temple ruins.

36 See Lalta Prasad Pandey, *Sun Worship in Ancient India*; V. C. Srivastava, *Sun Worship in Ancient India*; and Alice Boner, *New Light on the Sun Temple at Konārka*.

37 Pandey, *Sun Worship in Ancient India*, p. 189.

38 *Saura Purāna* 16.25–35 and 17. Cited in R. C. Hazra, *Studies in the Upapurānas*, p. 46.

39 Alice Getty, *Ganeśa*, p. xvii.

40 In *Mahābhārata* III.80–1, for example, there are numerous instances in which the guardian *yakshas* must be saluted in visiting various *tīrthas*. The *yakshas* as door-guardians also appear in the Purānas, for example, in *Vāmana Purāna* 13.

41 Victor Turner, *The Ritual Process*, Chapter 3.

42 *Shiva Purāna* II.4.13–18 tells Ganesha's story, for example.

43 *Harivamsha* I.29; *Vāyu Purāna* 92; *Brahmānda Purāna* 2.3.67.

44 The *linga* established by Gokarna and that of Bhārabhūta are along the borders of the Antargriha, the "Inner Sanctum." The *linga* of Tilaparna is housed in the temple

called Tilabhāndeshvara, one of the most venerable temples in Kāshī's southern sector.

⁴⁵ M. Sylvain Levi, "Le Catalogue Géographique des Yaksa dans la Mahāmāyūrī," pp. 19–138.

⁴⁶ KKh 57.

⁴⁷ The naming and locating of these fifty-six Vināyakas begin in KKh 57.59 and continue to the end of the chapter.

⁴⁸ Kāla Bhairava's story and *māhātmya* appear in KKh 31, and Dandapāni's is in KKh 32.

⁴⁹ According to Charlotte Vaudeville (conversation), the deities who are associated with peacocks (and this includes Krishna and Skanda) are gods of the wild areas, the hinterlands, in origin.

⁵⁰ *Tantrachudāmani*, cited in *Shakti Ank*, p. 645. J. N. Banerjea, *Development of Hindu Iconography*, pp. 466, 495.

⁵¹ KKh 31.43.

⁵² KKh 31.121–3.

⁵³ KKh 31.53.

⁵⁴ *Yājnavalkya Smriti* iii.243, quoted in David Lorenzen, *The Kāpālikas and Kālāmukhas*, p. 13.

⁵⁵ KKh 31.138.

⁵⁶ KKh 31.47, 142; *Shiva Purāna* III.8.51.

⁵⁷ KKh 31.149; TS, p. 194.

⁵⁸ KKh 31.153.

⁵⁹ Bhairava's punishment is described in the *Kāshī Moksha Nirnaya*, attributed to Sureshvara.

⁶⁰ KKh 31.138.

⁶¹ KKh 31.38–40; KKh 67.56. Sukul, *Vārānasī Vaibhava*, pp. 278–9.

⁶² KKh 31.42–6.

⁶³ The two pillars were near each other, according to Sukul. The Mahāshmashāna Stambha was destroyed and its sections are worshipped as Chakrapani Bhairava and Dandapāni Bhairava today. The Kula Stambha is the one that resembled an Ashokan pillar and was destroyed in the terrible riot of 1809. What is left of it is still honored at Lāt Bhairava. *Vārānasī Vaibhava*, pp. 120–1.

⁶⁴ Sherring, *Sacred City of the Hindus*, p. 191.

⁶⁵ Tavernier, *Travels in India*, vol. I, p. 119.

⁶⁶ Sherring, *Sacred City of the Hindus*, pp. 305–8.

⁶⁷ William Buyers, *Recollections of Northern India*, pp. 274–7.

⁶⁸ KKh 32.162.

⁶⁹ There is a mytho-historical Dandapāni, the son of Kāshī's King Paundraka, who was killed by Krishna. Dandapāni plotted revenge on Krishna and secured, with devotion, the aid of Shiva. The fire he sent to destroy Krishna boomeranged, however, and Kāshī was burned to ashes. (*Padma Purāna* 6.278.) It is unclear to me what the relation between this Dandapāni and our celebrated *yaksha* is.

⁷⁰ KKh 32.164–8.

⁷¹ *Matsya Purāna* 180.1–19, 80–100.

⁷² KKh 32.

⁷³ V. S. Agrawala, *Ancient Indian Folk Cults*, Chapter 15.

[74] See, for example, *Shiva Purāna* I.6–10, in which Brahmā gets a false witness to affirm that he has seen the top.

[75] KKh 52.68–9.

[76] *Linga Purāna* 92.72–8; 87–8.

[77] KKh 73.76–151.

[78] KKh 26; *Shiva Purāna* IV.22.8–23.

[79] KKh 98.24–33.

[80] KKh 58.17–18.

[81] KKh 58.23.

[82] KKh 58.30–62.

[83] Tulsī Dās, *The Petition to Rām*, F. R. Allchin, trans., No. 61.

[84] Tavernier, *Travels in India*, vol. II, pp. 230–5.

[85] KKh 58.200–2.

[86] KKh 60.48, 51, 61. The entire chapter tells Agni Bindu's story.

[87] KKh 60.73 ff.

[88] KKh 60.137.

[89] Sherring, *The Sacred City of the Hindus*, p. 277.

[90] *Ibid.*, pp. 271–87.

[91] The word *varkara/barkara* meaning "young goat" is offered in the Purānas as the source of the name Varkarī Kund, from which Bakariā is derived (KKh 47.56). Charlotte Vaudeville (conversation) makes another suggestion: *bak + ari* in Hindi means the "Crane's Enemy," an epithet for Krishna, who defeated a Crane demon in one of his famous exploits.

[92] *Nārada Purāna* II.48.11–12.

[93] KR 18.30; TS, p. 216.

[94] *Nārada Purāna* II. 48.14.

[95] KR 14.64; 6–41. Nārāyana is another of Vishnu's names.

CHAPTER 5

[1] KKh 53.43.

[2] The story of the descent of the Ganges is told in many places: *Rāmāyana*, Bāla Khanda 38–44; *Mahābhārata* III.104–8; *Bhāgavata Purāna* IX.8–9; *Brahmavaivarta Purāna* II.10; *Devībhāgavata Purāna* IX.11; and others.

[3] KKh 30.1–10a; KKh 52.69–70; TVK, p. 31; TS, p. 101.

[4] KKh 79.38.

[5] Water poured out over the tips of the fingers is for the gods, while water poured out between the thumb and the forefinger is for the ancestors.

[6] *Kūrma Purāna* I.44.28–33; *Brahmavaivarta Purāna* IV.34; *Bhāgavata Purāna* V.17.5–10; *Vishnu Purāna* II.2.30–7.

[7] *Matsya Purāna* 121.38–41; *Brahmānda Purāna* II.18.39–41; *Padma Purāna* I.3.65–6.

[8] The mother rivers are mentioned, for example, in Rig Veda I.32.12; I.34.8; I.35.8; II.12.12; IV.28.1. The Ganges is mentioned in Rig Veda X.75.

[9] KKh 28.91.

[10] Raj Bali Pandey, *Vārānasī: The Heart of Hinduism*, p. 30.

[11] From Jawaharlal Nehru's Last Will and Testament, quoted in Eric Newby and Raghubir Singh, *Gangā: Sacred River of India* (Hong Kong: The Perennial Press, 1974), p. 9.

[12] KKh 27.7–8.

[13] KKh 27.76.

[14] *Mahābhārata* III.85.94 (Bombay edition).

[15] KKh 28.38–83.

[16] Mary Douglas, *Purity and Danger* (London: Routledge & Kegan Paul, 1966), Introduction and Chapter 2.

[17] This type of Purānic exaggeration is called *arthavāda*. The great powers of the Ganges are praised in KKh 27 and 28.

[18] Jagannātha, *Gangā Laharī*, verse 1.

[19] *Gangā Laharī*, verse 24.

[20] *Gangā Laharī*, verse 47.

[21] The *Shrī Gangāshtaka*, "Eight Verses to the Ganges," begins, "O Mother! Co-wife of Pārvatī!" and the *Gangā Laharī*, verse 12, speaks of Pārvatī's envy of Ganga.

[22] KKh 28.84–8.

[23] KKh 28.9.

[24] KKh 27.19.

[25] KKh 84.107–10, 114.

[26] *Matsya Purana* 185.69.

[27] KKh 7.66.

[28] *Vāmana Purāna* 3.30–49.

[29] KKh 46.60.

[30] KKh 7.66; *Matsya Purāna* 185.69; *Vāmana Purāna* 3.40–3.

[31] *Mārkandeya Purāna* 8 tells Harishchandra's tale.

[32] There was a *shmashāna* connected with Kedāra temple called Ādi Manikarnikā in the *Kāshī Kedāra Māhātmya*. This is probably it.

[33] K. P. Jayaswal, *A History of India, 150 A.D. to 350 A.D.*, p. 57.

[34] KKh 61.21.

[35] Dharmesha's myth and *māhātmya:* KKh 78, 79, 81.

[36] Vīreshvara's myth and *māhātmya:* TVK, pp. 49–51; KKh 82–4.

[37] Agnīshvara's myth and *māhātmya*, related to Vīreshvara: KKh 10.40–11.165.

[38] Trilochana's myth and *māhātmya:* KKh 75, 76.

[39] Mahādeva's myth and *māhātmya:* TVK, pp. 41–2; KKh 69.26–35; KKh 97.7–8.

[40] *Matsya Purāna* 185.68; *Vāmana Purāna* 3.43–50.

[41] Roma Niyogi, *History of the Gāhadavāla Dynasty*, Appendix B.

[42] *Linga Purāna* 92.87–9.

[43] Motī Chandra, *Kāshī kā Itihās*, p. 226.

[44] Tavernier, *Travels in India*, pp. 230–5.

[45] *Ibid.*, p. 232.

[46] *Ibid.*, pp. 233–4.

[47] The myth and *māhātmya* of the "Five Rivers": KKh 59. This is followed by the myth and *māhātmya* of Bindu Mādhava in KKh 60 and 61.

[48] KKh 60.137–8.

[49] KKh 34.34; 61.73.

[50] KKh 26.1–65, summary.

[51] *Shiva Purāna* IV.22.1–17, summary.

[52] J.Ph. Vogel, *Indian Serpent-Lore*, pp. 218–19.

[53] KKh 26.66, 67, 69.

[54] KKh 26.70–99.

[55] KKh 26.101, 103.

[56] KKh 97.210.

[57] KKh 61.104–5.

[58] TVK, p. 103; KKh 61.85–105, quoted in TS, pp. 146–7; *Tīrtha Chintamāni*, pp. 200–1.

[59] This *shringāra* takes place on Akshaya Tritīyā, the third day of the waxing fortnight of Vaishākha, the day when the Himālayan *tīrthas* near the source of the Ganges open for the season, and Rangabhārī Ekādashī, the eleventh day of the waxing fortnight of Phālguna.

[60] Vaikunthanāth Upādhyāya, *Shrī Kāshī Khanda*, 22–6. On pp. 50–2 of this Hindu summary of the KKh, the author comments on the *shringāra* of the *kund*.

[61] *Padma Purāna* I.33.14.

[62] *Nārada Purāna* II.48.67.

[63] *Matsya Purāna* 182.23b–24.

[64] KKh 30.84–5.

[65] Edwin Greaves, *Kashi: The City Illustrious or Benares*, p. 47.

[66] The name Brahma Nāla, "The Brahman Vein," is sometimes said to be the third of the three mystical veins of the body of Kāshī, the other two being Varanā and Asi.

[67] I resist using the active voice in this matter ("the faithful wife immolates herself . . .") since most of the eyewitness accounts I have read hardly support such a view. In one famous Banāras incident, a *satī* leaped from the pyre in Rāmnagar and threw herself into the Ganges. When a British officer with a rowboat fished her out, there was a civil disturbance and a near riot.

CHAPTER 6

[1] This calendrical reckoning is called *pūrnimānta*, referring to months that "have the full moon at the end." In other parts of India, especially in the South, the months are reckoned with the new-moon day at the end of the month.

[2] KKh 14. Chandra's penance is also mentioned in the eighth-century inscription of Pantha found in Kāshī. See Motī Chandra 109–10. In KKh 15.1–20 the constellations, called *nakshatras*, do penance to win Chandra as their husband.

[3] Tuesday through Saturday are governed by the planets and their stories are told as follows: Mangala (Mars) also called Angāraka. KKh 17.4–21. (Angārakeshvara: in Sankatā Devī Temple.) Budha (Mercury). KKh 15.20–68. (Budheshvara: in Ātmavīreshvara Temple.) Brihaspati (Jupiter). KKh 17.23–66. (Brihaspatīshvara: near Ātmavīreshavara Temple.) Shukra (Venus). KKh 16. (Shukreshvara: in Kālikā Lane south of Ātmavīreshvara.) Shani (Saturn). KKh 18. (Shanaishchareshvara: south of Vishvanātha in Vishvanātha Lane.) Also TS, pp. 157–60 summarizes the days' *māhātmyas*.

[4] KKh 73.32–5, 45–7, 60–1.

[5] For the first group it is in the waning fortnight of Jyeshtha; the second in the same fortnight of Āshādha; and the third in Chaitra.

[6] *Kāshī Vārshika Yātrā* is the explanatory subtitle of *Kāshī Tattva Bhāskara*, The *Kāshī Yātrā Prakāsha* is a similar manual, organized around the temples themselves. The most recent such manual is Kuber Nāth Sukul's *Kāshī ke Yātrākrama*. TS, pp. 215–87 collects verses on Kāshī, according to the days of the month.

[7] KKh 24.76–8.

[8] KKh 66.9–12, 23–6. This entire first section of KKh 66 sets the *nāgas* of northern Kāshī (Vāsuki and Takshaka are also named) in geographical relation to the temples of this part of the city.

[9] According to popular tradition, the *kshatriya*'s special holiday is Vijaya Dashamī, the *vaishya*'s is Divālī, and the *shūdra*'s is Holī.

[10] V. S. Agrawala, *Ancient Indian Folk Cults*, p. 86.

[11] KKh 98.5.

[12] It would be possible to interpret this as Bhīshma, since the forehead of the figure fashioned from mud by the riverbank bears the name Bhīshma. He was the adviser of the Kauravas in the Mahābhārata War and a respected teacher. He was also the son of the River Ganga, which would explain his position here. When mortally wounded in the war, Bhīshma utilized a boon that enabled him to die when he pleased. He lay on his bed of arrows and waited for the auspicious half of the year to come round before he died. Perhaps this reclining figure is Bhīshma, the counselor, but according to most of my informants, this is Bhīma. Professor Charlotte Vaudeville attests that it is indeed Bhīma who is honored in this fashion in villages throughout India.

[13] KKh 22.86–7.

[14] *Padma Purāna,* quoted in TS, p. 94. The words used for "auspicious" here are *shubha* and *mangala.*

[15] *Kāshī Khanda,* quoted in TS, p. 80.

[16] For a discussion and description of the Kali Yuga, see R. C. Hazra, *Studies in the Purānic Records on Hindu Rites and Customs,* Chapters I and II. Among the Puranic descriptions of the Kali Yuga: *Vishnu Purāna* VI.1; *Matsya Purāna* 144; *Kūrma Purāna* I.29. See also KR 5.1–40.

[17] KKh 22.86. In KR 17.72–9 it is argued that Kali enters Kāshī in the karmic "tendencies" *(vāsanas)* that people bring with them, and in that sense alone Kali dwells in Kāshī.

[18] See, for example, KKh 53.112–14; KKh 32.74–83.

[19] KKh 32.74–8.

[20] KR 17.74, 79.

CHAPTER 7

[1] KR 13.54–5.

[2] TVK, p. 33.

[3] KR 13.54 commentary. *Kāshī Kedāra Māhātmya* 19.30 and Introduction, p. 10.

[4] TS, p. 139.

[5] *Charom Dhām Sapta Purī Māhātmya*, p. 131.

[6] Shiva Sharma's tale is found in KKh 6–24.

[7] *Tīrthānk*, p. 127.

[8] KR 13.25b–27a, 39.

[9] The locations are described in KR 13.28b–34a; the seasons of pilgrimage in KR 13.36b–39a.

[10] *Brahmānda Purāna* 35.15, as cited in *Tīrthānk*, p. 354.

[11] *Tīrthānk*, p. 413. One of the Sanskrit teachers at Shankhoddhāra also cited this story. In brief, it is the tale of a sea monster named Shankhu who was killed by Krishna but also saved by the sheer fact of having beheld Krishna. The shrine is on the island called Bet Dvārakā.

[12] J. Ph. Vogel, *Indian Serpent Lore*, pp. 210–17.

[13] Ujjain, for example, also has an extensive *māhātmya* in the *Skanda Purāna, Avantī Khanda*. Here Avantī (Ujjain) and the Mahākāla Forest are praised and the eighty-four great *lingas* of the sacred zone enumerated.

[14] Surajit Sinha and Baidyanath Saraswati, *Ascetics of Kāshī*, Chapter 4, "The Shaiva Sampradaya."

[15] J. Gonda, *The Meaning of the Sanskrit Term Dhāman*, p. 30.

[16] *Kāshī Yātra Prakāsha*, p. 64.

[17] In the *Skanda Purāna*, which is concerned from beginning to end with *māhātmyas* of sacred places, this story is cited many times, even in connection with places not among the twelve, such as Mt. Abu (Arbuda) in Rājasthān and Arunāchala mountain in Tamilnādu.

[18] KKh 22.64.

[19] KKh 61.29–30.

[20] KKh 61.41–5.

[21] KKh 10–13.

[22] There are many guardian deities included in the *mandala* of a temple. Stella Kramrisch's classic work, *The Hindu Temple*, has shown the complex pattern of temple architecture. See especially pp. 29–39, 91–4. Her first chapter, in a section on "Tīrtha and Temple," has made the symbolic connection between the structure of the *tīrtha* and that of a temple.

[23] KKh 22.83.

[24] KKh 44.30.

[25] KR 2.96–7.

[26] For example, KKh 26.27; 60.61; 44.29; KR 2.36–7, 106–23; TS, pp. 76–7.

[27] KKh 22.84–5.

[28] KKh 22.88; 25.57; *Kūrma Purāna* 1.29.26; *Padma Purāna* 1.33.13.

[29] KKh 52.30.

[30] KR 2.82 ff.

[31] *Kāshī Tattva Bhāskara*, pp.7–8.

[32] KKh 26.131.

[33] KR 17.14 ff.

[34] KKh 55.44.

[35] KKh 5.25–6; KKh 33.167 ff.; TS, p. 341.

36 *Jābāla Upanishad* 1–2. Quoted also by *Kāshī Moksha Nirnaya* and by Shankara, *Brahma Sūtra Bhāshya* I.2.32.

37 KR 3.21.

38 KR 2.31b.

39 TS, p. 83.

40 KKh 99.6; KR 2.97; KR 2.28 commentary; KR 7.65.

41 KR 2.25.

42 KR 2.28.

43 Shankarāchārya, "Kāshīpanchakam" in *Vedāntasamuchchaya*, Hareram Sharma, ed. (Bombay: Nirnaya Sagar Press, 1915). For a discussion of the authenticity of Shankara's authorship, see Robert E. Gussner, "Hymns of Praise."

CHAPTER 8

1 Literally *purushārtha* means "aims of man," and indeed they are intended for Hindu men, not women. The notion of the *purushārthas* as motivations to action as well as areas of activity has been articulated by Karl Potter, *Presuppositions of India's Philosophies*, and by Robert Lingat, *The Classical Law of India*.

2 KKh 74.29; KKh 17.29.

3 KKh 3.85.

4 KKh 4.97.

5 Motī Chandra, *The World of Courtesans*, p. 44.

6 *Ibid.*, pp. 34–6.

7 Dāmodara Gupta, *Kuttanīmatam*, edited by Dr. Sūryakānta (Vārānasī: Indological Book House, 1961). Also A. M. Shastri, *India as Seen in the Kuttanimata of Dāmodara Gupta* (Delhi: Motilal Banarsidass, 1975).

8 KKh 5.69–70.

9 KKh 44.14, 17.

10 KKh 44.1–8.

11 KKh 32.131, 134–5.

12 KR 3.34.

13 Kuber Nāth Sukul, *Varanasi Down the Ages*, p. 19. He cites here the *Mahābhāshya* IV.3.72. Motī Chandra, *Kāśī kā Itihās*, pp. 4, 5, 60.

14 Cited by M. A. Sherring, *The Sacred City of the Hindus*, p. 10.

15 Emma Roberts, *Scenes and Characteristics of Hindostan*, pp. 185–7.

16 Edwin Arnold, *India Revisited*, p. 220.

17 KKh 66.54–6.

18 Himālaya's story is told in KKh 66. Two *lingas* are related to his tale: Shaileshvara, the "Mountain's Lord," at Marhiyā Ghāt on the Varanā River, and Ratneshvara, the "Lord of Jewels," in the middle of the road leading from Maidāgin to Mrityunjaya.

19 TS, p. 131. Nārāyana Bhatta cites many examples of such equations here, a cross-section of what is truly a vast genre of Purānic literature.

20 *Matsya Purāna* 181.17b–18.

21 TS, p. 73; KR 2.42–4; KKh 26.133.

[22] Durdhara's story is told in the *Kāshī Kedāra Māhātyma* 16–18. In his next lifetime, Durdhara became Divodāsa, according to this account.

[23] KR 14.56.

[24] The term *vajralepa* refers to a kind of very hard cement. KKh 64.67; KR 5.72; KR 11.18–19.

[25] KKh 22.97, 102.

[26] KKh 22.95–6.

[27] KKh 74.41. Also KKh 35.2. KR 13.14–15 mentions nine *ūsharas* which, like the seven cities, are all located in Kāshī.

[28] KKh 64.52.

[29] These *prāyashchittas* are mentioned in KR 7 and 12.

[30] KR 9–11.

[31] *Sanatkumāra Samhitā* of *Skanda Purāna*, quoted in *Kāshī Moksha Nirnaya*.

[32] KR 2.34–35a.

[33] KKh 41.172–3.

CHAPTER 9

[1] KKh 94.43–4.

[2] KKh 63.71–2. Jaigishavya's story is told in KKh 63. *Matsya Purāna* 180.57–9; *Linga Purāna* 92.52–3.

[3] KKh 40.162. See also KKh 40.160–3, 170–1; KR 2.34–5.

[4] KKh 60.55, 57, 58.

[5] *Kūrma Purāna* I.29.59. The *tāraka mantra* is here, and sometimes elsewhere, referred to as the Tāraka Brahman, recalling one of the most ancient uses of the term Brahman, the sacred word.

[6] KKh 26.101, 103. See also KKh 33.105–8.

[7] TS, p. 292. He quotes the KKh here in the course of his wider discussion of this matter.

[8] *Kāshī Mriti Moksha Vichāra*, p. 5. This text is the same as the *Kāshī Moksha Nirnaya* and is more widely available.

[9] Sureshvara in the *Kāshī Moksha Nirnaya* cites sources identifying the *tāraka* as *Om*. In the TS (p. 291), Nārāyana Bhatta cities the *Rāmatāpanīya Upanishad* and the *Padma Purāna* equating the *tāraka* with *Rāma Rāma*.

[10] Tulsī Dās, *Vinaya Patrikā* 184.4, as translated by F. R. Allchin, *The Petition to Rām*, p. 206.

[11] TS, p. 292. Nārāyana Bhatta's own commentary on this subject is extensive and found primarily on pp. 292–8.

[12] *Kāshī Mriti Moksha Vichāra*, verses 3–4 on p. 1 and verse 20 on p. 9.

[13] TS, p. 308. Nārāyana Bhatta quotes the KKh and other sources in this regard. See also KKh 26.80; KKh 52.26; KR 2.32–3.

[14] *Matsya Purāna* 181.19–21. TS p. 299 quotes an almost identical passage in which women are listed as candidates for *moksha*, along with worms and foreigners.

[15] KKh 78–9 tells the birds' story.

[16] *Kāshī Mriti Moksha Vichāra*, p. 14. See also KR 18.6, 18.17.

[17] *Ibid.*, p. 2.

[18] *Ibid.*, pp. 12–14.

[19] *Ibid.*, p. 14.

[20] Alain Daniélou, *Hindu Polytheism*, pp. 213, 310.

[21] KKh 64.67–72; KKh 64.83 ff.; KR 7.65–75.

[22] KR 8.45.

[23] KR 14.40.

[24] KKh 30.72.

[25] KKh 74.40.

[26] Death rites in Kāshī have been studied by Meena Kaushik, "The Symbolic Representation of Death," and Jonathan Parry, "Death and Cosmogony in Kāshī."

[27] Meena Kaushik, "The Symbolic Representation of Death," p. 278.

[28] Raj Bali Pandey, *Hindu Samskāras*, p. 255. In Chapter 9, Pandey describes the whole of the Antyeshti Samskara.

[29] Veena Das in her article, "The Uses of Liminality: Society and Cosmos in Hinduism," discusses the liminal nature of death and death rites in a Hindu context.

[30] The observation that we in the West seem to consider death the opposite of life, while the Hindu and Buddhist traditions presuppose that death is the opposite of birth, was made during my years at the Center for the Study of World Religions at Harvard by a Japanese scholar, Kachiko Yokugawa.

APPENDIX II

[1] TS, p. 100.

[2] TS, pp. 100–1.

[3] KKh 74.45–6a.

BIBLIOGRAPHY

SANSKRIT TEXTS AND TRANSLATIONS
(in alphabetical order by title of text)

Aitareya Brāhmanam of the Rig Veda. Edited and translated by Martin Haug. Sacred Books of the Hindus Series. Allahabad: Sudhindra Nāth Vasu, 1922.

Śrīmad Bhāgavata Mahāpurāṇa (with Sanskrit text and English translation). Translated into English by C. L. Goswami. 2 vols. Gorakhpur: The Gītā Press, 1971.

——— Translated by J. M. Sanyal. 1930–34. Reprint, New Delhi: Munshiram Manoharlal, 1970.

Brahma Purāṇa. Gurumaṇḍala Granthamālāyā No. XI. 2 vols. Calcutta: 1954.

Brahmāṇḍa Purāṇam. Edited by J. L. Shastri. Delhi: Motilal Banarsidass, 1971.

Gaṅgā Laharī, by Jagannātha. Vārāṇasī: Thākur Prasād and Sons.

Harivamsha. Translated by Manmatha Nath Dutt. Calcutta: Elysium Press, 1897.

Kāśī Kedāra Māhātmya (Sanskrit text, with Hindi translation by Śrī Vijayānanda Tripāthī). Kāśī: Acyutagranthamālā Kāryālaya, 1920.

Kāśī Khaṇḍa (Skanda Purāṇa). Gurumaṇḍala Granthamālāyā No. XX, Vol. IV. Calcutta: 1961.

Kāśī Mokṣa Nirṇaya, by Sureśvara. (Sanskrit text, with Hindi translation by Ambika Datta Upādhyāya. Gorakhpur: Śrī Gaurīśaṅkar Ganerivālā, 1931.

Kāśī Mṛti Mokṣa Vicāra, by Sureśvara. Edited by Gopināth Kavirāj. The Princess of Wales Saraswati Bhavana Text No. 67. Allahabad: Government Printing, 1936.

Śrī Kāśī Pañcakrośī Māhātmya. Banāras: Victoria Press, 1906.

Kāśī Rahasya (Brahmavaivarta Purāṇa Pariśiṣṭa). Gurumaṇḍala Granthamālāyā No. XIV, Vol. III. Calcutta: 1957.

Kāśī Tattva Bhāskara. Edited by Munśī Harijanlāl. Banāras: Hitacintak Press, 1917.

Kāśī Yātrā Prakāśa. Banāras: Chandraprabha Press, 1913.

The Kūrma Purāṇa (Sanskrit text with English translation). Edited by A. S. Gupta. Vārāṇasī: All-India Kashi Rāj Trust, 1972.

Kuṭṭanīmatam, by Dāmodara Gupta. Vārāṇasī: Indological Book House, 1961.

The Liṅga Purāṇa. Edited by J. L. Shastri. Translated by a Board of Scholars. 2 vols. Ancient Indian Tradition and Mythology, Vols. 5–6. Delhi: Motilal Banarsidass, 1973.

Mahābhārata. Edited by Vishnu S. Sukthankar (and others). 19 vols. Poona: Bhandarkar Oriental Research Institute, 1933–59.

————. Translated by J. A. B. Van Buitenen. 3 vols. completed. Chicago: University of Chicago Press, 1973–78.

The Mārkaṇḍeya Purāṇa. Translated by F. Eden Pargiter. 1904. Reprint, Delhi: Indological Book House, 1969.

Matsya Purāṇa. Ānandāśrama Sanskrit Series No. 54. Poona: 1907.

————. Edited by Jamna Das Akhtar. Translated into English by various Orientalists. Sacred Books of the Aryans Series, Vol. I. Delhi: Oriental Publishers, 1972.

Nāradīya Purāṇa. Bombay: Veṅkateśvara Press, 1923.

Padma Purāṇa. Ānandāśrama Sanskrit Series No. 131. 4 vols. Poona: 1894.

Ṛg Veda Saṁhitā, Śripad Śarma, ed., Aundha: Svādhyāyamaṇḍala, 1940.

The Hymns of the Rigveda. Translated by Ralph T. H. Griffith. 2 vols. Banāras: E. J. Lazarus and Co., 1896, 1897. Reprinted, Delhi: Motilal Banarsidass, 1973.

The Śatapatha Brāhmaṇa. Translated by Julius Eggeling. Sacred Books of the East. Vols. 12, 26, 41, 43, 44. Oxford: The Clarendon Press, 1882.

Śrī Śiva Mahāpurāṇa. Banāras: Paṇḍita Pustakālaya, 1962.

————. Edited by J. L. Shastri. Translated by a Board of Scholars. 4 vols. Ancient Indian Tradition and Mythology, Vols. 1–4. Delhi: Motilal Banarsidass, 1971.

Skanda Purāṇa. Gurumaṇḍala Granthamālāyā No. XX, 5 vols. Calcutta: 1960–65.

Tīrthacintāmaṇi, by Vācaspati Miśra. Bibliotheca Indica, New Series, No. 1256. Calcutta: Asiatic Society of Bengal, 1912.

Tīrthavivecana Kāṇḍam, by Lakṣmīdhara. Vol. III of the *Kṛtyakalpataru,* K. V. Rangaswami Aiyangar, ed. Gaekwad's Oriental Series, Volume XCVIII. Baroda: Oriental Institute, 1942.

Tristhalīsetu, by Nārāyana Bhaṭṭa. Ānandāśrama Sanskrit Series No. 78. Poona: 1915.

Upaniṣatsaṅgraha. Edited by Pt. Jagadīśa Śāstri. Delhi: Motilal Banarsidass, 1970.

The Thirteen Principal Upanishads, translated by R. E. Hume. 2nd ed. rev., London: Oxford University Press, 1931.

The Vāmana Purāṇa (Sanskrit text with English translation). Edited by A. S. Gupta. Vārāṇasī: All-India Kashi Rāj Trust, 1972.

Vāyu Purāṇa. Gurumaṇḍala Granthamālāyā No. XIX. Calcutta: 1959.

Vedāntasamuccaya, by Śaṅkarācārya. Edited by Brahmarṣi Harerāma Śarma. Bombay: Nirṇaya Sāgara, 1915.

Vīramitrodaya: Tīrtha Prakāśa, by Vācaspati Miśra. Chowkhamba Sanskrit Series No. 239. Banāras: Chowkhamba Sanskrit Series Office, 1917.

Śrī Viṣṇu Purāṇa. Gorakhpur: Gītā Press, 1922.

————. Translated by Horace Hayman Wilson. *The Vishnu Purāṇa: A System of Hindu Mythology and Tradition.* 1840. Reprint of 3rd ed., Calcutta: Punthi Pustak, 1972.

Vividha Tīrthakalpa, by Jina Prabha Sūri. Śantiniketan: Sindhi Jaina Jñānapīṭha, 1934.

HINDI SOURCES

Chandra, Motī. *Kāśī kā Itihās*. Bombay: Hindi Granth-Ratnākar Private Limited, 1962.

Chaturvedī, Sitārām, ed. *Yaha Banāras Hai*. Vārāṇasī: Thaluā Club.

Kalyāṇ Śakti Aṅk, Vol. 1. Gorakhpur: The Gītā Press, 1934.

Kalyāṇ Tīrthāṅk, Vol. 31, No. 1. Gorakhpur: The Gītā Press, 1957.

Kavirāj, Śrī Gopināth. *Kāśī kī Sārasvat Sādhanā*. Patna: Bihār Rāṣṭrabhāṣā Pariṣad, 1965.

Rāmkṛṣṇajī, Śrī Paṇḍita, ed. *Kāśī Vārṣika Yātrā Prakāśa*. Banāras: Chandraprabha Press, 1913.

Sinha, H. B., ed. *Chāroṁ Dhām Sapta Purī Mahātma*. Hardvār: Harabhajan Sinha and Sons, n.d.

Sukul, Kuber Nāth. *Kāśī Ke Yātrākrama*. Vārāṇasī: Rām Ugraha Pāṇḍey, n.d.

_____. *Vārāṇasī ka Adhidaivik Vaibhava*. Vārāṇasī: Śrī Maheśvarī Press, 1968.

_____. *Vārāṇasī Vaibhava*. Patna: Bihār Rāṣṭrabhāṣā Pariṣad, 1977.

Tripāṭhī, Śrī Rāmpratāp. *Purāṇoṁ meṁ Gaṅgā*. Prayāga: Hindī Sāhitya Sammelan, 1952.

Tulsī Dās. *The Holy Lake of the Acts of Rāma*. Translated by W. D. P. Hill. London: Oxford University Press, 1952.

_____. *Kavitāvalī*. Translated by F. R. Allchin. London: George Allen and Unwin Ltd., 1964.

_____. *The Petition to Rām*. Translated by F. R. Allchin. London: George Allen and Unwin, 1966.

OTHER SOURCES

Agrawala, Prithvi Kumar. *Skanda-Kārttikeya: A Study in the Origin and Development*. Vārāṇasī: Banāras Hindu University, 1967.

Agrawala, Vasudeva S. *Ancient Indian Folk Cults*. Vārāṇasī: Prithivi Prakashan, 1970.

Ali, S. M. *The Geography of the Purāṇas*. New Delhi: People's Publishing House, 1966.

Altekar, A. S. *Benares and Sarnath: Past and Present*. 2nd ed. Vārāṇasī: Banāras Hindu University, 1947.

Arnold, Edwin. *India Revisited*. London: Trubner & Co., 1886.

Babb, Lawrence A. *The Divine Hierarchy: Popular Hinduism in Central India*. New York: Columbia University Press, 1975.

Banerjea, J. N. *The Development of Hindu Iconography*, 1956. 3rd ed., New Delhi: Munshiram Manoharlal, 1974.

Beal, Samuel, ed. and trans. *Buddhist Records of the Western World*. London: Trubner & Co., 1884. Reprint Delhi: Oriental Books Reprint Corporation, 1969.

Bernier, François. *Travels in the Mogul Empire, A.D. 1656–1668*. Translated by A. Constable. 2nd ed. revised by V. A. Smith. London: Oxford University Press, 1914.

Bharati, Agehananda. "Pilgrimage in the Indian Tradition," *History of Religions* 3, no. 1 (1963): 135–67.

————. "Pilgrimage Sites and Indian Civilization." In *Chapters in Indian Civilization,* edited by J. W. Elder, Vol. I, pp. 85-126. Dubuque: Kendall/Hunt Publishing Company, 1970.

Bhardwaj, Surinder Mohan. *Hindu Places of Pilgrimage in India.* Berkeley: University of California Press, 1973.

Bhattacharya, B. C. *The History of Sārnāth or the Cradle of Buddhism.* Banāras: Tara Printing Works, 1924.

Boner, Alice, and Sadā Śiva Rath Śarma. *New Light on the Sun Temple of Koṇārka.* Vārāṇasī: Chowkhambā Sanskrit Series Office, 1972.

Buyers, William. *Recollections of Northern India.* London: John Snow, 1848.

Caine, W. S. *Picturesque India, a Handbook for European Travellers.* London: George Routledge and Sons Limited, 1890.

Chandra, Motī. *The World of Courtesans.* New Delhi: Hind Pocket Books, 1976.

Chattopadhyaya, Sudhakar. *Early History of North India from the Fall of the Mauryas to the Death of Harṣa, c. 200 B.C.-A.D. 650.* Calcutta: Progressive Publishers, 1958.

————. *Evolution of Hindu Sects Up to the Time of Samkaracarya.* New Delhi: Munshiram Manoharlal, 1970.

Coomaraswamy, A. K. *Yakṣas.* 2 vols. 1928-31. Reprinted in one volume, New Delhi: Munshiram Manoharlal, 1971.

Cowell, E. B., ed. *The Jataka or Stories of the Buddha's Former Births.* Translated from the Pali by various hands. 1st ed., London: 1895. Reprinted Delhi: Cosmo Publications, 1973.

Daniélou, Alain. *Hindu Polytheism.* New York: Pantheon Books, 1964.

Das, Veena. "The Uses of Liminality: Society and Cosmos in Hinduism," *Contributions to Indian Sociology* (NS) 10, no. 2 (1976): 245-63.

Davidson, C. J. C. *Diary of Travels and Adventures in Upper India.* London: Henry Colburn, 1843.

Eliade, Mircea. *Cosmos and History: The Myth of the Eternal Return.* Translated by W. R. Trask, 1949. New York: Harper and Row, 1959.

————. *The Sacred and the Profane.* Translated by W. R. Trask. 1957, New York: Harcourt, Brace and World, 1959.

Elliott, Robert. *Views in India.* London: Fisher, Fisher, and Jackson, 1853.

Farquhar, J. N. *An Outline of the Religious Literature of India.* London: Oxford University Press, 1920.

Fausbøll, V., ed. *The Jātaka.* London: Kegan Paul Trench Trubner and Co., 1875-97.

Foster, William, ed. *Early Travels in India, 1583-1619.* London: Oxford University Press, 1921.

Getty, Alice. *Gaṇeśa. A Monograph on the Elephant-Faced God.* Oxford: Clarendon Press, 1936.

Glasenapp, Helmuth Von. *Heilige Stätten Indiens.* Munich: George Müller Verlag, 1928.

Gonda, Jan. *The Meaning of the Sanskrit Term Dhāman.* Amsterdam: N. V. Noord-Hollandsche Uitgevers Maatschappij, 1967.

————. *Viṣṇuism and Śivaism: A Comparison.* London: University of London, The Athlone Press, 1970.

Greaves, Edwin. *Kashi: The City Illustrious or Benares.* Allahabad: The Indian Press, 1909.

Grunebaum, Gustav Von. *Muhammadan Festivals.* 1951. Reprinted London: Curzon, 1976.

Gupte, Rai Bahadur. *Hindu Holidays and Ceremonies with Dissertations on Origin, Folklore, and Symbols.* Calcutta: Thacker, Spink, and Co., 1919.

Gussner, Robert E. "Hymns of Praise; A textual-critical analysis of selected Vedantic *stotras* attributed to Śaṅkara with reference to the question of authenticity." Ph.D. thesis, Harvard University, 1974.

Hara, Minoru. "Materials for the Study of Pāśupata Śaivism." Ph.D. Thesis, Harvard University, 1967.

Havell, E. B. *Benares, the Sacred City.* London: Blackie and Son Limited, 1905.

Hawley, J. S., and Wulff, D., eds. *The Divine Consort: Rādhā and the Goddesses of India.* Berkeley: Berkeley Religious Studies Series, forthcoming.

Hazra, R. C. *Studies in the Purāṇic Records on Hindu Rites and Cus.ɔms.* University of Dacca, Bulletin No. XX, 1940.

_____. *Studies in the Upapurāṇas,* Vol. I. Calcutta: Calcutta Oriental Press, 1958.

Heber, Reginald. *Narrative of a Journey Through the Upper Provinces of India from Calcutta to Bombay, 1824-1825.* London: John Murray, 1829.

Herbert, Jean. *Banāras Guide to Panch Krośī Yātrā.* Calcutta: Saturday Mail Publications, 1957.

"Homage to Varanasi" (a series of articles by various authors, in two parts), *The Illustrated Weekly of India* 85, nos. 6 and 7 (Feb. 9 and 16, 1964).

Jayaswal, K. P. *History of India 150 A.D. to 350 A.D.* Lahore: Motilal Banarsidass, 1933.

Kane, P. V. *History of Dharmaśāstra.* Government Oriental Series B.6. Poona: Bhandarkar Oriental Research Institute, 1930-62, 2nd ed. 1973-74.

Kapera, Constance. *The Worship of Kālī in Banāras: An Inquiry.* Delhi· Morilal Banarsidass, 1966.

Kaushik, Meena. "The Symbolic Representation of Death," *Contributions to Indian Sociology* (NS) 10, no. 2 (1976): 265-92.

Kennedy, James. *Life and Work in Benares and Kumaon.* New York: Cassell and Company, Ltd., 1885.

Kennedy, Colonel Vans. *Researches into the Nature and Affinity of Ancient and Hindu Mythology.* London: Longman, Rees, Orme, Brown, and Green, 1831.

Keyserling, Count Hermann. *Indian Travel Diary of a Philosopher.* Translated from the German by J. Holroyd-Reece. Bombay: Bharatiya Vidya Bhavan, 1969.

Kotker, Norman. *The Earthly Jerusalem.* New York: Charles Scribner's Sons, 1969.

Kramrisch, Stella. *The Hindu Temple.* Calcutta: University of Calcutta, 1946.

Levi, Sylvain M. "Le Catalogue géographique des Yakṣa dans la *Mahāmāyūrī,*" *Journal Asiatique* 11.5, no. 1 (janvier/février, 1905): 19-138.

Lingat, Robert. *The Classical Law of India.* Translated from the French by J. Duncan M. Derrett. Berkeley: University of California Press, 1973.

Lorenzen, David N. *The Kāpālikas and Kālāmukhas: Two Lost Śaivite Sects.* New Delhi: Thomson Press Limited, 1972.

Macleod, Norman. *Days in North India.* Philadelphia: J. B. Lippincott & Co., 1870.

Majumdar, R. C. *The History and Culture of the Indian People,* Vols. I–V. Bombay: Bharatiya Vidya Bhavan, 1951–57.

Mani, Vettam. *Purāṇic Encyclopaedia: A Comprehensive Dictionary with Special Reference to the Epic and Purāṇic Literature.* Delhi: Motilal Banarsidass, 1975.

Maury, Curt. *Folk Origins of Indian Art.* New York: Columbia University Press, 1969.

Mumford, Lewis. *The City in History: Its Origins, Its Transformations, and Its Prospects.* New York: Harcourt, Brace & World, Inc., 1961.

Nambiar, K. Damodaran. "Nārada Purāṇa: A Critical Study," *Purāṇa* 15, no. 2 (July 1973): 1–56.

Narain, A. K., and Lallanji Gopal, eds. *Introducing Vārāṇasi.* Vārāṇasī: Banāras Hindu University, 1969.

Nevill, H. R. *Benares: A Gazetteer.* District Gazetters of the United Provinces of Agra and Oudh, Vol. XXVI. Allahabad: Government Press, 1909.

Newell, Major H. A. *Benares: The Hindus' Holy City.* Bombay: Caxton Printing Works, n.d.

Niyogi, Roma. *History of the Gāhaḍavāla Dynasty.* Calcutta: Calcutta Oriental Book Agency, 1959.

O'Flaherty, Wendy Doniger. *Asceticism and Eroticism in the Mythology of Śiva.* London: Oxford University Press, 1973.

———. *The Origins of Evil in Hindu Mythology.* Berkeley: University of California Press, 1976.

———. *Women, Androgynes, and Other Mythical Beasts.* Chicago: The University of Chicago Press, 1980.

Pandey, L. P. *Sun-Worship in Ancient India.* Delhi: Motilal Banarsidass, 1971.

Pandey, Raj Bali. *Hindu Saṃskāras.* 2nd rev. ed. Delhi: Motilal Banarsidass, 1969.

———. *Vārāṇasī: The Heart of Hinduism.* Vārāṇasī: Orient Publishers, 1969.

Pargiter, F. E. *Ancient Indian Historical Tradition.* 1922. Reprint, Delhi: Motilal Banarsidass, 1962.

———. *The Purāṇa Text of the Dynasties of the Kali Age.* London: Humphrey Milford, Oxford University Press, 1913.

Parker, Arthur. *A Handbook of Benares.* Banāras: J. Lazarus and Co., 1895.

Parry, Jonathan. "Ghosts, Greed, and Sin: The Occupational Identity of the Benares Funeral Priests," *Man* 15, no. 1 (1980): 88–111.

———. "Death and Cosmogony in Kāshī." Forthcoming in *Contributions to Indian Sociology* 15 (1981).

Patil, Devendrakumar Rajaram. *Cultural History from the Vāyu Purāṇa.* 1946. Reprint, Delhi: Motilal Banarsidass, 1973.

Phatak, V. S. "Religious Sealings from Rajghat," *Journal of the Numismatic Society of India* 19, part II (1957): 168–79.

Potter, K. H. *Presuppositions of India's Philosophies.* Englewood Cliffs, N.J.: Prentice Hall, 1963.

Puri, B. N. *Cities of Ancient India.* Meerut: Meenakshi Prakashan, 1966.

Raghavan, V. "Tamil Versions of the Purāṇas," *Purāṇa* 2, nos. 1 and 2 (July 1960).

Rao, T. A. Gopinatha. *Elements of Hindu Iconography.* 2 vols, each of 2 parts. 2nd ed. Delhi: Motilal Banarsidass, 1968.

Raychaudhuri, Hemchandra. *Political History of Ancient India.* Calcutta: University of Calcutta, 1923.

Rhys-Davids, T. W., trans. *Buddhist Suttas.* The Sacred Books of the East, Vol. XI. Oxford: The Clarendon Press, 1881. Reprint, New York: Dover Publications, Inc., 1969.

Roberts, Emma. *Scenes and Characteristics of Hindostan.* London: William H. Allen and Co., 1837.

Robinson, Margaret L. "Santoshī Mā: The Development of a Goddess." Project Paper, University of Wisconsin, College Year in India Program, 1979.

Rowland, Benjamin. *The Art and Architecture of India: Buddhist, Hindu, Jain.* Baltimore: Penguin Books, Inc., 1953. 3rd rev. ed. 1967.

Salomon, Richard G. "The Sāmānya Praghaṭṭaka of Nārāyana Bhaṭṭa's *Tristhalīsetu:* Critical Edition and Translation." Ph.D. Thesis, University of Pennsylvania, 1975.

Saraswati, Baidyanath. *Kāshī: Myth and Reality of a Classical Cultural Tradition.* Simla: Institute of Advanced Study, 1975.

Schwartzberg, Joseph E., ed. *A Historical Atlas of South Asia.* Chicago: The University of Chicago Press, 1978.

Sen, Rajani Ranjan. *The Holy City (Benares).* Chittagong: Minto Press, 1912.

Sherring, M. A. "Benares Past and Present" in *Calcutta Review* 80, no. 40 (1864): 253–94. (This article, although published anonymously, is unquestionably Sherring's.)

———. *The Sacred City of the Hindus: An Account of Benares in Ancient and Modern Times.* London: Trubner and Co., 1868.

Shulman, David Dean. *Tamil Temple Myths.* Princeton: Princeton University Press, 1980.

Singer, Milton, ed. *Traditional India: Structure and Change.* Bibliographical and Special Series, Vol. X. Philadelphia: The American Folklore Society, 1959.

———, *When a Great Tradition Modernizes: An Anthropological Approach to Indian Civilization.* New York: Praeger Publishers, 1972.

Sinha, Surajit, and Saraswati, Baidyanath. *Ascetics of Kāshī, an Anthropological Exploration.* Vārāṇasī: N. K. Bose Memorial Foundation, 1978.

Sircar, D. C. "The Sakta Pithas," *Journal of the Royal Asiatic Society of Bengal* 14 (1928): 1–108.

———. *Studies in the Religious Life of Ancient and Medieval India.* Delhi: Motilal Banarsidass, 1971.

Smith, Vincent A. *The Oxford History of India.* 3rd ed. edited by Percival Spear. Oxford: The Clarendon Press, 1958.

Smith, Wilfred Cantwell. *The Meaning and End of Religion: A New Approach to the Religious Traditions of Mankind.* New York: The Macmillan Company, 1962.

Srivastava, V. C. *Sun Worship in Ancient India.* Allahabad: Indological Publications, 1972.

Stevenson, Margaret. *The Rites of the Twice Born.* 1920. Reprint, New Delhi: Oriental Books Reprint Corporation, 1971.

Stutley, Margaret and James. *Harper's Dictionary of Hinduism.* New York: Harper and Row, 1977.

Sukul, Kuber Nāth. *Varanasi Down the Ages.* Vārāṇasī: Bhargava Bhushan Press, 1974.

Tavernier, Jean Baptiste. *Travels in India.* Translated by V. Ball. 2 vols. London: Macmillan and Co., 1889.

Tiwari, Jagdish Narain. "Studies in Goddess Cults in Northern India, with Special Reference to the First Seven Centuries A.D.," Ph.D. Thesis, Australian National University, 1971.

Tripāṭhī, Rām Śaṅkar. *The Chequered History of the Golden Temple of Kāshī Vishwanath.* Kāśī, n.d.

Tucci, Giuseppe. *The Theory and Practice of the Mandala.* Translated from the Italian by A. H. Brodrick. New York: Samuel Weiser, Inc., 1969.

Turner, Victor. "The Center Out There: Pilgrim's Goal," *History of Religions* 12, no. 3 (Feb. 1973): 191–230.

———. *The Ritual Process: Structure and Anti-Structure.* Chicago: Aldine Publishing Co., 1969.

Twain, Mark. *Following the Equator, A Journey Around the World.* Hartford: The American Publishing Company, 1898.

Vaudeville, Charlotte. "Braj, Lost and Found," *Indo-Iranian Journal* 18 (1976): 195–213.

———. "The Govardhan Myth in Northern India," *Indo-Iranian Journal* 22 (1980): 1–45.

———. *Kabīr.* Oxford: Oxford University Press, 1974.

Vidyarthi, L. P.; Saraswati, B. N.; and Jha, Makan. *The Sacred Complex of Kāshī.* Delhi: Concept Publishing Company, 1979.

Vogel, J. Ph. *Indian Serpent Lore, or the Nāgas in Hindu Legend and Art.* London: Arthur Probsthain, 1926.

Wheatley, Paul. *City As Symbol.* London: H. K. Lewis and Co. Ltd., 1969.

———. *The Pivot of the Four Quarters.* Chicago: Aldine Publishing Company, 1971.

Winternitz, Maurice. *A History of Indian Literature.* Calcutta: University of Calcutta, 1927. Reprinted in three volumes, New Delhi: Oriental Books Reprint Corporation, 1972.

Zimmer, Heinrich. *The Art of Indian Asia. Its Mythology and Transformations.* 2 vols. Bollingen Series XXXIX. Princeton: Princeton University Press, 1955.

———. *Myths and Symbols in Indian Art and Civilization.* New York: Pantheon Books, Inc., 1946.

ACKNOWLEDGMENTS

I first want to thank those Banārsīs to whom I have dedicated this book. Kuber Nāth Sukul, who has worked for years on Kāshī and written books in both English and Hindi on the city, appointed me his pupil the first time we met, and has helped and corrected me at every step. Pandit Ambika Datta Upādhyāya, who has taught Sanskrit to Western students for over forty years, patiently discussed the *Kāshī Khanda* with me, day after day, for a whole year. Professor J. L. Mehta and Mrs. Vimalā Mehta, whom I knew for six years at Harvard, gave me help, support, and hours of conversation and above all gave me the benediction that only Banārsīs can give to an outsider who presumes to know something of their native place.

In Banāras my work was completed with the help of many others as well: J. N. Tiwari, Lallanji Gopal, K. K. Sinha, and A. K. Narain of the Department of Ancient Indian History and Culture at Banāras Hindu University; Satyanarayan Pandey, Purānic Research Scholar at B.H.U.; R. L. Singh of the Department of Geography at B.H.U.; Ananda Krishna, the late Rai Krishna Das, and Kamala Giri of the Bhārat Kalā Bhavan Museum; V. R. Nambiar and his staff at the American Institute of Indian Studies in Rāmnagar; A. S. Gupta and Giorgio Bonazzoli of the All-India Kāshī Rāj Trust Purānic Research Institute; and Dr. Bhanu Shankar Mehta, Banārsī *par excellence.* I owe a special debt of gratitude to some of the city's religious leaders: Ram Shankar Tripathi, *mahant* of the Vishvanātha Temple; Virabhadra Mishra, *mahant* of the Sankat Mochan Temple; Anand Shankar Dave of the Ādi Vishveshvara Temple; Chandra Nath Vyas of the Jnāna Vāpī; Swami Karpatri, Hindu scholar and renowned *sannyāsin;* and many other priests and *pūjārīs* whose names I do not know. For gracious hospitality and hours of discussion about Banāras, I would like to thank Shrimati Upadhyaya, Dr. Sarojini Varshney, Prahlad Das Shapuri and family, and Krishna Mankhand and family. Finally, I wish to thank His Highness, the Maharaja Vibhuti Narain Singh.

At Harvard University, I am especially grateful for the advice and encouragement of John B. Carman, Director of the Center for the Study of World Religions, who has seen this work emerge over the course of many years. Wilfred Cantwell Smith, Professor of the Comparative History of Religion; Daniel H. H. Ingalls, Professor of Sanskrit; and John Rosenfield, Professor of Fine Arts, have also given their generous help and support. In the final stages of this work I was fortunate to have Pramod Chandra, Professor of Fine Arts, who is from a long line of great Banārsīs, read the manuscript and offer his comments. With my colleagues, Professors William Graham and Richard Niebuhr, I have spent many fruitful hours thinking through the meanings of Pilgrimage. Finally, I am deeply grateful to Professor Charlotte Vaudeville of the Sorbonne, who was a Visiting Professor at Harvard in 1980. Professor Vaudeville spent many days with me, discussing what I had written and helping me to see its significance in the wider context of popular Hinduism, which she knows so well.

My students at Harvard have also been important to me as this work has emerged. In particular, I want to thank Robert Hueckstedt, my research assistant, and Andrew McCord of Harvard College and Annie Wilson of Williams College, who both helped me with some aspects of my research in Banāras.

Through the years this work has been supported by many institutions and foundations, going back to 1965–66, when the University of Wisconsin's India Program first introduced me to India and to Banāras. In 1972, a summer grant from the American Institute of Indian Studies enabled me to study Hindi in Delhi. In 1973–74, the Foreign Area Fellowship Program of the Social Science Research Council supported a year of research in Banāras. In 1974–75, the Danforth Foundation supported me while writing my doctoral dissertation, and in the summer of 1978, the Indo-U.S. Sub-Commission on Education and Culture enabled me to return to Banāras for further research. In the summer of 1979, the American Council of Learned Societies provided support while I began the writing of this book. Throughout, the Center for the Study of World Religions at Harvard has been supportive in countless ways.

I want especially to thank my editor at Knopf, Toinette Lippe, who has been generous with her support and encouragement ever since she received this manuscript. I am grateful for her insight, her gentle editing, and her knowledge of Sanskrit.

It is also a pleasure to thank my family. My parents, Hugo and Dorothy Eck, have shared their spirit of adventure with me in Montana, in Mexico, and in India. My grandmother, Ida Fritz, who died while I was in Banāras in January 1978, first set me on a literary path. And my grandfather, Ira Fritz, continues to embody the great oral tradition of storytelling. My many relations, Ecks, Concas, and Millers, have endured more slide lectures on Banāras than any other family in North America.

Finally, I want to thank those few rare and wonderful people who are both colleagues and dear friends, with whom I have been fortunate to share my work through the years, both in India and Cambridge—Jack Hawley, Laura Shapiro, and Frédérique Marglin. Most especially, I would like to thank Dorothy Austin, who has been twice with me to Banāras and has become something of a Banārsī herself. Dorothy's love of India and her own experience of Banāras, as both a theologian and psychologist, have given me an important perspective on my work. Through the many months of writing this book, Dorothy has read and discussed the manuscript with me at every stage, as only one who has had the *darshana* of Kāshī could do.

ILLUSTRATIONS

Munshī Ghat   Frontis

The narrow lanes and lofty houses of Banaras   7

"Munikurnika Ghat" as drawn by James Prinsep. Courtesy of the American Institute of Indian Studies   10-11

James Prinsep's view of "Dusaswumedh Ghat"   14-15

Bathing in the Ganges   16

The riverfront near Manikarnikā   22-3

"View of the City of Benares" by William Hodges. Courtesy of the American Institute of Indian Studies   30

Kāshī pilgrims   40

Pilgrims leaving Kapiladhārā   41

"Benares from the Mundakinee Tulao" as drawn by James Prinsep. Courtesy of the Yale University Library.   48-9

The Buddha from Sārnāth. Courtesy of the Archaeological Survey of India   64

Krishna lifting Mt. Govardhana. Courtesy of Bhārat Kalā Bhavan   67

Gudimallam linga. Courtesy of the American Institute of Indian Studies and the Archaeological Survey of India   70

The fiery appearance of the linga. Courtesy of Bhārat Kalā Bhavan   71

Durgā, Slayer of the Bull Demon. Courtesy of Bhārat Kalā Bhavan   73

Skanda Kārttikeya. Courtesy of Bhārat Kalā Bhavan and the American Institute of Indian Studies.   77

Dancing Ganesha from Dehalī Vināyaka. Courtesy of Bhārat Kalā Bhavan   78

Decorating the Ādi Vishveshvara linga *for the evening* āratī   96

Shiva seated in meditation. Banāras folk art   98

Shiva and Parvatī, in the Himālayas   99

Four-faced linga *from Panna, Madhya Pradesh. Courtesy of the American Institute of Indian Studies*   104

Linga *at Kedāra Ghāt*   105

Rāma and Lakshmana. Banāras folk art   111

Omkāreshvara Temple   114

"View of the Gyan Bapee Well" by James Prinsep. Courtesy of the American Institute of Indian Studies   125

Jnāna Vāpī pavilion   126

The Jnāna Vāpī Mosque today   127

"Temple Vishveshwur" drawn by James Prinsep. Courtesy of the American Institute of Indian Studies   128

Kedāra Temple from the Ganges   138

The entry to Kedāra Temple from the city-side lane   139

The Well of Dharma, Dharma Kūpa, ringed with small shrines   156

Durgā's image painted by the door at the Durgā Temple   165

Standing for the darshana *of Durgā*   167

Shītāla's Dashāshvamedha temple   172

A popular Shītāla shrine   173

The Goddess Kālī standing upon the body of Shiva   175

Lolārka Kund   178

Sun discs at Sūrya Kund   181

Ganas *posted along the Panchakroshī Road*   186

Ganesha shrine   188

Kāla Bhairava   191

The image of Lahurā Bīr   201

Vishnu, seated upon the serpent called Ananta. Banāras folk art   204

Offering the waters of the Ganges to the ancestors   213

The great steps of Chaumsathī Ghāt   224-5

Bathers at Dashāshvamedha Ghāt   229

The great mosque at Panchagangā Ghāt. Courtesy of the Widener Library, Harvard University   236

Panchagangā Ghāt, with its myriad riverfront shrines. Courtesy of the American Institute of Indian Studies   237

Manikarnikā Ghāt. Courtesy of the American Institute of Indian Studies   240-1

A satī *stone*   250

"Eve of an Eclipse of the Moon, 23 November, 1823," by James Prinsep. Courtesy of the Yale University Library   254-5

A nāga *or serpent stone*   265

The temple of Pishāchamochana   268

Panchagangā Ghāt on the full moon day of Kārttika   272-3

The riverfront, looking toward Panchagangā   287

Brass merchant in Thatherī Bazaar   305

The "burning ghāts*" at Manikarnikā*   326-7

The Kāshīvāsī, "bound for moksha"   330

The riverfront at Manikarnikā Ghāt   342-3

MAPS

1. *The City of Banāras*   2

2. *Sacred Sites in India*   37

3. *The Ponds and Lakes of Kāshī*   47

4. *Vishvanātha, Manikarnikā, Dashāshvamedha and Vicinity*   121

5. *Vishvanātha Temple*   122

6. *Zones of the Sacred City*   351

7. *The Three Sectors (Khandas) of Kāshī*   356

All these maps were drawn by Robert C. Forget

INDEX

Adampura, 112

Ādi Keshava, 3, 44, 46, 81, 154 and n., 181, 187, 203, 204, 205, 209, 210, 212, 220, 221, 232-4, 353, 354, 357

Ādi Manikarnikā, 144, 225, 355

āditya, 151 and n., 176 7, 180, 181, 255; *māhātmya*, 176, 362; the twelve, list and location, 362. *See also* Sun

Ādi Vishveshvara, 96, 133, 135

Agastya, 145, 199, 308-9, 355

ages of cosmic time, 139-40, 159-60, 207, 219-20, 279, 280-2. *See also* Kali Age

Aghorī, 59, 328

Agni, 101, 230, 295, 310, 341

Agni Purāna, 348

Agnīshvara, 230, 355

Aitareya Brāhmana, 21

Ajātashatru, 45, 58

Akbar, 83, 134

Amareshvara, 226

Amarnāth, 35

amāvasyā, 253, 270, 275

ānanda, 29-31, 300, 301

Ānandamayī Mā, 4, 223

Ānandavana, 29-31, 98. *See also* Forest of Bliss

ancestors. See *pitri*, ancestor

Annakūta, 162, 163-4, 271

Annapūrnā, 90, 136, 144, 159, 160-4, 165, 168, 174, 192, 195, 198, 220, 264, 269, 271, 274, 305, 332, 352, 355

Annapūrnā Vrat Kathā, 162-3

Antargriha, Inner Sanctum of Vishveshvara, 25 n., 112, 136, 145, 160, 228; limits of sacred zone of, 354-5

antyeshti. See cremation rites

āratī, 12, 106, 121-2, 157

Arka Vināyaka, 187, 223

Arnold, Edwin, 15-16, 311-12

artha, 304-5, 306, 310; forest of, 310-14

Arunāditya, 181

ascetics, asceticism, 43, 55, 56, 60, 69, 71, 86, 94, 97, 192, 195, 200, 242, 243, 244, 289, 326, 328-9

Āshādha, 258, 260-2, 285, 290

Ashoka, 57, 61-2

Ashokan pillar, 197

āshram (retreat), 4, 29, 59, 286, 316

āshrama (stage of life), 100 and n.,
102
ashvamedha, 62 and n., 68, 140, 152,
202, 226-7
Āshvina, 174, 215, 257, 258, 267-9
Asi: Ghāt, 3, 221, 222-3, 278, 290;
River, 25, 26-7, 167, 177, 220, 222,
248, 286, 299, 300-1, 317, 353, 356
Asisangameshvara, 222
astrology, 253, 257
asura, 101-2 and n.
Athens, 4, 5, 16
ātman, 300-1, 303; knowledge of,
333, 334
Ātmavīreshvara, 131, 230. *See also*
Vīreshvara
Aurangzeb, 12, 83-4, 120, 127, 134-5,
143, 196-7, 206, 207, 235
āvāhana, 219
Avantikā. *See* Ujjain, ancient Avantikā
avatāra, 35, 61, 65 and n., 205, 209-
10
Avimukta, 25 n., 28-9, 95, 130, 157,
180, 242, 249, 300-1; limits of sa-
cred zone of, 354
"Avimukta Māhātmya," 221, 348
Avimukta Vināyaka, 123
Avimukteshvara, 109, 124, 129, 130-1,
133-5, 277, 348, 354, 359. *See also*
Vishvanātha, Vishveshvara
Ayodhyā, 38, 74, 247, 269, 284; in
Kāshī, 285

Badrīnāth, 38, 289, 294; in Kashi, 289
Bakariā Kund, 66, 179, 207-8, 294
Balarāma, 66
bali, 52, 54, 159, 166, 184
Ban Kati, 29
Banāras, name, 26. *See* Kāshī,
Banāras, Vārānasī
Banāras Hindu University, 28, 91
Bārānasi, 26, 45, 54
Bare Ganesha, *illus.* 48, 188-9, 266

Batuk Bhairava, 190, 356
Bengāl, and Banāras, 137, 138, 329
Bengāli Tolā, 158, 226, 329
Beniā Tālāb, 48, 50, 227
Bernier, François, 16, 84
Besant, Annie, 44, 91
Bhādrapada, 179, 258, 260-1, 266-7,
269, 288
Bhāgavata Purāna, 348
Bhagīratha, 31, 211-12, 215, 237, 239,
260
Bhairava, 108, 119, 144, 189-97, 255,
256, 257, 268, 337; Kāla Bhairava,
84, 90, 143, 144, 146, 162, 173, 189-
95, *illus.* 191, 198, 201, 223, 274,
313, 317, 320, 339, 344, 357; the
eight Bhairavas, 223, 274; list and
location, 362
bhairavas, 51, 173, 189, 190, 201
Bhairavāshtamī, 195, 274
bhairavī yātanā, 143, 193, 337-9
bhakti, 61, 67, 85-7, 223
bhāng, 277, 278, 304
Bhārabhūteshvara, 355
Bhāra Shiva dynasty, 62, 68, 227
Bhārat Kalā Bhavan, 61, 63, 64, 66,
illus. 67, 68, 70 and n., *illus.* 71,
illus. 73, 75 n., *illus.* 77, *illus.* 78,
80, 180
Bhārat Mātā Temple, 38-9
Bhārat Milāp, 269
Bhavānī, 80, 158, 159, 160, 164, 169,
302
Bhavānī, Queen, 113
Bhīma, 271-2
Bhīmachanda Vināyaka, 187
Bhīmachandī, 187, 321, 352
Bhīma Dvitīyā, 271-2
Bhīma Shankar, 291
Bhīshmachandikā, 353
bhukti, 131, 306
Bhūta Bhairava, 190
Bimbisāra, 45
Bindu Mādhava, 12, 83, 88, 204, 206-
7, 221, 234-5, 238, 272, 286, 292. *See
also* Panchagangā Ghāt

bīr, 76, 168, 200–1
bodhisattva, 45, 54, 63
Brahmā, 70, 107-8, 116 n., 135, 190,
    194, 202-3, 213, 249, 285, 290, 293,
    298, 310; in Divodāsa myth, 148,
    151-2, 202, 226-7. *See also* Brah-
    meshvara, Brahmesha
Brahmadatta, 54
Brahmā Ghāt, 231
Brahman, 24, 31-2, 58-9, 136, 241,
    243, 285, 318, 328, 332-4, 335
Brahma Nāla, 33, 189, 239, 251, 299
Brahmānda Purāna, 52-3, 348
Brahma Purāna, 52, 348
Brahmavaivarta Purāna, 23, 142, 347
Brahmavardhana, 59
Brahmeshvara, Brahmesha, 110, 145,
    152, 203, 228, 354, 355; at Ādi Ke-
    shava, 233
brahmin, 11-12, 58, 92-3, 252, 256-7,
    264-5, 284, 289, 314, 315
Brindāvan, 35
Buddha, 4, 25, 44-5, 54, 56-7, 60, 61,
    62-4, 177, 261, 288, 310
Buddhism, Buddhist, 53, 55-7, 61,
    62-4, 72, 81, 154, 181, 197, 208, 209
    10, 288
Burhwa Mungal, 278, 304
Buyers, William, 92

Caine, W. S., 14-15
Chaitra, 174, 257, 258, 277-8, 285
Chakrapushkarinī Kund, 239-43
Chāmundā, 74, 75
Chandikā, 74, 321; *chandikās*, 165
Chandra, Motī, 56
Chandreshvara, 110, 160, 358
chaturmāsa, 261-2, 272
Chauk, 133
Chaukhambā, 29, 67, 72, 73, 193, 266
Chaukī Ghāt, 226
Chaumsathī Devī, 150 n., 158, 356
Chaumsathī Ghāt, 158, *illus.* 224-5,
    226, 278

Chitragupta, 192, 216, 317
Christians, Christianity, 91-3, 335,
    336
commerce in Banāras, 9-10, 44, 45,
    310, 311
communal tension, 127-9, 196-7
courtesans, 305, 307-8
cremation grounds: Aghorīs and,
    328; Banāras as "Great Crema-
    tion Ground," 32-33, 98, 314, 324;
    at Harishchandra Ghāt, 4, 33,
    223-5; as home of Shiva, 33, 97,
    102, 312; inauspiciousness of, 4,
    32-3; at Manikarnikā Ghāt, 4, 33,
    225, 248-51
cremation rites, 32, 248-9, 340-3

Daksha, 33, 99-100
dakshinā, 156, 223, 226
Dāl Mandī, 132
dāna, giving, 81, 226, 314, 315, 322
Dandapani, 76, 124, 130, 136, 144, 146,
    198-201, 337
Daniell, William, 29
Dārā Shikoh, 217
darshana, meaning of, 12, 20-1, 110;
    as philosophy, 58-9; use of term,
    39, 58-9, 121, 123, 127, 136, 160, 163,
    164, 167, 170, 173, 174, 189, 193, 195,
    207, 220, 227, 228, 229-30, 231, 233,
    238-9, 246, 258, 262, 263, 266, 267,
    268, 269, 271, 272, 274, 275, 276, 282,
    290, 316, 321
Dashahara, 174
Dashakumāracharita, 130
Dashāshvamedha Ghāt, *illus.* 14-15,
    48, 50, 68, 117, 138, 140, 144-5, 152,
    171, 202-3, 211, 220, 221, 226-8,
    illus. 229, 233, 257, 260, 275, 291,
    292, 355, 356
Dashāshvamedheshvara, 172, 203, 228
Davidson, Lt. Col., 17
days, lunar, 253, 255
days, solar, 253, 255-6

death: and Ganges, 215–16; and
Kāla Bhairava, 143, 190, 192–3, 194,
337–9; in Kāshī, liberation by, 4,
18, 24, 28–9, 32, 87, 91, 161, 249–51,
279, 324–5, 331–7; and life, 238,
251, 304–6, 343–4; rites, 4, 32, 215,
267–8, 273, 340–3. See also *moksha;*
Shiva: gives *moksha* in Kāshī
Dehalī Vināyaka, 78, 321, 351, 352,
353
devadāsīs. See courtesans
Devī, Mahādevī, 60, 72–5, 115, 158,
159, 166–7, 169, 245, 259. *See also*
Goddess, Great Goddess
Devī Māhātmya, 72, 74–5, 163, 166
devīs, goddesses, 36, 51, 61, 72–5,
157–74, 201, 218–19, 231, 247, 256,
266–7
devotion. See *bhakti*
dhāmas, the four, 38, 288–90
Dhanteras, 270
dharma, 85, 97, 102, 149, 150, 151, 155,
197, 209, 280, 305, 306, 313, 314–16,
318, 325, 343; Buddhist, 56;
varnāshrama, 100, 154, 200, 209
Dharma Kūpa, *illus.* 156, 229
Dharmesha, 229, 358
Dhundhirāja Vināyaka, 136, 182, 187,
188, 352
directional regents, guardians, 146,
230, 294–6; list and location of, 363
Divālī, 269–71, 304
Divodāsa, 25, 52–4, 95, 130, 148–57,
185–6, 202, 203, 209–10, 226–7, 229,
271, 348
Divodāseshvara, 155, *illus.* 156
Doms, 249, 341
Douglas, Mary, 216–17
Duncan, Jonathan, 90
Durgā, 36, *illus.* 73, 74, 75, 157, 158,
160, 164–7, *illus.* 165, *illus.* 167,
169, 171, 255, 263, 275; cycle of
nine, 174, 258, 268–9, 360; destruction of bull demon, 166–7, 269;
temple, 50, 164–8, 263
Durgā Ghāt, 231

Durgā Kund, 29, 50, 164, 167, 168,
187, 255, 269, 354, 356
Durgā Pūjā, 268–9
Durgā Vināyaka, 187
Dvārakā, 38, 284, 290; in Kāshī,
287–8

Eliade, Mircea, 35, 108
Elliott, Captain Robert, 235, *illus.*
236

festivals, 252, 253, 257, 258–78, 279;
calendar of, 364–6
Fitch, Ralph, 9–12
Forest of Bliss, 29–31, 33, 46, 50–1,
55, 80, 84, 85, 168, 170, 199, 200,
212, 231, 242, 287, 309, 314, 319. *See
also* Ānandavana; Kāshī, Banāras,
Vārānasī

Gabhastīshvara, 231, 238
Gāhadavāla, 46, 79–82, 118, 132, 133,
174, 177, 233
gana, 51, 53, 61, 78, 95, 146, 183, 185–
7, *illus.* 186, 189, 199, 200; in
Divodāsa myth, 152–3
Gāndhi, Mahātma, 135
Ganesha, Vināyaka, 36, 53–4, *illus.*
78, 78–9, 95, 101, 115, 144, 146, 147,
182–9, *illus.* 188, 190, 198, 199, 200,
266, 270, 275; in Divodāsa myth,
153–5, 185–7; the fifty-six, 154, 182,
187–8, 198, 223, 234
Ganesha Chaturthī, 189, 256, 266,
275
ganeshas, 51, 53–4, 61, 69, 95, 183, 186,
189, 198, 201
Gangā, goddess, 74, 160, 212, 217–19,
259
Gangā Dashahara, 259–60

Gangā Keshava, 229, 239
Gangā Laharī, 85, 217-18, 235
"Gangā Māhātmya," 219
Gangā Sāgara, 211, 212
Gangā Saptamī, 259-60
Ganges: Banāras riverfront along,
14-16, 17, 24-5, 26-7, 34, 43-4, 46-7,
111, 187, 211-12, 245; bathing in, 3,
9, 11-12, 15-16, 39, 46, 124, 136, 137,
152, 175-6, 212-17, 220, 221, 222,
226-7, 233, 238, 243, 249, 259-60,
272, 274, 275, 278, 304, 314-15, 322;
descent of, 3, 30-1, 84, 211-12, 213,
239-40; festivals of, 257, 259-60,
274, 275; flood of, 50, 117-18, 119,
218-19, 245, 260-1; in Himālayas,
136, 212-13, 240, 284, 285; Panchatīrthī pilgrimage along, 220-1;
prototype of sacred waters, 41,
212-15; purification by, 197, 216-
18, 305; ritual use of, 13, 120, 121,
137, 139, 248-9, 262, 340, 341; and
sacred geography, 36, 38, 39; salvation of dead by, 214, 215-16; as
Shakti, 149, 218-20, 309; temple of,
229. See also *ghāts*; Panchatīrthī
pilgrimage
Garuda Purāna, 202
Gaurī, 74, 142, 144; cycle of nine,
158, 174, 258, 268-9, 360-1
Gaurī Shankar, 246
Gayā, 44, 56, 85, 134, 267, 302
Gāya Ghāt, 231, 289
Getty, Alice, 183
ghātiā, 11, 21, 226
ghāts, 3, 21, 46-7, 176, 197, 222, 232,
234, 235, 239, 245, 257, 259, 260,
274; along Ganges, 222-51 *passim*;
"burning," 224-5, 248, 324, 333.
See also cremation grounds
Godauliā, 48, 50, 92, 117, 133, 180,
227, 267, 293, 355
Godāvarī River, 48, 213-14, 227, 293,
309. *See also* Godauliā
Goddess, Great Goddess, 61, 72-5,
80, 146, 147, 158-9, 161, 169, 172,

174, 247, 255, 256, 257, 258, 269. *See
also* Devī, Mahādevī; *devīs*, goddesses
goddesses. See *devīs*, goddesses
Gokarneshvara, Gokarna, 145, 354,
355
Golden Temple, 125, 133. *See also*
Vishvanātha, Vishveshvara
Gopāla Temple, 67, 88, 266, 271
Govardhana, 66, *illus.* 67, 76, 207,
208, 271
Govindachandra, 81, 118
Greaves, Edwin, 250
guardian deities, 146-7, 318; *chandikā
devīs*, 165, 317; Dandapāni, 198,
200; directional guardians, 294-5;
ganas, 186-7, 317, 318; Ganesha,
78, 146, 184, 185, 187, 317; Varanā
and Asi, 27, 317
Gupta, 61-2, 63-4, 66-7, 68, 71, 72,
74-9 *passim*, 129, 133, 179, 207

Haihaya, 52, 348
Hanumān, 54, 87, 255, 263, 270, 271
Hanumān Ghāt, 223
Hardvār, 38, 212, 218, 260, 284, 295;
in Kāshī, 285-6
Harishchandra, King, 223-4, 239,
249, 348
Harishchandra Ghāt, 4, 33, 223-5
Harishchandra Mandapa, 239
Haritālikā Tīj, 266
Harivamsha, 52-3
Hastings, Warren 89, 90
Havell, E. B., 176, 182
Heber, Bishop Reginald, 12-13, 91
Hiuen Tsiang, 50, 57, 71, 79, 132, 208
Himālayas, 39, 40, 94, 97, 136, 140-2,
211, 212, 240, 260, 285, 289, 291,
295; journey of, to Kāshī, 312-13
Hodges, William, 29, 30
Holī, 197, 275, 276, 277-8, 304
Holkar, Queen Ahalyabāī of In-
dore, 120, 135, 248

images, divine, 19-20; of Bhairava, 189-90, 193; of *bīrs*, 200; of Buddha, 63; of Ganesha, 78-9, 182, 184; of Goddess, 72-3, 80, 161, 164, 165-6, 167, 174, 247-8, 269, 275, 299; of Govardhana, 271; of Krishna, 66-7; of Shiva, 69-70, as *linga*, 103-6, 109; of Skanda, 76-7; of Vishnu, 12, 205, 234, 245; Western perception of, 9-11, 18-19; in worship, 6, 16, 60, 79, 234-5, 257, 303, 311, 316
Indra, 65, 66, 245, 285, 295
Indus Valley Civilization, 72, 75, 96, 217
Īshāna, 295

Jābāla Upanishad, 27, 130, 300-1
Jagannāth, 290
Jagannātha, poet, 85, 217-18, 235
Jahān, Shāh, 83-216
Jaigishavyeshvara, 110, 145, 327-8, 357
Jain, Jainism, 55, 57-58
Jalasaī Ghāt, 249-50
Jātaka tales, 25, 44-5, 54, 307, 310
Jayaswal, K. P., 227
Jerusalem, 4, 5-6, 19, 36
jīvan mukta, 32, 328
Jīvit Putrikā Vrata, 267
jñāna, 58, 126, 300, 333
Jnāna Vāpī, 124-8, *illus.* 125, *illus.* 126, 130, 131, 136, 162, 246, 251, 277, 354-5
Jnāna Vāpī Mosque, 127-9, *illus.* 127, 133, 134, 197, 198, 276
Jyeshtha, 257, 258, 259-60, 285
Jyeshtheshvara, 357
jyotirlinga. See *linga* of light, *jyotirlinga*

Kabīr, 86-7, 235, 324
Kabīr Panth, 59, 87

Kachaurī Lane, 252, 291
Kajali Tīj, 266
Kāla Bhairava. *See* Bhairava
Kāla Kūpa, 262
Kāleshvara, 286, 357
Kālī, 74, 158, 174, *illus.* 175
Kali Age, 160, 219-20, 247, 280-2
Kāma, 304, 306-7, 309; Kāshī as City of, 307-10
Kamacchā, 158, 291, 354
Kāmākshī, Kāmākhyā, 158, 162, 163, 173, 286, 293, 356
Kāmeshvara, 117, 354, 358
Kanauj, 79, 80
Kānchī, 38, 173, 284; in Kāshī, 286
Kanishka, 62
Kanyā Kumārī, 38
Kapālamochana, "Where the Skull Fell," 108, 109, 117-19, 192, 193, 196, 221, 348, 357
Kapālī Bhairava, 190, 196-7
Kāpālikas, 190-2, 195
Kapiladhārā, *illus.* 41, 321, 352, 353
Kardameshvara, 181, 321, 352
karma, 143, 152, 155, 319-20, 337, 338
karmakāndī, 21
Karpātrī, Swāmī, 261, 282, 336
Kārttika, 163, 207, 237, 257, 258, 259, 269-73, *illus.* 272-3, 286
Kārttikeya. *See* Skanda
Kāshī, Banāras, Vārānasī: as Brahman, 31, 301-3; as center of earth, 6, 254, 284, 294-6, 323; as City of Light, 3, 24, 25-6, 59, 107, 109, 175, 211, 244, 281, 282, 289, 300, 301, 302, 344; as City of Shiva, 4, 5, 24, 31-2, 68, 94-5, 109-12, 140-2, 145, 158, 244, 298, 299; as City of Vishnu, 65, 81 n., 203, 209-10; creation of, 242, 243; destroyer of sins, 316-17; duplication of, 40-1, 283; education, learning, wisdom in, 4, 29, 55-60, 84-5, 299, 300-1, 331-4; fulfiller of aims of life, 304, 306-16; as goddess, 74, 159, 299;

includes all *tīrthas*, 39, 41-2, 146-
7, 283-4, 284-94; interior place, 27,
300-2; no Kali Age in, 279-82; as
linga of light, 109, 282, 291, 298-9;
māhātmya of, 22, 23-4, 149-50, 210,
244, 280; *mandala* of all gods, 41,
146-7, 157, 182, 210; measurement
of sacred zone of, 350-3; *moksha*
in, 242-4, 284-5, 325, 331-7; as refuge, 281; on top of Shiva's trident, 24, 28, 132, 207, 243, 296-8,
301, 355
Kāshī Devī, 74
Kāshī Karavat, 291
Kāshī Kedāra Māhātmya: discussion
of text, 85, 142-3, 347; quotations,
137, 140, 355
Kāshī ke Yātrākrama, 355
Kāshī Khanda: discussion of text,
xiv, 22, 85, 347; quotations, 26, 32,
33, 53, 76, 82, 94, 107, 108, 110, 111,
115, 117, 130, 131, 147, 159, 160, 164,
166, 170, 176, 177, 181, 186, 187, 189,
193, 194, 198, 199, 205, 209, 210, 215,
216, 219, 222, 240, 244, 247, 249, 256,
261, 262, 284, 288, 293, 294, 296, 298,
308, 310, 312, 319
Kashi Lābh Mukri Bhavan, 329-31
Kāshī Moksha Nirnaya, 332, 333, 334,
337
Kāshī Rahasya: discussion of text,
xiv, 31, 85, 347; quotations, 164,
281, 288, 296, 298, 301-2, 320-1
Kāshīvāsa, 28, 226, 329, *illus.* 330
Kāshī Yātra Prakāsha, 296, 354, 355
Kātyāyanī Devī, 230
Kāverī River, 213, 214
Kedāra, Kedāreshvara, 4, 132, 136-
44, *illus.* 138, *illus.* 139, 276, 289,
291, 355, 358; in Himālayas, 39,
136-7, 140-2; *māhātmya* of, 142-4;
as prototype, 137; and Vishveshvara, 143
Kedāra Ghāt, 137-9, 142, 144, 261,
262, 354, 355
Kedāra Khanda, 112, 137, 143, 274;

death in, 143, 340; limits of sacred
zone of, 355-6
Kennedy, Reverend James, 17, 20,
92-3, 122 n.
Keshava. *See* Vishnu; Krishna
Keshavāditya, 181
Keyserling, Count Hermann, 17
Kharva Vināyaka, 234, 353
Koshala, 45, 55-6
kotwāl, police chief, 189, 196
Kotwālpurī, 189, 195
Krishna, 35, 60, 61, 65-7, *illus.* 67, 85,
207-8, 223, 264, 266-7, 271, 284, 285,
290; lifting Govardhana, 179, 207-
8, 271
Krishna Janmāshtamī, 266-7
krishna-paksha, waning fortnight,
253, 256, 258, 266, 267, 274, 275, 276,
278
Krittikās, 101, 169
Krittivāsa, Krittivāseshvara, 83, 84,
119, 131, 144, 276, 286, 348, 351, 357,
358
Krityakalpataru, 81, 348
kshatriya, 58, 258, 269
Kshemaka, 52-4, 185-6
kshetra, 26, 56, 299
kshetra sannyāsa, 28, 151
Kubera, 52, 184, 270, 295
Kulu Stambha, 196
Kumāra. *See* Skanda
Kumbha Melā, 286, 292
kunds, 50; Bakariā, 179, 207-8;
Chakrapushkarinī, 239-43; Durgā,
164, 167; Lolārka, 177-9; Manikar-
nikā, 239-45, 247-8; Nāg Kuān,
264; Sūrya, 179-80
Kūrma Purāna, 26, 107, 348
Kurukshetra, 50, 293
Kushāna, 62, 76
Kushmānda Vināyaka, 354
Kuttanīmata, 132, 307-8

Lahurā Bīr, 29, 200, *illus.* 201
Lakshmana, 263, 285

Lakshmanabālā Ghāt, 231, 237
Lakshmana Pura, 285
Lakshmī, 160, 171, 219, 245, 267, 269,
    270
Lakshmīdhara, 81-2, 85, 130, 131-2,
    172, 347, 348
Lakshmī Kund, 50, 158, 267
Lalitā Devī, 229, 269
Lalitā Ghāt, 229-30, 239
Lāt Bhairava, 196-7, 357
liberation. See *moksha*
linga of light, *jyotirlinga*, 36, 38, 39,
    70-1, *illus.* 71, 94, 107-9, 119, 135,
    136, 144, 190, 203, 289; Kāshī as,
    109, 291-2, 298-9; the twelve, 109,
    136, 290-1, 293
linga of Shiva: 4, 9, 19, 25-6, 28, 29,
    68-71, *illus.* 70, 75, 101, 103-6,
    illus. 104, *illus.* 105, 110, 148, 155,
    199, 264, 289; groups of fourteen,
    358-9; in Kāshī, 109-12, 112-16,
    120-25, 129-30, 134-6, 139-42, 143,
    144-5, 152, 153, 155, 168, 171, 186,
    203, 222, 228-31 *passim*, 233, 235,
    246, 254, 256-7, 262, 276, 296, 299,
    327-8; *kshanika*, 110; *sthāpita*, 110;
    svayambhū, 38, 115, 135, 139, 144,
    231-2, 290
Linga Purāna, 130, 233, 247, 348
Lodī dynasty, 83, 134
Lolārka Kund, xv-xvi, 177-9, *illus.*
    178, 221, 222-3, 233; *melā*, 177-9;
    Shashthī, 267

Macaulay, Thomas Babington, 311
Macchodarī. *See* Matsyodarī Tīrtha,
    Sangam
Macleod, Norman, 13, 17, 19
Madhyameshvara, 30, 42, 84, 119,
    348, 351, 352
Madurai, 74, 173
Magadha, 45, 56
Māgha, 189, 257, 259, 266, 275,
    286

Mahābhārata, 26, 34, 36, 44, 74, 79,
    130, 170, 184, 216, 353
Mahādeva, 84, 119, 232, 358
Mahākāla, *gana*, 124, 130, 152
Mahākāla, Mahākāleshvara, 144, 262-
    3, 286, 291, 351
Mahāmāyūrī, 186
mahant, xv; of Annapūrnā, 163; of
    Vishvanātha, 106, 129, 163, 300
Mahārāja, of Banāras, 88, 90, 91, 246,
    269, 278; Balwant Singh, 89; Chet
    Singh, 89, 223; Īshvarī Prasād
    Nārāin Singh, 90; Mansārām, 89;
    Vibhūti Nārāin Singh, 90
Mahārāja Vināyaka, 188-9
Mahāshmashāna, 32-3, 98, 314, 324.
    See also cremation grounds
Mahāshmashāna Stambha, 196, 198
māhātmya, xiv, 22-5, 26, 35, 40; ex-
    amples of, 28, 29, 30-1, 32, 66, 130,
    131, 135-6, 142-3, 147, 164, 176, 177,
    205, 210, 215, 223, 280, 286, 288, 312,
    328, 341, 347-8
Mahāvīra, 57-8, 64
Maheshvara Shiva, 54, 68, 69, 71, 95,
    185
Mahisha, bull demon, 36, 72, *illus.*
    73, 75 and n., 166-7, 169, 259,
    269
Maidāgin, 193, 262, 266, 276, 355. *See
    also* Mandākinī Kund
Makara Sankrānti, 274-5
Mālavīya, Madan Mohan, 90, 91
Mānasarovara, lake, 226, 293
Mandākinī Kund, 48, *illus.* 48-9, 50,
    117-18, 351, 355; river of heaven,
    136
mandala, 6, 25 n., 41, 146-7, 182, 186,
    203, 208, 210, 294-6
Mandara, Mount, 148, 149, 151, 153,
    156, 209, 309
Māndhātri, 140-1, 142
Mangalā Gaurī, 231, 234, 238, 256,
    266
Manikarnī Devī, 247-8
Manikarnikā Ghāt, 4, *illus.* 10-11,

illus. 22–3, 33, 130, 136, 188, 203, 211, 220, 221, 225, 230, 233, 238–51, *illus.* 240–1, 302, 321, 324, *illus.* 326–7, 332, 340, *illus.* 342–3, 344, 348, 352, 353, 354

Manikarnikā Kund, 203, 238, 239–48, 251, 259, 267

Manikarnikeshvara, 246, 359

Mān Mandir Ghāt, 228, 289, 291

mantra, 34, 41, 55, 106, 235, 247, 332–3. *See also* Om

Marāthās, in Banāras, 85, 90, 113, 222, 329

Mārgashīrsha, 163, 164, 195, 257, 258, 274, 286

Mārkandeya Purāna, 348

mastī, 304

matha, monastery, 4, 163, 261, 266, 289

Mathurā, 35, 38, 62, 65, 266, 284; in Kāshī, 179, 208, 285

mātrikās, 51, 158–9, 168–9, 171, 183; Vikata Mātrikā, 168, 170

Mātritīrtha, 171

Matsya Purāna, 74, 199, 221, 249, 348

Matsyodarī Tīrtha, Sangam, 48, 50, 112, 116–18, 119, 299, 355, 356

Maurya, 61, 62, 74, 174

māyā, 103, 241, 338–9

Mayūkhāditya, 231, 238

Mecca, 5, 6, 17, 86

melā, 177–9, 262, 263, 264, 267, 269, 275, 278, 288, 290

Mīr Ghāt, 135, 158, 229, 355

Mishra, Mitra, 130, 349

Mishra, Vāchaspati, 131, 348

Moda Vināyakas, 188, 353, 355

moksha, 3, 24, 26, 28 n., 32, 59, 80, 136, 140, 150–1, 161, 206, 212, 242, 244, 304, 306, 325–31, 332–7, 340; justice in gaining, 336–40; in Kedāra Khanda, 143, 340; recipients of, in Kāshī, 32, 206–7, 244, 334–7; seven cities of, 36–8, 284–8. *See also* death: in Kāshī, libera-tion by; Shiva: gives *moksha* in Kāshī

mokshada: Kāshī as, 306; seven cit-ies as, 36–8

Monkey Temple, 165. *See also* Durgā

months, lunar, 253, 258–78

Mrityunjaya, 120, 262–3, 276, 286

Mughal, 88, 89, 217, 311

Muhammad Ghūrī, 46, 82, 132

Mukhanirmālikā Devī, 231

mukti, 28 n., 32, 131, 306, 336. *See also moksha*

Müller, Max, 40

Mumford, Lewis, 5

mūrti, 60, 109, 299. *See also* images, divine

music, 278, 304, 307

Muslim: destruction of temples, xv, 46, 66, 77, 82, 120, 129, 134–5, 143, 164, 179, 196, 206, 351; liberation in Kāshī, 335, 336; mosques, 127–9, 133, 134, 196, 206, 207, 208, 276–7; neighborhoods, 112, 113, 114, 207, 232; piety and Kabīr, 86–7, 235; rulers of Banāras, 83–4, 132, 134, 217

mysterium tremendum, 97, 109

nāga, 36, 51, 54, 55, 61, 66, 146, 177, 226, 244, 264, *illus.* 265, 288, 344

Nāga Panchamī, 226, 264

Nāgeshvarī Devī, 231

Nāg Kuan, Nāga Kūpa, 196, 226, 264, 357

Nārada, 338–9

Nārada Ghāt, 226

Nārada Purāna, 210, 249, 348

Nārāyana Bhatta, 85, 118, 131, 134, 333, 348–9

Narmadā River, 119, 213, 291, 293

Nātī Imlī, 269

Navarātra, "Nine Nights," 163, 174, 258–9, 268–9, 275

Nepālī Temple, 230, 293
Nevill, H. R., 112
nibandha, 81, 348–9
Nikumbha, 52–4, 95, 184, 185–6;
  shrine of, 124
nirguna, 31, 85
Nirriti, 230, 295
nivritti, 102, 105–6

Om, 113–14, 115–16, 333
Omkāra, Omkāreshvara, 84, 109,
  112–120, *illus.* 114, 193, 203, 291,
  348, 354, 357, 358; as "five-fold,"
  115–16; on Narmadā, 119, 291
Omkāra Khanda, 112, 119; limits of
  sacred zone of, 356–7
Otto, Rudolf, 97

Padma Purāna, 26, 170, 249, 348
Pādodaka Tīrtha, 154, 205
pān, 304, 305
Panchagangā Ghāt, also Panchanada, 86, 88, 155, 206–7, 212, 217,
  220, 221, 231, 233, 234–8, *illus.* 236,
  illus. 237, 257, *illus.* 272–3, 278,
  286, *illus.* 287, 313, 329
Panchakroshī, five *kroshas*, 25 n.,
  41–2, 75, 94, 109, 116, 147, 181, 187,
  242, 243, 244, 259, 289, 291, 299, 300,
  302, 307, 354; as five *koshas*, 116,
  300, 302, 350; *linga* of five *kroshas*,
  321, 352; *māhātmya*, 320–1, 347, 352
  n.; of other *tīrthas*, 119, 283; pilgrimage around, 41–2, 320–1,
  350–3
panchānga, 252–3, 286
Panchatīrthī pilgrimage, 220–51, 259
panchāyatana, 115–16
pandā, xv, 11–12, 21, 24, 221, 226
Pāndavas, 36, 137, 170, 271–2; temples of the five, 353

Pantha, 80
pāpa, 316. *See also* sin
Pāpamochana, 117
Parshvanātha, 57–8
Parvateshvara, 353, 355
Pārvatī, 53, 74, 88, 94–5, 97–8, *illus.*
  99, 101, 111, 149, 150, 161, 169, 172,
  185, 200, 219, 242, 244, 245, 247, 266,
  312–13
Pāshapāni Vināyaka, 187, 353, 354
Pashupata, 71
Pashupateshvara, 230
Pashupatināth, 293
Pātan Darvāzā, 231
Patanjali, 59, 264
Pausha, 258, 274, 286
Peking, 4, 5, 6
Phālguna, 258, 276
pilgrimage, 6, 10, 20–2, 36–43, 60, 82,
  86–7, 136, 184, 215, 257, 280–1, 283,
  286, 313, 314, 316, 329; Antargriha,
  136, 354–5; around Avimukta, 354;
  daily, 134, 136; to eight Bhairavas,
  190, 274; to eight directions, 296;
  to four *dhāmas*, 288–90; of gods to
  Kāshī, 148–57; to interior, 302–3;
  Kabīr and, 86–7; around Kedāra
  Khanda, 143, 274, 355–6; of
  Māndhātri, 140–1; around Omkāra
  Khanda, 119, 356–7; around Panchakroshī, 41–2, 320–1, 350–3;
  along Panchatīrthī, 220–51; *sakāma*
  and *nishkāma*, 221; and Sākshī
  Vināyaka, 188, 251; to seven cities, 285–8, 293; of Shivasharma,
  284–5; to twelve *ādityas*, 181; to
  twelve *lingas*, 291, 293; around
  Vārānasī, 353–4; of Vasishtha,
  141–2
pilgrims, 14, 18, 20–2, 28, 39–42, 192,
  210, 218, 220–51 *passim*, 302–3, 311,
  317, 320–1
pindā, 118, 215–16, 341–2
pindadāna, 314
pindapradāna, 215

pishācha, 267-8; *rudra-pishācha,* as punishment, 320, 339-40, 342
Pishāchamochana, 267-8, *illus.* 268, 340, 354
pītha, 38, 39, 73, 74, 105, 141, 158, 162, 163, 172, 173, 190
pitri, ancestor, 215, 267, 342
pools and lakes, 29, 48-51, 227, 242; draining of, 90
Prabodhinī, 262, 272
Prahlāda, 277; Ghāt, 205, 356, 357
pralaya, 28, 280, 297, 298
prasāda, 12, 20, 123 and n., 162, 164, 262
pravritti, 102, 105-6
Prayāga, 85, 134, 212, 229, 267, 286, 292-3, 302; Ghāt, 228, 292; in Kāshī, 292-3
prāyashchitta, 264, 314, 316
preta, 342
Prinsep, James, 49-50, 124-5, 128, 227, 231, 246, 250, 355; illustrations, 10-11, 14-15, 48-9, 125, 128, 254-5
pūjā, 12, 52, 60, 247-8, 315
pūjārī, xv, 21; of Ādi Keshava, 209-10, 233; of Kedāra, 138-9; of Omkāra, 113-15; of Tārakeshvara, 243
punya, 34, 292, 316, 318, 325
Purī, 38, 290
pūrnimā, full moon, 253; *guru pūrnimā,* 261; of Kārttika, 272; of Phālguna, 277; of Shrāvana, 264-5
purushārtha, 304, 306, 310, 314, 315, 325

Qutb-ud-din Aibak, 46, 57, 82, 132

Rājaputra Vināyaka, 234
Rājghāt, 26, 29, 43-6, 132, 205, 232, 355, 357; excavations at, xv, 46, 75, 130
Rājputs, 83; and Ādi Vishveshvara, 135
Rakshā Bandhana, 265-6
rākshasa, 51-3, 130-1, 183, 184, 198, 201
Rām, *mantra* and name, 86-7, 324, 333
Rāma, 36, 85, 87-9, 247, 258-9, 263, 269, 284, 285, 289
Rāma Ghāt, 230-1, 234, 271
Rāmakrishna, 332
Rāma Kund, 50, 285, 289, 329, 357
Rāmānanda, 86, 235, 287
Rāma Navamī, 258
Rāmānuja, 59, 86
Rāma Pura, 285
Rāmāyana, 36, 87, 261, 263
Rāmcharitmānas, 87-9
Rāmeshvaram, 38, 285, 289, 294; Rāmeshvara in Kāshī, 289, 321, 352, 353
Rām Līlā, 87-8, 269
Rāmnagar, 161, 269, 278
Rānā Mahal Ghāt, 158
Rangabhārī Ekādashī, 277
Ratha Yatra, 290
Ratnāvalī, 308
Ratneshvara, *illus.* 99, 358
Rāvana, 184, 259, 269, 289
Razia (Raziyyat-ud-din): Razia's Mosque, 120, 132-3
Revarī Tālāb, 293
Rinamochana, 117
Rishipatana, 56-7. *See also* Sarnāth
ritual, 6, 11-14, 20, 106 n., 121-3, 212-13, 220-1, 247-8, 252, 314-15. *See also* death: rites; cremation rites
rivers, India's sacred, 48, 212-15, 283; as "mothers," 73-4
Roberts, Miss Emma, 13-14, 311
Rudra, 31-2, 60, 69, 96, 97, 117, 151, 295

Rudrasarovara, 227-8, *illus.* 229
Rudravāsa, 31-2. *See also* Kāshī,
    Banāras, Vārānasī
Ruru Bhairava, 190, 223

sacred: meaning of, 34, 98, 99; cit-
    ies, the seven, 36-7, 284-8; city,
    5-6, 16-17, 41-2, 296-8, 300; geog-
    raphy, xiv-xv, 38-9, 147, 157, 284,
    285, 290, 296, 323; place, 17-18, 34-
    41, 283, 293, 295; rivers, waters,
    215-16. See also *tīrtha*
sacrifice. See *yajna,* sacrifice; cre-
    mation rites
sādhu, 20, 21, 261, 281
saguna, 85
Sākshī Vināyaka, 90, 188, 220, 251,
    353
Sambāditya, 179-80
Sambhrama and Udbhrama, 198, 200,
    337
samsāra, 3, 24, 34, 106, 154, 306, 340
Sangameshvara, 203, 233
sankalpa, 126, 220-21, 226, 315
Sankatā Devī, 159, 160, 168-70, 171,
    230, 232, 256, 269
Sankatā Ghāt, 168, 230, 239
Sankatā Vrat Kathā, 169, 170
Sankat Mochan Temple, 255, 263-4
sannyāsin, 4, 20-22, 59-60, 161, 163,
    261, 289, 325-6
Sanskrit College, 90-1, 269
Santoshī Mātā, 160, 170, 230, 256
saptapurī, 36-7, 284-8
Sarasvatī, goddess, 219, 275; River,
    212, 213, 228, 237
Sarnāth, 56-7, 61, 62-3, 196, 197; mu-
    seum, 61, 62, 63
satī, 33, *illus.* 250, 251
Satī, 172-3
seeing, 6-8, 19-25, 282, 297, 300, 303.
    See also *darshana,* meaning of
Shaileshvara, 313, 354, 357

Shakti: cycle of nine, 174; divine
    female powers, 72-4, 80, 158, 159,
    160, 173; Gangā as, 218-19; as
    Goddess, 38, 100, 105-6, 159, 174,
    illus. 175, 241-3
Shālakatankata Vināyaka, 354
Shanīshvara, Shani, 256
Shankara: Shankarāchārya, 116, 163;
    Shiva, 31, *illus.* 98; teacher, 4, 59,
    115, 289, 302
Shankhoddhāra, 50, 287, 294, 356
Sharqī, dynasty, 83, 134
Sherring, the Reverend M. A., 4-5,
    18-19, 133, 179, 196-7, 208, 235
Shītalā, 75, 159, 160, 171, *illus.* 172,
    illus. 173, 231, 256, 259; temple,
    171-2, 203, 228, *illus.* 229
Shītalāshtamī, 256, 259
Shiva: and calendar, 256, 257, 262,
    271, 276; dwells in Kāshī, 4, 5, 24,
    28, 31-2, 94-5, 284, 302, 209-10; em-
    bodied in Kāshī, 31-2, 299; faces
    of, 96, 100-3, *illus.* 104; gives *mok-
    sha* in Kāshī, 161, 242, 244, 249,
    300, 331-5, 344; mythology of, 52-4,
    94-5, 97-8, 107-8, 126, 148-57, 160,
    172-3, 181, 183, 185, 189, 190-1, 199-
    200, 203-4, 209, 211, 219, 241-3, 266,
    309-10, 312-13; nature of, 33, 95-
    100, 202, 314; rise of, 60, 61, 69-71,
    96, 177, 182, 185, 200; Sadā Shiva,
    106, 115, 219, 298; *sakala* and *nish-
    kala,* 106, 109, 298; and Shakti, 100,
    103, 105-6, 174, 203, 218, 241-3, 299.
    See also *linga* of Shiva
Shiva Kāshī, 38
Shivālā Ghāt, 90, 223
Shiva Purāna: discussion of text, 348;
    quotations, 33, 97, 107, 194, 242
Shivarātri, 113, 131, 256; Mahāshi-
    varātri, 276
shmashāna. See cremation grounds
shrāddha, 215, 267, 314, 341
Shrāvana, 138-9, 167-8, 226, 257, 258,
    260-1, 262-6, 288

Shrāvanī, 264
shukla paksha, waxing fortnight,
253, 256, 258, 259, 261, 264, 266, 267,
268, 270, 271
Shūlatankeshvara, 144, 228
Shunga, 61-2
Siddha Kshetra, 230
Siddheshvarī Devī, 160, 230
siddhi, in Kāshī, 195, 327-8
Siddhi Vināyaka, 187-8, 251
sin: of brahmin-killing, 80, 108, 119,
190-2; destruction of, 27, 144, 191-
3, 195, 216, 217, 218, 260, 264-5, 279,
292-3, 316-18, 319-21, 354; the five
"great sins," 108 n.
Sindhiā Ghāt, 230, 246-7
Singh, Mahārāja Īshvarī Prasād
Nārāin, 90
Singh, Jai, 228
Singh, Mahārāja Mān, 234
Singh, Rājā Ranjit, 123
Singh, Mahārāja Vibhūti Nārāin, 90
Sītā, 36, 89, 247, 263, 289
Skanda, 76, *illus.* 77, 101, 102, 144,
169, 190, 199, 219
Skanda Purāna, 76, 347. See also
Kāshī Khanda
snakes. See *nāga*
Someshvara, 228, 291
Somnath, 291
Sorahiā Melā, 267
South India, 137, 138, 173, 223, 284,
286, 289, 329
sthala purāna, 35
sukhada, 306
Sukul, Kuber Nāth, 164, 171, 193
Sun, 76-7, 151, 175-82, 254-5, 274.
See also *āditya*; Sūrya
Sureshvara, 333, 337, 338, 339
Sūri, Jina Prabha, 57-8
Sūrya, 76, 81, 115, 151, 176, 180, 181,
285; Kund, 50, 179-80, *illus.* 181,
355
Svargadvāra, 239, 251
svastika, 170, 180

svayambhū, self-manifest: goddess
images as, 167, 170. See also *linga*
of light

Tantra, 72, 75, 80, 146, 247
tapas, 69, 149, 220, 230, 231, 244. See
also ascetics, asceticism
Tāraka, 102
tāraka mantra, 246, 331, 332-4; called
Tāraka Brahman, 333
Tārakeshvara, *illus.* 10-11, 130, 243,
246
Tavernier, Jean Baptiste, 12-13, 197,
206, 234-5
thandāī, 304
Thatherī Bazaar, 29, 270, *illus.* 305,
311
theism, theistic religion, 60-2, 79
tīrtha, 4, 34-4, 80, 81-2, 109, 123, 157,
184, 192, 211, 212, 214, 232, 244-5,
293-4, 299, 316-17, 332; the "five
tīrthas" of the Ganga at Kāshī,
220-1; the interior, 27, 300-1, 302;
Kāshī contains all, 39, 41-2, 146-7,
283-4, 285, 288-94; Kāshī as prototype, xvi, 40, 213
Tīrtha Chintāmani, 131, 348
tīrthankara, 57, 64
Tīrtha Prakāsha, 82, 131, 348
Tīrthavivechana Kānda, 82, 131, 348
tīrthayātrā, 314. See also pilgrimage
Todar Mal, 134
transposition of place, 40-1, 144-5,
283-4
Trilochana, Trilochaneshvara, 90,
112, 113, 119, 120, 144, 159, 181,
231-2, 276, 356, 358
Trilochana Ghāt, 231, 237, 289, 354
Tripāthī, Rām Shankar, 123, 300
Tripurabhairavī Ghāt, 228-9
Tristhalīsetu, 85, 131, 134, 333, 348-9
Tughluq, Firūz Shāh, 83-134
Tulsī Dās, 87-9, 206, 235, 263

Tulsī Ghāt, 88, 222-3
Tulsī Mānas Temple, 89, 263
Twain, Mark, 5, 14, 19, 36

Uddanda Vināyaka, 187
Ujjain, ancient Avantikā, 74, 144,
    262, 284, 286-7
Unmatta Bhairava, 352
Upashānteshvara, 230
ūshara, Kashi as, 319-20
Uttara Kāshī, 40
Uttarārka, 179

Vāgīshvarī Devī, 354
Vaidyanātha, 291, 294, 356
Vaishākha, 258, 259, 285, 286
Vallabha, 59, 223, 266
Vāmana Purāna, 27, 221, 348
Varanā River, 25 n., 26-7, 29, 44, 48,
    117, 118, 187, 203, 205, 220, 221, 232,
    233, 299, 300-1, 317, 321, 353, 354,
    357
Vārānasī, 25 n., 26-7, 29, 45-6; as
    goddess, 74; limits of sacred zone
    of, 353-4. *See also* Kāshī, Banāras,
    Vārānasī
Vārānasī Devī, 74, 159, 232
"Vārānasī Māhātmya," 348
Vārānasī River, 26-7
Varuna, 295
Vasanta Panchamī, 275, 277
Vasishta, 141-2
Vaudeville, Charlotte, 160
Vāyu, 295
Vāyu Purāna, 52-3, 95, 348
Vedas, 55, 58-9, 73, 96
Venī River, also Beniā, 48, 118
Vijaya Dashamī, 258-9, 269
Vijaya Lakshmī, 174, 269
Vināyaka. *See* Ganesha, Vināyaka
Vindhyavāsinī Devī, 159, 166, 167,
    266

vīra. See bīr
viraha, 308-9
Vīra Shaiva, 59, 110
Vīreshvara, 160, 168, 230, 232, 355,
    358. *See also* Ātmavīreshvara
Virupāksha, 130, 181
visarjana, 219
Vishālākshī, 157, 160, 172-3, 229, 266,
    269, 355
Vishnu: as *āditya*, 176; and Buddha,
    209-10; and calendar, 256, 267,
    261-2; and Divodāsa myth, 148,
    153-5, 203; and Ganges, 219; and
    linga of light, 70, 107-8, 115, 135,
    194, 202, 298-9; locations in Kāshī,
    123, 202-8, 287, 290, 292-3; as lord
    of Kāshī, 65, 81, 209-10, 332; and
    Manikarnikā, 238, 240-5, 246-7,
    310; rise of, 60, 61, 65-7, 69, 97,
    200, *illus.* 204. *See also* Bakariā
    Kund; Bindu Mādhava; Pancha-
    gangā Ghāt
Vishnu Purāna, 348
Vishnu Shayanī Ekādashī, 256, 261
Vishvakarman, 310; Vishvakarmesh-
    vara, 359
Vishvanātha, Vishveshvara: and
    Annapūrnā, 160, 161, 162, 192, 305;
    and Avimukteshvara, 129-32, 133-
    4, 135; at Banāras Hindu Univer-
    sity, 135; at center of Antargriha,
    mandala, 25 n., 147, 187, 188, 354-
    5, 359; destruction of, 83, 84, 132,
    134, 135; duplication of, 120, 283;
    and festivals, 271, 276, 277; hilltop
    of, 132-3; interior, 302; and
    Kedāra, 143; *linga* of light, 109,
    135-6, 291, 299; lord of all, popular
    temple, 120, 132; Mahārāja as rep-
    resentative of, 90, 246; *māhātmya*
    of, 135-6; and Manikarnikā, 136,
    238-9; "New" Vishvanātha at
    Mīr Ghāt, 135, 229; the "origi-
    nal" Ādi Vishveshvara, *illus.* 96,
    133, 135; pilgrimage routes, 220,
    221, 227, 238-9, 251, 321, 323, 352,

354; reconstruction by Ahalya Bāī Holkar, 135, 248; reconstruction by Nārāyana Bhatta, 85, 88, *illus.* 128, 134, 193, 198; and Vishālākshī, 173; and Vishnu, 123, 204; worship of, 120-4

Vishvanātha Lane, 120, 182, 198, 256, 271, 311

Vishveshvara Khanda. *See* Antargriha, Inner Sanctum of Vishveshvara

Vividha Tīrtha Kalpa, 57-8

vrat, vrata, 162, 163, 164, 169, 170, 191, 192, 256, 261, 274, 314

Vriddhakāleshvara, 144, 262-3, 291, 386

Vrishabhadhvaja, 156, 307, 308, 321, 353

Vyāsa, 161, 164, 348

"Where the Skull Fell." *See* Kapālamochana

widows, 4, 138, 158, 329

yajna, sacrifice, 60, 152, 314. See also *ashvamedha*

yaksha, 36, 51-2, 54, 55, 61, 62, 66, 69, 74, 124, and *illus.,* 146, 182, 183-4, 185, 186, 189, 194, 198-201, 244, 270, 271, 295, 344; Harikesha, 69, 199-200

yakshī, 51-2, 54, 72, 74, 158

Yama, 24, 32, 193, 216, 229, 271, 295, 325, 338, 344

Yama Dvitīyā, 271

Yamunā River, 212, 213, 228, 236, 271

yantra, 75, 170

yoga, 58, 102, 111, 195; success in, in Kāshī, 327-8; unnecessary in Kāshī, 322-3, 328-9

yoginīs, 51, 150-1, 157-9, 183; the sixty-four, 150, 158, 159, 190, 278

yogīs, 43, 55, 60, 244, 297, 299, 327-9; Gorakhnāthī, 59, 86, 195, 328; Shiva as, 68-9, 96, 102, 195

yoni, 75

yuga. See ages of cosmic time; Kali Age

About the Author

DIANA L. ECK is Associate Professor of Hindu Religion in the Department of Sanskrit and Indian Studies at Harvard University, where she also works with the undergraduate honors program in the Comparative Study of Religion and is affiliated with the Center for the Study of World Religions. She holds a B.A. in Religion from Smith College, an M.A. in South Asian Studies from the University of London, School of Oriental and African Studies, and a Ph.D. in the Comparative Study of Religion from Harvard University.

A Note on the Type

This book was set on the Harris Photosetter in a film version of Janson, originally a recutting made direct from type cast from matrices long thought to have been made by the Dutchman Anton Janson, who was a practicing type founder in Leipzig during the years 1668–1687. However, it has been conclusively demonstrated that these types are actually the work of Nicholas Kis (1650–1702), a Hungarian, who most probably learned his trade from the master Dutch type founder Dirk Voskens. The type is an excellent example of the influential and sturdy Dutch types that prevailed in England up to the time William Caslon (1692–1766) developed his own incomparable designs from them.

Composed by New England Typographic Service, Inc., Bloomfield, Connecticut

Book design by Margaret McCutcheon Wagner

Maps by Robert C. Forget